AQA Geography

Foundation Edition

Kirsty Taylor

Judith Canavan

Alison Rae
Simon Ross

Editor

Simon Ross

Nelson Thornes

Published in 2012 by:
Nelson Thornes Ltd
Delta Place
27 Bath Road
CHELTENHAM
GL53 7TH
United Kingdom

12 13 14 15 16 / 10 9 8 7 6 5 4 3 2 1

A catalogue record for this book is available from the British
Library

ISBN 978 1 4085 1709 3

Cover photograph by thinair28/iStockphoto

Illustrations by David Russell Illustration, Tim Jay,
Peters & Zabransky and GreenGate Publishing

Page make-up by GreenGate Publishing, Tonbridge, Kent

Printed and bound in Spain by GraphyCems

Contents

2014001128

About these resources

Nelson Thornes has developed these resources to ensure that the book and the accompanying online resources offer you the best support for your GCSE course.

All resources have been reviewed by subject experts so you can feel assured that they closely match the specification for this subject.

These print and online resources together **unlock blended learning**; this means that the activities in the book and the activities online blend together to maximise your understanding of a topic and help you achieve your potential.

These online resources are available on Kerboodle which can be accessed via the internet at **www.kerboodle.com/live**, anytime, anywhere. If your school or college subscribes to Kerboodle you will be provided with your own personal login details. Once logged in, access your course and locate the required activity.

For more information and help on how to use Kerboodle visit **www.kerboodle.com**.

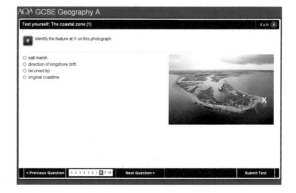

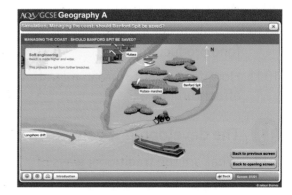

How to use this book

This specification focuses on the physical and human processes and factors that have shaped the environment in which we live. You will learn about the interdependence of physical environments and how human activity affects the environment, and vice versa. You will also gain an understanding of the need for sustainable management of both physical and human environments. You will learn to appreciate the differences and similarities between people, places and cultures and improve your understanding of societies and economies.

Your GCSE geography course has three units (Unit 1: Physical Geography; Unit 2: Human Geography, and Unit 3: Local Fieldwork Investigation, which will be based on a topic covered in the first two units). Units 1 and 2 each have two sections, A and B, and the chapters of this book take their titles from the topic titles in these sections.

■ Unit 1 Physical Geography

In the exam, you must answer three questions. One question should be taken from Section A, one from Section B and the third question from either section.

Section A

- ■ The Restless Earth
- ■ Rocks, Resources and Scenery
- ■ Challenge of Weather and Climate
- ■ Living World

Section B

- ■ Water on the Land
- ■ Ice on the Land
- ■ The Coastal Zone

These topics are intended to provide you with a solid foundation in physical geography to enable you to fully appreciate the physical world in which you live.

A great deal of emphasis has been placed on topicality, using up-to-date case studies and examples to explore themes and concepts, such as the 2011 Japanese tsunami and recent floods in Boscastle and Cockermouth.

All of the physical geography topics have a link to human activities. For example, in *The Restless Earth* you will study the impact of tectonic hazards on people's lives. The impacts of climate change are also discussed in *Challenge of Weather and Climate*.

Sustainable development is a key concept in all topics. For example, in *The Coastal Zone*, strategies for coastal defence and coastal zone management are underpinned by the need for a sustainable approach. In *Living World*, sustainability is at the heart of ecosystem management, whether it is hot deserts or tropical rainforest.

■ Unit 2 Human Geography

In the exam, you must answer three questions. One question should be taken from Section A, one from Section B and the third question from either section.

Section A

- ■ Population Change
- ■ Changing Urban Environments
- ■ Changing Rural Environments

Section B

- ■ The Development Gap
- ■ Globalisation
- ■ Tourism

These topics have been chosen to reflect current thinking and interests in geography in the 21st century. They all involve the study of recent issues and extensive use is made of up-to-date case studies and examples. For example, in *Population Change*, detailed consideration is made of the implications of China's controversial 'one child policy'. The current (and future) issue of ageing populations in Europe is also considered.

Sustainable development is a significant consideration in human geography. For example, in *Tourism*, you will discuss the issues surrounding mass tourism as well as examining recent trends such as ecotourism and adventure tourism. In *Globalisation*, topics such as renewable energy and pollution control are also tackled.

As you study human geography there will be many opportunities for you to discuss and debate real world issues, such as Fairtrade in *The Development Gap* and organic farming in *Changing Rural Environments*. You will be able to formulate and share your own opinions and, hopefully, you will be able to make a positive difference to the world around you.

1.1 Why is the earth's crust unstable?

The structure of the earth

The **crust** – the outer layer of the earth – is quite thin (diagram **A**). The crust is not one single piece of skin, like that of an apple. Instead, it is split into **plates** of different sizes. The boundary between two plates is called a **plate margin**. Currents of heat in the **mantle** called **convection currents** cause the plates to move. Plate boundaries are zones of seismic (earthquakes) and volcanic activity. There are two types of crust: oceanic and continental (diagram **B**). The location of the plates, plate boundaries and direction of movement of the plates is shown in map **C**.

In this section you will learn

about the structure of the earth and the difference between oceanic and continental crust

how and why destructive, constructive and conservative plate margins are different

how the earth's crust is unstable, especially at plate margins.

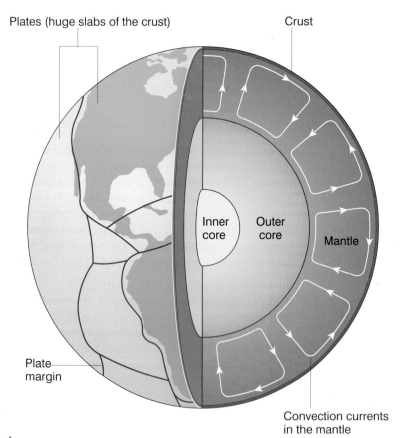

Plates (huge slabs of the crust)

Crust

Inner core

Outer core

Mantle

Plate margin

Convection currents in the mantle

A *The structure of the earth*

Key terms

Crust: the outer layer of the earth.

Plate: a section of the earth's crust.

Plate margin: the boundary where two plates meet.

Mantle: the dense, mostly solid layer of the earth between the outer core and the crust.

Convection currents: the circular currents of heat in the mantle.

Did you know ???????

The earth's crust is divided into 14 major plates and 38 minor plates, making a total of 52 jigsaw pieces altogether.

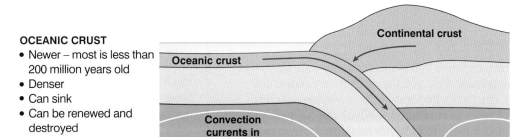

OCEANIC CRUST
- Newer – most is less than 200 million years old
- Denser
- Can sink
- Can be renewed and destroyed

CONTINENTAL CRUST
- Older – most is over 1500 million years old
- Less dense
- Cannot sink
- Cannot be renewed or destroyed

B *Contrasts between oceanic and continental crust*

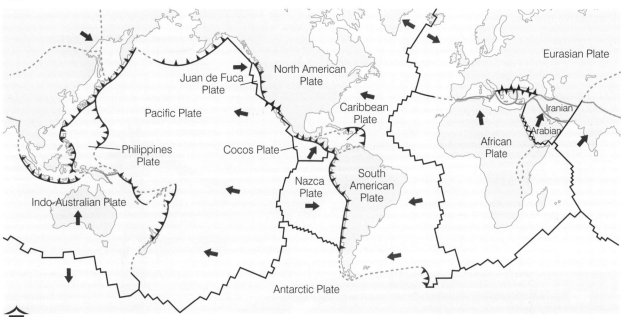

C *World tectonic plates and margins*

Activities

1 Look carefully at diagram **A**, which shows the structure of the earth.

a Which of these four words describes the outer layer of the earth?

    mantle   inner core   outer core   crust

b Explain what a plate margin is.

2 Study diagram **B**.

a Use the diagram to list four differences between continental crust and oceanic crust.

b Explain how convection currents cause plate movement.

3 Study map **C** which shows the plates and their margins. Copy this table below and fill it out. You need to use the map to find examples of each type of plate margin. The first one has been done for you.

Map key

→ Direction of plate movement

⤙⤙ Destructive margin – one plate sinks under another (subduction)

⌣ Destructive (collision) margin – two continental plates move together

ⱱⱱ Constructive margin – two plates move away from each other

⤫ Conservative margin – two plates slide alongside each other

·-·-· Uncertain plate boundary

Plate margin	Direction of plate movement	Example of plate margin
Destructive – subduction	towards each other	Nazca/South American
Destructive – collision		
Constructive		
Conservative		

Types of plate margin

Destructive plate margins

Destructive plate margins are when two plates move towards each other. If one plate is made from oceanic crust and the other from continental crust, the denser oceanic crust sinks under the lighter continental crust (see diagram **D**). This is known as **subduction**. Where this happens the oceanic crust is destroyed as it melts to form hot liquid rock called magma.

If two continental plates meet each other, they collide rather than one sinking beneath the other. This **collision** boundary is a different type of destructive margin.

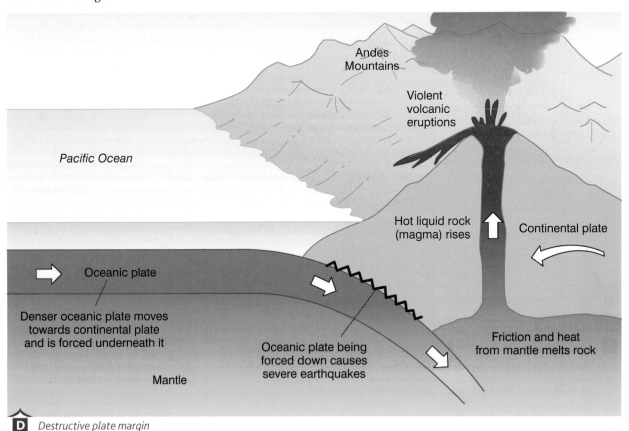

Andes Mountains

Violent volcanic eruptions

Pacific Ocean

Hot liquid rock (magma) rises

Continental plate

Oceanic plate

Denser oceanic plate moves towards continental plate and is forced underneath it

Oceanic plate being forced down causes severe earthquakes

Friction and heat from mantle melts rock

Mantle

D Destructive plate margin

Constructive plate margins

Constructive plate margins form when plates move apart. This usually happens under the oceans, as shown in map **C**. As these **oceanic plates** pull away from each other, cracks and fractures form between the plates. Magma forces its way into the cracks and makes its way to the surface to form **volcanoes**. In this way new land is formed as the plates gradually pull apart.

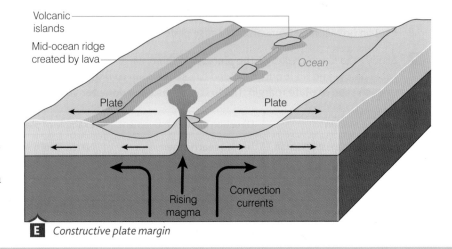

Volcanic islands

Mid-ocean ridge created by lava

Ocean

Plate

Plate

Rising magma

Convection currents

E Constructive plate margin

Conservative plate margins

At **conservative plate margins**, the plates are sliding past each other. They are moving in a similar (though not the same) direction, at slightly different angles and speeds. As one plate is moving faster than the other and in a slightly different direction, they tend to get stuck. Eventually, the build-up of pressure causes them to be released. This sudden release of pressure causes an **earthquake**. At a conservative margin, crust is not being destroyed or made. There is no magma being produced, so there are no volcanoes.

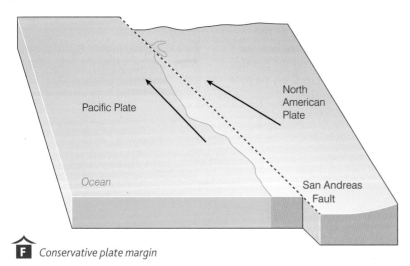

F *Conservative plate margin*

∞ links

You can find out more about plates and the different types of crust at **http://en.wikipedia.org/wiki/List_ of_tectonic_plates**.

Activity

4   Study diagrams **D**, **E** and **F**. These show what happens at three different types of plate margin: destructive, constructive and conservative plate margins.

a   At what type of plate margin does this process happen: 'As the oceanic crust is destroyed, it produces magma'?

b   At what type of plate margin does this process happen: 'As the plates slide past each other they sometimes get stuck, which can produce an earthquake'?

c   At what type of plate margin does this process happen: 'As the plates pull apart, magma forces itself into the cracks and volcanoes form'?

5   For each plate margin described in diagrams **D**, **E** and **F**, draw a labelled cross-section to describe the characteristics of the boundary and the processes that are occurring there.

Key terms

Collision: when two plates of continental crust meet 'head on' and buckle.

Constructive plate margin: a plate margin where two plates are moving apart.

Oceanic plate: a tectonic plate made of dense iron-rich rock that forms the ocean floor.

Volcano: an opening in the earth's crust through which molten lava, ash and gases are ejected.

Conservative plate margin: a plate margin where two plates are sliding alongside each other.

Earthquake: a sudden and often violent shift in the rocks forming the earth's crust, which is felt at the surface.

1.2 What landforms are found at different plate boundaries?

Fold mountains and ocean trenches

Fold mountains are the highest areas in the world. All peaks over 7,000 metres high are in central Asia, including Mount Everest at 8,850 m. This is much bigger than the highest mountain in England – Scafell Pike at 978 m. Fold mountains include ranges such as the Himalayas, the Rockies, the Andes and the Alps. **Ocean trenches** are some of the deepest parts of the ocean. The location of fold mountains and ocean trenches is shown in map **A**. Look back at map **C** on page 9 to see the link between these landforms and plate margins.

In this section you will learn

why fold mountains and ocean trenches form at destructive plate margins

the differences between composite volcanoes and shield volcanoes.

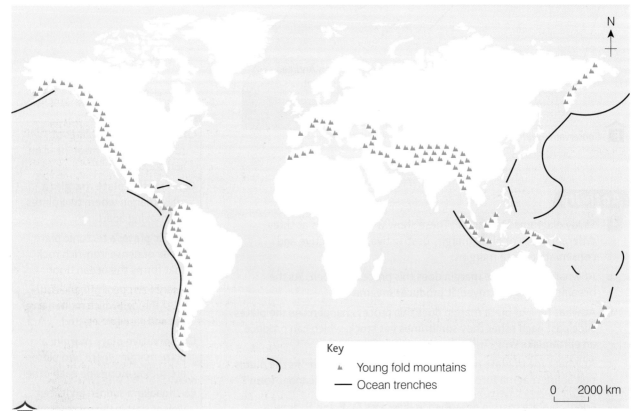

Key

▲ Young fold mountains

— Ocean trenches

0   2000 km

N

A *Young fold mountains and ocean trenches*

Activities

1. Study map **C** on page 9 and map **A** on this page. You will need a world map outline showing the plates and plate boundaries which your teacher will give you.

    a. On your map, draw the young fold mountains shown in map **A**.

    b. Then draw the ocean trenches on your map as well.

    c. At what type of plate boundary do fold mountains and ocean trenches form?

⊙⊙ links

Investigate further facts and figures about landforms resulting from plate movements at **www.geology. com** and **www.extremescience.com**.

Both fold mountains and ocean trenches happen where plates move together.

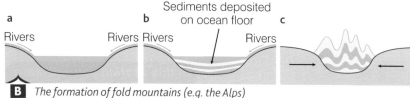

B   *The formation of fold mountains (e.g. the Alps)*

Composite and shield volcanoes

There are two types of volcano: **composite volcanoes**, which happen at destructive plate margins, and **shield volcanoes**, which happen at constructive plate margins (diagrams **C** and **D**).

Key terms

Fold mountains: large mountain ranges where rock layers have been crumpled as they have been forced together.

Ocean trenches: deep sections of the ocean, usually where an oceanic plate is sinking below a continental plate.

Composite volcano: a steep-sided volcano that is made up of a variety of materials, such as lava and ash.

Shield volcano: a broad volcano that is mostly made up of lava.

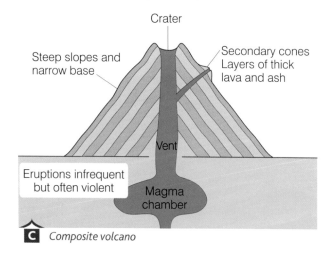

C   *Composite volcano*

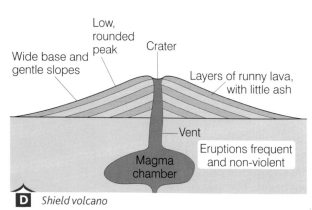

D   *Shield volcano*

Activities

2   Study diagram **B** which shows how fold mountains are formed. Use this diagram to help you answer these three questions.

a   Describe what happens in the first stage of how fold mountains are formed (this is shown in part a of the diagram).

b   Describe what happens in the second stage of how fold mountains are formed (part b of the diagram).

c   Describe what happens in the third stage of how fold mountains are formed (part c of the diagram, where the plates are moving together).

3   Study diagrams **C** and **D**. These show the main differences between shield volcanoes and composite volcanoes. Use this information to complete this table. You should copy out the table first and then complete it. The first row has been completed for you.

Volcano feature	Composite volcano	Shield volcano
Very violent eruptions, but eruptions do not happen that often	✓	✗
Frequent eruptions but not very violent eruptions		
Gentle slopes to the volcano		
The volcano sides are steep and the volcano has a narrow base		
Volcano made up of layers of thick lava and ash		
Volcano made up of runny lava, not much ash		

1.3 How do people use an area of fold mountains?

The Andes and its people

The Andes is a range of young fold mountains formed about 65 million years ago (map **A**, page 12). It is the longest range of fold mountains in the world: 7,000 kilometres long. It covers the length of South America. The Andes are about 300 km wide and have an average height of 4,000 m.

Farming

The Andes are very high and steep, they don't get much rain and the soil is thin. Even so, the mountain slopes are used for farming. Many **subsistence** farmers grow a variety of crops on the steep slopes, including potatoes which are a main source of food. Areas of flat land, called **terraces**, are created on the slopes (photo **A**) which helps the farmers in many ways:

- They stop water running down the slope.
- They stop soil sliding down the slope.

Most crops are grown in the lower valleys (photo **B**). Some cash crops are produced such as soybeans, rice and cotton.

Llamas are very important in the Andes. These surefooted animals can carry over 25 per cent of their body weight (125–200 kg). For hundreds of years they have been pack animals, carrying materials to areas where even horses cannot reach. The mining industry often relied on them as a form of transport. Male llamas are still used for transport today. The females are used for meat and milk, and their wool is used for making clothes and rugs.

A Farming on terraces in the Andes

Activities

1   Study photo **A**. This shows farming on the mountain slopes in the Andes.
   a   Describe the terraces that have been made on the mountain side.
   b   Why would farmers in this area make these terraces? What would farming be like here without the terraces?

2   Now compare photo **A** with photo **B**, which shows farming conditions in the lower valleys of the Andes fold mountains.

   Give two reasons why farming would be easier in the lower valleys than on the terraces on the mountain slopes.

   If farming is easier in the lower valleys, give one reason why farmers bother farming the difficult mountain slopes.

B   The lower valleys where the patchwork of fields shows the variety of crops shown

Mining

The Andes has a range of important minerals. Countries in the Andes rank in the top 10 for tin (Peru and Bolivia), silver (Peru and Chile) and gold (Peru). More than half of Peru's exports are from mining. The Yanacocha gold mine (map **C**) is the largest gold mine in the world. It is an open pit mine. The rock which contains the gold is blasted loose with dynamite. The rock is then sprayed with cyanide which dissolves everything except for the gold. This can, however, lead to contamination of water supplies.

The nearby town of Cajamarca has grown from 30,000 inhabitants (when the mine began) to about 300,000 in 2010. This brings with it lots of different jobs. However, this growth also brings many problems, including a lack of services and an increased crime rate.

Hydroelectric power

In many ways, the Andes are good places for **hydroelectric power** (HEP) because:

- it is often cheaper to put dams across narrow valleys than wide ones
- the steep mountain sides make the water flow very quickly to generate electricity
- melting snow creates plenty of water to generate electricity in the spring.

The Yuncan project dams the Paucartambo and Huachon rivers in north-east Peru. In 2009 the El Platanal HEP power plant began to generate electricity. Involving a huge dam across the Cânete River, the $US200 million project is the second largest in Peru (map **C**).

Key terms

Subsistence: farming to provide food and other resources for the farmer's own family.

Terraces: steps cut into hillsides to create areas of flat land.

Irrigation: artificial watering of the land.

Hydroelectric power: the use of flowing water to turn turbines to generate electricity.

Study tip

Make sure that you can list and explain the different ways people use a specific range of fold mountains.

Activities

3 Study map **C**.

a Work in pairs to produce a short presentation to include:

- a map showing where the Yanacocha gold mine is located in Peru
- how the mine is good for the local area and good for Peru as a whole
- how the mine is possibly damaging the local area around it.

b Show your presentation to another group.

C The location of Yanacocha gold mine and the El Platanal HEP project

D *A llama looks over Machu Picchu*

Tourism

There are many natural attractions which people want to visit in the Andes such as mountain peaks, volcanoes, glaciers and lakes. Some tourist attractions show how people settled in these places, such as the remains of early settlements built by the Incas like Machu Picchu (photo **D**). The Inca Trail combines both (extract **E**).

∞ links

Investigate further facts and discussion about gold mining by searching on **www.google.co.uk**. For more on the Inca Trail, go to **www.incatrailperu.com**.

The Inca Trail is South America's best-known trek

The Inca Trail is South America's best-known trek. It combines a stunning mix of Inca ruins, mountain scenery, lush forest and tropical jungle. Over 250 species of orchid exist in the Machu Picchu historic sanctuary, as well as many species of birds. The sanctuary is an important natural and archaeological reserve – it is only one of 23 UNESCO world heritage sites to be classified as important for both culture and nature.

The Inca Trail is a hike that finishes at Machu Picchu, the sacred mysterious 'Lost City of the Incas'. The 45 km trek is usually covered in four days, arriving at Machu Picchu at daybreak on the final day before returning to Cusco by train in the afternoon. It is best to do the trek between April and October, when the weather is drier. Any fit person should be able to walk the route. It is fairly challenging and altitudes of 4,200 m are reached, so it is important to be well acclimatised.

E *The Inca Trail*

1.4 How do volcanoes affect people?

The distribution of volcanoes

Volcanoes are an example of a **natural hazard**. They are usually located at plate margins (map **A** and map **C**, page 9). The area around the Pacific Ocean is known as 'the Pacific Ring of Fire' because there are so many volcanoes there. Occasionally, active volcanoes are found away from plate margins. We are going to study two recent volcanic eruptions that have had significant impacts on people's lives.

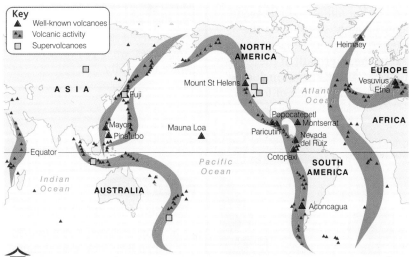

A *The distribution of active volcanoes and supervolcanoes (see topic 1.5, page 22)*

Key terms

Natural hazard: an event over which people have little control, which threatens people's lives and possessions. This is different from a natural event as volcanoes can erupt without being a hazard.

Primary effects: the immediate effects of the eruption, caused directly by it.

Secondary effects: the after-effects that occur as an indirect effect of the eruption on a longer timescale.

Aid: money, food, training and technology given by richer countries to poorer ones, either to help with an emergency or for long-term development.

Activities

1. Study map **A**. This shows where the world's active volcanoes are located.

   a. Describe the distribution of the world's active volcanoes. Is there a pattern to their location, or does it look like they just occur in random places?

   b. Where would you go if you were really interested in seeing a volcano?

   c. How about if someone you knew was terrified of volcanoes. Where would you recommend they went on holiday?

2. Compare the distribution of the world's volcanoes with map **C** on page 9. This shows the world's main plates and plate boundaries.

   a. Would you agree or disagree with this statement: 'Volcanoes usually occur at plate boundaries'?

   b. What type of plate margin looks to be most closely associated with active volcanoes?

The eruption of Nyiragongo, Africa (2002)

On 17 January 2002, Nyiragongo volcano in the Democratic Republic of Congo erupted. It is one of several volcanoes formed along the East African rift valley. Lava spilled south in three streams. The speed of the lava reached 60 kilometres per hour, which is especially fast. The lava flowed across the runway at Goma airport (photo **C**) and through the town, splitting it in half (map **B**). **Primary effects** of the eruption included:

- The lava destroyed many homes as well as roads and water pipes.
- There were explosions in fuel stores and power plants which killed 45 people.

There were also many **secondary effects**. Half a million people went to Rwanda to escape the lava. They spent the night sleeping on the streets of Gisenyi. Here, there was no shelter, electricity or clean water. Diseases such as cholera were a real risk. In the aftermath of the eruption, water had to be supplied in tankers. **Aid** agencies, including Christian Aid and Oxfam, were involved in the distribution of food, medicine and blankets.

C *Lava on the runway at Goma airport*

Study tip

Be clear about the differences between the terms 'effects' and 'responses' when you write about volcanic activity.

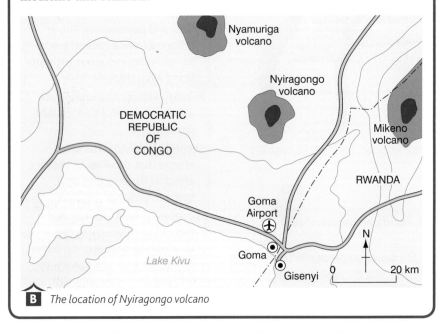

B *The location of Nyiragongo volcano*

Activities

3 Study map **B** and photo **C**.

a Draw a sketch map based on map **B** to show the location of the volcano, the countries and the main towns. Use an arrow to show the flow of the lava towards Goma.

b Label your sketch map to show the primary and secondary effects of the eruption at Nyiragongo.

The eruption of Eyjafjallajökull, Iceland (2010)

Iceland lies on the Mid-Atlantic Ridge, a constructive plate margin separating the Eurasian plate from the North American plate (map **C** on page 9). As the plates move apart, magma rises to the surface to form several active volcanoes located in a belt running through the centre of Iceland (map **D**). Eyjafjallajökull (1,666 m high) is located beneath an ice cap in southern Iceland 125 km south east of the capital, Reykjavik.

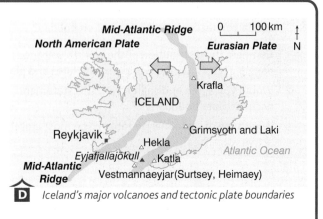

D *Iceland's major volcanoes and tectonic plate boundaries*

The eruption

In March 2010 magma broke through the crust beneath the Eyjafjallajökull glacier. This was the start of two months of dramatic and powerful eruptions that would affect people all over the world. The eruptions in March were mostly lava eruptions. Whilst they were spectacular and fiery they were of little threat to local people.

However, on 14 April a new phase began which was much more explosive. Over a period of several days in mid-April violent eruptions sent huge quantities of ash into the atmosphere (photo **E**).

E *Ash cloud from the eruption of Eyjafjallajökull*

Impacts and responses

The heavier particles of ash (like black gritty sand) fell to the ground close to the volcano, covering land with a thick layer of ash (photo **F**). The **immediate response** was to evacuate local people from their farms and villages. Rescuers wore face masks to prevent them choking on the dense cloud of ash.

F *Ash falls (impact on farming) or flood wiping out road*

One of the most damaging secondary effects of the eruption was flooding. As the eruption happened underneath a glacier, a huge amount of meltwater was produced which flooded the coastal plains at the foot of the mountains destroying roads and crops.

The eruption of Eyjafjallajökull became an international event as the cloud of ash spread south-eastwards towards the rest of Europe (map **G**). Scientists were worried about aeroplane engines being jammed by the ash so aeroplanes were not allowed to fly over a large area of Europe. The knock-on effects were felt across the world.

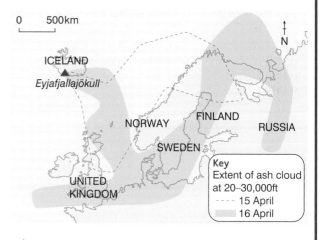

G *The spread of the ash cloud over Europe*

Some people felt that the closures were an over-reaction and that aeroplanes could fly safely through low concentrations of ash. However, a scientific review conducted after the eruption concluded that it had been right to close the airspace. Further research will be carried out as a **long-term response** to find better ways of monitoring ash concentrations and improving forecast models. This should minimise disruption in the future.

It's not all bad news though! Eyjafjallajökull has become a new tourist attraction which benefits local people and industries. Lava and ash help to make the soils very fertile and good for agriculture. The rocks themselves can be used for building. Geothermal energy just below the surface of the earth can be used to produce electricity and provide hot water for industry, heating swimming pools and even melting snow. Small quantities of valuable minerals such as copper, gold, silver, lead, and zinc are often found in volcanic regions. Deposits of sulphur can be mined from volcanic craters and used to bleach sugar and make matches and fertiliser.

H *Impacts of the Eyjafjallajökull explosion*

Local	National	International
Some 800 local people living close to the volcano had to leave their homes	Tourism was affected with the number of international tourists dropping during summer 2010. This affected the Icelandic economy as well as local people's jobs and incomes.	Over a period of 8 days, some 100,000 flights were cancelled. Ten million business people and tourists were stranded. Airlines and airports lost huge amounts of money (estimated at £80 million).
Local flood defences were destroyed	Road transport was disrupted as roads were washed away by floods.	Industries and businesses were affected as workers, raw materials and products couldn't reach factories and shops e.g. Honda stopped making cars.
Crops (particularly grass used for hay) were damaged by heavy falls of ash	Agricultural production was affected as crops were smothered by a thick layer of ash.	Fresh food could not be imported, affecting supermarkets and producers across the world e.g. farm workers in Kenya lost their jobs or suffered pay cuts as flowers and beans couldn't reach Europe.
Local water supplies were contaminated with fluoride	Reconstruction of roads and services was expensive.	In sport, a number of international events were affected by the flight ban including the Japanese Motorcycle Grand Prix, French rugby league teams competing in the Challenge Cup and the Boston Marathon on 19 April, which took place without a number of international athletes.

Activities

4 Use the information on these pages to complete a table like this about primary and secondary effects. You should copy out this table first. Some answers have been added already to get you started.

Impacts of the Eyjafjallajökull eruption	Primary effect	Secondary effect
Risk of choking from the thick fall of ash	✓	
Flooding produced by the volcano melting glacier ice		✓
Airplanes unable to fly through the ash cloud		
Ash covering agricultural land, making farming impossible		
Fresh food couldn't be imported to Iceland due to the airplane flying ban		
Road transport disrupted when roads were washed away by the meltwater floods		

5 Think back to plate margins and volcano types. Is Eyjafjallajökull an example of a:
- ◼ composite volcano on a destructive plate margin?
- ◼ shield volcano on a constructive plate margin?
- ◼ shield volcano on a conservative margin?
- ◼ composite volcano on a constructive margin?

6 Compare the responses to the Nyiragongo volcanic eruption and the Eyjafjallajökull eruption. Think about the following for your answer:
- ◼ were the immediate responses to the eruption the same or different?
- ◼ were the long term responses different (think about the role of aid agencies here)?
- ◼ Congo is a poorer country and Iceland is a richer country. Did this affect these responses?

7 Tourism is one positive effect of volcanoes. Use the internet to find answers to these questions.

a How has Eyjafjallajökull become a tourist attraction?

b Research two other positive effects of volcanic activity in Iceland. Describe each positive effect and give an example of where this occurs.

Monitoring and predicting volcanoes

Volcanoes usually give warning signs that they are going to erupt. Scientists monitor active volcanoes using high technology equipment and warnings are given if a volcano seems likely to erupt.

- An increase in the number of earthquakes shows that magma is rising beneath a volcano, causing rocks to crack and break. Earthquakes are recorded using instruments called seismometers that are placed in the ground.

- Digital cameras (photo I) can be placed on the rim of craters to record small eruptions or landslides that might indicate rising magma (e.g. White Island, New Zealand). The cameras are controlled by people far away so it's safe.

- Tiltmeters can be placed on the ground to measure slight changes in the tilt of the ground caused by rising magma (diagram J). Just before Mount St Helens erupted in 1980 (in the USA) one side of the volcano bulged as magma rose inside. Global positioning systems (GPS) use satellite technology to measure very slight changes of as little as 1 mm. Laser beams can also be used to measure changes in distance between two fixed points on a volcano. If the volcano swells, the distance between two places will increase.

- Gases emitted from a volcano, such as sulphur dioxide, can change in concentration prior to an eruption. Continuous gas monitoring stations are used by scientists to monitor activity at Kilauea volcano on Hawaii.

Historic information from previous eruptions, such as evidence of ash falls, lava flows and **lahars** can be used to construct **hazard maps**. These identify zones at risk from particular hazards. They can be used in deciding which areas are safe for developments such as housing and also in making plans for evacuations.

Key terms

Immediate responses: how people react during a disaster and straight afterwards.

Long-term responses: later reactions that happen in the weeks, months and years after the event.

Hazard map: a map that shows areas that are at risk from hazards such as earthquakes, volcanoes, landslides, floods and tsunamis.

Lahar: mudflows resulting from ash mixing with melting ice or water – a secondary effect of a volcano.

∞ links

Further information with many suberb links about the eruption of Eyjafjallajökull can be found at www.geographyinthenews.rgs.org. Search for Eyjafjallajökull.

Activities

8   Study the text together with photo I and diagram J.

a   Make a list of the different ways in which volcanoes are monitored and predicted.

b   Pick one of these methods of monitoring volcanoes. Explain how it works to monitor changes in or around the volcano.

c   Imagine you were chief of police in a town near an active volcano when a warning came through that an eruption looked likely in the next three days. What information would you want to know to best protect your townspeople? You could play out this scenario as a role play.

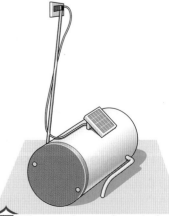

J   Tiltmeters detect a change in slope caused by shifting magma beneath the surface.

I   Time-lapse cameras in the crater allow geologists to make safe observations

1.5 What is a supervolcano?

A **supervolcano** is a massive volcano. If a supervolcano erupted today it would cause a global catastrophe. Look back at map **A** on page 17 to see where the world's supervolcanoes are.

Characteristics of a supervolcano

Supervolcanoes are on a much bigger scale than volcanoes. They emit at least $1,000\,km^3$ of material – a thousand times bigger than a volcano like Mt. St. Helens or Eyjafjallajökull. Supervolcanoes do not look like a volcano. Instead of a cone, they are large depressions called **calderas**, often marked by a rim of higher land around the edges (diagram **A**).

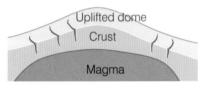

1 Rising magma cannot escape, and a large bulge appears on the surface

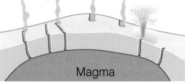

2 Cracks appear in the surface and gas and ash erupt from the magma chamber

3 The magma chamber collapses, forming a depression called a caldera

A The formation of a supervolcano

In this section you will learn

what a supervolcano is and how it differs from a volcano

the potential impact of a supervolcano eruption in contrast to a volcano eruption

Key terms

Supervolcano: a mega colossal volcano that erupts at least $1,000\,km^3$ of material.

Caldera: the depression of the supervolcano marking the collapsed magma chamber.

Geothermal: water that is heated beneath the ground, which comes to the surface in a variety of ways.

Geyser: a geothermal feature in which water erupts into the air under pressure.

Hot spot: a section of the earth's crust where plumes of magma rise, weakening the crust. These are away from plate boundaries.

Activities

1 Study map **A** on page 17. This shows where the main volcanoes and supervolcanoes are located around the world.
  a Describe the distribution of supervolcanoes.
  b How is the distribution of supervolcanoes different from that of volcanoes?

2 Study diagram **A**.
  a Draw simple diagrams of a volcano and a supervolcano.
  b Label your diagrams to show the characteristics and contrasts between them.

The Yellowstone supervolcano

Map **B** shows the area of Yellowstone and some of its attractions. Many visitors stand in awe looking at Old Faithful and the **geothermal** features of the Norris **Geyser** basin without realising they are standing on a supervolcano! This supervolcano could threaten the existence of people in America and around the world.

Did you know ? ? ? ? ? ?

The last supervolcano eruption occurred on Sumatra when Toba erupted 74,000 years ago. It is thought world temperatures fell by between 3 and 5 °C. Toba exuded $3,000\,km^3$ of magma and covered India in a layer of ash 15 cm deep.

Study tip

Make notes to reinforce your understanding of the differences between a volcano and a supervolcano.

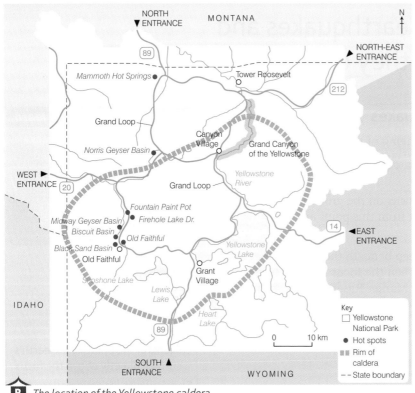

B The location of the Yellowstone caldera

C Cascade Geyser in Yellowstone National Park

Three eruptions have occurred at this **hot spot** during the last 2 million years. An eruption today would have a catastrophic effect.

There is evidence that the magma beneath Yellowstone is shifting. The caldera is bulging up beneath Lake Yellowstone. There are signs of increasing activity at Norris and the ground has risen 70 cm in places. Is this just part of a natural cycle? The magma chamber beneath Yellowstone is believed to be 80 km long, 40 km wide and 8 km deep.

An eruption is likely to destroy 10,000 km² of land and kill 87,000 people. An estimated 15 cm of ash would cover buildings within 1,000 km and 1 in 3 people affected would die. The ash would affect transport, electricity, water and farming. High level atmospheric winds would transfer the ash cloud to the UK in just 5 days. Global climates would change, crops would fail and many people would die.

∞links

Investigate the Yellowstone supervolcano further at **www. discovery.com** and **www.bbc.co.uk**. Enter Yellowstone supervolcano into the search box in both websites.

Activities

3 Study map **B**, which shows the location of the Yellowstone caldera.

a Use the key to measure the size of the caldera at its widest point north to south and west to east.

b There are several geysers shown on the map. What are geysers? Write a description that explains how geysers are related to the supervolcano.

c What is the evidence that Yellowstone might soon erupt again?

4 Produce a front-page report for a newspaper published in the UK describing the local, national and global impacts as 'Yellowstone supervolcano erupts'.

1.6 What are earthquakes and where do they occur?

Characteristics of earthquakes

An earthquake is a sudden, violent shaking of the ground.

- The place where earthquakes begin, deep within the earth's crust, is called the **focus**.
- The point immediately above the focus on the ground surface is called the **epicentre**. Radiating out from this point are **shock waves** (called seismic waves).

When the focus of an earthquake is deep beneath the surface, they are felt less and cause less damage than when the focus is closer to the surface. This is why the earthquake at Market Rasen in Lincolnshire on 27 February 2008, was felt a long way away but not severely. The focus was 18.6 km below the surface.

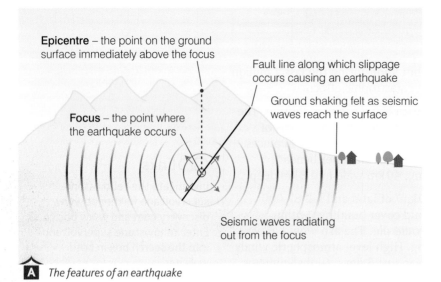

Epicentre – the point on the ground surface immediately above the focus

Fault line along which slippage occurs causing an earthquake

Ground shaking felt as seismic waves reach the surface

Focus – the point where the earthquake occurs

Seismic waves radiating out from the focus

A *The features of an earthquake*

Where and why do earthquakes occur?

Map **B** shows the location of areas which have many earthquakes. Look back at map **C** on page 9, and you will see a close link between plate margins and where earthquakes happen. The friction and pressures that build up where the plates meet causes earthquakes.

- Destructive margins – here the sinking of the subducting plate can trigger strong earthquakes as this pressure is periodically released.
- Constructive margins – here earthquakes tend to be less severe than those at destructive or conservative plate margins. The friction and pressure caused by the plates moving apart is less intense than at destructive plate margins.

In this section you will learn

the features of an earthquake and how they are measured

where volcanoes occur and why they are found at constructive, destructive and conservative plate margins

Key terms

Focus: the point in the earth's crust where the earthquake begins.

Epicentre: the point at the earth's surface directly above the focus.

Shock waves: seismic waves generated by an earthquake that pass through the earth's crust.

- Conservative margins – here the plates tend to stick for periods of time as they try to slide past each other. This causes stresses and pressure to build. The release of the pressure occurs in a sudden, quick release of the plates and this often produces powerful earthquakes.

Study tip

Ensure that you can describe and explain the distribution of earthquakes – where they occur and why.

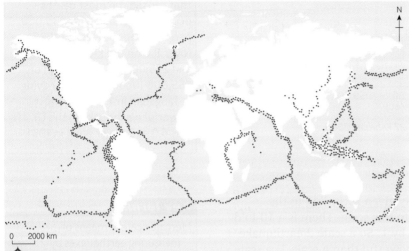

0   2000 km

B   *The location of earthquake zones*

Activities

1   Study diagram **A**, which shows the features of an earthquake.

a   Draw your own diagrams based on this one to illustrate:
- the focus of an earthquake
- the epicentre of an earthquake.

b   On your diagram, next to where you have shown the focus, write a definition of what the focus is.

c   Do the same thing for the epicentre. Write a definition of this term next to the epicentre on your diagram.

2   Study map **B**, above, and map **C** on page 9.

a   On an outline map of the world, shade in the areas that experience earthquakes.

b   Using an atlas to help you, add the locations of the following recent earthquakes to your map:
- Christ Church, New Zealand (2011)
- Port-au-Prince, Haiti (2010)
- Sichuan, China (2008)
- Kashmir, Pakistan (2005)
- Bam, Iran (2003)
- Kobe, Japan (1995).
- Add any additional recent earthquakes.

c   'Earthquakes mostly occur at plate boundaries.' Do you think this statement is correct? Give two reasons to back up your answer.

links

There are many facts and figures available at **http://earthquake. usgs.gov** and **www.earthquakes. bgs.ac.uk**.

Measuring earthquakes

When earthquakes occur, seismographs record the extent of the shaking by a pen identifying the trace of the movement on a rotating drum. The line graph produced is called a seismogram (graph **C**).

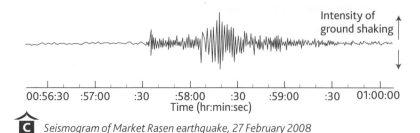

Intensity of ground shaking

| | | | | | | | |
00:56:30 :57:00 :30 :58:00 :30 :59:00 :30 01:00:00
Time (hr:min:sec)

C *Seismogram of Market Rasen earthquake, 27 February 2008*

The Richter scale

The strength of earthquakes is generally given according to the **Richter scale**. There is no upper limit to this scale. There is a 10-fold increase every time the scale increases by 1. So a scale 2 earthquake on the Richter scale is 10 times more powerful than a scale 1; a scale 3 earthquake is 10 times more powerful than a scale 2 and 100 times more powerful than a scale 1.

The Mercalli scale

The **Mercalli scale** measures the effects of earthquakes using a scale from I to XII. It uses descriptions of the resulting damage (table **D**).

Key terms

Mercalli scale: a means of measuring earthquakes by describing and comparing the damage done, on a scale of I to XII.

Richter scale: a scale ranging from 0 to 10 used for measuring earthquakes, based on scientific recordings of the amount of movement.

D *The Mercalli scale*

I	Barely felt
II	Felt by a few people; some suspended objects may swing
III	Slightly felt indoors as though a large truck were passing
IV	Felt indoors by many people; most suspended objects swing; windows and dishes rattle; standing cars rock
V	Felt by almost everyone; sleeping people are awakened; dishes and windows break
VI	Felt by everyone; some are frightened and run outside; some furniture moves; slight damage
VII	Considerable damage in poorly built structures; felt by people driving; most are frightened and run outside
VIII	Slight damage to well-built structures; poorly built structures are heavily damaged; walls, chimneys and monuments fall
IX	Underground pipes break; foundations of buildings are damaged and buildings shift off foundations; considerable damage to well-built structures
X	Few structures survive; water moved out of banks of rivers and lakes; avalanches and rockslides; railroads are bent
XI	Few structures remain standing; total panic; large cracks in the ground
XII	Total destruction; objects thrown into the air; the land appears to be liquid and is visibly rolling like waves

Activity

3 Study table **D**. The Mercalli scale describes the damage done by different scales of earthquake.

a Read the Mercalli description for level V (5). Draw a picture of what that sort of damage would look like in your school.

b Now read the Mercalli description for level XI (11) and draw a picture of what your school would look like after suffering that scale of earthquake.

1.7   How do the effects of earthquakes differ in countries at different stages of development?

Case study

The Kobe earthquake, Japan

At 5.46am on 17 January 1995 there was an earthquake near Kobe in Japan which measured 7.2 on the Richter scale, with tremors lasting 20 seconds.

The effects of the Kobe earthquake

In this short time, the earthquake:

- killed 6,434 people, injured over 40,000 and made 300,000 people homeless
- broke gas mains, electric works and water pipes, leaving two million homes without electricity and one million homes without water for 10 days
- caused fires which swept through the city, destroying wooden structures (photo **C**)
- destroyed part of the transport system as roads collapsed (photo **B**) and railway lines buckled.
- Afterwards people huddled in blankets on the streets and in tents in parks because they were scared to return to buildings which might fall down.

The damage caused was over $220 billion and the economy suffered. Companies such as Panasonic had to close temporarily.

In this section you will learn

case studies of earthquakes in countries at different stages of development – their causes, effects and responses
how and why the effects and responses are different in these two areas
the ways of trying to reduce the impact of earthquakes: the three Ps.

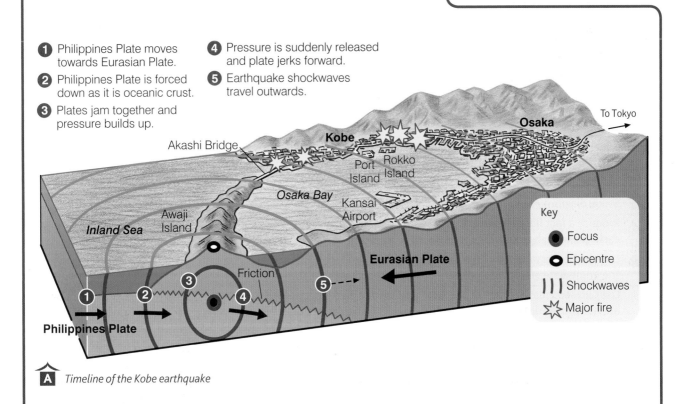

❶ Philippines Plate moves towards Eurasian Plate.
❷ Philippines Plate is forced down as it is oceanic crust.
❸ Plates jam together and pressure builds up.
❹ Pressure is suddenly released and plate jerks forward.
❺ Earthquake shockwaves travel outwards.

Akashi Bridge
Kobe
Osaka
To Tokyo
Port Island
Rokko Island
Osaka Bay
Kansai Airport
Inland Sea
Awaji Island
Friction
Eurasian Plate
Philippines Plate

Key
● Focus
◎ Epicentre
|│| Shockwaves
✺ Major fire

A   Timeline of the Kobe earthquake

Responses to the Kobe earthquake

- Friends and neighbours searched through the rubble for survivors, joined by the emergency services when they could reach the area.
- Hospitals struggled to cope with the numbers of people injured.
- Shops such as 7-Eleven helped to provide food and water for survivors.
- Motorola maintained telephone connections free of charge.
- The railways were 80 per cent operational within a month. It was not until September 1996 that the Hanshin Expressway was fully open again. A year later, the port was 80 per cent operational, but much of the container shipping business had been lost.

Buildings that had survived the earthquake had been built to a 1981 code, whereas earlier buildings had collapsed. This led to changes. New buildings were built further apart. High-rise buildings had to have flexible steel frames. Others were built of concrete frames reinforced with steel instead of wood. Rubber blocks were put under bridges to absorb shocks.

B *The Great Hanshin Expressway*

C *Fire in the area west of Kobe port*

Did you know ??????

The Japanese practise an earthquake drill every year to prepare them for an event such as that at Kobe. Over 800,000 people took part in a drill in August 2006.

Activity

1 Study diagram **A** and photos **B** and **C**.

a Produce a fact file to summarise the main points about the Kobe earthquake such as the date, time, focus and epicentre.

b List two primary effects of the Kobe earthquake. Primary effects are the immediate effects of the earthquake, caused directly by it.

c List two secondary effects of the Kobe earthquake. Secondary effects are not caused directly by the earthquake but happen as a result of what it does, after the earthquake.

d List two immediate responses to the Kobe earthquake. Immediate responses are how people react as the disaster happens and in the period immediately after it.

e List two long-term responses to the Kobe earthquake. These are later reactions that occur in the weeks, months and years after the event.

The Haiti earthquake (2010)

At 16:53 on 12 January 2010 the Caribbean island of Haiti was struck by a powerful 7.0 earthquake. The epicentre of the earthquake was very close to the capital Port-au-Prince. Following the main earthquake there were several minor tremors measuring up to 5.0 on the Richter scale.

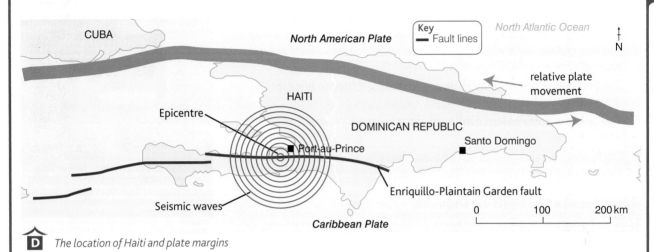

D   *The location of Haiti and plate margins*

The effects of the Haiti earthquake

The Haiti earthquake was one of the most destructive earthquakes of all time.

- Approximately 230,000 people were killed.
- Over 2 million people were affected by the earthquake and 1.5 m were made homeless.
- About 180,000 homes were destroyed by ground shaking – this is an example of a primary effect (photo **E**).
- The homeless lived in over 1,100 squalid camps with limited services such as water and sanitation. Many remained in these camps for well over a year. Storms and flooding caused further hardship in the camps (photo **F**).
- Cholera claimed the lives of several hundred people, mainly children in the aftermath of the earthquake. This is a good example of a secondary effect.
- Some 19 million cubic metres of rubble and debris remained in Port-au-Prince – enough to fill a line of shipping containers stretching end to end from London to Beirut.
- Approximately 5,000 schools were damaged or destroyed.
- Services such as electricity, water, sanitation and communications were badly disrupted or destroyed.
- The total cost of repairing the damage done by the earthquake is $US 11.5bn over a period of 5–10 years.

E   *The impacts of the earthquake*

Why did Haiti suffer so much?

There are several reasons why Haiti suffered so much death and destruction:

- Haiti is a very poor country. It was unprepared for an earthquake and could not cope after it happened.
- Most people lived in poorly constructed buildings which were very close together. The buildings simply fell apart when the earthquake struck.
- The earthquake was very close to the capital city Port-au-Prince and had a shallow focus. This meant that the city experienced very severe ground shaking.
- The port and airport were badly damaged making it hard to bring in emergency supplies.
- The lack of a stable government meant that organising rescue and recovery was very slow.
- There were not enough doctors, hospitals (most were destroyed) and medical supplies. Many people died from their injuries or from diseases.

Responses to the Haiti earthquake

The main short-term response was looking for survivors. Teams with sniffer dogs and high tech equipment were flown into the country to help local people rescue those trapped by the collapsed buildings. Food, water, medical supplies and temporary shelter were also brought in. The United Nations and USA helped to maintain law and order and help give out aid. The UK's Disasters Emergency Committee (DEC) raised over £100 m. This money was used to support over 1.2 million people by providing emergency shelter, medical help, clean drinking water and sanitation.

In the weeks and months that followed there were several longer-term responses:

- Three-quarters of the damaged buildings were inspected and repaired.
- Some 200,000 people have received cash or food for public work, such as clearing the many tonnes of rubble.
- Several thousand people have decided to leave Port-au-Prince.
- The World Bank pledged $US 100 m to help Haiti recover.

F *Refugee camp Acra in Delmas, Port-au-Prince*

Activity

2 Work in pairs to copy and complete the table below to summarise the main facts about the two earthquakes.

Feature	Kobe earthquake	Haiti earthquake
Cause		
Primary effects		
Secondary effects		
Immediate responses		
Long-term responses		

■ Prediction, protection and preparation

The **three Ps** provide the key to trying to reduce the impact of earthquakes.

Prediction

Prediction tries to work out when and where an earthquake will happen. Experts know that earthquakes happen at plate margins but cannot pinpoint exactly where. They also cannot tell when. Even looking at the time between earthquakes in a particular area does not seem to work. Even when they do, this often does not leave enough time to warn people.

Protection

Building solid structures using special designs is the main method of **protection** (diagram **G**). Man-made structures such as houses and bridges need to be able to absorb stresses or sway to avoid breaking apart.

Preparation

Preparation involves hospitals, emergency services and local people practising for major disasters. A code of practice helps people to know what to do to reduce the impact and increase their chance of survival.

Computer-controlled weights on roof to reduce movement

'Birdcage' interlocking steel frame

Steel frames that can sway during earth movements

Outer panels flexibly attached to steel structure

Fire-resistant building materials

Automatic window shutters to prevent falling glass

Roads to provide quick access for emergency services

Open areas where people can assemble if evacuated

Foundations sunk into bedrock, avoiding clay

Rubber shock-absorbers to absorb earth tremors

G *Earthquake-proofed building*

⚭ links

To research Kobe, go to **www.seismo.unr.edu**; for Haiti go to **http://earthquake.usgs.gov**.

For information on earthquake preparation and drills, visit **www.bbc.co.uk** and **www.sfgate.com**. Enter 'earthquake drill' into the search box.

Activities

3 Prediction, protection and preparation are three ways of trying to reduce the impact of an earthquake.

a Write down what each term means: prediction, protection and preparation.

b Which of the three Ps do you think is the most useful in reducing the impact of earthquakes? Explain your answer.

4 Why do you think richer countries are often more successful in reducing the impact of earthquakes than poorer countries? Think about:

■ The availability of enough doctors, hospitals and emergency supplies to cope with an earthquake.

■ How important money would be in constructing earthquake-proof buildings.

■ What sort of systems you need to run earthquake drills and make sure everyone knows what to do if there is an earthquake.

1.8 Why is a tsunami hazardous?

How tsunamis form

Tsunamis are caused by earthquakes, volcanic eruptions or underwater landslides. The movement of the plates during an earthquake causes the water above to move upwards. This is the start of a tsunami, a giant wave or wall of water

- A normal, wind-driven wave may be 100 m long from crest to crest, but a tsunami may be 200 km in length.
- The heights are also different: 2 m for a normal wave versus 1 m for a tsunami out at sea.
- Tsunamis move at speeds of around 800 kph (500 mph), rapidly approaching the coast almost unnoticed.
- As they get close to land tsunamis slow down and get shorter and higher (diagram **A**).

In this section you will learn

what a tsunami is and why it is a secondary effect of an earthquake

the causes and effects of, and responses to, a tsunami.

Key term

Tsunami: a special type of wave where an event, often an earthquake, moves the entire depth of the water above it.

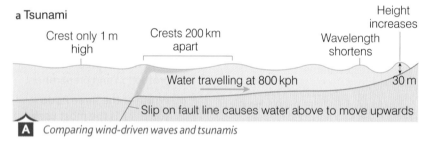

a Tsunami

Crest only 1 m high — Crests 200 km apart — Wavelength shortens — Height increases

Water travelling at 800 kph — 30 m

Slip on fault line causes water above to move upwards

b Normal wave

Wind speed 32 kph →

Crests 100 m apart — Wave height 2 m — Breaking wave

A *Comparing wind-driven waves and tsunamis*

The Tohoku tsunami, Japan 2011

On 11 March 2011 a very powerful earthquake measuring 9.0 on the Richter scale happened about 100 km east of Sendai on Honshu, Japan. In just 30 minutes a wall of water up to 40 m high hit the coast of north western Japan. It was followed in places by up to nine more 'waves' of up to 10 m in height.

Causes

The earthquake that caused the tsunami happened at the destructive plate margin where the Pacific plate is moving under the North American plate.

Scientists believe that a 200 km section of solid crust slipped suddenly making the earth's crust move upwards by between 5–10 m. It was this sudden uplift that triggered the tsunami (diagram **C**).

Effects

- Over 20,000 people were killed as the waves swept up to 10 km on shore.
- 500 km² of coastal plains were flooded and farmland, buildings and communications were destroyed.

B *Aerial view of the impact of the Japanese tsunami*

- The port city of Sendai (population 100,000) was almost totally swept away. 200,000 buildings were damaged or destroyed by the earthquake and tsunami.
- Ruptured gas pipes led to fires that raged for days.
- Explosions occurred at the Fukushima nuclear power plant as seawater came over the flood defences.
- Electricity was cut off in almost six million homes and over one million people were left without running water.
- Relief efforts were held back by heavy snow, roads blocked by debris and landslides and over 1,000 aftershocks. In some areas food, water and medical supplies ran out.
- Japan's economy was hit very hard. Stock markets around the world fell.

Responses

- Over 100,000 Japanese soldiers were used in search and rescue. They gave out blankets, water and food to the people affected by the disaster.
- Specialist search and rescue teams were flown in to the area from overseas.
- An exclusion zone was set up around the Fukushima nuclear plant and people were forced to leave the area.
- In the longer-term, a huge re-building and reconstruction programme is planned.
- The system of tsunami defences may well be made higher than they were before.

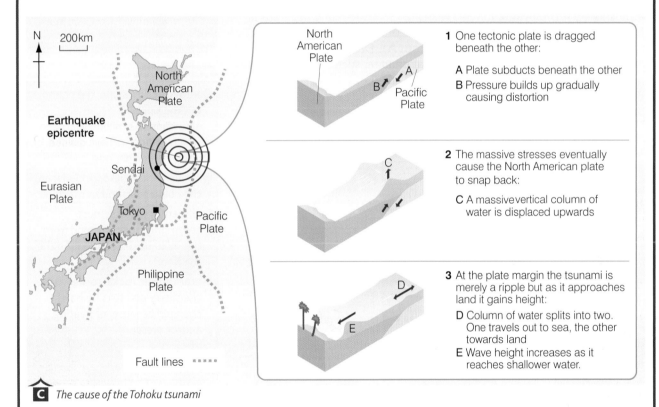

C *The cause of the Tohoku tsunami*

Activity

Working in small groups of three or four, produce a report or presentation on the Japanese tsunami to include the following:

a A definition of 'tsunami'.

b An explanation of what caused the Tohoku tsunami of 2011. A labelled diagram would be a good way to do this.

c A description of three primary effects of the Tohoku tsunami. Primary effects are the immediate effects, caused directly by the tsunami.

d A description of two secondary effects of the Tohoku tsunami. Remember, these are things that happen because of what the tsunami did, but were not directly caused by the tsunami.

e Describe two immediate responses to the Tohoku tsunami.

f Describe two long-term responses to the Tohoku tsunami.

2 Rocks, resources and scenery

2.1 How were rocks formed?

What is the geological timescale?

Although we measure time in minutes and hours, geologists are not often interested in anything less than hundreds of thousands of years! Scientists believe that the earth is about 4,600 million years old. For much of that time the earth was cooling and forming a basic atmosphere. It is only 542 million years ago that life really began. It is from this time that geologists have divided time into eras and periods to form the **geological timescale** (diagram **A**). Each period starts and ends at a stage when there was great change, such as periods of mountain building or widespread sea level change.

Era	Millions of years ago	Period	Major UK events
Cenozoic	23	Quaternary* / Neogene	Ice Age
	65	Palaeogene	Formation of Alps caused folding of rocks in UK
Mesozoic	145	Cretaceous	Much of England covered by sea
	199	Jurassic	Limestone deposited that now forms the Cotswold Hills
	251	Triassic	Much of the UK would have been desert
Palaeozoic (Late)	299	Permian	
	359	Carboniferous	Tropical conditions affected the UK. Coal formed
	416	Devonian	
	443	Silurian	
Palaeozoic (Early)	488	Ordovician	Volcanoes active in Wales. Great Glen Fault formed in Scotland
	542	Cambrian	
		Pre-Cambrian	* The Quaternary period is divided into the PLEISTOCENE (ICE AGE) and the most recent period (from 10,000 years ago until the present day) called the HOLOCENE

A The geological timescale

In this chapter we will be focusing on four rocks that are common in the UK. They were formed at different times on the geological timescale:

- granite – formed about 280 million years ago
- Carboniferous limestone – formed some 340 million years ago
- chalk – formed during the Cretaceous period
- clay – formed on many occasions throughout geological time but especially during the Jurassic, Cretaceous and Tertiary periods. We will look at landscapes formed on clay deposited during the Cretaceous period.

Rock types

The earth's crust is the thin outer layer of the earth, surrounding the mantle and the core. Look at diagram **A** on page 8 to see the structure of the earth and plate margins.

Three types of rock make up the earth's crust: **igneous**, **sedimentary** and **metamorphic** (see table **B**).

Activity

Study diagram **A**.

a   Use a ruler to draw your own geological timescale.

- If you measure out 4 cm for each 100 million years, that should work well.
- Notice how the youngest periods are at the top and the oldest at the bottom.

b   Write the names of the eras and periods onto your timescale diagram.

c   Use arrows to locate the times when granite, Carboniferous limestone, chalk and clay were formed.

B   *Formation and characteristics of igneous, sedimentary and metamorphic rocks*

Rock type	Formation	Characteristics	Examples	Photo
Igneous	Formed by the cooling of molten magma either underground (intrusive) or on the ground (extrusive) by volcanic activity.	Igneous rocks are made up of interlocking crystals. They are generally tough rocks and are resistant to erosion.	Basalt and andesite are examples of extrusive lavas. Granite and dolerite are intrusive rocks.	
Sedimentary	Formed when sediments are compacted and cemented, usually in the sea. Also includes organic material (e.g. coal) and rocks precipitated from solutions (e.g. limestone).	Sedimentary rocks usually form layers called beds. They often contain fossils. Although some rocks can be tough (e.g. limestone), most are weaker than igneous and metamorphic rocks.	Common sedimentary rocks include sandstone, limestone, shale, clay and mudstone. Chalk is a form of limestone.	
Metamorphic	Formed when igneous, sedimentary or metamorphic rocks are changed by heat and/or pressure.	Metamorphic rocks are also made of crystals. They are often banded or split along lines of weakness called cleavage planes. Metamorphic rocks tend to be very tough and resistant to erosion.	Slate is one of the most common metamorphic rocks. Other examples include gneiss (pronounced 'nice') and schist.	

The British Geological Survey has a good website at www.bgs.ac.uk

2.2 The rock cycle

Rocks are constantly being recycled. For example, igneous rocks are broken down by weathering and transported to the sea as sediment. On the sea bed the sediment is turned into sedimentary rock. When uplifted to form a new mountain range, the sedimentary rock is put under enormous pressure. Some of it is changed into metamorphic rock. Some might be completely melted to form magma and, on cooling, a brand-new igneous rock will be formed.

The connections between the main rock groups can be described as the **rock cycle** (diagram **A**).

In this section you will learn

the three types of rock which can be linked by the rock cycle.

Key term

Rock cycle: connections between the three rock types shown in the form of a diagram.

A The rock cycle

Labels on diagram: Weathering; Uplift to surface; Transportation; Intrusive igneous rock; Crystallisation; Metamorphic rock; Melting; Squashing, heating; Deposition, sedimentation; Burial, compression; Sedimentary rock; Magma – Molten rock from the mantle; Radioactive processes within the earth's core provide heat energy

Did you know ???????

What is thought to be the oldest rock on earth was discovered encased in gneiss (metamorphic rock) in Canada. It is over 4,000 million years old.

Activity

Study diagram **A**.

a Make a large copy of the rock cycle diagram.

b Draw lava coming out of the volcano and add the label 'extrusive igneous rock'.

c If extrusive igneous rock is igneous rock that has come out of a volcano, what do you think intrusive igneous rock would be?

d Using diagram **A** to help you, explain how sedimentary rocks are formed.

e Describe in your own words how a metamorphic rock can turn into a sedimentary rock.

Study tip

Make sure you learn the three definitions of rock types and practise labelling the parts of the rock cycle.

2.3   What is weathering and how does it operate?

What is weathering?

Weathering is the breaking up or decay of rocks. As the name suggests, it is largely caused by the weather such as rainfall and changes in temperature.

Weathering affects rocks in their natural state as well as in buildings such as churches, bridges and schools. Looking at a wall closely often shows small pits, flaking of the outer surface or changes in colour. This is weathering.

Types of weathering

There are three types of weathering:

1   Mechanical weathering – also known as physical weathering. This is where rocks are broken up without any chemical changes taking place. It often results in piles of angular rock fragments called **scree** found at the foot of bare rocky outcrops.

2   Chemical weathering – is when a chemical change happens when weathering takes place. Rainwater is slightly acidic. Therefore it slowly dissolves certain rocks and minerals. Those minerals or particles unaffected by chemical weathering are usually left behind to form a fine clay deposit.

3   Biological weathering – this is where plants and animals affect rocks. Plant roots can grow and expand in cracks in the rocks (photo **A**). Rabbits can burrow into weak rocks such as sands.

A *Biological weathering involving the expansion of tree roots*

Mechanical weathering

Freeze–thaw weathering

Freeze–thaw weathering is sometimes known as frost shattering. It is where water freezes and thaws in a crack or hole in the rock. It is a common process and happens where temperatures change often. Look at diagram **B**.

- The process of freeze–thaw starts with water collecting in cracks or holes (**pores**) in a rock.
- At night, this water freezes and expands (grows) by approximately nine per cent. If the water is in a small space, the expansion creates stresses within the rock and cracks can get bigger.
- When the temperature rises and the ice thaws, the water moves deeper into the rock along newly formed cracks.
- After repeated cycles of freezing and thawing, bits of rock may fall off and become scree.

Exfoliation

Look at photo **C**, which shows a rock that has been affected by **exfoliation**. The outer 'skin' of the rock looks like it is flaking away from the rest of the rock. You can see why exfoliation is sometimes known as onion-skin weathering.

Exfoliation is most common where they are large changes in temperature, such as in hot deserts. Rock is a bad conductor of heat. This means that only the outer part of a rock warms and cools in response to changes in temperature. As it warms during the day it expands (gets bigger) and as it cools at night it contracts (gets smaller). This keeps repeating and can lead to the outer skin peeling away from the rest of the rock. Water is also important for exfoliation to take place as it weakens the rock, making it more open to flaking.

☀ Day

Water collects in cracks in rock

★☾ Night

Water freezes to form ice

Expansion makes stresses and cracks get bigger

☀/★☾ Repeated freezing and thawing

Rock fragment breaks off and collects as scree at the foot of the rockface

B *The process of freeze–thaw weathering*

C *Exfoliation in rocks exposed in Antrim, Northern Ireland*

Chemical weathering

Solution

In the same way that sugar dissolves in tea, some minerals and rocks dissolve in rainwater. This dissolving process is called **solution**. Rock salt is a sedimentary rock that formed where salt crystals built up on a dried-up lake bed. Deposits of rock salt are found deep underground in Cheshire. It is taken out of the ground and used on roads and pavements to thaw ice in winter. Just like table salt, rock salt dissolves in water and is therefore vulnerable to the weathering process of solution.

Carbonation

Carbonation is similar to solution in that it involves dissolving. It affects rocks that are made up of calcium carbonate ($CaCO_3$) such as limestone and chalk. Look at diagram **D** to see how the process of carbonation works. Carbonation formed some of the landforms which can be seen in limestone landscapes (see section 2.6, page 45).

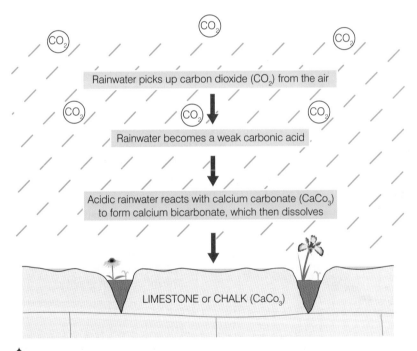

Rainwater picks up carbon dioxide (CO_2) from the air

Rainwater becomes a weak carbonic acid

Acidic rainwater reacts with calcium carbonate ($CaCO_3$) to form calcium bicarbonate, which then dissolves

LIMESTONE or CHALK ($CaCO_3$)

D *The process of carbonation*

> ### Did you know ???????
>
> Rock salt put on roads as a de-icer is a powerful weathering agent. It can damage steel structures, for example those supporting bridges. At the coast, salt from the sea makes paint on the walls of houses flake and cars rust.

> ### Study tip
>
> Learn the definition of weathering and of the various processes. Using diagrams to describe weathering processes is effective and makes them easier to learn.

Activities

2 Study diagram **B**. Draw your own series of diagrams to describe the process of freeze–thaw weathering.

3 Make a sketch of photo **C**. Add annotations to explain how the process of exfoliation operates.

4 Work in pairs to produce a PowerPoint presentation to describe either freeze–thaw, exfoliation or carbonation. Use labelled photos and diagrams to describe the process you have chosen. Do not use more than six slides.

∞ links

Further information and links can be found at www.geographypages.co.uk/weathering.htm.

2.4 What are the characteristics of granite landscapes?

The formation and distribution of granite

Granite is an intrusive igneous rock that was formed deep underground. The movement of plates lifting the rock and erosion of the rocks on top of granite, means that in some places granite can be seen on the earth's surface.

In south-west England it looks like there are lots of separate outcrops of granite (map **A**). Actually they are all part of the same huge igneous rock mass called a **batholith**. Gradually, rock above the granite is being eroded. One day, south-west England will appear to be almost completely granite.

Apart from south-west England, granite is only found in parts of north-west England, Scotland and Ireland (map **A**).

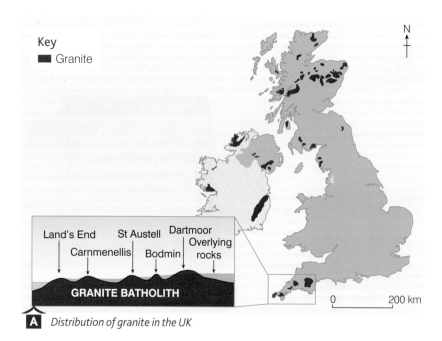

N

Key
■ Granite

Land's End · St Austell · Dartmoor · Overlying rocks
Carnmenellis · Bodmin

GRANITE BATHOLITH

0   200 km

A *Distribution of granite in the UK*

In this section you will learn

the formation and characteristics of granite

the distinctive landforms associated with granite.

Key terms

Batholith: a huge irregular-shaped mass of igneous rock that only reaches the surface when the overlying rocks are removed.

Joints: cracks that may run vertically or horizontally through rock.

Impermeable rock: a rock that does not allow water to pass through it.

Tor: an isolated outcrop of rock on a hilltop, usually in granite landscapes.

Mass movement: the downhill movement of material under the influence of gravity.

The characteristics of granite

Granite is a tough rock resistant to the processes of weathering and erosion. This explains why it forms upland areas such as Dartmoor and Bodmin in south-west England. Granite is an **impermeable rock** – it does not allow water to pass through it. Therefore, granite landscapes are often wet and marshy with plenty of rivers. Granite moorlands tend to be bleak, wet and windswept. As upland areas, they experience heavy rainfall and snow in winter. Low grasses with a few trees mostly cover the moors, which are split up by rivers.

Granite contains cracks or **joints**. Vertical joints (from top to bottom) were made when the granite cooled and contracted (got smaller). Horizontal joints (from side to side) were made when the granite

Study tip

Tors are one of the main features of a granite landscape and you should be able to describe their features. A labelled diagram can often be the best way to learn and also to explain these features.

expanded (got bigger) as the pressure from the rock on top was reduced as they eroded away. All joints makes granite vulnerable to freeze–thaw weathering and, in some places, exfoliation.

Horizontal joints formed by pressure release when the overlying rocks were removed

Rounded edges caused by chemical weathering

Vertical joints formed when the granite cooled

Broken rocks at the foot of the tor resulting from freeze–thaw weathering

Enlarged joints caused by freeze–thaw weathering

B   *Haytor, one of Dartmoor's most impressive tors*

a Horizontal cracks caused by pressure release

Soil

Zone of widely spaced joints

Vertical joints caused by cooling

Zone of closely spaced joints

b Deep chemical weathering under warm and wet conditions

Weathered granite

Zone of widely spaced joints is weathered less rapidly than where the joints are closely spaced

Granite landforms

The most distinctive granite landform is called a tor (photo **B**). Tors are found on the tops of hills. They look like a pile of rocks dumped on the ground. They are, however, part of the solid geology.

There are several theories about the formation of these desolate rocky outcrops. The most widely accepted theory was suggested by Linton in 1955 (diagram **C**).

■ Linton suggested that the spacing of the vertical joints in granite varied across an area.

■ While underground and when the climate was warmer and wetter, the closely spaced joints were weathered faster than more widely spaced joints.

■ The granite was lifted up and the rock above it was eroded away so it appeared on the earth's surface. The parts of granite which had more closely spaced joints was taken away by erosion and **mass movement** (slumping). This left behind the largely unweathered part of the granite to form a tor.

■ Under current conditions, the tor keeps being weathered by physical and chemical processes.

c Weathered granite removed by surface processes to leave the tor exposed

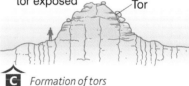

Tor

C   *Formation of tors*

Activities

1   Study map **A**, which shows where granite is located in the UK.

a   On a blank outline map of the UK, draw the areas of granite shown on the map.

b   Write a few sentences describing the distribution of granite in the UK.

2   Study photo **B**, which shows Haytor in Dartmoor.

a   Draw a sketch of Haytor from the photo.

b   Use arrows to locate the features listed in the photo.

c   Describe the main features of the tor.

∞links

Further information about granite and Dartmoor can be found at **www.dartmoor-npa.gov.uk**. Enter 'geology and landforms' into the search box.

2.5 What are the characteristics of chalk and clay landscapes?

Chalk and clay are two examples of sedimentary rocks. They were both formed under the sea and then lifted up by plate movement to form land. Although they are similar in terms of their formation, they are rocks with very different characteristics.

Map **A** shows the distribution of chalk in the UK. It is found in the south and east of England, and tends to form bands rather than the isolated outcrops that we saw with granite (map **A**, page 40). This is because, being a sedimentary rock, chalk forms beds (layers) that cover large areas. When exposed at the surface, these beds appear as bands. Clay is a very common rock, formed throughout geological time, and is found all over the UK.

> **In this section you will learn**
>
> the formation and characteristics of chalk and clay
>
> the distinctive landforms associated with chalk and clay.

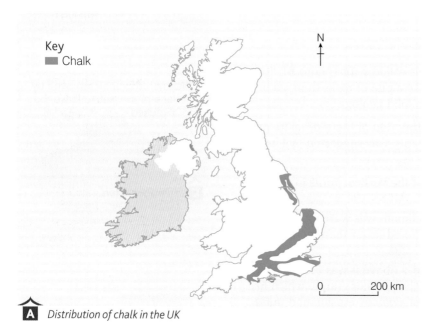

Key
■ Chalk

N

0   200 km

A Distribution of chalk in the UK

> **Key terms**
>
> **Permeable rock**: a rock that allows water to pass through it.
>
> **Water table**: the upper surface of underground water.
>
> **Spring**: water re-emerging from the rock onto the ground surface. Springs often occur as a line of springs (springline) at the base of a scarp slope.
>
> **Vale**: in the landscape, a flat plain typically formed on clay.

■ Characteristics of chalk and clay

Chalk is a tough rock although it is not as strong as granite. Chalk is famous for forming the 'white cliffs of Dover'. It does form upland areas, such as the Chilterns (photo **C** and Map **D**), Yorkshire Wolds and the South Downs, but this is partly because chalk is a **permeable rock**. This means that it does not really support rivers, and a lack of rivers means a lack of erosion.

Chalk is permeable because it is heavily jointed and porous (it contains holes or pores). Rainwater soaks through the joints and pores until it reaches the **water table** (diagram **B**). This is the upper surface of underground water. Water stored within the chalk is a valuable resource, as you will find out later. Where the water table reaches the ground surface, **springs** are formed.

> **Did you know** ??????
>
> Classroom chalk is not the same as rock chalk. It is made of a much softer mineral called gypsum, which is the same as the substance used to make plaster boards in buildings and the plaster used to mend broken bones.

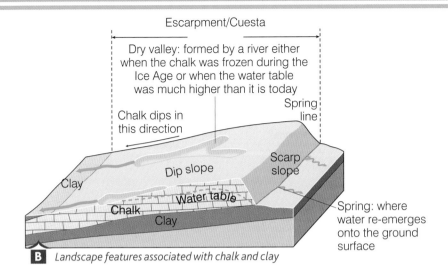

Escarpment/Cuesta

Dry valley: formed by a river either when the chalk was frozen during the Ice Age or when the water table was much higher than it is today

Chalk dips in this direction

Spring line

Dip slope

Scarp slope

Clay

Water table

Chalk

Clay

Spring: where water re-emerges onto the ground surface

B   *Landscape features associated with chalk and clay*

Chalk is a pure form of limestone and rich in calcium carbonate ($CaCO_3$). This means that it is vulnerable to the chemical weathering process of carbonation (page 39). As it contains many joints and pores, chalk is also vulnerable to freeze–thaw weathering.

In contrast, clay is a weak and impermeable rock. Rivers easily erode clay, which explains why it mainly forms low, flat ground called **vales**.

▣ Chalk and clay landscapes

Look at diagram **B**, which describes the main landscape features of chalk and clay. The key thing to note is that the rocks are exposed at the ground at a slight angle rather than being flat. This is due to the rocks being folded by **tectonic activity**. As you can see, this has had a big effect on the landscape features.

C   *The Chilterns*

Activities

2 Study map **D**, which is a 1:50,000 OS map extract of part of the Chiltern Hills. The chalk **escarpment/cuesta** is the hilly area to the south-east of the map extract. The steeper scarp slope is at the north-western edge of the chalk. The clay vale is the flatter area to the north-west of the map extract.

a What is the highest point and what is its six-figure grid reference?

b What is the lowest point on the clay and what is its six-figure grid reference?

c Give an example of a springline settlement.

d Locate the grid square 7498. What evidence is there on the map to suggest that this is a scarp slope?

e In pairs, compare the **physical landscape** and **human land uses** of the **chalk** and the **clay** on the map extract.

> **Key term**
>
> **Escarpment/cuesta:** an outcrop of chalk made up of a steep scarp slope and a more gentle dip slope.

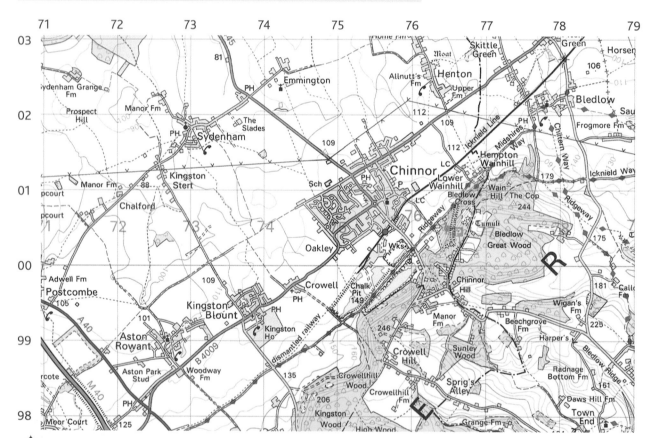

D 1:50,000 OS map extract of the Chiltern Hills near Chinnor, part of map sheet 165

⚭ links

Further information about the Chiltern Hills can be found at **www.chilternsaonb.org**.

The White Cliffs Countryside Project has information on chalk at **www.whitecliffscountryside.org.uk**. Click on the 'Chalk' link.

> **Study tip**
>
> Practise your map reading skills so that you are able to recognise the key features and landforms shown on Ordnance Survey mapping.

2.6   What are the characteristics of Carboniferous limestone landscapes?

Carboniferous limestone is a sedimentary rock. It was given its name because it was formed during the Carboniferous geological period about 340 million years ago. It was formed by the build up of calcium carbonate ($CaCO_3$) in warm tropical seas, rather like the present-day Caribbean. The corals and shellfish of these ancient seas are often found in the limestone as fossils.

Map **A** shows the distribution of Carboniferous limestone. Like chalk (map **A**, page 42), limestone forms bands across the UK. One of the main exposures of Carboniferous limestone runs down the spine of England to form the Pennine Hills.

The characteristics of Carboniferous limestone

Carboniferous limestone is a tough and resistant rock. It forms upland areas in the UK such as the Pennine Hills and the Mendips. When exposed at the coast, as it is in parts of south Wales, it forms dramatic towering cliffs.

Despite being physically strong, it is chemically weak. As it is made up of calcium carbonate, it is vulnerable to the slow dissolving action of carbonation. It has lots of joints. The horizontal joints are called bedding planes and are between the layers (beds) of limestone. Having lots of joints makes carboniferous limestone prone to freeze–thaw weathering. They also mean that limestone is a permeable rock.

Carboniferous limestone landscapes

Carboniferous limestone tends to form high ground, often with bare rock showing and steep-sided valleys or **gorges** (photo **B**). Weathering produces thin soils that support grass, used for grazing by sheep, and just a few trees.

In this section you will learn

about the formation and characteristics of Carboniferous limestone

about the distinctive landforms associated with Carboniferous limestone.

∞ links

Find out more at **www.bbc.co.uk**. Enter 'upland limestone' into the search box.

Study tip

Be aware of the various advantages and disadvantages of quarrying. Facts and figures from case studies help to reinforce your argument.

Key term

Gorge: a narrow steep-sided valley.

Hard, grey, full of fossils (e.g. coral), well jointed and permeable

A *Distribution of Carboniferous limestone in the UK*

B *Limestone landscape near Malham, Yorkshire*

There are many features found in Carboniferous limestone landscapes (diagram **C**). Some are found on the surface whereas others are underground.

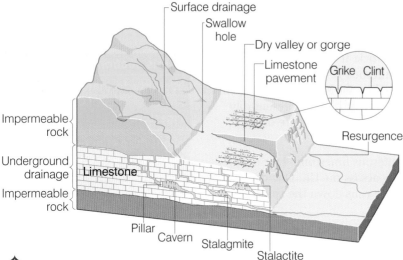

 Features associated with Carboniferous limestone landscape

Surface features

■ Bare rocky surfaces called **limestone pavements** are common features. A limestone pavement is often an extensive rocky surface with lots of joints making it look like a pavement. Blocks called clints are separated by enlarged joints called grikes. Chemical weathering causes the surface of the limestone pavement to be quite smooth.

■ Water flowing over nearby impermeable rocks disappears down holes in the limestone called **swallow holes**. These are found where joints meet. They are made bigger by weathering processes and river erosion.

■ **Dry valleys** are common in limestone areas. They are formed in much the same way as the dry valleys in chalk. Most were probably formed by water melting at the end of the last ice age. Some of the limestone was still frozen and impermeable and water tables were much higher than today. Occasionally very narrow gorges can be found. These may result from the collapse of roofs of underground **caverns**. Springs or **resurgences** happen where water flowing underground emerges onto the ground surface, often from a small cave. (A good example of a dry valley can be seen in grid square 7799 on map **D** on page 44.)

Underground features

As water flows through the joints in the limestone, weathering and erosion make the joints much bigger and create tunnels and caverns. When water, rich in calcium carbonate, drips from the roofs of caverns it leaves a very small deposit of calcite as it evaporates. Over hundreds and thousands of years an icicle-like **stalactite** forms hanging down from the roof. The drips on the floor of the cavern also deposit calcite. This forms shorter and stubbier **stalagmites**. In rare cases, the two features join together to make a **pillar**. Calcite can be deposited over a wider surface where water flows over a rock face or drips occur in many places along a crack in a wall. This can result in the formation of a sheet-like **curtain** rather than an individual stalactite.

Key terms

Limestone pavement: a bare rocky surface, with blocks (clints) and enlarged joints (grikes).

Swallow hole: an enlarged joint into which water falls.

Dry valley: a valley formed by a river during a wetter period in the past but now without a river.

Cavern: a large underground cave.

Resurgence: a stream that emerges from underground.

Stalactite: an icicle-like calcite feature hanging down from a cavern roof.

Stalagmite: a stumpy calcite feature formed on a cavern floor.

Pillar: a calcite feature stretching from floor to ceiling in a cavern.

Curtain: a broad deposit of calcite usually formed when water emerges along a crack in a cavern.

Activities

1 Study photo **B** and diagram **C**. Photo **B** shows a limestone landscape and diagram **C** describes typical features of limestone landscapes.

a What limestone feature from diagram **C** can you identify in photo **B**? Is it:

   ■ cavern

   ■ dry valley

   ■ swallow hole?

2 Study diagram **C**.

a Why is the swallow hole located where it is? Use the terms 'impermeable rock' and 'surface drainage' in your answer.

b Draw your own diagrams to show how stalactites, stalagmites, pillars and curtains are formed.

2.7   What are the uses of rocks?

Rocks have many uses to people. They can be dug out of the ground to provide raw materials for industry or used as building stone or for **cement**. They can help with water supply. Water can be stored underground in cracks and pores or, if the rocks are impermeable, reservoirs can be constructed. Soils that develop from rocks help farming to take place. Rocks also create distinctive landscapes and scenery, providing a very wide range of opportunities for leisure and recreation.

Table **A** outlines some of the main uses for the four types of rock that you have been studying in this chapter.

In this section you will learn

the opportunities for human use of granite, chalk, clay and Carboniferous limestone.

Key term

Cement: mortar used in building, made from crushed limestone and shale.

A   *Uses of granite, chalk, clay and Carboniferous limestone*

Rock type	Resource for extraction	Farming	Water supply	Scenery
Granite	Building stone used throughout Cornwall. Aberdeen is known as the 'city of granite'. Commonly used for kitchen surfaces. In the past, granite contained valuable veins of tin and other metals.	Mainly extensive sheep farming on poor pastures and in harsh environmental conditions. This is because granite forms upland areas.	Impermeable rock. Several reservoirs have been constructed in steep valleys, such as the Burrator Reservoir which supplies Plymouth.	Bleak and windswept, granite forms wild and attractive moorland scenery. Attractive for outdoor activities especially walking, bird watching, mountain biking and climbing. Water sports (fishing, sailing) on the reservoirs.
Chalk	Quarried to be made into cement. Source of lime for industry and farming, to neutralise acidic soils.	Quite fertile land used for sheep farming and some arable crops such as wheat and barley.	Important store of underground water (aquifers). Supplies large parts of the south-east of England including London.	Rolling hills. Popular with naturalists due to rich wildlife, particularly flowers and birds. Opportunities for walking and horse riding.
Clay	Used in making bricks and for pottery.	Fertile soils but with a tendency to become waterlogged. Mostly used as pasture for sheep and dairy cattle.	Impermeable rock. Some reservoirs have been constructed but flat land is not ideal.	Featureless landscape is not especially attractive.
Carboniferous limestone	Quarried to be made into cement. Source of lime for industry and farming, to neutralise acidic soils. Used as a building stone and in dry-stone walls as field boundaries. Popular stone for gardens, which has led to some destruction of limestone pavements.	Generally thin, upland soils (most of the limestone dissolves when weathered) so mostly used for sheep.	Spring water flowing out of the limestone can be a source of water.	Attractive upland scenery is popular with tourists. A number of National Parks and Areas of Outstanding Natural Beauty are on limestone areas, e.g. Peak District and Yorkshire Dales. Many opportunities for walking, mountain biking, climbing and potholing.

Farming on Dartmoor

Over the last 5,000 years farming has been the main land use on Dartmoor. Today, over 90 per cent of the land in the National Park is farmed. Half of this is open moorland, which is used for grazing animals, and the rest is made up of marginal farmland and improved grassland.

The whole of Dartmoor is now designated as an Environmentally Sensitive Area. Farmers are paid to carry out agricultural practices that conserve the landscape and wildlife habitats. This may include reducing the numbers of animals grazing in sensitive areas. They must also restrict the use of fertilisers and pesticides. They must maintain stone walls and hedgerows, develop hay meadows and adopt agricultural practices that help to protect the area's archaeological and historic interest.

B *A sheep farm on Dartmoor*

The London Basin chalk aquifer

The rocks underneath London form a basin called a **syncline** (diagram **C**). Water soaks into the chalk where it is exposed on either side of London and then seeps through the chalk to form a huge underground reservoir called an **aquifer**. For hundreds of years this has supplied London with its water. The aquifer is carefully managed by the Environment Agency to make sure that its use is sustainable. In the 1960s, industrial use caused the water table to drop to 88 m below sea level, which resulted in some seawater contamination. Following careful management and reduced demand from industry since the 1990s, the water table has risen by as much as 3 m a year.

> **Key terms**
>
> **Syncline**: the lower arc of the fold in fold mountains.
>
> **Aquifer**: an underground reservoir of water stored in pores and/or joints in a rock, e.g. chalk.

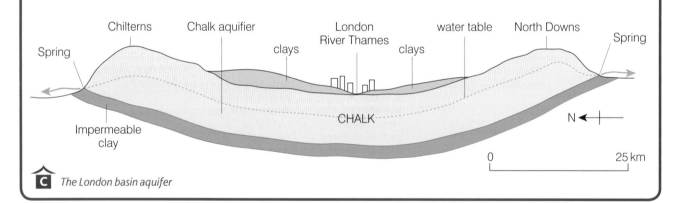

C *The London basin aquifer*

Limestone scenery: recreation in the Yorkshire Dales

The Yorkshire Dales is a National Park largely made up of Carboniferous limestone. The landscape is amazing, with steep valleys, cliffs and lots of raised grassland. This means there are lots of things to do!

Walking: the area has many footpaths including the long-distance footpath known as the Pennine Way.

Nature tourism: lots of birds, animals and wildflowers for people to enjoy.

> **Study tip**
>
> Table **A** is probably the best way of learning this topic. You could add to it from your own research and from additional articles.

Outdoor pursuits such as climbing (limestone is an excellent rock for climbing with its many joints), mountain biking and caving.

The area around Malham (map **E**) is a particular focus for tourism. For this reason it is referred to as a honeypot site (think bees and honeypot!). Tourism brings both benefits and costs to the Yorkshire Dales (Table **D**). Thoughtful and sustainable management is vital if the area is to retain its special beauty in the future.

D   *Benefits and costs of tourism to the Yorkshire Dales.*

Benefits	Costs
Tourists bring money into the area, which they spend in shops, cafés and hotels.	Traffic jams form in the narrow roads and cause pollution.
Many local people benefit from work opportunities, in restaurants and hotels or acting as guides.	People leave litter, which spoils the area and can be harmful to wildlife.
Local craft industries and farms also benefit from the visitors.	Farm gates may be left open and animals worried by dogs.
Money raised from tourism can be used to protect and conserve the landscape.	Shop prices may be higher than elsewhere as people cash-in on the tourists, which is bad news for local people. House prices may also be higher than elsewhere due to a demand for holiday homes.

Activities

1   Study map **E**. This map shows Malham, which is in a limestone landscape.

a   Using grid references or place names, suggest some activities available for visitors in this area.

b   What facilities have been provided for tourists? You may need to check what these symbols mean with the key from an OS map.

c   Look closely at the roads. What challenges does the landscape create for travelling in the area?

d   Suggest two problems that might occur in the area resulting from the high number of visitors.

e   Suggest two benefits that tourism might bring to the area.

2   Use the internet to find out more about climbing and caving activities available in the Yorkshire Dales. A good starting point is the Yorkshire Dales National Park website at **www.yorkshiredales.org.uk**. Present your information in the form of a single-page advertisement encouraging climbers and cavers to visit the Yorkshire Dales.

links

A number of excellent farm case studies are available at the Farming and Countryside Education (FACE) site at **www.face-online.org.uk**.

Further information about Malham can be found at **www.malhamdale.com**.

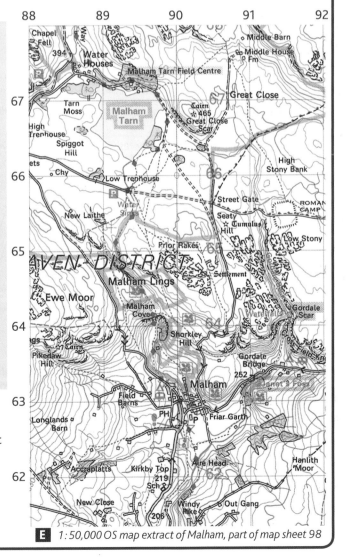

E   *1 : 50,000 OS map extract of Malham, part of map sheet 98*

2.8 What are the issues associated with quarrying?

Limestone quarrying in the Peak District

As early as Roman times, limestone was quarried in the Peak District. It has many uses including building stone, cement, lime for use in farming, and as **aggregate** (crushed stone) for road building and the construction industry (Table **A**). In 2008 there were 13 active quarries in the Peak District. The amount of limestone taken from the area has increased from 1.5 m tonnes in 1951 to 7.9 m tonnes in 2008. This is mainly because of increasing demand for aggregate.

Case study

Hope Quarry, Castleton

Hope Quarry is one of the largest limestone quarries in the Peak District. It is located on the outskirts of Castleton in the Peak District National Park (map **B**). It supplies 2 m tonnes of limestone a year to the nearby Hope Cement Works, which produces 1.3 m tonnes of cement a year.

The cement works was opened in 1929 near to reserves of limestone and shale, both of which are needed to make cement.

The quarry and cement works, now owned by the Lafarge Group, employs around 200 local people, many of whom live in Hope. The local economy enjoys huge benefits. Local people have work and are able to support shops and services nearby. This is called the multiplier effect.

The quarry is estimated to have reserves for another 30 to 35 years and is working to a planned programme of extraction and restoration.

> **In this section you will learn**
>
> the advantages and disadvantages of a quarry.

> **Key term**
>
> **Aggregate:** crushed stone made from tough rocks such as limestone, used in the construction industry and in road building.

A Main uses of limestone in the Peak District

Use	%
Aggregate	56
Cement	23
Chemicals	17
Iron and steel	4

> **Study tip**
>
> Be aware of the various advantages and disadvantages of quarrying. Facts and figures from case studies help to reinforce your argument.

> **Did you know ??????**
>
> In 2003 Hope Cement Works started to use chipped tyres as a fuel to preserve fossil fuels and recycle materials.

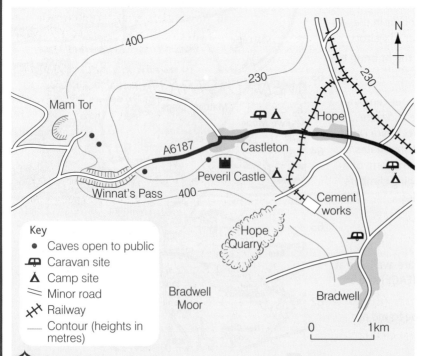

Key
- • Caves open to public
- ⌂ Caravan site
- ▲ Camp site
- ≋ Minor road
- ✕✕ Railway
- — Contour (heights in metres)

B Location map of Hope Quarry

Quarrying and the environment

In 1951 the Peak District became a National Park. The Park Authority has to find a balance between conserving the environment and the economic and social needs of the area.

Hope Quarry is a huge hole in the ground (photo **C**) and it has a huge visual impact on the landscape. Several things have been tried to minimise the effects of the quarry and the cement works on the environment:

- Landscaping and tree planting have reduced the visual impact of the quarry.
- Efforts have been made to reduce dust, such as washing down roads.
- Around £20 m has been spent to improve transport. Rail is used rather than road to reduce the impact of heavy traffic. A single train carries the load of 57 lorries.
- Hope Cement Works produces 1m tonnes of carbon dioxide a year. In 2003, in an attempt to offset some of this, 7,000 trees were planted.
- One old quarry area is now managed as a wetland reserve.
- In 2010 Lafarge, the quarry owners, got permission to use processed sewage pellets as fuel in the cement works. This will reduce **carbon emissions.**

> ### Key term
> **Carbon emissions:** release of carbon (usually in the form of carbon dioxide) often by burning fossil fuels.

C *Hope Quarry*

∞ links

The Virtual Quarry site offers a great deal of related information at **www.virtualquarry.co.uk/text/textlimestonelandscapes.htm**.

The Peak District National Park has a quarrying factsheet available at **www.peakdistrict.gov.uk**. Search for 'education factsheets'.

Activities

1   Study table **A**. This shows the main uses of quarried limestone in the Peak District.

a   What is aggregate and what is it used for?

b   What sort of activities might increase the demand for aggregate?

2   Work in pairs or small groups for this activity.

a   Draw a table with two columns. At the top of one column write the heading 'Benefits of quarrying' and at the top of the other 'Problems caused by quarrying'.

b   With reference to Hope Quarry and the cement works, complete the table using the text and the resources in this section.

   Think about the economic (money), social (people) and environmental impacts of quarrying.

c   Do you think quarrying should be allowed to continue at Hope Quarry or should it be stopped? Give reasons for your answer.

2.9 How can quarries be restored?

Quarrying can cause environmental damage. It can cause pollution of rivers and underground aquifers and can also destroy habitats when trees and vegetation are dug out.

There are now strict controls on quarrying. Quarrying companies should restore or improve on the original environmental qualities of the area. This is called **quarry restoration**.

Quarry restoration can begin while work is still in progress. Parts of a quarry that have been exhausted can be restored while other parts keep being worked. However, most of the repair work takes place when quarrying has stopped completely.

There are many uses for exhausted quarries. They can be turned back into farmland by having the topsoil replaced. They can create good courses for motocross or mountain bikes. Waste tips can be used as dry ski slopes. Often quarries contain lakes and these are ideal for wildlife reserves, fishing or water sports.

In this section you will learn

the options for quarry restoration during extraction and after the resource has been exhausted.

Key term

Quarry restoration: restoring or improving the environment of a quarry, either during its operation or afterwards.

Did you know ???????

The National Watersports Centre near Nottingham has been created on the site of an old quarry.

Case study

Restoration during extraction

Drayton Sand and Gravel Quarries are near Chichester in West Sussex. There are two quarries: Drayton North and Drayton South. Drayton North has been worked for some time and the site is now being extended to Drayton South.

Even before extraction started on the new site, restoration had begun. This involved planting hedgerows and creating an avenue of oak trees in between the two quarries. Much of the site is waterlogged and it will be worked wet to retain and deepen the existing lake.

When quarrying has been completed, an extensive lake covering some 15 ha will have been created. It will have reed beds, deep and shallow areas to provide a range of habitats and small islands. The edges of the lake will be grassland and woods (photo **A**). Nesting boxes will be sited to encourage birds into the area. The operators expect to have increased biodiversity in an area that was previously species-poor intensive farmland.

A *Quarry restoration at Drayton Quarries, Chichester*

Restoration after extraction

Hollow Banks Quarry is a quarry near Catterick, North Yorkshire where sand and gravel were extracted between 1999 and 2003. Soon after the quarry closed in 2003, the owners Tarmac Ltd. began restoration (photo **B**):

- The site was changed into a gently rolling landscape with small ponds bordered by grass and woodland.
- After soil had been added, it was loosened and had stones removed. It was then divided into separate parcels of land, some of which were sown with grasses for pasture (farming) and others with trees for woodland. By planting a variety of plants and trees, a number of different habitats were created for animals and birds.
- Woodland areas have been fenced to prevent trees being damaged by farm animals.
- Over 20,000 trees and shrubs raised locally were planted during 2004 and 2005.
- Aquatic plants have been planted at the margins of the ponds.
- Footpaths have been created so people can go to the woods and ponds.

∞ links

Information on the sustainability of the cement industry can be found at http://cement.mineralproducts.org

Further information on Drayton Quarries is at the West Sussex County Council website at **www. westsussex.gov.uk**. Type 'Drayton quarries' into the search box.

For more information on Tarmac Ltd, go to **www.tarmac.co.uk**.

> **Study tip**
>
> Be prepared to debate various options for quarry restoration.

B *Restoration of Hollow Banks Quarry, Catterick*

Activities

1 Study photo **B**, which shows the restoration of Hollow Banks Quarry.

a List three things you can see that have been done to turn the quarry back into a more natural-looking habitat

b What other improvements would you make to this site to make it a really popular place for local people to go to?

2 Study photo **C** on page 51, which shows Hope Quarry as it is now.

How do you think Hope Quarry could be restored after it stops being a quarry?

a Draw a sketch of the quarry as it is now.

b Use detailed labels to show how you would restore the quarry. Consider how people might use the restored quarry (e.g. picnics, walking, fishing). Refer to these uses in your labels (and draw them on your sketch if you wish).

3 Challenge of weather and climate

3.1 What is the climate of the UK?

The **climate** of the UK is a result of where it is in the world (diagram **A**). It lies between warm tropical air and cold polar air. These 'fight' each other for control. This is why the UK has such contrasting and changeable **weather** conditions – sometimes the cold polar air wins and sometimes the tropical air wins.

The location of the UK also affects where the sun is in the sky and the impact of the seasons. During the summer, the sun is high in the sky bringing long days, sometimes with warm sunshine. Occasionally the high temperatures can trigger **convectional rainfall**, and thunderstorms. During the winter, the sun is much lower in the sky. This means it is less powerful and temperatures are much lower.

A number of other factors control our climate:

- **Ocean currents** – a warm ocean current called the North Atlantic Drift brings warm conditions to the west of the UK. This makes the UK milder (less cold) than would be expected for our **latitude**.

- **Prevailing winds** – the prevailing winds in the UK are south-westerly so they come from a warm ocean. This is one reason why the UK's climate is quite mild (not too hot or cold) and damp.

- **Maritime influence** – the sea has a great effect on the climate of the UK. Being an island, the air over the UK tends to be humid. This is why there are high amounts of rainfall and lots of cloudy weather.

- **Continentality** – inland areas away from the sea tend to be drier than the coast. In summer, energy from the sun (insolation) heats up the land quicker than the sea. This is why summer temperatures inland are higher. In winter, the land loses heat faster than land close to the sea. This is why winter temperatures inland are colder.

- **Altitude** – upland areas tend to get more **precipitation** (rain and snow), as air is forced to rise up and over them (diagram **B**). The temperature also decreases with altitude, which is why it is often colder in upland areas.

In this section you will learn

the difference between weather and climate

the characteristics and factors affecting the climate of the UK.

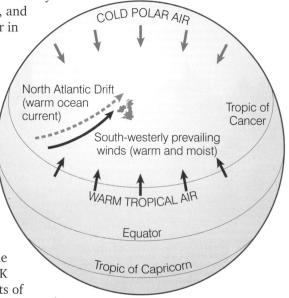

 A Factors affecting the climate of the UK

Key terms

Climate: the average weather conditions recorded over a period of at least 30 years.

Weather: the day-to-day conditions of the atmosphere involving, for example, temperature, cloud cover and wind direction.

Convectional rainfall: intense rainfall often in the form of thunderstorms resulting from very high temperatures and rapidly rising and cooling air.

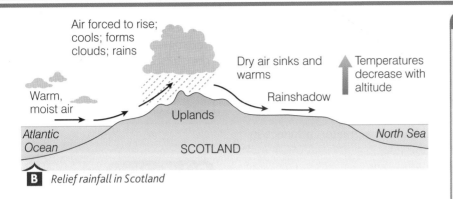

B Relief rainfall in Scotland

Characteristics

The maps in **C** show some of the characteristics of the climate of the UK. Take time to study the key for each of the maps and look closely at the overall patterns and some of the anomalies (exceptions to the general rule). Some features are explained on the next page.

Key terms

Latitude: determines the geographic north-south position of a point on the earth. 0° is at the Equator and 90° are at the poles.

Prevailing winds: the dominant wind direction.

Maritime influence: the influence of the sea on climate.

Continentality: the influence of being close to or far away from the sea. Inland areas well away from the coast have a continental climate.

Altitude: height above sea level, usually given in metres.

Precipitation: the transfer of water from the atmosphere to the ground, for example rain and snow.

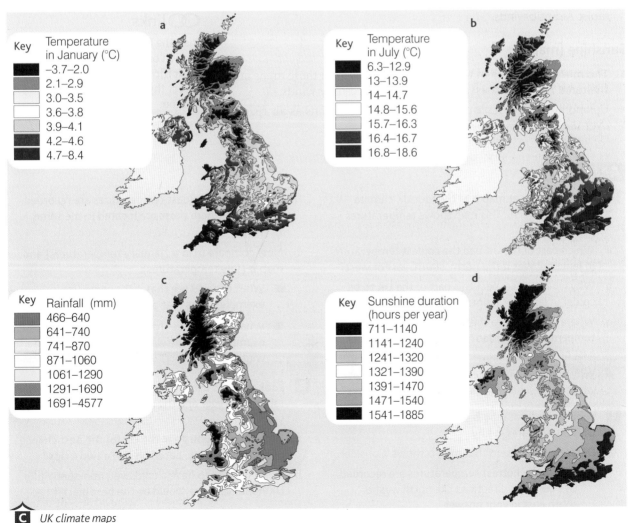

C UK climate maps

Temperature in January (map a):

- In winter, the warmest parts of the UK are in the west and the south where the North Atlantic Drift has a big influence.
- The coldest areas are in the north where the sun is at a lower angle in the sky. It is particularly cold over the mountains because of altitude.
- Cold polar air moving south is likely to have a greater influence in the north of the UK than in the south.
- The sea warms up the coastal parts of the UK.

Temperature in July (map b):

- In summer, the warmest places are in the south. Here the sun is more powerful than in the north.
- Warm air from southern Europe often moves into the south of the UK during the summer.

Precipitation, or rainfall (map c):

- The prevailing south-westerly winds explain why there's more rainfall in the west. Upland areas also receive more rainfall.
- The driest areas are in the east, sheltered by the uplands from the moist Atlantic winds.

Sunshine (map d):

- The most sunshine is in the south and east because these areas are sheltered from the moist and cloudy south-westerly winds.
- Upland areas have less sunshine than lowland regions as air rising over the mountains cools to form clouds.

Study tip

Take time to study the patterns on the climate maps. It will extend your knowledge if you are able to describe and explain these patterns on similar maps.

Did you know ??????

The highest temperature ever recorded in the UK was 38.5 °C at Faversham in Kent on 10 August 2003 during the European heatwave. The lowest recorded temperature was -27.2 °C, which was recorded at Altnaharra in the Scottish highlands on 30 December 1995.

links

Visit the Met Office education section on UK climate at www.metoffice.gov.uk/education/teens. Select the 'Climate of the UK' section.

Activities

1 Look carefully at map **a** of the four UK climate maps on page 55. This map shows temperatures in January.

a Which part of the UK had the coldest temperature in January? Was it the north, south, east or west?

b Why would you expect this part of the UK to be colder in January? (Hint: cold, polar air.)

c Where in the UK are the highest January temperatures recorded? Again, is it north, south, east or west?

d Why would the North Atlantic Drift help explain why this area has warmer January temperatures?

2 Look carefully at map **b**. This shows the pattern of UK temperatures in July.

a Describe the pattern that map **b** shows. Consider:

- Where the hottest temperatures are recorded. Use compass directions like north west or south east in your answer.

- Where the coldest temperatures are recorded. Explain where these are located in the same way.

b Now compare map **a** (January temperatures) and map **b** (July temperatures).

- What can you see that is the same (for example, areas that are always the coldest)?

- What can you see that is different (for example, does the warmest area move from winter to summer)?

3 Look at maps **c** and **d**, which show the amount of rainfall per year and the amount of sunshine per year.

a Where would you go in the UK for the best chance of a sunny holiday, based on these two maps?

b If you wanted to have a cold, wet, non-sunny July UK holiday, where would be the best place to go?

3.2   What causes the weather in the UK?

The formation and development of depressions

A **depression** is an area of low atmospheric **pressure**. In a depression, air rises which leads to clouds forming and then rain. In the UK most of our weather is caused by depressions. They form over the Atlantic Ocean and then move across the UK from west to east driven by the prevailing winds.

Look at satellite photo **B**. It shows a satellite image of an intense depression over the UK in 1998. Look closely at the labels to see the main features of the depression.

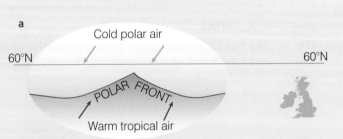

Depressions form where cold polar air moving south and warm tropical air moving north meets. This boundary is called the polar **front**.

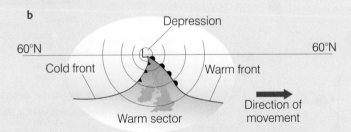

Where the air meets it starts to sprial (move round in circles) upwards and forms cloud and rain. All boundaries between the warm and the cold air are called fronts. The **warm front** marks the front of warmer air and the **cold front** represents the front of colder air.

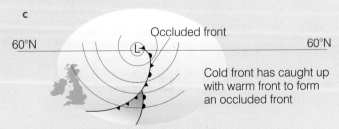

Cold front has caught up with warm front to form an occluded front

Over time the cold front catches up with the warm front to form a single boundary called an **occluded front**. Eventually the depression fizzles out and dies.

A   *The formation and development of a depression*

In this section you will learn

the formation and development of a depression

the sequence of weather associated with a depression

the characteristics of an anticyclone and the contrasting weather conditions between winter and summer.

Key terms

Depression: an area of low atmospheric pressure.

Pressure (atmospheric): pressure exerted on the Earth's surface by the mass of the overlying atmosphere.

Front: a boundary between warm and cold air.

Warm front: a boundary with cold air ahead of warm air.

Cold front: a boundary with warm air ahead of cold air.

Occluded front: a front formed when the cold front catches up with the warm front.

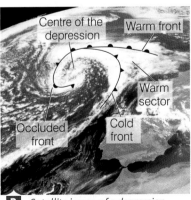

B   *Satellite image of a depression, 26 December 1998*

Weather associated with depressions

When a depression passes over the UK it brings a sequence of weather conditions. Look at satellite photo **C**. There is a depression centred off Northern Ireland to the west coast of Scotland. The warm front stretches through the North Sea and the cold front runs through the centre of England. Note on chart **D** that weather symbols have been used to describe the weather at a number of locations. The symbols are explained in the key (**E**).

Ahead of the warm front, it slowly becomes cloudier before steady rain sets in for a long time (diagram **F** and table **G**). Behind the warm front the temperature increases in the **warm sector**. It stays cloudy with patchy rain and drizzle. The cold front brings a short period of heavy rain, often with strong winds. Behind the cold front the temperature drops sharply. The rain stops but heavy showers may occur. A frontal system like diagram **D** would usually take between 12 and 18 hours to cross the UK.

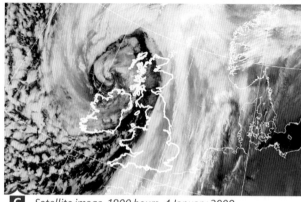

C *Satellite image, 1800 hours, 4 January 2008*

Key term

Warm sector: an area of warm air between a warm front and a cold front.

∞ links

The Met Office has regularly updated weather charts and satellite images at **www.metoffice.gov.uk**.

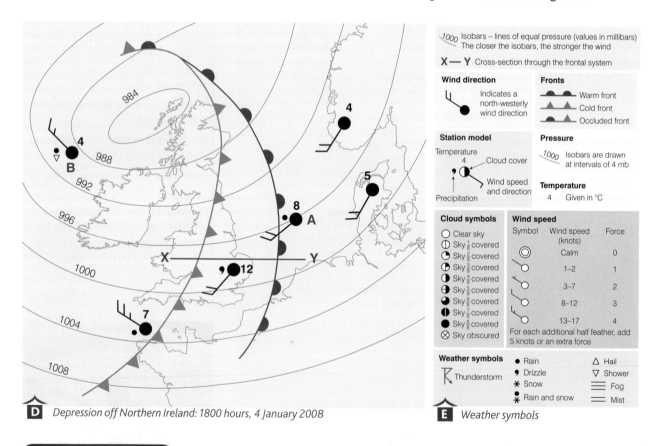

D *Depression off Northern Ireland: 1800 hours, 4 January 2008*

E *Weather symbols*

Did you know ??????

On 29 January 2008 a cold front caused temperatures to drop from +6 °C to –23 °C in a few hours at La Crosse in Minnesota, USA.

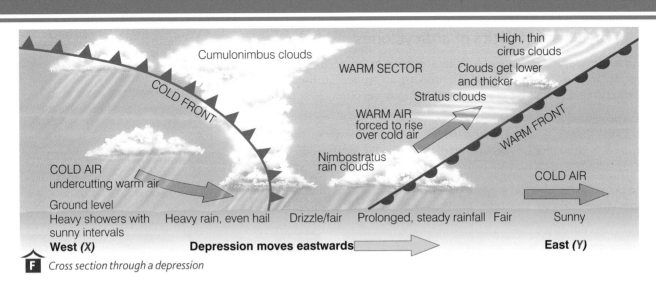

F *Cross section through a depression*

G *Weather associated with the passage of a depression*

	Cold sector	Passage of the cold front	Warm sector	Passage of the warm front	Ahead of the warm front
Pressure	Continues to rise	Starts to rise	Steadies	Continues to fall	Starts to fall steadily
Temperature	Remains cold	Sudden drop	Quite mild	Continues to rise	Quite cold, starts to rise
Cloud cover	Clouds thin with some cumulus	Clouds thicken (sometimes with large cumulonimbus)	Cloud may thin and break	Cloud base is low and thick (nimbostratus)	Cloud base drops and thickens (cirrus and altostratus)
Wind speed and direction	Winds are squally	Speeds increase, sometimes to gale force, sharp change in wind direction	Remain steady	Wind changes direction and becomes blustery with strong gusts	Speeds increase
Precipitation	Showers	Heavy rain, sometimes hail, thunder or sleet	Rain turns to drizzle or stops	Continuous, and sometimes heavy rainfall	None at first, rain closer to front, sometimes snow on leading edge

Activities

1 Look carefully at the weather symbols shown in Figure **E**.

a Draw the symbol for a warm front. Label it 'warm front'.

b Draw the symbol used to show rain. Label this symbol 'rain'.

c Use the key to describe the weather recorded at A and B on map **D**. Can you suggest why the weather differs?

d Look at the 'station model' in the key to see how symbols are used to describe the weather recorded at a weather station. Use the key to draw the correct station model for the following.

Station	Wind speed and direction	Temperature	Cloud	Weather
X	Calm (no wind)	−2 °C	Clear sky	Mist
Y	Force 2 wind from a south direction	8 °C	8/8 covered	Rain
Z	Force 4 wind from a north east direction	12 °C	2/8 covered	Shower

2 Place the following statements in their correct order to describe the weather associated with the passage of a depression (diagram **F** and table **G**):

- short period of heavy rain and gusty winds
- cloud gradually thickens and sun becomes hazy
- cold and showery
- warm and cloudy with light patchy rain
- prolonged period of steady rain.

The characteristics of anticyclones

An **anticyclone** is an area of high atmospheric pressure. It is caused by air sinking towards the ground. The sinking air stops warm pockets of air from rising. Rainfall is unlikely and conditions are often clear and sunny.

In the winter, anticyclones can mean sunny days. Nights can be **frosty** because there is no cloud to stop the heat escaping. However, the air over the UK is often moist. When it is cold, this moist air forms cloud and **fog**. This is known as 'anticyclonic gloom' can last for several days at a time.

In the summer, the sun is more powerful and it is able to burn off any low cloud and fog. This often leads to warm and sunny days.

H *Typical winter's day under the influence of an anticyclone*

I *Warm sunny day during a summer anticyclone*

Case study

Winter anticyclone, 2 February 2006

At the end of January and into the start of February 2006, there was a large anticyclone over the UK (chart **K**). The air was moist. Temperatures were low and there was little wind (see how the isobars are far apart in the UK). This meant the weather was dull and overcast with mist and fog (satellite photo **J**). If the air had been drier continental air, the weather would have been different with cold, crisp and sunny days and frosty nights.

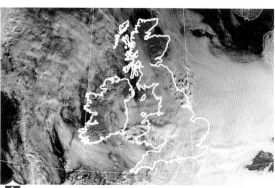

J *Foggy weather associated with anticyclone*

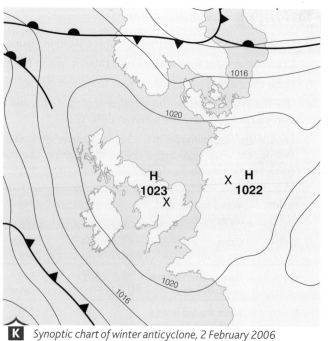

K *Synoptic chart of winter anticyclone, 2 February 2006*

Summer anticyclone, 24 July 2008

In mid-July 2008 an anticyclone settled to the east of the UK (satellite photo **L**). This brought warm easterly winds to much of the UK. Map **M** shows the weather experienced in the UK on 24 July 2008. Notice the following points:

- There is very little cloud in the centre of the anticyclone. This is because air is sinking, stopping clouds from forming.
- The lack of cloud means there is nothing stopping the summer sun. Temperatures are high in much of the UK.
- There is more cloud at the edge of the anticyclone where it is slightly less settled. This is why it is cloudier in south-west England and Wales.
- It is cooler and cloudier over parts of the north-east coast. This is because the wind has travelled over the cooler (and wetter) North Sea.

L   *Satellite image of summer anticyclone, 24 July 2008*

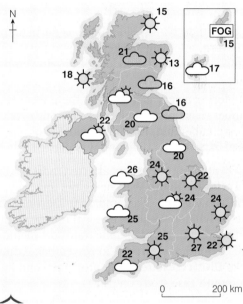

M   *Weather chart of summer anticyclone, 24 July 2008*

Activities

3   Study chart **K** and satellite photo **J**. These show conditions during a winter anticyclone in the UK.

a   Look really carefully at the satellite photo. One part of the UK has got clear skies? Which part of the UK is this?

b   Would you expect it to be very windy or pretty calm? Explain your answer.

c   Which parts of the UK were most affected by low cloud and foggy conditions?

d   Describe some of the typical weather experienced by a winter anticyclone in the UK.

4   Study satellite photo **L** and map **M**. These show conditions during a summer anticyclone in the UK.

a   Where was the sunniest part of the UK during this summer anticyclone?

b   Describe the temperatures experienced in south-east England during this summer anticyclone.

c   In the centre of an anticyclone, high pressure pushes the air downwards. Explain why this leads to a clear sky, without clouds forming? (Hint: rising air forms clouds, especially if it is wet air.)

3.3 Is the weather in the UK becoming more extreme?

Extreme weather events

In recent years there have been a number of **extreme weather** events in the UK:

- 2003 – Europe suffered from an intense heatwave (photo **A**). The UK recorded its highest ever temperature of 38.5°C in Kent.

- 2007 – flooding across the UK. Several people were killed and many thousands left homeless. In the north, Hull and Sheffield were badly hit. In the village of Toll Bar near Doncaster some people couldn't return to their homes for over a year. In the south of the UK, several rivers burst their banks. Flooding was particularly serious along the River Severn, affecting Tewkesbury and parts of Gloucester. Huge areas of farmland were flooded, destroying crops and drowning animals.

- 2008 – during a very wet summer there were several floods. In September rivers burst their banks in south Wales, Worcestershire and Northumberland, flooding hundreds of properties. The town of Morpeth in north-east England was particularly badly affected.

- 2009 – heavy February snow affected most of Great Britain and Ireland with the South West being the most severely affected. Over 55cm of snow fell on Okehampton in Devon. Around 20cm settled in parts of London which is unusual for the capital. Widespread disruption was caused to public transport including the temporary closure of Heathrow Airport. In November, extreme flooding in the Lake District resulted from prolonged and heavy rainfall (see Cockermouth case study on p114).

- 2010 – severe winter weather hit the UK unusually early in December. The very low temperatures and snowfall caused much disruption. There was a record low temperature in Northern Ireland of -18.7 °C at Castlederg on 23 December.

In this section you will learn

the range and frequency of extreme weather events in the UK

the impacts of extreme weather events on people's lives.

Key terms

Extreme weather: a weather event such as a flash flood or severe snowstorm that is significantly different from the average.

Global warming: an increase in world temperatures as a result of the increase in greenhouse gases (carbon dioxide, methane, CFCs and nitrous oxide) in the atmosphere brought about by the burning of fossil fuels, for example.

Climate change: long-term changes in the climate, such as cooling leading to an Ice Age or the current trend of global warming.

A A forest fire caused by the 2003 European heatwave

Study tip

Make sure you understand the causes and effects of extreme weather. Details from a case study can be invaluable in clarifying your understanding.

■ Links to global warming and climate change

Some people, particularly in the media, have linked these recent extreme weather events (particularly the European heatwave of 2003) to **global warming**. Although extreme weather events may happen more often as the atmosphere warms up, no individual event can be blamed on global warming. Evidence would have to be drawn from a much longer period of time – hundreds of years – before any reliable links can be made.

'You can say that due to the Earth getting warmer there will be, on average, more extreme events,' said Malcolm Haylock of the University of East Anglia's Climate Research Unit, UK, 'but you can't attribute any specific event to climate change.'

Source: BBC

> **Did you know** ???????
>
> An estimated 1,422 m litres of water flowed through Boscastle in just two hours during the flood of 2004. This is equal to 21 petrol tanker loads of water every second.

Case study

The Boscastle flash flood, 2004

During the afternoon of Monday 16 August, the small pretty village of Boscastle in Cornwall (map **B**) was hit by a huge thunderstorm. About 200 mm of rain fell in 24 hours, most of it in just five hours. The average rainfall in Boscastle for the whole of August is 75 mm.

This huge quantity of rainfall poured down the steep-sides of the valley into the River Valency. The banks of this small river burst as it flowed towards the harbour. The floodwaters quickly spread across the car park before going down the narrow streets towards the harbour (photo **C**). Many cars were picked up and carried by the floodwaters. These cars, together with tree trunks and large branches acted like battering rams smashing into bridges and buildings.

Luckily, no one was killed, but a number of people had to be airlifted to safety.

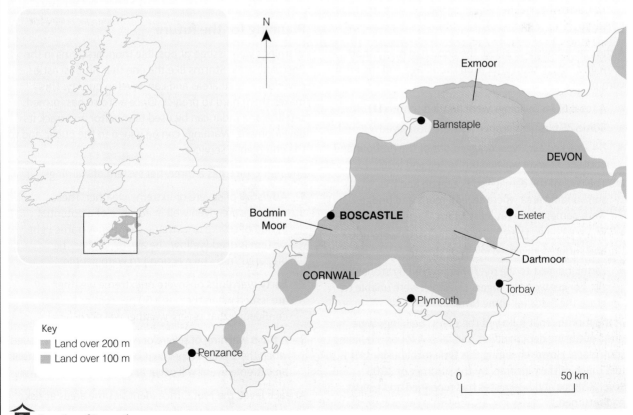

N

Exmoor

Barnstaple

DEVON

Bodmin Moor   **BOSCASTLE**   Exeter

Dartmoor

CORNWALL   Torbay

Plymouth

Key
- Land over 200 m
- Land over 100 m

Penzance

0   50 km

B *Location of Boscastle*

C *The flood in Boscastle*

Effects

Although nobody was killed, the flood had many short-term and longer-term effects on the village and the local community:

- A total of 58 buildings were flooded (photo **D**).
- Some 25 business properties were destroyed.
- 84 wrecked cars were dragged out of the harbour and another 32 were washed out to sea and lost.
- The cost of the damage to Boscastle and the surrounding area where several roads and bridges were damaged was at least £15m.
- Many people – both locals and tourists – were upset and suffered increased levels of stress.
- Farmland next to the river was covered by stones and silt. Fences were damaged. Livestock were unable to graze the fields for some time.

In the months that followed the event, buildings were dried out using dehumidifiers and fans. A lot of rebuilding took place. However, during this time local businesses lost much of their income. By the summer of 2005 several shops and businesses had reopened and tourists had returned.

Planning for the future

Warnings were issued of possible thunderstorms in the Boscastle area. Storms like the one that hit Boscastle cover only small areas and can develop quickly. This makes them hard to predict. Once a storm has formed, satellite and radar can be used to monitor and track its development. Warnings can be issued to the public and to the emergency services.

The Met Office has a three-tier system of warnings:

1 **Advisory** of severe or extreme weather. These warnings are given well in advance of a potential period of severe or extreme weather. A traffic light system is used (yellow: 'be aware'; amber: 'be prepared'; red: 'take action') to warn people.

2 **Early warnings** of severe or extreme weather are issued when there is a 60 per cent or greater confidence that severe weather will occur.

3 A **flash warning** of severe or extreme weather is issued when there is an 80 per cent or greater confidence that an extreme event will occur in the next few hours.

At each level, the Met Office identifies the areas at risk, the level of risk and the likely time the risk will last.

The Environment Agency is in charge of flood management. A telephone Floodline offers warnings, help and advice to people. It is possible to use the Environment Agency's website to identify 'at-risk' areas based on postcodes.

The Boscastle flood event was a 1-in-400-year event. This means that it happens only once every 400 years.

For such a rare event it is not worth building expensive flood defences. However, the stream channel has been enlarged and the bridges have been widened. People have been allowed to rebuild their homes and their lives with the knowledge that a similar event is unlikely to happen again for hundreds of years.

This is the site of a historic building, which was completely destroyed

Youth hostel badly damaged

Fire brigade searching for people

Gifts flushed out from nearby shops and deposited here

D   *The immediate effects of the Boscastle flood*

∞links

There are several extreme weather events that would make excellent research projects. The Met Office has a dedicated website at **www. metoffice.gov.uk/education/teens**. Look for relevant headings or enter 'Boscastle' or 'extreme weather' into the search box to find out some useful information.

The Environment Agency flood pages are at **www.environment-agency.gov.uk/homeandleisure/floods/**.

Activities

1   Read the case study about Boscastle and use this information to answer these questions.

a   Write down at least three facts about the Boscastle flash flood, for example the date it happened and, how much rain fell in 24 hours that day, how much the damage cost to put right.

b   Boscastle is situated at the confluence of two rivers, both of which flow through steep valleys.

■   explain what the word confluence means

■   how did Boscastle's location (the confluence, the steep valley sides) contribute to the flash flood?

2   Study photo **C**.

Work in pairs to make a list of what is happening in the photo. Consider the following:

■   What has happened to the river? Describe the extent of the flooding.

■   What damage has the flooding caused?

■   What are the rescue services doing?

■   What do you think will happen next?

3   Write a few sentences outlining the long-term impacts of the flood on the people of Boscastle.

3.4 What is the evidence for global warming?

The world's climate has been changing since the beginning of time and will do so in the future. During the **Pleistocene period** (the so-called Ice Age), changing temperatures meant that there were cold periods called glacials and warm periods called interglacials (page 124). At the end of the last glacial period about 10,000 years ago, the climate began to warm up. We are living in this warm period today.

Throughout the last few hundred years, temperatures have continued to change (graph **A**). During the medieval period, the climate became warmer. From about 1550 to 1750, there was a period of lower temperatures that became known as the 'Little Ice Age'. These changes are considered to be completely 'natural'.

Since about 1950, there is evidence of a very steep increase in temperatures. It is this recent dramatic increase in global temperatures that is known as global warming.

In this section you will learn

the principles of climate change and global warming

the debate surrounding the evidence for global warming

the greenhouse effect and its connection with global warming.

Key terms

Pleistocene period: a geological time period lasting from about 2 million years ago until 10,000 years ago. Sometimes this period is called the Ice Age.

Glacial retreat: melting of the ice causes a glacier to retreat up-valley.

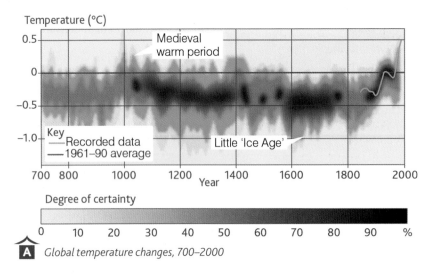

A Global temperature changes, 700–2000

Assessing the evidence for global warming

Evidence for global warming comes from measuring temperatures using thermometers (mostly after 1850 as shown on graph **A**), together with historical records, ice cores and sea-floor sediment samples.

Instrument readings

Measurements from thermometers suggest a clear warming trend in the last few decades (graph **B**). Average global temperatures have risen by 0.74 °C during the last 100 years and by 0.5 °C since 1980.

Glacial retreat

Photographs prove that many of the world's glaciers have been retreating (getting smaller) over the last 50 to 100 years (photo **C**, page 127). In 2001 the World Glacier Monitoring Service reported a significant retreat of glaciers since 1980. It suggests that up to 25 per cent of glacier ice around the world could disappear by 2050.

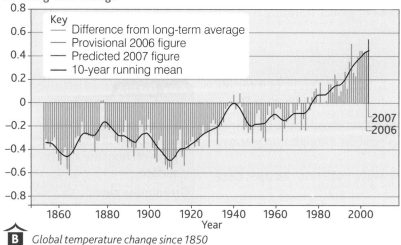

Temperature difference (°C)
from long-term average

Key
— Difference from long-term average
— Provisional 2006 figure
— Predicted 2007 figure
— 10-year running mean

2007
2006

Year

B   *Global temperature change since 1850*

Arctic ice cover

Over the last 30 years, ice in the Arctic has got thinner. It is almost half its earlier thickness. The Arctic could be completely ice-free by the end of this century. As the ice gets thinner less of the sun's radiation is reflected back into space. Instead, the darker sea will absorb more radiation, increasing temperatures further.

Ice cores

Some of the most compelling evidence for global warming comes from the study of deep ice cores from Greenland and Antarctica (photo **C**). When snow falls year on year, it builds up a record going back thousands of years, just like rings in a tree. Water molecules and trapped air can be analysed for changes in temperatures and atmospheric gas concentrations at the time when each layer of snow fell. Scientists have found clear evidence that temperatures have been increasing rapidly in recent decades.

Early spring

In the last 30 years, there have been many signs that the seasons are changing. Spring in particular seems to arrive earlier than in the past. Birds are nesting earlier and bulbs such as crocuses and daffodils are flowering earlier. Winters also appear to be less severe, with fewer frosts and days of snow cover.

C   *Ice cores reveal scientific evidence about global warming*

Activities

1 Study graph **B**. This shows global temperature variations from the long term average every year from 1850 up to 2007. Concentrate on the black line in this graph, which shows the average global temperature variation each year.

a When was the lowest temperature recorded? Was it:

- between 1900 and 1920
- between 1860 and 1880
- between 1940 and 1960?

b There are two sections of the graph that show temperatures going up steadily over a period of several years. One is from the late 1970s to 2007. When is the other one? Is it:

- from around 1880 to 1910
- from around 1910 to 1940
- from around 1940 to 1970?

Causes of climate change and global warming

Many scientists believe that the recent trend of global warming is to some extent caused by the actions of people.

The greenhouse effect

The atmosphere which surrounds the earth, naturally keeps in some of the sun's heat. This is known as the **greenhouse effect** (diagram **D**).

- Just like a greenhouse, the atmosphere allows most of the heat from the sun (short-wave radiation) to pass straight through it to warm up the earth's surface.
- Some of the heat from the Earth (long-wave radiation) escapes back through the atmosphere.
- Gases in the atmosphere absorb some of the heat and stop it escaping. These gases are called **greenhouse gases** (table **E**).

In the same way that glass keeps heat inside a greenhouse, the greenhouse effect keeps the earth warm. Without this it would be far too cold for life to exist on earth.

> **Key terms**
>
> **Greenhouse effect**: the blanketing effect of the atmosphere in retaining heat given off from the earth's surface.
>
> **Greenhouse gases**: gases such as carbon dioxide and methane, which are effective at absorbing heat given off from the earth.

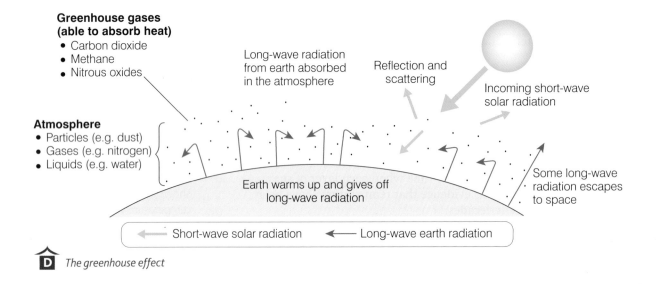

D *The greenhouse effect*

E *Greenhouse gases*

Greenhouse gas	Sources
Carbon dioxide: accounts for an estimated 60 per cent of the 'enhanced' greenhouse effect. Global concentration of carbon dioxide has increased by 30 per cent since 1850	Burning fossil fuels (e.g. oil, gas, coal) in industry and power stations to produce electricity, car exhausts, deforestation and burning wood
Methane: very effective in absorbing heat. Accounts for 20 per cent of the 'enhanced' greenhouse effect	Decaying organic matter in landfill sites and compost tips, rice farming, farm livestock, burning biomass for energy
Nitrous oxides: very small concentration in the atmosphere. Up to 300 times more effective in capturing heat than carbon dioxide	Car exhausts, power stations producing electricity, agricultural fertilisers, sewage treatment

Human activities and global warming

In recent years, the amount of greenhouse gases in the atmosphere have increased (graph **F**). Many scientists believe that this because of human actions such as burning fossil fuels in power stations, dumping waste in landfill sites and burning trees.

This means that there has been an increase in greenhouse gases in the atmosphere. This is what scientists believe is causing global warming. For the first time in history, human activities appear to be changing the atmosphere. This could have dramatic effects on the world's climate. In 2007 the IPCC (Intergovernmental Panel on Climate Change) stated that global climate change is 'very likely' to have a human cause. It predicted that by the end of the 21st century temperatures would rise by between 1.8 °C and 4 °C. This would lead to a sea-level rise of 18–59 cm.

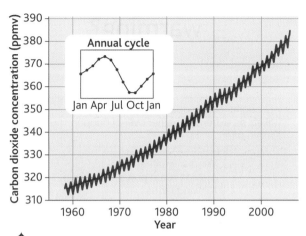

F *Increases in carbon dioxide obtained from direct readings at the Mauna Loa Observatory, Hawaii*

Activities

2 Study diagram **D**. This explains the greenhouse effect.

a Make a large copy of the diagram.

b Use table **E** to add the main sources of greenhouse gases to your diagram. Use simple sketches if you prefer.

3 Study graph **F**. This shows how the concentration of carbon dioxide in the atmosphere has increased since 1960.

a Describe the overall trend (the black line) from 1960–2007. Refer to carbon dioxide concentration values in your answer.

b Can you suggest why concentrations of carbon dioxide go up and down annually? (Hint: think about plant growth).

4 There are some people who believe that global warming is not in any way related to human activities. Work in pairs using the internet to find out why some people do not believe that human actions are affecting the climate.

links

An excellent summary of global warming can be found on the Met Office's website at **http://www.metoffice.gov.uk/climate-change**.

The Met Office Hadley Centre for Climate Change is at **http://www.metoffice.gov.uk/climate-change/resources/hadley/**.

Search for 'climate change' at **www.bbc.co.uk**.

3.5 What are the possible effects of global warming?

In this section you will learn

the possible impacts of global warming in the UK and the world.

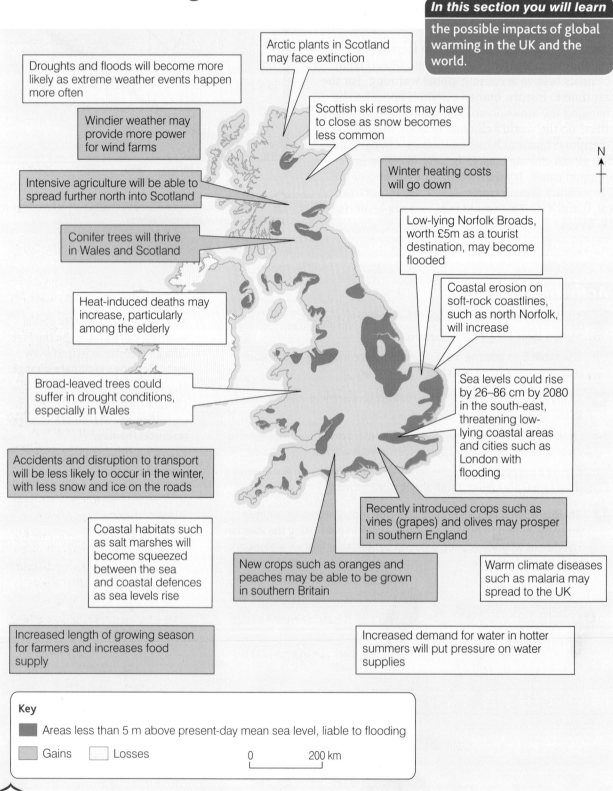

Arctic plants in Scotland may face extinction

Droughts and floods will become more likely as extreme weather events happen more often

Scottish ski resorts may have to close as snow becomes less common

Windier weather may provide more power for wind farms

Winter heating costs will go down

Intensive agriculture will be able to spread further north into Scotland

Low-lying Norfolk Broads, worth £5m as a tourist destination, may become flooded

Conifer trees will thrive in Wales and Scotland

Coastal erosion on soft-rock coastlines, such as north Norfolk, will increase

Heat-induced deaths may increase, particularly among the elderly

Broad-leaved trees could suffer in drought conditions, especially in Wales

Sea levels could rise by 26–86 cm by 2080 in the south-east, threatening low-lying coastal areas and cities such as London with flooding

Accidents and disruption to transport will be less likely to occur in the winter, with less snow and ice on the roads

Recently introduced crops such as vines (grapes) and olives may prosper in southern England

Coastal habitats such as salt marshes will become squeezed between the sea and coastal defences as sea levels rise

New crops such as oranges and peaches may be able to be grown in southern Britain

Warm climate diseases such as malaria may spread to the UK

Increased length of growing season for farmers and increases food supply

Increased demand for water in hotter summers will put pressure on water supplies

N

Key

Areas less than 5 m above present-day mean sea level, liable to flooding

Gains   Losses

0   200 km

A Possible impacts of global warming in the UK

Impacts of global warming in the UK

The Department for Environment, Food and Rural Affairs (Defra) estimates that temperatures in the UK will rise by between 2 °C and 3.5 °C by 2080. This could have big impact on the UK (Map **A**). Temperatures are expected to rise the most in the south and east. Summers are expected to become hotter, and winters colder. Winters will become wetter and summers drier. The amount of snow is expected to decline.

Impacts of global warming in the world

Table **B** lists some of the advantages and disadvantages that global warming may have. Always consider these impacts to be 'possible' rather than 'probable'.

B

Advantages of global warming	Disadvantages of global warming
Frozen regions of the world such as Siberia and northern Canada may be able to grow crops in a milder climate.	Higher sea levels may flood low-lying parts of the world such as Bangladesh, Myanmar and the Netherlands. 80 million people live in these areas at the moment.
Canada's North-west Passage may become ice-free and can be used by shipping.	Tropical storms affecting the Caribbean and the USA may increase in size.
As it will get warmer in some parts of the world (such as northern Europe), people won't need to heat their houses so energy use will go down.	Islands such as the Maldives and Tuvalu may completely disappear as sea levels rise.
Fewer deaths or injuries due to cold weather.	Loss of glaciers (fresh water) in the Himalayas may threaten agriculture and water supply in India, Nepal and China.
Longer growing season in areas such as Europe and North America will increase the amount of food grown.	Parts of Africa may become drier and more prone to droughts, leading to starvation and civil war.
	Hazards such as landslides, floods and avalanches may become more common in mountainous areas such as the Alps.
	Crops are expected to decrease in Africa, the Middle East and India.
	Arctic ice may melt completely
	220–400 million more people may be at risk from malaria, particularly in China and central Asia.
	Some species, may become extinct (die out), for example, polar bears.
	Ski resorts may be forced to close due to lack of snow.

⚭ links

More about global warming can be found at **www.defra.gov.uk/ environment/climate/**

Activities

Study table **B**. This table summarises some of the advantages and disadvantages of global warming.

a Which of the advantages of global warming do you think is the best one for the world – the one that would help the most people? Explain why you think this.

b Which of the disadvantages of global warming do you think is the worst one for the world – the one that would hurt the most people? Again, give your reasons for this.

c These impacts are described as possible rather than probable. Do you think:

■ we should wait until we definitely know they are going to happen before we try to slow down global warming, or

■ should we do something now to slow down global warming, even if these impacts might never happen at all?

There isn't a single right answer to this question, but it's a good one to think about and discuss!

3.6　What are the responses to global warming?

Individual and local responses

What can one person do to help solve a world crisis? People often feel helpless but individuals are important as they set the trends for others to follow. Individual actions include:

- Saving energy at home by using low-energy light bulbs, switching off electrical items, insulating lofts and wearing an extra sweater rather than turning up the heating.
- Walking or cycling to work or school rather than using cars.
- Reducing waste by reusing materials or **recycling** (page 211).
- Buying organic food to cut the use of chemical fertilisers.
- Air passengers can pay money to offset the carbon used by a plane. This money is often used to plant trees, which absorb carbon dioxide from the atmosphere.

Local authorities are trying to reduce carbon emissions:

- They promote public transport by using park-and-ride schemes in towns and cities.
- They give money (grants) for people to insulate their homes.
- They provide recycling collections and encourage people to recycle rubbish at domestic refuse sites.
- Some cities, such as London and Edinburgh, have **congestion charging** to try and reduce the number of cars in the city centre (photo **A**). Bus lanes and car-sharing lanes encourage people to save energy.

National responses

The UK government:

- has introduced tougher MOT tests on vehicle exhausts and has set higher road taxes for 'gas-guzzling' vehicles
- supports plans such as bus lanes and cycle ways
- encourages recycling and waste reduction
- has passed laws so power stations have to cut the amount of greenhouse gases they send into the atmosphere.

The government says it will cut the amount of carbon dioxide Britain puts in the atmosphere by 34 per cent by 2020 and 80 per cent by 2050. These targets are against the levels of carbon dioxide in 1990. To meet this target, the government wants people to save energy as well as using renewable sources of energy such as wind and wave power.

In this section you will learn

the individual, local, national and international responses to global warming.

Key terms

Recycling: using materials, such as aluminium or glass, time and again.

Congestion charging: charging vehicles to enter cities, with the aim of reducing the use of vehicles.

Kyoto Protocol: an international agreement to try to reduce carbon emissions from industrialised countries.

Carbon credits: a means of trading carbon between organisations or countries in order to meet an overall target.

A Congestion charging in London

Did you know ??????

In London, drivers of most vehicles have to pay to enter the centre of the city. All of the money raised is used to improve London's transport system.

International responses

On 16 February 2005, after seven years of debate, the **Kyoto Protocol** became international law. It states that:

- The 37 industrialised countries that have signed the treaty have to reduce their carbon emissions by an average of 5.2 per cent below their 1990 levels by 2012.
- The USA and Australia are the only countries who have refused to sign the treaty. Those that have signed it emit over 60 per cent of carbon dioxide into the atmosphere. Over 190 countries have signed the agreement.
- The USA would not sign because reducing carbon emissions would harm its economy. It is also unhappy that the agreement only applies to industrialised countries.

Carbon credits can be used to trade carbon between organisations or countries. Governments set the amount of carbon a company can emit. Those companies or countries that have not used their set amount can sell it to other companies or countries which have used their set amount.

B   *Tree planting buys carbon credits*

C   *Individual, national and international responses to global warming*

Gas	Sources	Individual responses	National responses	International responses
Carbon dioxide				
Methane				
Nitrous oxides				

Study tip

Be clear about the different levels of responses to global warming.

Activities

For this activity you should work in pairs or small groups.

a   Make a large copy of table **C**.

b   Look back at table **E** on page 68 to remind yourself of the sources of the three main greenhouse gases. Write these in your table.

c   Discuss the individual, national and international responses that would lead to reductions in the emissions of each of the gases.

d   Complete your table with your suggestions.

links

An excellent summary of the Kyoto Protocol can be found at **www.bbc.co.uk/climate/policies/kyoto.shtml**.

3.7   What is the hurricane hazard?

■ How are hurricanes formed?

A **hurricane** is a deep area of low pressure (satellite photo **C**). In other parts of the world it is known as a cyclone (south-east Asia) or a typhoon (Japan and the Philippines). Hurricanes are very powerful storms which form in the Tropics (hot parts of the world). They can destroy large areas, damage property and kill people.

Scientists are not sure what triggers a hurricane. However, they tend to form:

- over warm water (over 26.5 °C)
- in summer and autumn when sea temperatures are at their highest
- at a latitude over 5° N or S of the Equator.

Look at diagram **A**. It is a cross-section through a hurricane. The sequence of events leading to the formation of the hurricane are shown by the numbers 1–4. Notice that the rising warm, moist air 'fuels' the hurricane, leading to the formation of cloud and rain.

When winds reach an average of 120 kph (75 mph), the storm officially becomes a hurricane. Once formed, the hurricane is carried across the ocean by the prevailing winds. The path (**tracks**) of hurricanes are shown in map **B**. As it moves it continues to pick up moisture from the sea, becoming more powerful. When it reaches land the supply of water is cut off and the storm begins to weaken.

In this section you will learn

how hurricanes are formed

the effects of hurricanes, with particular reference to a rich country and a poor country

how to reduce the hurricane hazard.

Key terms

Hurricane: a powerful tropical storm with sustained winds of over 120 kph (75 mph). Also known as a tropical cyclone, a cyclone or a typhoon.

Eye: the centre of a hurricane where sinking air creates clear conditions.

Eye wall: a high bank of cloud either side of the eye where wind speeds are high and heavy rain falls.

Track: the path or course of a hurricane.

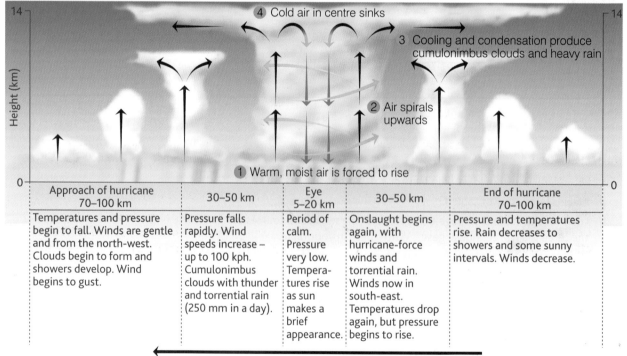

Approach of hurricane 70–100 km	30–50 km	Eye 5–20 km	30–50 km	End of hurricane 70–100 km
Temperatures and pressure begin to fall. Winds are gentle and from the north-west. Clouds begin to form and showers develop. Wind begins to gust.	Pressure falls rapidly. Wind speeds increase – up to 100 kph. Cumulonimbus clouds with thunder and torrential rain (250 mm in a day).	Period of calm. Pressure very low. Temperatures rise as sun makes a brief appearance.	Onslaught begins again, with hurricane-force winds and torrential rain. Winds now in south-east. Temperatures drop again, but pressure begins to rise.	Pressure and temperatures rise. Rain decreases to showers and some sunny intervals. Winds decrease.

Direction of hurricane movement

A   *The structure of a hurricane (in the northern hemisphere)*

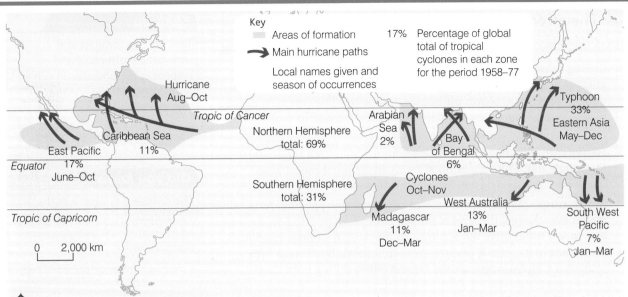

B *The location and tracks of hurricanes*

This is the eye of the hurricane. Here, it's calm and clear.

On either side of the eye is a large bank of cloud called the **eye wall**. Here are the strongest winds and the heaviest rain.

C *The distinctive shape of a hurricane in the Caribbean*

Activities

1 Study map **B**. this shows the location and tracks of hurricanes.

a On a blank map of the world, make a copy of the areas of hurricane formation and the main hurricane paths.

b Use an atlas to label some of the countries most at risk from hurricanes.

c What do you notice from this map about where most hurricanes are formed? Do hurricanes usually start:

■ near the polar regions, where cold air falls (anticyclones common)

■ in the middle of continental land masses, where hot summers heat the dry air

■ in a band either side of the equator, where water vapour from the oceans is drawn up as the warm air rises

■ none of the above options?

d A geographer wants to combine a Caribbean holiday with some hurricane-spotting. When should she travel to the Caribbean to have the best chance of experiencing a hurricane?

■ between January and April

■ between June and October

■ Christmas/New Year.

The effects of hurricanes

Hurricanes can cause great destruction. The main causes of destruction are:

- **Strong winds** – with wind speeds of over 120 kph (75 mph) and gusts over 200 kph (125 mph), hurricanes can cause a great deal of damage. Roofs are blown off houses and power lines are torn down. Flimsy houses will be totally destroyed. The damage to crops could have long-lasting effects.

- **Heavy rainfall** – huge amounts of rain can fall, often up to 200 mm in a single day. This causes flooding as rivers burst their banks. Landslides may be triggered in upland regions.

- **Storm surge** – a hurricane is an area of intense low pressure. As it moves over the sea, the level of the sea rises, often by 3 to 5 metres. The strong winds drive the sea towards the land. A storm surge flattens everything in its path. It destroys crops and floods huge areas with salty water. Storm surges are the biggest killers during hurricanes.

Reducing the hurricane hazard

Hurricanes can be clearly seen and tracked by satellites (see map **D**). Computers can predict the course of a hurricane. People living in hurricane-prone areas can be taught how to prepare.

Hurricanes are more destructive in poorer parts of the world. Emergency services are often unable to cope with the aftermath of a hurricane.

Following terrible disasters in Bangladesh:

- Hurricanes are carefully monitored by the Bangladesh Meteorology Department.
- Warnings are broadcast over the radio.
- Trained wardens help to spread the word in remote villages.
- Cyclone shelters have been built to provide shelter.

In 2007 Cyclone Sidr caused the deaths of 3,000 people in Bangladesh. This is much lower than previous death tolls.

> **Study tip**
>
> Take time to compare and contrast the effects of and responses to hurricanes in rich and poor countries.

> **Did you know** ??????
>
> The deadliest cyclone was the 1970 Bhola Cyclone, which killed an estimated 500,000 people in Bangladesh.

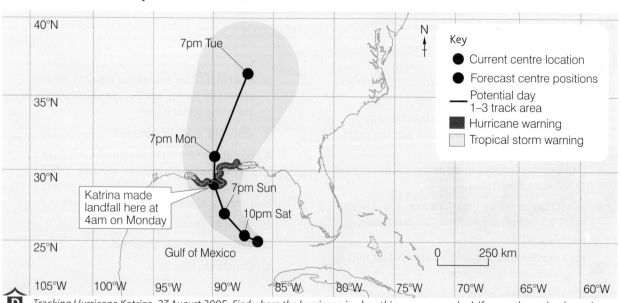

D *Tracking Hurricane Katrina, 27 August 2005. Find where the hurricane is when this map was made. A 'forecast' zone has been drawn ahead of it.*

E *Comparing Hurricane Katrina and Cyclone Nargis*

Impact	Hurricane Katrina, 2005 (USA)	Cyclone Nargis, 2008 (Myanmar)
Event details	• Sixth most powerful North American hurricane ever recorded. Formed over the Bahamas and then passed over Florida. It hit the land near to New Orleans, Louisiana. Strongest winds recorded were 280 kph. Over 200 mm of rain fell. The system of levees (waterway embankments) failed, resulting in widespread flooding.	• Cyclone developed in the Bay of Bengal in April and made landfall in the south-west of Myanmar on 2 May 2008. • Winds of up to 215 kph battered the coastline. • The Irrawaddy delta region was particularly badly affected by a storm surge.
Deaths	• 1,836 confirmed dead.	• 138,000 confirmed dead.
Homeless	• Hundreds of thousands displaced from their homes; many evacuated.	• Hundreds of thousands were made homeless. • In the Irrawaddy delta region an estimated 95 per cent of all homes destroyed.
Number affected	• 3 million people left without electricity. 80 per cent of New Orleans flooded.	• 2.4 million.
Economic losses	• $89 bn (the costliest US hurricane ever).	• Approximately $4 bn. 42 per cent of food stocks were destroyed and 200,000 farm animals were killed.
Time for help to arrive	• A few hours.	• The government refused to let foreign aid into the country for several weeks.
Services damaged	• All services (electricity, water, sanitation) severely affected in New Orleans.	• Almost total destruction of services (electricity, telephones, water).
Short-term responses	• Rescuing people from the water. • Treating the injured. • Providing food, water and shelter for those left in New Orleans.	• Identification and burial of the dead. • Treating the injured. • Providing safe water, food and medicines.
Long-term responses	• Massive rebuilding of New Orleans. • Some evacuees have still not returned. • Strengthening of levees.	• Rebuilding homes and workplaces. • Reclaiming farmland from salty water. • Rebuilding services and transport networks.
Environmental effects	• Floodwaters became very polluted. • Physical changes to the Mississippi delta. • Some coastal habitats lost or damaged.	• Salt water flooded farmland and polluted water sources. • Burst sewage pipes caused pollution.
Warnings	• Katrina had been monitored and predictions were accurate. • 80 per cent evacuated. • Public transport closed down ahead of the storm.	• Most people had no idea that the cyclone was approaching.

Activities

2 Conduct a research project comparing the impacts of hurricanes in rich and poor countries. You could compare Hurricane Katrina and Cyclone Nargis (table **E**) or choose other examples using the internet. Describe the events and the impacts using maps and photos. Compare the social, economic and environmental impacts of your chosen hurricanes.

4 Living world

4.1   What is an ecosystem?

An **ecosystem** is a natural system that is made up of plants, animals and the natural environment in which they live. There are often complex relationships between the living and non-living parts in an ecosystem. Non-living parts include the climate (mainly the temperature and rainfall), soil, water and light.

There are different scales of ecosystem. A local ecosystem can be a pond (diagram **A**) or a hedge. Larger ecosystems can be lakes or woodlands. It is possible for ecosystems to be global, such as tropical rainforests or deciduous woodland. These global ecosystems are called **biomes**.

Case study

The freshwater pond ecosystem

Freshwater ponds provide a variety of habitats for plants and animals (diagram **A**). There is a lot of variation in the amount of light, water and oxygen in different parts of a pond. Animals living at the bottom in deep water need different **adaptations** to those living near the edge of the pond. Some plants such as water lilies can be covered in water because they send their flowering stems to the surface of the water. Reeds and other plants are better adapted to being right on the edges where it is drier.

There are a number of important ecological concepts that you need to understand:

- **Producers** and **consumers** – organisms can be either producers or consumers. Producers convert energy into sugars. The most obvious producers are plants, which convert energy from the sun. Consumers get their energy from the sugars made by the producers. The grasses on the edge of the pond in diagram **A** are good examples of producers. A pond snail is a good example of a consumer because it eats the plants.
- **Food chain** – this shows the links (or 'chain') between producers and consumers. Diagram **B** shows a food chain for a pond.
- **Food web** – this shows the connections between producers and consumers in a more detailed way, than a food chain (diagram **C**).
- **Scavengers** and **decomposers** – when living things in an ecosystem die, scavengers and decomposers break them down and recycle their nutrients. Scavengers eat dead animals and plants. A rat-tailed maggot is a good example of a freshwater pond scavenger. Flies and earthworms are examples of scavengers found on land. Decomposers are usually bacteria and fungi. They break down the last bits of plant and animal material, often returning the nutrients to the soil.

Key terms

Ecosystem: the living and non-living parts of an environment and the interrelationships that exist between them.

Biomes: global-scale ecosystems.

Adaptations: the ways that plants evolve to cope with environmental conditions such as lots of rainfall.

Producers: organisms that get their energy from a primary source such as the sun.

Consumer: organisms that get their energy by eating other organisms.

Food chain: a line of linkages between producers and consumers.

Food web: a diagram that shows all the linkages between producers and consumers in an ecosystem.

Scavengers: organisms that consume dead animals or plants.

Decomposers: organisms such as bacteria that break down plant and animal material.

Nutrient cycling: the recycling of nutrients between living organisms and the environment.

- **Nutrient cycle** – nutrients are foods that are used by plants or animals to grow. Examples are nitrogen, potash and potassium. Nutrients come from two main places: rainwater and weathered rock. When plants or animals die, the scavengers and decomposers recycle the nutrients. This means other plants and animals can use them to grow.

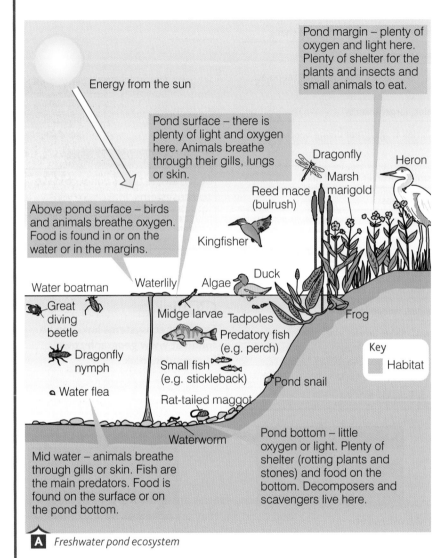

Pond margin – plenty of oxygen and light here. Plenty of shelter for the plants and insects and small animals to eat.

Energy from the sun

Pond surface – there is plenty of light and oxygen here. Animals breathe through their gills, lungs or skin.

Above pond surface – birds and animals breathe oxygen. Food is found in or on the water or in the margins.

Dragonfly

Marsh marigold

Heron

Reed mace (bulrush)

Kingfisher

Water boatman   Waterlily   Algae   Duck

Great diving beetle

Midge larvae   Tadpoles

Frog

Dragonfly nymph

Predatory fish (e.g. perch)

Small fish (e.g. stickleback)

Water flea

Rat-tailed maggot

Pond snail

Key

Habitat

Waterworm

Mid water – animals breathe through gills or skin. Fish are the main predators. Food is found on the surface or on the pond bottom.

Pond bottom – little oxygen or light. Plenty of shelter (rotting plants and stones) and food on the bottom. Decomposers and scavengers live here.

A *Freshwater pond ecosystem*

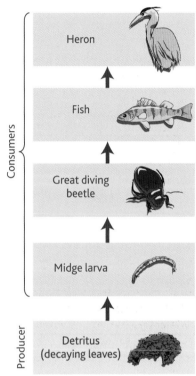

Consumers

Heron

Fish

Great diving beetle

Midge larva

Producer

Detritus (decaying leaves)

B *Freshwater pond food chain*

The impact of change on the freshwater pond ecosystem

Ecosystems can change over time. This can be caused by natural factors such as a flood, fire, drought or something caused by humans, like overfishing or draining land.

If some types of fish are introduced into the pond in diagram **A** they will eat more of the smaller fish and small animals such as frogs. This will affect the numbers of those creatures, which will mean there is less food for creatures further up the food chain. At the same time, with fewer frogs in the pond, there will be more creatures below frogs in the food chain as they are not being eaten by frogs.

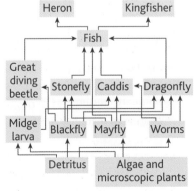

Heron   Kingfisher

Fish

Great diving beetle   Stonefly   Caddis   Dragonfly

Midge larva   Blackfly   Mayfly   Worms

Detritus   Algae and microscopic plants

C *Freshwater pond food web*

D *Freshwater pond species and energy sources*

Species	Energy source (sunlight or food)
Algae	Sunlight
Dragonfly	Other adult insects
Dragonfly nymph	Tadpoles, young fish, water fleas, beetles
Duck	Water plants, insects, tadpoles, small fish, pond snails
Frog	Insects, water worms, snails
Great diving beetle	Water fleas, midge larvae, pond snails, nymphs, tadpoles, water boatmen
Heron	Fish, frogs and tadpoles, larger insects
Kingfisher	Small fish, tadpoles, small frogs, great diving beetle
Marsh marigold	Sunlight
Midge larvae	Microscopic plants, small particles of dead plants
Perch	Small fish, beetles, water fleas
Pond snail	Large water plants, algae
Rat-tailed maggot	Decaying plants
Reed mace	Sunlight
Sticklebacks	Tadpoles, young fish, water fleas, beetles
Tadpole	Microscopic plants, algae, midge larvae
Water boatmen	Tadpoles, water worms, midge larvae, water fleas
Water flea	Microscopic plants, small particles of dead plants
Water lily	Sunshine
Water worm	Small particles of dead animals

> **Study tip**
>
> Learn all the terms connected to ecosystems. Make sure you understand how ecosystems can change.

⬭ **links**

Excellent ecosystems links can be found at **www.geography.pwp. blueyonder.co.uk**

Activities

1 Study diagram **A** and table **D**.

a Which two of these organisms from a freshwater pond are producers?
- pondweed
- pond snail
- algae.

b Which two of these organisms from a freshwater pond are consumers?
- marsh marigold
- dragonfly
- pond snail.

c Which pond species are at the top level in the food chain, i.e. they are not eaten by any other species in the ecosystem?

d Draw a food chain diagram with a heron at the top. Include sunlight in your diagram and add sketches to make it look more interesting.

e Imagine that disease wipes out all the frogs in this pond. How would this affect the ecosystem in the short term and the long term?

f Suggest another change that could happen to this ecosystem and describe the effects that it could have on the species living in the pond.

4.2   What are the characteristics of global ecosystems?

■ The distribution of global ecosystems

Global ecosystems are called biomes. A biome is usually named after the main type of vegetation, e.g. tropical rainforest. Map **A** shows where the major world biomes are.

The biome in the UK is **temperate deciduous forest**. This is the natural vegetation of the UK. If all building and land management stopped for 100 years or so, then the landscape would return to natural deciduous woodland.

In this section you will learn

the distribution of temperate deciduous forests, tropical rainforests and hot deserts

the characteristics and adaptations of vegetation in these three biomes to climate and soils.

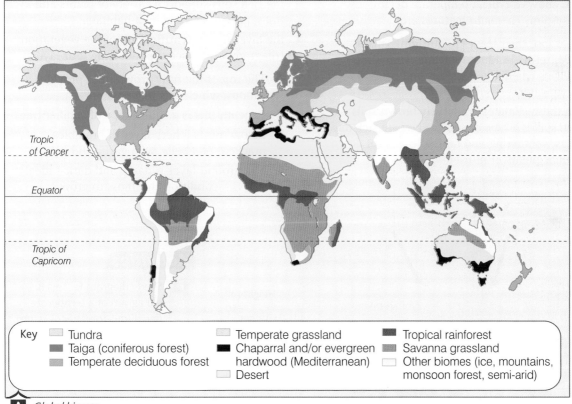

Key
- Tundra
- Taiga (coniferous forest)
- Temperate deciduous forest
- Temperate grassland
- Chaparral and/or evergreen hardwood (Mediterranean)
- Desert
- Tropical rainforest
- Savanna grassland
- Other biomes (ice, mountains, monsoon forest, semi-arid)

A Global biomes

Activities

1   Study map **A**. This shows the distribution of the global biomes.

a   On a blank outline map of the world, draw the distribution of temperate deciduous forest.

b   Use an atlas to identify some of the main regions and countries where this is the natural type of vegetation.

Key term

Temperate deciduous forest: forests made up of broad-leaved trees such as oak that drop their leaves in the autumn.

Did you know ??????

The tallest tree in the world is in Redwood National Park, California. It measures 115.55 m. The oldest tree in the world is said to be a Norway spruce in Sweden. It's 9,550 years old.

Temperate deciduous forests

Location

Temperate deciduous forests occur across most of north-west Europe, eastern North America and parts of East Asia (Map **A**).

Climate

Temperate deciduous forests are found in areas with a moderate climate. (graph **B**). There is rain all through the year. Summers are warm but not too dry and winters are cool but not too cold. There is a long growing season lasting up to seven months.

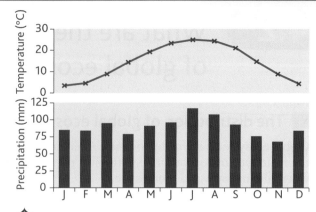

B *Climate graph for Greensborough, North Carolina, USA – a temperate deciduous forest biome*

Main features

Diagram **C** shows a typical temperate deciduous forest ecosystem. The main features are:

- the trees lose their leaves in autumn. This is what the term 'deciduous' means. They drop their leaves when it gets darker and cooler to conserve water.

- soils in these climates are mostly brown soils ('brown soil' is a type of soil!). They are rich and fertile as weathering and falling leaves rot down to produce plenty of nutrients.

- the rich soils support a variety of plants and trees, providing a range of habitats.

- the layering or **stratification** of the vegetation (diagram **C**). Notice the following four layers:

  1. The top of the fully grown trees provides a canopy, which acts like an umbrella.

  2. Beneath this is a sub-canopy of smaller trees.

  3. Below this is a herb layer of brambles, bracken, bluebells, wild garlic and ivy.

  4. The ground layer is damp and dark – ideal conditions for moss to grow.

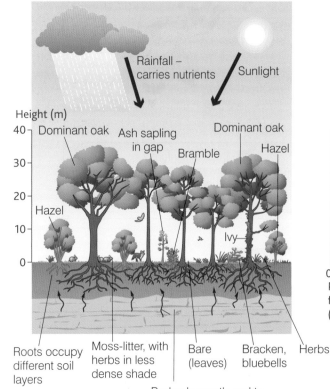

C *A temperate deciduous forest ecosystem*

Activities

2 Study diagram **C**. This is a diagram of a temperate deciduous forest ecosystem.

a Does this diagram show that this ecosystem:

- does not support much wildlife

- supports a lot of wildlife?

Give evidence from the diagram to justify your answer.

b What does stratification mean? Draw a diagram to help explain your answer.

c Why do you think stratification exists? (Hint: think about where plants get their energy from.)

◼ Tropical rainforests

Location

Tropical rainforests are found in the tropics (map **A**), from Central and South America, through central parts of Africa, in South-east Asia and into the northern part of Australia.

Climate

This biome has lots of rainfall (over 2,000 mm a year) and high temperatures (averaging 27 °C) throughout the year. This climate (graph **D**) provides ideal conditions for plant growth.

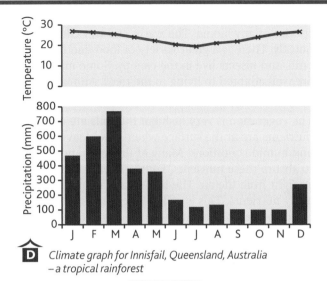

D Climate graph for Innisfail, Queensland, Australia – a tropical rainforest

Main features

- Lush and dense vegetation. It is dark and damp.
- Very tall trees, often up to 45 m in height. There is a great variety of trees. The wood is a very valuable resource.
- A clear stratification (diagram **E**). Most plants and animals live in the canopy where there is maximum light. Some tree leaves are specially adapted to twist and turn to face the sun as it arcs across the sky. In contrast, rainforest floors are often too dark to support many plants.

> **Key terms**
>
> **Stratification**: layering of forests, seen particularly in temperate deciduous forests and tropical rainforests.
>
> **Tropical rainforests**: the natural vegetation found in the tropics, well suited to the high temperatures and heavy rainfall of these latitudes.

Fast-growing trees such as capoc out-compete other trees to reach sunlight – such trees are called emergents

Many leaves have flexible bases so that they can turn to face the sun

Many leaves have a 'drip tip' to allow the heavy rain to drip off the leaf

Water drips off leaves

Thin, smooth bark on trees to allow water to flow down easily

Buttresses – massive ridges help support the base of the tall trees and help transport water.

Lianas – woody creepers rooted to the ground but carried by trees into the canopy where they have their leaves and flowers

Plants called epiphytes can live on branches high in the canopy to seek sunlight – they get nutrients from water and air rather than soil

 E *Stratification and vegetation adaptations in a tropical rainforest*

Tropical rainforests have the largest number of plant and animal species of any biome. The warm and wet climate makes plants grow quickly. There is a great variety of food and natural habitats. Many birds and insects live in the canopy. Some mammals, such as monkeys, are well adapted to living in the trees. Animals such as deer live on the forest floor eating seeds and berries.

The vegetation is very lush but the soils are quite infertile. Most of the nutrients are at the surface where dead leaves rot quickly in the hot and humid conditions. Many of the trees and plants have shallow roots to absorb these nutrients. Fungi growing on the roots transfer nutrients straight from the air. The heavy rainfall quickly dissolves and carries away nutrients. This is called **leaching**. It leaves behind an infertile red-coloured soil called latosol. Latosol is red because it is rich in iron and very acidic (photo **F**).

Key terms

Leaching: the dissolving and removal of nutrients from the soil, often in tropical rainforests because of the heavy rainfall.

Arid: dry conditions typically associated with deserts.

Hot deserts: deserts have a rainfall of less than 250 mm per year. Hot deserts are generally found between 30°N and 30°S

Activities

3 Study diagram **F**. This is a diagram of a tropical forest ecosystem.

a What name is given to the tall trees that break through the canopy? Give an example of one of these types of tree.

b How high can the tallest trees grow?

c On the ground in a tropical rainforest, in which layer of the forest would you be in?

d How have the leaves of the tallest trees adapted to gain maximum sunlight?

e Describe how leaves are designed to shed water quickly during torrential downpours.

f What are lianas and how have they adapted to live successfully in tropical rainforests?

g What is a buttress and what are the possible reasons why some trees have them?

4 In the past, some people cut down rainforest trees and replaced them with commercial crops expecting a wonderful harvest. Instead, the new plants grew poorly. Explain why this happened.

F Latosol: a typical soil found in the tropical rainforest biome

◼ Hot deserts

Location

Hot deserts are generally found away from the coast in a belt between 30°N and 30°S of the equator.

Climate

A hot desert is an area that has less than 250 mm of rainfall per year. Temperatures are hot during the day. Because there is no cloud cover to trap the heat, it can be very cold at night.

Main features

- The **arid** (dry) conditions control life in the desert.
- Desert soils are often sandy or stony and are not very fertile. Soils are dry but can soak up water quickly after rainfall. Salt is drawn to the surface, often leaving a white residue on the ground.
- There is little vegetation but some plants can survive in these tough conditions (fact file **G**).
- Lack of water and vegetation means there are not many animals or birds that can live here.

⚭ links

For more information on plant adaptations in arid environments, go to **www.cwnp.org/adaptations.html**.

Activities

5 Use the information in fact file **G**, together with your own internet research and the text here, to complete a short research project on desert ecosystems. You should include the following information:

- ■ Draw a map to show the main areas of hot desert. Use an atlas to name the deserts.
- ■ Using a climate graph, describe the climatic conditions experienced in hot deserts. Why are hot deserts hostile environments?
- ■ Describe how a plant or an animal of your choice has adapted to hot desert conditions. You could draw a picture of the plant or the animal and label its adaptations. A good website to get you started is www.cwnp.org/adaptations.html

Study tip

The key aspect in this section is the way that plants respond to climate and soils. Learn some of the ways that plants have adapted to the challenges presented by living in particular environments.

G *Desert ecosystem fact file*

Death Valley, California

	J	F	M	A	M	J	J	A	S	O	N	D
Average temperature (°C)	11	15	19	24	29	35	38	37	32	25	17	10
Average precipitation (mm)	0.8	1.2	0.8	0.4	0.2	0.1	0.3	0.2	0.4	0.3	0.6	0.4

Plant adaptations

1 Desert yellow daisy – small linear leaves that are hairy and slightly succulent.

2 Great basin sagebrush – tap roots up to 25 m long and small needle-like leaves to reduce water loss.

3 Giant saguaro cactus – roots very close to the surface so that it can soak up water before it evaporates. Outside skin is pleated so that it can expand when water is soaked up. Grows very slowly.

4 Joshua tree – needle-like leaves coated with a waxy resin

1

2

3

4

4.3 What are temperate deciduous woodlands used for?

Epping Forest, Essex

Epping Forest is a very old deciduous forest near London. It is about 19 km long and 4 km wide. It is the largest area of public open space near London.

Although 70 per cent of Epping Forest is deciduous woodland, there are also grasslands and marshes. It is home to a rich variety of wildlife including woodpeckers, wood-boring stag beetles and fallow deer.

Early uses and management

Since Norman times, kings and queens of England have used Epping Forest for hunting deer. Local people grazed their animals and collected wood for firewood and building.

For many years, **pollarding** was used to manage the woodland. This involves cutting the trees at about shoulder height, so that animals such as deer cannot harm them (photo **A**). Pollarded trees reshoot at this height and keep growing. This is a good example of **sustainable management** as it means there is a supply of wood for the future. It also explains why there are some very old trees in Epping Forest.

In the 19th century, landowners tried to buy parts of the forest. To stop this, in 1878 the Epping Forest Act of Parliament said that the forest should never be shut off or built on. It must always be kept as an open space for people to enjoy.

Recent management

Epping Forest is an excellent example of a natural deciduous forest that is being managed sustainably for the future. A large part of the forest has become a Site of Special Scientific Interest and a European Special Area of Conservation. This means that many of the ancient trees, which support lots of plants and animals, are protected from being cut down.

A *An ancient pollarded tree, Epping Forest*

Key terms

Pollarding: cutting off trees at about shoulder height to encourage new growth.

Sustainable management: a form of management that ensures that developments are long lasting and non-harmful to the environment.

Did you know ??????

Epping Forest is home to the very rare stag beetle due to the presence of dead and decaying wood.

Activities

1. Study photo **A**. This shows an ancient pollarded tree in Epping Forest.

   a. What is pollarding? Draw a sketch of the tree in the photo to illustrate your answer.

   b. Why are trees pollarded?

   c. 'Pollarding is an example of sustainable management.' Is this statement true or false? Explain your choice, making sure you say what sustainable management means in your answer.

Since 1878 Epping Forest has been managed by the City of London Corporation. It tries to make sure that the forest is looked after while still allowing the public to enjoy it by:

- providing car parks, toilets and refreshment facilities and by looking after footpaths (photo **B**)
- providing three easy-access parks so people with disabilities can enjoy the forest
- allowing old trees to die and collapse naturally unless they are dangerous
- controlling where people can ride and mountain bike to protect areas and other people
- re-pollarding trees so they grow new shoots – since 1981, over 1,000 ancient trees have been re-pollarded
- encouraging grazing to look after the grassland and the plants and animals which use it
- looking after old earthworks and buildings
- maintaining ponds to stop them silting up
- taking care of the fallow deer.

B   *Recreation in Epping Forest*

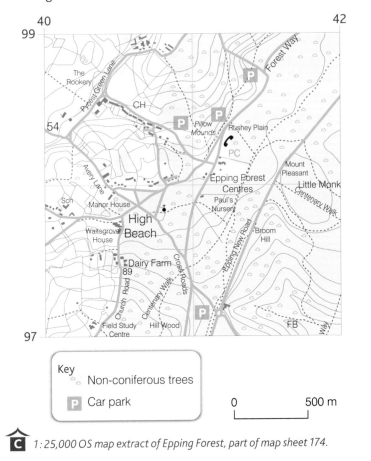

Key
- Non-coniferous trees
- **P** Car park

0 —————— 500 m

C   *1 : 25,000 OS map extract of Epping Forest, part of map sheet 174.*

Activities

2   Study map extract **C**. This map is from a 1 : 25,000 Ordnance Survey map of Epping Forest.

a   Is this area of Epping Forest flat or is it quite hilly? Explain how the map shows you this.

b   You'll see in this map that the houses are mostly outside the wooded part of the map. Why do you think this might be? Try and come up with three possible reasons.

c   Name a couple of features from the map that suggest people use this area for recreation. (Hint: travel.)

d   Why do you think it is important to have properly designated car parking?

e   Find the field study centre on this map. What sort of geography fieldwork could you do in a place like this, do you think?

links

Further information about Epping Forest can be found at **www.bbc.co.uk**. Type 'Epping Forest' into the search box.

The Epping Forest Information Centre can be found at High Beach, Loughton, Essex IG10 4AF.

Deforestation in Malaysia

Malaysia's tropical rainforests

Malaysia is a country in south-east Asia. It is made up of two parts, peninsular Malaysia and Eastern Malaysia, which is part of the island of Borneo (maps in **A**). The natural vegetation in Malaysia is tropical rainforest. Nearly 60 per cent of Malaysia is forested and commercial tree crops, mainly rubber and oil palm, take up a further 13 per cent. Trees and forest cover an area the same size of the whole of the UK.

In this section you will learn

the causes of deforestation in tropical rainforests

the effects of deforestation in tropical rainforests.

a World location map

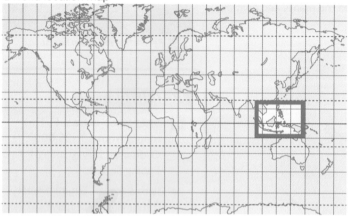

Key terms

Primary (virgin) rainforest: rainforest that represents the natural vegetation in the region unaffected by the actions of people.

Deforestation: the cutting down and removal of forest.

Clear felling: absolute clearance of all trees from an area.

Selective logging: the cutting down of selected trees, leaving most of the trees intact.

b Regional location map

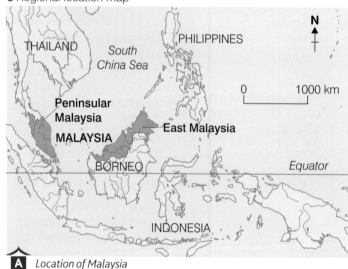

A *Location of Malaysia*

In the past most of the country was covered by **primary (virgin) rainforest**. In Peninsular Malaysia most of this has now gone and little is left on Borneo. Today an estimated 18 per cent of Malaysia's forest is virgin forest.

Malaysian rainforests support over 5,500 species of plants (the UK has 1,350), 2,600 species of tree (UK 35) and over 1,000 species of butterflies (UK 43). Of the 203 species of mammals, 78 per cent live only in forests. Malaysia's rainforests are very special places.

■ Threats to Malaysia's rainforests

The rate of **deforestation** in Malaysia is increasing faster than in any other tropical country in the world. Since 2000, some 140,200 hectares of forest have been lost on average every year. This destroys the trees and leaves animals and people without homes. There are several threats to the rainforests in Malaysia.

Logging

During the 1980s, Malaysia became the world's largest exporter of tropical wood. **Clear felling**, where all trees are cut down in an area, was common. This led to the total destruction of forest habitats. In recent years the main logging practice has been **selective logging**. This is when only fully grown trees are cut down. Although selective logging is far less damaging, it reduces biodiversity. All types of logging need roads to be built which bring in machinery and take away the timber (photo **B**).

B *Road construction and logging in Sarawak, East Malaysia*

Malaysia has one of the best rainforest protection policies in the region. Even so, environmental groups claim to have found evidence of illegal logging in Borneo. Here, increasingly marginal slopes have been logged. This has led to problems of soil erosion and mudslides.

Energy

The $2 billion Bakun Dam project in Sarawak was completed in 2011 and is designed to supply hydroelectric power for Malaysia. Thousands of hectares of forest have been flooded and 230 km² of virgin rainforest has been cut down. Around 10,000 indigenous people have been forced to move from the flooded area. They are traditional subsistence farmers with very little money. Even though they are poor, they have to pay to be rehoused. Many now suffer from depression and alcoholism.

Mining

Tin mining has been widespread in Peninsular Malaysia. Areas of rainforest have been cleared to make way for mining and for roads leading to and from the mines. In some places, the mining has led to pollution of the land and rivers. Drilling for oil and gas has started on Borneo.

> **Did you know** ??????
>
> The orang-utan is a great ape found only in the rainforests south-east Asia. It is the largest tree-living mammal in the world. It is also one of our closest relatives, sharing 97 per cent of human DNA.

Commercial plantations

Malaysia is a major producer of oil palm and rubber. In the early 20th century, forest was cleared for the rubber plantations. In recent decades, however, demand for natural rubber has got much smaller. Many plantations have either been abandoned or converted to oil palm (photo **C**).

Today, Malaysia is the largest exporter of palm oil in the world. During the 1970s, large areas of rainforest were cut down and turned into palm oil plantations. Plantation owners get a 10-year tax break, so increasing amounts of land have been converted to plantations.

Resettlement

In the past, poor people were encouraged to move into the countryside to relieve pressure on cities. This policy is called **transmigration** (see page 184). Between 1956 and the 1980s, an estimated 15,000 ha of rainforest was cut down for the new settlers, many of whom set up plantations.

Fires

Fires are common on Borneo. Some are caused by lightning strikes, whereas others are caused by people. Sometimes, '**slash and burn**' agriculture – where local people clear small areas of land so they can grow food – results in wildfires.

C Oil palm plantation in Malaysia

(see page 184)

Activities

1 Study this section on the threats to Malaysia's rainforest.

a List and write a sentence about each of the six main causes of deforestation in Malaysia.

b 'Deforestation in Malaysia is because people want to make money from forests and forest lands.' To what extent do you agree with this statement: 100% agree, 80% agree or only 50% agree? Explain your decision.

2 Complete a large revision diagram to summarise the threats to Malaysia's rainforests, using an A3 sheet of paper if possible. Include some internet research information if you can.

a At the centre of your diagram, place a photo or sketch to show the features of Malaysia's rainforest. You could include a map too.

b Around the central feature, create a series of illustrated text boxes describing the main threats to the rainforest. Use arrows to link these boxes to the central image. Use plenty of colour and make use of photos if you can.

Key terms

Transmigration: a population policy that aims to re-distribute people from densely populated areas to sparsely populated areas and provide them with opportunities to improve the quality of their lives.

Slash and burn: a form of subsistence farming in tropical rainforests where some trees are felled and land is cleared by burning before being replanted.

Study tip

Be sure to identify the difference between 'threats', 'causes' and 'effects' of deforestation and make sure that you use each term correctly.

∞ links

Further information on Malaysia's rainforests, go to **http://rainforests. mongabay.com/20malaysia.htm**.

For information on deforestation in Brazil, go to **www.mongabay.com/ brazil.html**.

4.5   Sustainable rainforest management in Malaysia

■ National Forest Policy

Logging on a large-scale started in Malaysia after the Second World War. This was because of new technology such as trucks and chainsaws. The government responded by passing the National Forestry Act in 1977. This had the following aims:

■ Develop timber processing to increase the amount of money made from wood and cut down on demand for raw timber. The export of low-value logs is now banned in most of Malaysia.

■ Encourage alternative timber sources (e.g. from rubber trees).

■ Increase public awareness of forests.

■ Increase research into forestry.

■ Involve local communities in forest projects.

One of the main initiatives of the 1977 Act was to introduce a new approach to forest management known as the **Selective Management System** (diagram **A**). This is seen as one of the most sustainable approaches to managing tropical rainforests in the world.

Key term

Selective Management System: a form of sustainable forestry management adopted in Malaysia.

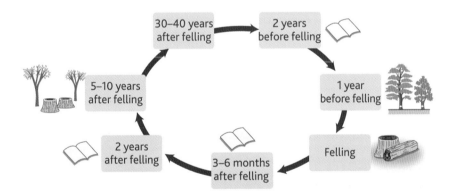

Stage	Actions
2 years before felling	Study the area to find out what is there.
1 year before felling	Trees which will make money marked for cutting down. Arrows painted on trees to show direction of felling to avoid damaging other trees.
Felling	Felling is done by licence holders.
3–6 months after felling	Survey to check what has been felled. Prosecution may result from illegal felling.
2 years after felling	Treatment plan drawn up to re-grow the forest.
5–10 years after felling	New trees planted by state forestry officials.
30–40 years after felling	Cycle begins again.

A *Malaysia's Selective Management System*

Unfortunately, there are not many trained officials to enforce the system across this country. This means that trees are still being cut down illegally and replanting, has not always been carried out well. Deforestation is still taking place in Borneo where land is being converted to oil palm plantations.

Permanent Forest Estates and National Parks

Land-use surveys carried out in the 1960s and 1970s have helped the government to identify Permanent Forest Estates. These areas are protected, with no development allowed. However, large areas of forest are used for commercial logging. Around 10 per cent of the forested land (the primary forest areas) has special **conservation** status. This is to make sure that the rainforest habitats and species survive.

Forest Stewardship Council

The Forest Stewardship Council (FSC) is an international organisation that promotes sustainable forestry. The FSC label is used to show that products come from sustainably managed forests. The FSC tries to educate people about the need to buy wood from sustainable sources. It also aims to reduce demand for rare tropical wood.

Developing tourism

In recent years, Malaysia has promoted its forests as places for **ecotourism** ('green tourism'). This aims to help people see the natural world without damaging it (photo **B**). The great benefit of ecotourism is that it creates a source of income for local people without damaging or destroying the environment.

> **Key terms**
>
> **Conservation**: the thoughtful use of resources; managing the landscape in order to protect ecosystems and cultural features.
>
> **Ecotourism**: tourism that focuses on protecting the environment and the local way of life. Also known as green tourism.

Features of ecotourism

- Usually involves small groups.
- Local guides used.
- Buildings use local materials and are environmentally friendly (sustainable water, energy and waste management). Local people build and maintain the buildings.
- Mostly nature-based experiences (walks, birdwatching).
- Limited transport involved.

B Ecotourism in Borneo

■ Recent worldwide initiatives

Rainforests are valuable resources particularly for poor countries trying to expand their economies. Apart from the timber itself, rainforests take up land that could be used for large-scale farming, such as plantations (e.g. Malaysia) or ranching (e.g. Brazil). Valuable mineral resources such as bauxite, copper or iron may be in the rock beneath the forests. Of course, countries will try to use their rainforest resources to help improve the lives of their people. However, there are alternatives to clearing forest for timber, agriculture and mining.

Debt relief

One approach is to pay countries to look after their rainforests. This could take the form of **debt relief**. For example, a country would not have to pay back some of its **debt** in return for looking after their rainforests.

Carbon sinks

Rainforests reduce global warming by acting as a **carbon sink**. In 2008 the Gola Forest in Sierra Leone became a National Park which protects it from deforestation (photo **C**). The park is supported by money from the European Commission, the French government and **non-governmental organisations** (NGOs), such as the Royal Society for the Protection of Birds (RSPB) and Conservation International.

C   *Scientists in Sierra Leone's Gola Forest*

∞ links

For further information on the Forest Stewardship Council, **http://www.fsc.org/about-fsc.html**.

More details about a National Park, Taman Negara in Malaysia, can be found at **www.geographia.com/malaysia/taman.html**.

Ecotourism information can be found at **www.about-malaysia.com/adventure/eco-tourism.htm**.

Activities

1. Study photo **B**. This shows an ecotourism development in Borneo.

   a   What does ecotourism mean?

   b   What ecotourism features can you see in the photo?
   - Are the buildings large and imposing or low and blended into the landscape?
   - Is there a lot of natural vegetation around the complex or has it all been cleared away?
   - Are there extensive road, rail and air links in the area to bring in the maximum number of tourists, or are communications quite restricted?
   - Is the complex designed to entertain large numbers of people, or quite small groups?

   c   How does ecotourism offer opportunities to protect rainforests from deforestation? (Hint: think about how tourism can contribute to the economy of a country.)

4.6 What are the opportunities for economic developments in hot deserts?

Case study

The Thar Desert, Rajasthan, India

The Thar Desert is one of the major hot deserts of the world. It stretches across north-west India and into Pakistan (map **A**). The desert covers an area of 200,000 km².

Rainfall in the Thar Desert is low – typically between 120 and 240 mm per year – and summer temperatures in July can reach 53 °C. Much of the desert is sandy hills with lots of sand dunes. There are clumps of thorn forest vegetation and a mixture of small trees, shrubs and grasses (photo **B**). The soils are generally sandy and not very fertile. They drain quickly so there is little surface water.

In this section you will learn

the economic opportunities of deserts in rich and poor areas of the world

the challenges faced by desert communities and the management responses.

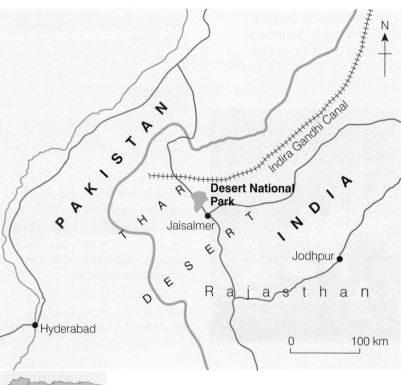

A *Location map of the Thar Desert*

Key terms

Subsistence farming: farming to produce food for the farmer and his/her family only.

Hunter-gatherers: people who carry out a basic form of subsistence farming by hunting animals and gathering fruit and nuts.

Commercial farming: a type of farming where crops and/or livestock are sold to make a profit.

Did you know ?????

The Thar Desert National Park in India is home to the rare great Indian bustard, a large ground-dwelling bird.

Economic opportunities in the desert

Subsistence farming

Most of the people living in the desert are farmers. The climate presents huge problems. There are often droughts. The most successful basic farming systems involve keeping a few animals on the grassy areas and growing vegetables and fruit trees. Although most of the farming is subsistence farming, some crops are sold at local markets.

Over the border in Pakistan's Thar region, the Kohlis tribe are descendants of **hunter-gatherers**. They survived in the desert by hunting animals and gathering fruit and natural products such as honey. This type of subsistence farming is the most basic form of farming and is rarely found in the world today.

Irrigation

Irrigation (artificial watering) in parts of the Thar Desert has really improved farming in the area. The main form of irrigation in the desert is the Indira Gandhi (Rajasthan) Canal (map **A**). The canal was built in 1958 and is 650 km long. Two of the main areas to benefit are the cities of Jodhpur and Jaisalmer, where over 3,500 km² of land is irrigated. **Commercial farming**, growing crops such as wheat and cotton, now flourishes in an area that used to be scrub desert. The canal also provides drinking water to many people in the desert.

Mining and industry

The state of Rajasthan is rich in minerals. The desert region has valuable reserves of gypsum (used in making plaster for the building industry and in making cement), feldspar (used to make ceramics) and kaolin (used as a whitener in paper).

There are also reserves of stone in the area. At Jaisalmer the Sanu limestone is the main source of limestone for India's steel industry. Limestone is also quarried for making cement. The livestock reared in the area are easily sold to local hide and wool industries.

Tourism

In the last few years, the Thar Desert, with its beautiful landscapes, has become a popular tourist destination. Desert safaris on camels, based at Jaisalmer, have become particularly popular with foreigners as well as wealthy Indians from elsewhere in the country. Local people benefit by acting as guides or by rearing and looking after camels.

B   *The natural desert environment near Jaisalmer*

Future challenges

The Thar Desert faces a number of challenges for the future:

- Population pressure – the Thar Desert is the most densely populated desert in the world and the population is increasing. This is putting pressure on the fragile ecosystem and leading to overgrazing and overcultivation.

- Water management – too much irrigation in some places has led to waterlogging of the ground. This leaves salt, which poisons plants on the ground surface. This is called **salinisation** and is a big problem in deserts (diagram **C**). In other places, the huge demand for water has caused a fall in water tables.

- Soil erosion – overcultivation and overgrazing have damaged the vegetation in places, leading to soil erosion by wind and rain. Once eroded away, the soil takes thousands of years to re-form.

- Fuel – firewood is the main source of fuel but it's running out so people are using manure as fuel rather than using it to improve the soil.

- Tourism – although tourists bring benefits such as employment and money, they can also harm the environment.

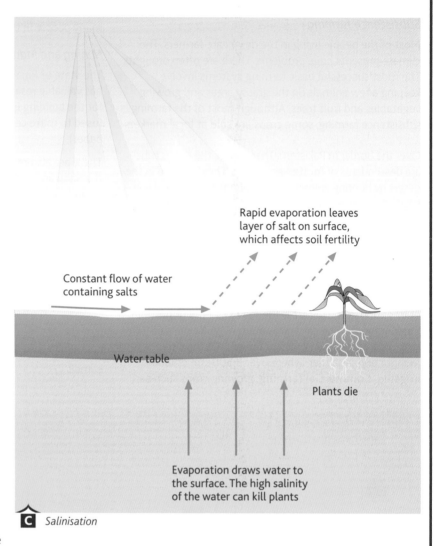

Rapid evaporation leaves layer of salt on surface, which affects soil fertility

Constant flow of water containing salts

Water table

Plants die

Evaporation draws water to the surface. The high salinity of the water can kill plants

C   *Salinisation*

Thar Desert National Park

The Thar Desert National Park has been created to protect 3,000 km² of land and its wildlife.

Sustainable management

A number of approaches have been tried to address the challenges of living in the Thar Desert. In 1977 the government-funded Desert Development Programme was started. Its main aims are to create an ecological balance in the region by looking after and developing land, water, livestock and people in a sustainable way. In Rajasthan forestry has been developed and sand dunes have been stabilised.

Stabilising sand dunes

The sand dunes in the Thar Desert move around a lot. In some areas they can move onto farmland, roads and waterways. Planting blocks of trees and fences alongside roads and canals are two ways in which people are trying to stabilise the sand dunes.

> **Key term**
>
> **Salinisation**: the deposition of solid salts on the ground surface following the evaporation of water. Also, an increase in the concentration of salts in the soil, reducing fertility.

Forestry

The most important tree in the Thar Desert is the *Prosopis cineraria*. It is very well suited to the hostile conditions of the desert and has many uses (photo **D**). Scientists at the Central Arid Zone Research Institute have developed a hardy breed of plum tree called a Ber tree. It produces large fruits and can survive in low rainfall conditions. The fruits can be sold and there is the potential to make a decent profit.

Uses of the Prosopis Cineraria tree

- A lot of foliage is produced, which can be used to feed animals, especially in the drier winter.

- The trees can provide good-quality firewood.

- The wood is strong and can be used for building.

- Its pods provide animal fodder.

- Crops can benefit from shade and moist growing conditions if grown between the trees.

- This and other tree species are planted in blocks to help stabilise the sand dunes.

D   *Sustainable qualities of the* Prosopis cineraria *tree*

Activities

1 Study photo **B**, which shows a natural desert environment in the Thar Desert

a Describe the environment of the Thar Desert as shown in the photo.

b What are the challenges of this environment for local people?

c Copy and complete the table. The first column lists some of the economic opportunities of the Thar Desert. In the next column, for each opportunity, suggest a possible negative impact on the desert environment. The first one has been done for you.

Economic opportunity	Negative impacts on desert environment
Subsistence farming	Population pressure means subsistence farmers graze too many sheep and goats on the fragile desert land, and cut down too many trees and bushes for firewood.
Irrigation and commercial farming	
Mining and industry	
Tourism	

Case study

The Sonoran Desert, Arizona, USA

The Sonoran Desert is one of North America's largest and hottest deserts. It is also one of the wettest, with over 300 mm of rain falling in some places. It is in the south-west of the USA (map **E**). The Sonoran Desert is very beautiful and has a great diversity of plants and animals including the saguaro cactus (fact file H, page 85).

The USA has the money to overcome some of the problems of a desert environment compared with poorer countries such as India (Thar Desert):

- Air conditioning for vehicles, houses, workplaces and shopping centres means people can live in comfort. With lots of relatively cheap energy, this is perfectly possible in the USA.

- Water is piped into the area for irrigating crops, to supply drinking water and for filling swimming pools and watering golf courses.

- A recent trend in the Sonoran Desert has been **retirement migration**. This is where people decide to retire to newly built housing complexes with swimming pools and golf courses.

Marana: the tale of one town in the Sonoran Desert

Marana is a town of around 35,000 people in Arizona (map **E**). Over the years it has developed into a thriving business town and leisure resort.

The town began as a mid-19th century ranching and mining community. In 1920 a new irrigation system meant that it became an agricultural centre growing cotton, wheat and barley. Families moved to the town to work in the fields.

Since the 1990s farming in the area has declined. By 2005 there were only six large cotton farms. Durum wheat is grown and exported to Italy to make pasta.

Migration accounts for much of the growth of the town. It is a thriving and wealthy business community with lots of housing developments.

In 2007 Marana began hosting golf's PGA Matchplay Championship (photo **F**).

Managing the Sonoran Desert

In 1998 the Sonoran Desert Conservation Plan began. This is a plan to look after the environment while allowing the economy to grow and the population to increase.

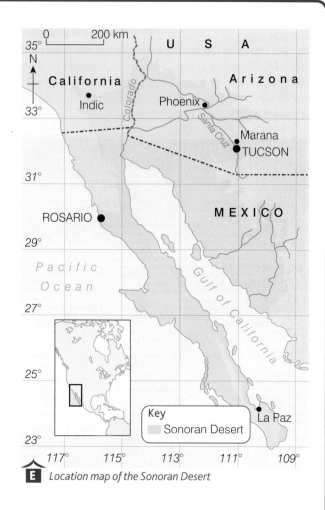

E *Location map of the Sonoran Desert*

The plan was started because of concern for wildlife habitats as housing developments expanded into the desert. An endangered species of pygmy owl was considered to be particularly at risk.

The plan has led to:

- detailed mapping and listing of the county's natural and cultural heritage

- development of protected buffer zones around areas of natural vegetation

- native plant protection

- control of hillside developments

- home designs which conserve energy and water.

Key term

Retirement migration: migration to an area for retirement.

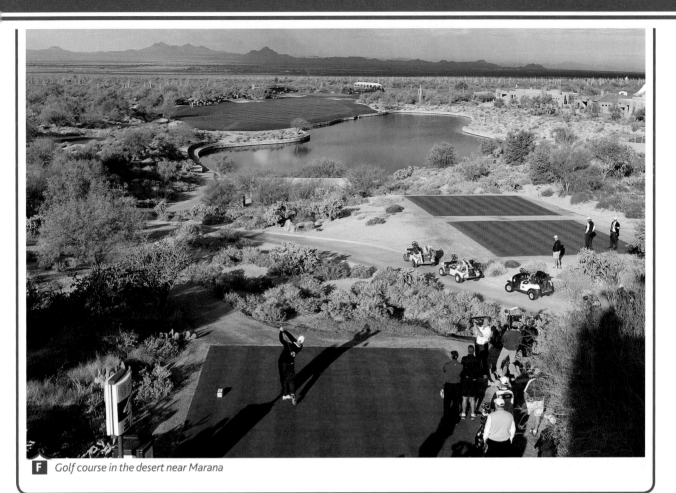

F   *Golf course in the desert near Marana*

Activities

2   Study photo **F** and the information in the text about Marana.

a   Which features of this landscape do you think are natural parts of the desert environment, and which are artificial? Try to list at least two examples of each.

b   Desert environments are dry, dusty, difficult to cultivate (farm) and are often very hot in the day and very cold at night. How do the inhabitants of Marana get round these challenges? (Talk about air conditioning, irrigation and energy in your answer.)

c   Why would Americans want to retire to Marana? List some of the attractions for older people.

3   **a**   What would life be like in Marana if the people could no longer afford to pump in thousands of gallons of water every day, and weren't able to run their air conditioning units night and day?

b   How would the inhabitants of Marana need to change their lives to survive in a natural desert environment? Use your knowledge and imagination to list some advice to help the people of Marana.

Study tip

Be sure to separate the themes of economic opportunities, challenges and management options when studying deserts. Think carefully about the contrasts between poor countries such as India and rich countries such as the USA.

∞ links

Some excellent maps are available at www.mapsofindia.com/geography and www.mapsofindia.com/maps/rajasthan.

Information about the Sonoran Desert can be accessed at http://alic.arid.arizona.edu/sonoran.

Marana Town's website is at www.marana.com.

5.1 How and why do river valleys change downstream?

There are three main processes that shape river valleys. These are **erosion**, **transportation** and **deposition**.

Processes of erosion

Near to the start of a river (its source) (photo **A**) the main process in a river **channel** is erosion. There are four ways in which a river erodes.

- **Hydraulic action** is the sheer force of the water hitting the bed and the banks. This is most effective when the water is moving fast and there is a lot of it.
- **Abrasion** is when the **load** the river is carrying keeps hitting the river bed and the banks. This causes some of the material to break off.
- **Attrition** happens when the stones and boulders carried by the river knock against each other. Over time they get weaker so bits fall off and the stones get smaller.
- **Solution** only happens when the river flows on some types of rock, such as chalk and limestone. These become part of the water as they are dissolved by it.

Rivers usually erode downwards (vertically) or sideways (laterally). As a river gets further down its course, **vertical erosion** becomes less important and **lateral erosion** takes over.

A *Golden Clough, Edale*

Activities

1. Look carefully at photo **A**, which shows the Golden Clough river in Edale.

   Choose the right words to complete this description of the river shown in the photo. Copy out the description, adding in the right words as you go.

   Words to use in your answer

   channel   vertical   source   steep   erosion

   This photo shows the river near where it starts. The place where a river starts is called the ____ of the river. At this point, _____ is the main process in the river channel. Most erosion is happening in a _____ direction. You can see this from the _____ valley sides. The water in the river _____ is moving quickly.

2. Draw a diagram to illustrate each of the four processes of erosion: hydraulic action, abrasion, attrition and solution. Label your diagrams so it is clear what is happening in each process.

Processes of transportation

Transportation involves the river moving its load downstream. There are four methods of transportation. These are **traction**, **saltation**, **suspension** and **solution** (diagram **B**). Photo **C** shows the same river in **A** but further downstream where the gradient has become less steep. By photo **D** it is much more gentle.

- Traction is the way the largest material is moved by the river. Material such as boulders is rolled along the river bed.
- Suspension carries very small material in the water, so that it floats in the river and is moved as it flows.
- Saltation moves the small stones and grains of sand by bouncing them along the bed. This lighter load leaves the river bed in a hopping motion.
- Solution cannot be seen. This is because it's carrying material that has been dissolved in the water.

Traction

Saltation

Suspension

Solution

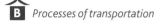
B *Processes of transportation*

C *Grindsbrook Clough, Edale*

D *River Noe, Edale*

Deposition

This is where the river dumps or leaves behind material that it has been carrying. It deposits the largest material first as this is the heaviest to carry. The smaller the load, the further it can be transported, so this is deposited much further downstream than the larger load. So you can see large boulders in photo **A**, but there aren't any in photo **D**.

Long and changing cross profiles

The **long profile** shows how the river changes in height along its course. Diagram **E** shows a long profile from the river's source to its mouth. Near the source it's very steep but this becomes a more gentle slope as it moves downstream.

As the river flows downstream, its valley changes shape and the **cross profile** from one side of the valley to the other clearly shows this. Generally, the cross profile shows the valley becoming wider and flatter, with lower valley sides. Map extract **F** shows part of the course of the River Noe and some of its tributaries, where photos **A**, **C** and **D** were taken.

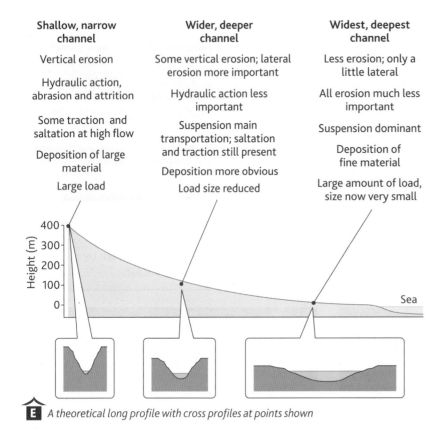

Shallow, narrow channel	Wider, deeper channel	Widest, deepest channel
Vertical erosion	Some vertical erosion; lateral erosion more important	Less erosion; only a little lateral
Hydraulic action, abrasion and attrition	Hydraulic action less important	All erosion much less important
Some traction and saltation at high flow	Suspension main transportation; saltation and traction still present	Suspension dominant
Deposition of large material	Deposition more obvious	Deposition of fine material
Large load	Load size reduced	Large amount of load, size now very small

E A theoretical long profile with cross profiles at points shown

links

You can find out more facts about large rivers at **http://ga.water.usgs.gov/edu/riversofworld.html** and **http://en.wikipedia.org/wiki/Rivers_of_England**. On this website, it would be worth searching for Durham and then the Tees as preparation for the next section.

Key terms

Vertical erosion: downwards erosion, for example when a river gouges out a deep valley.

Lateral erosion: sideways erosion, for example in a river channel at the outside bend of a meander.

Load: material of any size carried by the river.

Traction: the rolling along of the largest rocks and boulders.

Saltation: the bouncing movement of small stones and grains of sand along the river bed.

Suspension: small material carried (suspended) within water.

Long profile: a line representing the course of the river from its source (relatively high up) to its mouth where it ends, usually in a lake or the sea, and the changes in height along its course.

Cross profile: a line that represents what it would be like to walk from one side of a valley, across the channel and up the other side.

Did you know ??????

The Mississippi River is 3,800 km long. It carries on average 42,002 tonnes of sediment each day and 130 million tonnes a year.

Activities

3 Draw a diagram to illustrate each of the four processes of transportation: traction, suspension, saltation, solution. Label each diagram so it is clear what is happening.

4 Study photos **A** and **D** and diagram **E**.

a Draw your own sketch of photo **A**, which shows a river near its source.

b Using diagram **B** to help you, label the features of a river at this point: for example, 'shallow, narrow river channel'.

c Now study photo **D**, which shows the river lower down its course. How has the river and its channel changed compared with photo **A**?

5 Study map extract **F**. This is a map of the area around the River Noe.

a Find the three points on the map where each of the photos **A**, **C** and **D** were taken. They are marked for you as x A, x C and x D.

b Study the contour lines to find out how high the place is where photo **A** was taken. Is it:

■ around 340 metres above sea level

■ around 550 metres above sea level

■ around 650 metres above sea level?

c Study the contour lines to find out how high the place is where photo **D** was taken. Is it:

■ around 220 metres above sea level

■ around 350 metres above sea level

■ around 410 metres above sea level?

d Describe how the cross profiles of the river change downstream.

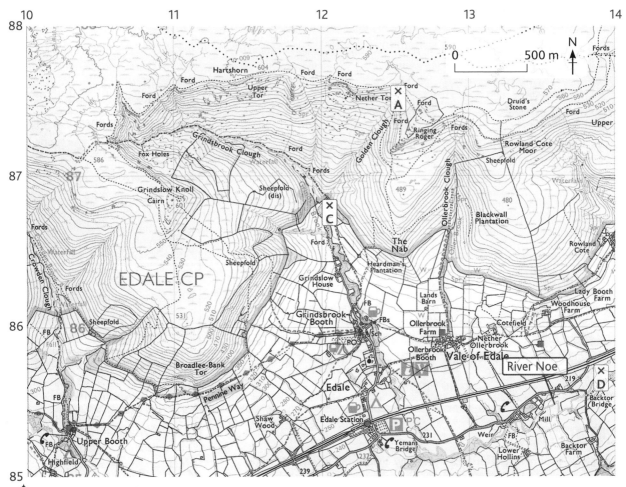

F 1 : 25,000 OS map extract of the River Noe and its tributaries, part of map sheet OL1

5.2 What distinctive landforms result from the changing river processes?

Different river processes lead to different landforms.

- Near the source where the main process is downwards vertical erosion there are **waterfalls** and **gorges**.
- Further down, where lateral erosion and deposition become more important, **meanders** and **oxbow lakes** develop.
- Nearer to the mouth, where the main process is deposition, **floodplains** and **levees** become a key part of the landscape.

The River Tees will be used here to show the different landforms and how they change downstream.

■ Landforms resulting from erosion: waterfalls and gorges

Waterfalls and gorges are formed by downwards vertical erosion. Diagram **A** shows how waterfalls form and how they leave gorges as they cut back into the rock. One of the best-known waterfalls in the UK is High Force on the River Tees (photo **B** and map extract **C**). High Force is formed where whinstone (a resistant igneous rock) lies on top of weaker limestone.

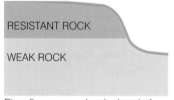

River flows over a harder band of rock and forms a waterfall

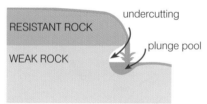

Erosion scoops out a plunge pool and undercutting of the waterfall occurs

c

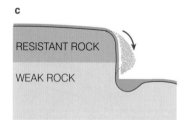

The overhanging rock collapses.

d

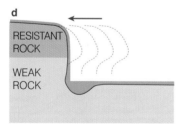

Over time the waterfall retreats upstream leaving behind a steep-sided gorge.

 A *The formation of waterfalls and gorges*

Key terms

Waterfall: the sudden, and often vertical, drop of a river along its course.

Gorge: a narrow, steep-sided valley.

Meander: a bend or curve in the river channel.

Oxbow lake: a horseshoe or semi-circular area that used to be a meander. Oxbow lakes are cut off from a supply of water and so will eventually become dry.

Floodplain: the flat area next to the river channel, especially in the lower part of the course. This is a natural area for water to spill onto when the river reaches the top of its banks.

Levees: raised banks along the course of a river in its lower course. They are formed naturally but can be artificially increased in height.

Activities

1. Draw your own diagrams to show how a waterfall is formed. Study diagram **A**. Label your diagrams so it is clear what is happening at each stage.

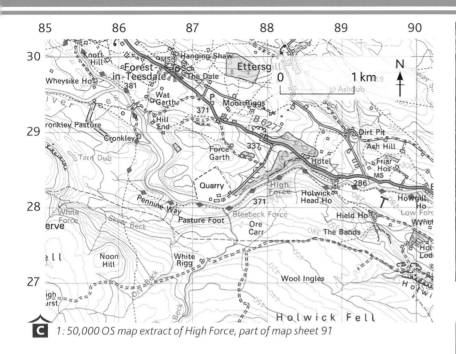

C   1 : 50,000 OS map extract of High Force, part of map sheet 91

B   High Force, River Tees

Landforms resulting from erosion and deposition: meanders and oxbow lakes

Meanders and oxbow lakes are found in the middle part of the river. The formation of meanders leads eventually to the development of oxbow lakes, as shown in diagram **E** on page 106.

Map extract **D** shows meanders on the River Tees. Where do you think an oxbow lake may form?

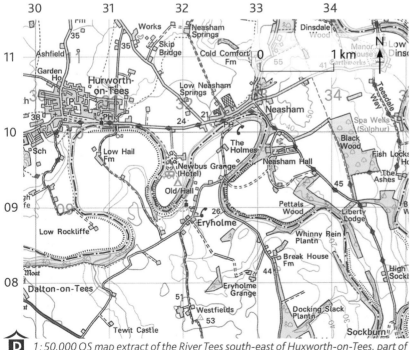

D   1 : 50,000 OS map extract of the River Tees south-east of Huxworth-on-Tees, part of map sheet 93

Study tip

When writing answers to questions about the formation of river landforms such as waterfalls and oxbow lakes, make sure that you describe how they are formed in order and refer to river processes.

Activities

2 Look carefully at diagram **E**, which shows how meanders and oxbow lakes are formed.

The following list has the stages all mixed up. Arrange them in the correct order.

A Eventually, the bend is so exaggerated that it forms a loop.

B In a river with a sinuous (bendy) course, water flows fastest around the outside of a bend and slowest on the inside of a bend.

C Erosion on the outside of a bend, and deposition on the inside widens the meander.

D Finally the two ends of the loop are so close that they erode into each other and the loop gets cut off from the rest of the river to form an oxbow lake.

3 Study map extract **D**. This shows part of the River Tees, in the lower part of its course. The river is flowing from west to east.

a Draw a sketch of the meanders on this map and then label the following features:

■ an inside bend

■ an outside bend

■ the neck of a meander

■ the meander most likely to be cut off first.

b Locate Low Hail Farm (309097) and The Holmes (325098). Describe the location of these two farms, thinking about:

■ how flat or hilly the land they are situated on is

■ how near the farms are to water

■ how the farms are connected to the main road and other housing in the area

■ the farms' location in relation to the meander loops.

c Why do you think the farms are in these locations? What are the benefits of these locations for farmers?

d Do you think the farms are at risk from flooding?

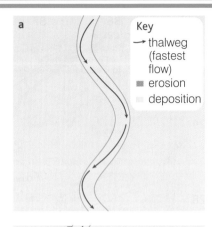

a

Key
→ thalweg (fastest flow)
■ erosion
□ deposition

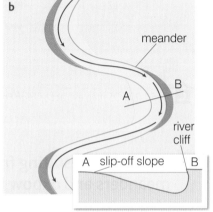

b

meander
A
B
river cliff
A slip-off slope B

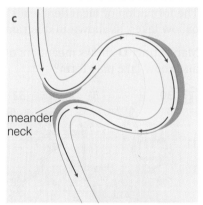

c

meander neck

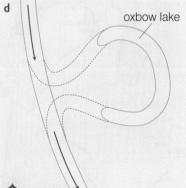

d

oxbow lake

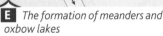

E The formation of meanders and oxbow lakes

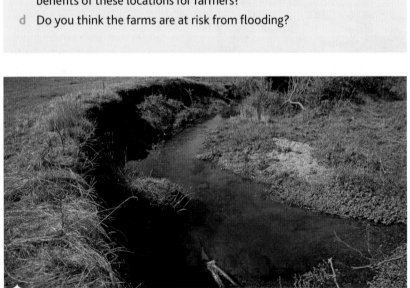

F Inside bend of a meander

Landforms resulting from deposition: levees and floodplains

Levees are raised river banks formed at the edges of the river channel. A floodplain is a wide, flat area of land on either side of a river typically found in lowland regions. Floodplains are usually used as farmland but in some places they are developed for housing or transport.

Levees and floodplains both form because of repeated flooding. Usually a river stays within its banks. However, when there's a lot of rain it may burst its banks. When this happens, sediment is deposited on the river banks to form levees. Water and finer sediment then floods across the river's floodplain, (diagram **G**).

H *Artificial levees on the Mississippi*

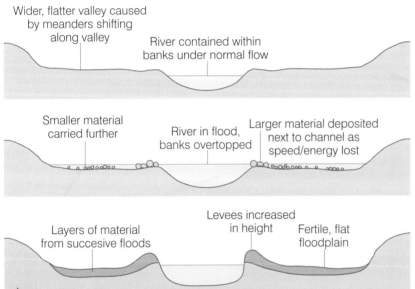

Wider, flatter valley caused by meanders shifting along valley

River contained within banks under normal flow

Smaller material carried further

River in flood, banks overtopped

Larger material deposited next to channel as speed/energy lost

Layers of material from succesive floods

Levees increased in height

Fertile, flat floodplain

G *The formation of levees and floodplains*

⬤⬤**links**

You can find out more about the River Tees at **http://en.wikipedia. org/wiki/River_Tees**.

I *1 : 50,000 OS map extract of the floodplain of the River Tees, part of map sheet 93*

Activities

3 Study diagram **G**. These show how levees and floodplains are formed, and the link between levees and floodplains

a Working in pairs, produce a short PowerPoint presentation to include the following:

■ the formation of levees

■ the formation of floodplains

■ the links between the two landforms.

b Show your presentation to another group in the class.

5.3 How and why does the water in a river fluctuate?

In this section you will learn

how the amount of water in a river varies

the reasons for this variation.

The **discharge** of a river is the volume of water flowing down a river. Discharge changes a lot during a year. It can even change in a matter of hours when there is a lot of rain. The **drainage basin** hydrological cycle (diagram **A**) is useful in explaining how and why the amount of water in a river changes.

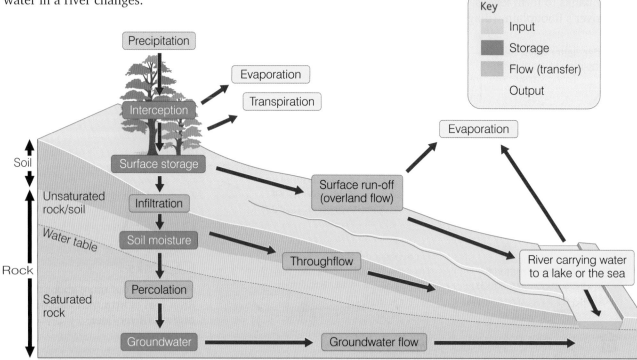

Key
- Input
- Storage
- Flow (transfer)
- Output

Precipitation: any source of moisture reaching the ground, e.g. rain, snow, frost

Interception: water being stopped from reaching the ground by trees or grass

Surface storage: water held on the ground surface, e.g. puddles

Infiltration: water sinking into soil/rock from the ground

Soil moisture: water held in the soil layer

Percolation: water seeping deeper below the surface

Groundwater: water stored in the rock

Transpiration: water lost through pores in vegetation

Evaporation: water lost from ground/vegetation surface

Surface run-off (overland flow): water flowing on top of the ground

Throughflow: water flowing through the soil layer next to the surface

Groundwater flow: water flowing through the rock layer next to the surface

Water table: current upper level of saturated rock/soil where no more water can be absorbed

 Drainage basin hydrological cycle

The storm hydrograph

The **flood or storm hydrograph** is used to show what happens to a river when it rains (graph **C**). Rivers that respond quickly to rainfall have a high peak and short lag time and are referred to as **flashy**. A lower peak and long lag time shows a delayed hydrograph.

Did you know ??????

Some places in England had over 380 mm of rain in May, June and July 2007 – more than double the average for the three months. This was more than the previous high of 349 mm in 1789.

B *Discharge of River Eden, Carlisle*

Date	Time	Discharge in cubic metres per second (cumecs)
7 January	0000 hours	90
	1200 hours	130
8 January	0000 hours	820
	1200 hours	1,400
	1500 hours	1,520
9 January	0000 hours	1,000
	1200 hours	430

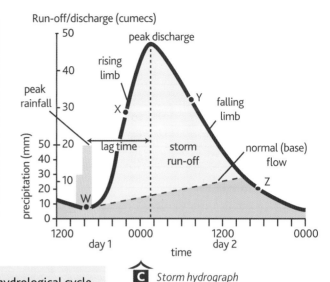

C *Storm hydrograph*

Activities

1 Study diagram **A**, which shows the drainage basin hydrological cycle. Work in pairs to produce a series of flash cards for the key terms in the diagram.

a On one side of the card, there should be a definition and an illustration of the term.

b On the other side, the term should be given so that the answer is clear.

c Use your completed flash cards with another pair to see how many terms you got correct and how good your definitions are.

2 Study table **B**

a On a sheet of graph paper draw a line graph to show the changing discharge of the River Eden.

b Use graph **C** to add labels to your graph to identify the main features of the hydrograph.

c Do you think the River Eden can be described as 'flashy'? Explain your answer.

Factors affecting river discharge

The discharge of a river is influenced by many factors.

Weather

- Heavy rainfall causes high river levels and may result in flooding. Less intensive rainfall, such as drizzle has little effect on a river's discharge.

- When temperatures are higher (table **D**), there is greater water loss via evaporation and transpiration, so river levels go down.

- Previous weather conditions also have an impact on river discharge. If it has been dry, the ground will soak up rainwater. If, however, there has been a wet period and the soil is saturated, further rain may lead to flooding. Look at table **E**. Notice that a lot of rain had fallen in mid-June before the heavy rain that fell in Sheffield on 24th and 25th June 2007.

Key terms

Discharge: the volume of water passing a given point in a river at any moment in time.

Drainage basin: area from which a river gets its water. The boundary is marked by an imaginary line of highland known as a watershed.

Flood or storm hydrograph: a line graph drawn to show the discharge in a river in the aftermath of a period of rain.

Flashy: a hydrograph that responds quickly to a period of rain so that it characteristically has a high peak and a short lag time.

Relief: height and slope of land.

Impermeable: rock that does not allow water to pass through.

Porous: rock that allows water to soak into it via spaces between particles.

Pervious: rock that allows water to pass through it via vertical joints and horizontal bedding planes.

Urbanisation: the increase in the proportion of people living in cities, resulting in their growth.

D *Average rainfall and temperature in Sheffield*

Month	Rainfall (mm)	Maximum temperature (°C)
January	87	6.4
February	63	6.7
March	68	9.3
April	63	11.8
May	56	15.7
June	68	18.3
July	51	20.8
August	64	20.6
September	64	17.3
October	74	13.3
November	78	9.2
December	92	7.2

E *Rainfall in Sheffield, June 2007*

Date	Rainfall (mm)
13 June	30.3
14 June	88.2
15 June	16.9
16 June	0.0
17 June	2.2
18 June	0.0
19 June	14.7
20 June	0.1
21 June	9.6
22 June	6.9
23 June	0.2
24 June	36.0
25 June	51.1
26 June	0.0

Relief

Relief describes the height and slope of the land. Steep slopes mean fast run-off as the water runs quickly downhill. Gentle slopes allow time for water to soak into the ground. Sudden, flash floods often occur in areas with steep slopes.

Rock type

- Water can soak into some permeable rock types, such as limestone and chalk. This usually slows down the transfer of water to rivers.
- Water cannot soak into **impermeable** rock like granite so there is more run-off which reaches the river quicker.

Land use

How people use the land can have a huge effect on the amount of water in local rivers.

- When trees are cut down, (deforestation (photo **F**)) water reaches the ground faster and the trees do not soak up any water.
- **Urbanisation** (photo **G**) means there are more impermeable surfaces like roads which do not soak up water. This is made even worse by building drains to take the water away from buildings quickly – and equally quickly into rivers!

F *Deforestation in Tayside, Scotland*

G *Urbanisation in Leicester*

Activities

3. Study tables **D**, **E** and photos **F**, **G**. Work in pairs to produce an A3 spread around the central title 'Factors affecting river discharge'.

   a. In the central box, give the meaning of 'river discharge'.

   b. Place the factors around the central title.

   c. Add information to each factor to explain how discharge is affected. Each factor should be illustrated by diagrams, sketches or photos. You should use data provided in the tables.

   Your finished spread should be informative and accurate but also interesting, colourful and original.

5.4 Why do rivers flood?

In this section you will learn

why flooding occurs – the natural causes and the ways in which people make it worse

where floods have occurred in the UK

how the frequency of flooding seems to be increasing.

Floods happen when a river cannot be kept in its channel. Flooding is not a normal condition for the river. It is an extreme situation caused by high levels of flow. Flooding is a natural event but it can be a **hazard** when it affects people's lives.

Causes of floods

Rivers usually flood due to a combination of physical and human factors (extract **A**). Physical factors include steep slopes, heavy rainfall and snowmelt. Human factors include urbanisation and deforestation. Look at table **B** and extract **C**. They describe flooding that occurred in Sheffield in 2007. What was the main cause of the floods?

Key terms

Floods: these occur when a river carries so much water that it cannot be contained by its banks and so it overflows on to surrounding land – its floodplain.

Hazard: an event where people's lives and property are threatened and deaths and/or damage result.

Soil erosion: the removal of the layer of soil above the rock where plants grow.

News   Home | Contact | Sitemap | News | Forum | Shop

Home
Contact
Sitemap
News
Forum
Shop

Snowmelt is a main contributing factor to flooding. It was partly responsible for floods in Malton (N. Yorkshire) in November 2000 and is frequently important in Bangladesh. An extract from 'Why Bangladesh floods are so bad' (BBC News website news.bbc.co.uk) on the 2004 floods states 'Bangladesh receives enormous amounts of water from four major rivers. All are filled up from melting snow in the Himalayas.' The Himalayas provide some of the steepest relief worldwide and this is also important in ensuring that water reaches the rivers quickly, increasing the flood risk.

Deforestation has an impact on the water cycle in a drainage basin. It is frequently seen as one reason for the increasing severity of flooding in Bangladesh. Chopping trees down in higher-lying areas, including neighbouring countries, such as Nepal, can have unintentional effects elsewhere. As well as increasing rates of surface runoff, **soil erosion** is a consequence. Much of this is washed into rivers, where, when deposited, the amount of water the channel can hold is reduced. Thus, the flood risk is increased.

Building construction can increase flooding. New houses built next to the river in Malton are clearly susceptible to flooding. Building on floodplains is an issue, as outlined in Lincoln.

A *Causes of flooding*

B *Rainfall in Sheffield*

Month	Average rainfall (mm), 1971–2000	Actual rainfall (mm), 2007
March	67.9	44.5
April	62.5	5.8
May	55.5	83.8
June	66.7	285.6

The city experienced the most rain in a single month since records began 125 years ago. A resident said, 'The rain had been almost constant for a week. On the morning the flooding started, the rivers were almost visibly rising. By lunchtime, the city was at a standstill as bridges became impassable and underpasses flooded. We were stranded in the north of the city – it took six hours to travel four miles. By the evening much of the city centre was under water, many roads had collapsed and were impassable and electricity supplies were limited for almost a week.'

Adapted from the Sheffield Star

 Prolonged rain in Sheffield, 2007

Frequency and location of flood events

In the past large floods in the UK did not happen very often:

- In 1607 a great flood affected Devon, Somerset and South Wales.
- In March 1947 major floods affected many areas of southern, central and north-eastern England.
- In January 1953 storms and high tides led to severe flooding on the east coast, including Suffolk, Essex and Kent. Huge waves washed away sea defences and 307 people died.
- In 1968 another Great Flood affected counties in south-east England.

Today, flooding seems to be happening more often. Table **D** shows some of the most serious floods since 1998.

Did you know ???????

Brize Norton in Oxfordshire recorded 115 mm of rainfall in 12 hours on 20 July 2007; some places received between 30 and 40 mm in one hour. One unofficial rain gauge in Hull recorded 94 mm.

D   *Major flood events, 1998–2009*

Date	Location	Rivers
April 1998	Warwickshire, Gloucestershire, Herefordshire, Worcestershire, Leicestershire, south-east Wales	Avon, Severn, Wye
	Northamptonshire, Bedfordshire and Cambridgeshire	Nene, Great Ouse
October 1998	Course of River Severn from mid-Wales to Gloucester	Severn
March 1999	Malton and Norton flooded by Derwent and its tributaries	Derwent
May 2000	Uckfield, Petworth, Robertsbridge, Horsham (Sussex)	Uck, Rother
June 2000	Calder Valley, Yorkshire and York	Calder, Ouse
August 2004	Boscastle (Cornwall)	Valency
January 2005	Carlisle	Eden
June 2007	Large areas of south and east Yorkshire including Doncaster, Sheffield and Hull	Don, Hull, Witham
	Parts of Lincolnshire including Lincoln and Louth	Witham, Ludd
July 2007	Large areas of Gloucestershire including Upton-upon-Severn, Tewkesbury, Gloucester	Avon, Severn
	Oxfordshire including Oxford, Banbury and Witney	Thames, Windrush, Cherwell
November 2009	Cockermouth and the Derwent Valley to Workington	Derwent, Cocker

Activities

1. Study extract **A**. This explains some of the reasons behind flooding in Bangladesh.

    a. Using the example of Bangladesh, explain to a younger student how snowmelt, relief and deforestation are responsible for flooding. You could draw a diagram for each reason to help your explanation.

    b. 'Flooding happens because it rains really heavily.' Does this statement sum up all you need to know about why floods happen, or are there other factors? Write out a short statement that does a better job of explaining floods.

2. Study table **D**. This lists some of the major UK floods in recent years.

    a. On an outline map of the UK, mark and label the places that flooded.

    b. Add the major rivers to your map.

    c. Maybe there have been more floods since this book was published. If so, add them onto your map, too.

    d. Use the internet to find some photos to add to your map.

5.5   How and why do the effects of flooding and the responses to it vary?

The effects of flooding depend on their size and location. Poorer countries are often more severely affected than richer ones.

- Countries at further stages of development usually respond quicker and the attempts made to reduce the effects come from within the affected area or country.

- In countries at lesser stages of development, attempts made to reduce the effects may take longer and require help from other countries.

Long-term responses are likely to show similar differences as richer countries can afford flood protection measures.

Flooding in England (2007)

The flooding in parts of England in the summer of 2007 were the most extensive ever experienced. Diagram **A** shows the main areas affected and the damage done after record levels of rainfall.

In this section you will learn

the effects of flooding and the responses to it in both richer and poorer countries

how and why the effects and responses vary.

Did you know ? ? ? ? ? ?

The sale of women's raincoats at John Lewis in July 2007 was over 11 times higher than in July 2006, while the sale of umbrellas was 184 per cent higher.

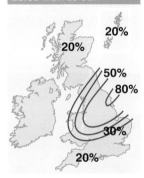

RISK OF DISRUPTION
21:00 Sun 24 Jun to
23:00 Mon 25 Jun

20%
20%
50%
80%
30%
20%

- Surface water flooding in Hull.
- Widespread disruption and damage to more than 7,000 houses and 1,300 businesses in Hull.
- River Don burst its banks, flooding Sheffield and Doncaster.
- Flooding in Derbyshire, Lincolnshire and Worcestershire.
- Highest official rainfall total was 111 mm at Fylingdales (North Yorkshire). Amateur networks recorded similar totals in the Hull area.
- There were fears that the dam wall at the Ulley Reservoir near Rotherham would burst.

B   *Flooding in Hull*

RISK OF DISRUPTION
00:00 Fri 20 Jul to
12:00 Sat 21 Jul

20%
20%
30%
20%
50%
80%
30%   70%

- Widespread disruption to the motorway and rail networks.
- In the following days the River Severn and tributaries in Gloucestershire, Worcestershire, Herefordshire and Shropshire broke banks and flooded surrounding areas.
- River Thames and its tributaries in Wiltshire, Oxfordshire, Berkshire and Surrey flooded.
- Flooding in Telford and Wrekin, Staffordshire, Warwickshire and Birmingham.
- The highest recorded rainfall was 157.4 mm in 48 hours at Pershore College (Worcestershire).

 Flooding in England, 2007

C   *Victims of the Tewkesbury floods*

Cockermouth, 2009

Causes of the flood

On 19 November 2009 the highest amount of rain ever recorded in a 24-hour period fell on the hills of the Lake District in NW England. That autumn had already been very wet. So the heavy rain fell on ground that was already full of water. Most of the rainwater therefore swept quickly down the steep hillsides and into the streams and rivers.

Cockermouth is a small town on the western side of the Lake District (map **D**). It lies where two rivers meet, the Derwent and the Cocker. The huge amount of water was too much for the channels and the rivers burst their banks. This caused widespread and devastating flooding.

D *Location of Cockermouth in the Lake District*

Effects of the flood

In Cockermouth itself shops, offices and homes were flooded and many were badly damaged (photo **E**). The flood had a big impact on the local community:

- More than 1,300 people were directly affected by the floods. A policeman died when a bridge collapsed beneath him.

- Many homes had no power or water supply and local schools had to close.

- All of Cumbria's 1,800 bridges had to be checked that they were safe to use. Several bridges were destroyed by the flood.

- Roads were blocked all over Cumbria, causing lots of difficulties to local people.

- The cost of the damage was expected to be over £100 million.

- Farmers suffered greatly. Livestock were drowned and fields were flooded or coated with rocks carried down by the swollen rivers. Fences and walls were destroyed, farm buildings damaged and machinery ruined.

- Local businesses, such as shops, pubs and hotels suffered. Many businesses suffered directly from flood damage with up to 1 m of mud and silt needing to be cleared from downstairs rooms.

Responses

The main focus after the flood was search and rescue. Some 200 people had to be airlifted from the roofs of their houses by RAF helicopters. Several people were rescued from their homes by boat. People were taken to temporary shelters to be looked after.

In the days that followed, flooded buildings were checked for their safety before people were allowed back into them. Some small businesses got temporary trading accommodation in the town centre while their shops were refitted. For days, the streets were lined with skips full of stuff damaged by the flood.

Most of the people whose homes were flooded had to live elsewhere for several months. The main road bridge over the River Derwent was closed for two months. Several roads in the town centre were so broken up by water that they had to be completely re-surfaced.

E *Aerial photo of floods*

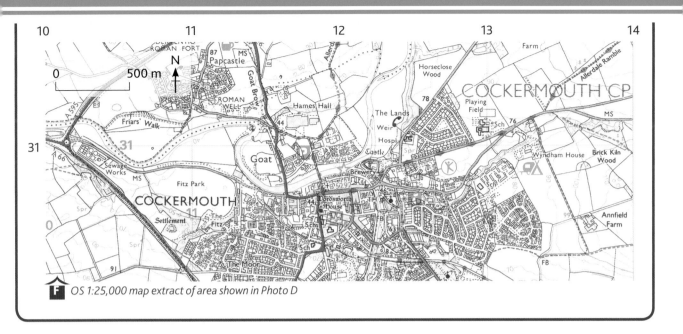

F   OS 1:25,000 map extract of area shown in Photo D

■ Flooding in Bangladesh

Bangladesh is often affected by serious floods. Flooding is expected every year in this low-lying country, much of which lies on the delta of the River Ganges.

Bangladesh, 2004

The 2004 floods happened from July to September. Map **G** shows the areas of Bangladesh under water and the depth of the water

Effects

At the time of the July 2004 floods:

- 40 per cent of Dhaka (the capital city) and 60 per cent of the country was under water
- 600 deaths were reported and 30 million left homeless out of a population of 140 million.
- Many people suffered from diarrhoea as the floodwaters left mud and raw sewage behind.

Then, Bangladesh had its heaviest rain in 50 years with 35 cm falling in one day on 13 September.

- The death toll rose to over 750.
- Dhaka airport was flooded as were many roads and railways. Bridges were also destroyed.
- In rural areas, rice, vegetables and cash crops were washed away.

Case study

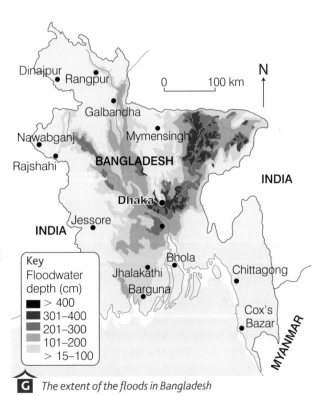

Key
Floodwater depth (cm)
■ > 400
■ 301–400
■ 201–300
■ 101–200
  > 15–100

G   The extent of the floods in Bangladesh

Responses – short-term

- Food, medicines, clothing and blankets were handed out but it was difficult to reach everyone (photo **H**).
- People began to rebuild their homes.
- International help began to arrive. The United Nations launched an appeal for $74 million, but had received only 20 per cent of this by September.

Responses – long term

- Embankments were built along the river to try to stop flooding but they have not really worked.
- Food shelters have been built on raised land where people can move with their cattle. Here they have access to items such as dried food and water when flooding happens. This has been quite successful.

H *The effects of flooding in rural areas of Bangladesh*

∞ links

You can find out more about flooding in the UK and Bangladesh at **www.bbc.co.uk**.

The website **www.bangladesh.gov.bd** has information about Bangladesh.

Study tip

When comparing two case studies, record information in a simple table like the one on this page and then use this as a writing frame to help write your answer.

Activities

1 Study photo **E** and map **F**. These show a photo of the Cockermouth floods in 2009 and a map of the area.

a In which direction is the photograph looking?

b What is the name of the area of land at **X**?

c Describe the extent of the flooding in Cockermouth.

d Describe the likely effects of the flooding on the following people:

- A shopkeeper on the High Street
- A homeowner at **Y**
- A farmer whose land has been flooded at **Z**

e Locate the castle on the map and photo. How does the choice of site for the castle suggest that flooding has been a problem here in the past?

2 Study map **G** and photo **H**. Imagine you are working as a volunteer for an aid agency in Bangladesh during the floods of 2004. Write a letter home, describing the floods. Describe the effects and the responses of the people. Try to make your account as real as possible so that the reader can imagine the experience.

3 Consider the Cockermouth flood (2009) and the Bangladesh flood (2004).

a Compare these two floods by copying out and completing the table below.

b Think about the differences between the effects and responses. How much do you think these differences were due to Cockermouth being in a rich country and Bangladesh being a poor country?

	Cockermouth	Bangladesh
Location		
Date		
Causes		
Effects		
Responses		

5.6 Hard and soft engineering: which is the better option?

Hard engineering involves the use of technology to control rivers. **Soft engineering** tries to work with natural processes. Hard engineering approaches tend to give fast results and control the river, but are expensive. However, in the future, they may make problems worse or create other ones. Soft engineering is much cheaper and offers a more sustainable option as it does not interfere directly with the river's flow.

Hard engineering

Dams and **reservoirs** are ways to control a river. The natural flow of water is stopped by a dam (often a concrete barrier across the valley). Water then fills the area behind the dam which is known as a reservoir. Water is held or let go depending on things like how much rain is expected. Dams and reservoirs are normally built as part of a multipurpose project rather than with just a single aim in mind (see case study on page 118).

Straightening meanders is a smaller scale approach to managing rivers. Like following a route in a car, lots of bends takes longer and is slower than a straight route. Therefore, water in a meander takes longer to clear an area than water in a straight section of a river. A possible solution to flooding in areas where there are many meanders is to straighten them. In this way, the river is made to follow a new shorter, straight section and stop its natural meandering course (diagram **A**).

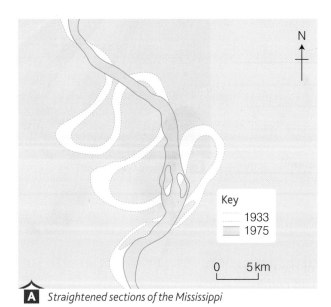

Key
..... 1933
— 1975

0   5 km

A *Straightened sections of the Mississippi*

> **Study tip**
>
> Learn the arguments for and against hard and soft engineering strategies used to manage river flow. Back up these arguments with examples.

> **In this section you will learn**
>
> how hard and soft engineering are used to try to manage rivers and flooding
>
> why there is debate about the two options
>
> how to evaluate the two strategies and come to a supported view about them.

> **Key terms**
>
> **Hard engineering**: building artificial structures aimed at controlling natural processes.
>
> **Soft engineering**: this option tries to work with the natural river system and involves avoiding building on areas especially likely to flood, warning people of a possible flood and planting trees to increase lag time.
>
> **Dam**: an artificial structure designed to hold back water to create a reservoir.
>
> **Reservoir**: commonly an artificial lake formed behind a dam and used for water supply.
>
> **Straightening meanders**: making the river follow a more direct, rather than its natural course, so that it leaves an area more quickly.

> **Did you know** ??????
>
> The Hoover Dam over the Colorado River near Las Vegas was the biggest concrete structure when it was completed in 1935. There would have been enough concrete to make a two-lane road between San Francisco and New York.

The Three Gorges Dam, China

The Three Gorges dam was built at Yichang on the River Yangtse (map **B**, photo **C** and table **D**). The reservoir should reduce the risk of flooding downstream. This will benefit over 15 million people living in high-risk flood areas and protect over 25,000 ha of farmland.

The dam is already having a positive impact on flood control and it is also used to generate electricity, but it has caused problems. The Yangtse used to carry over 500 million tonnes of silt every year. Up to 50 per cent of this is now deposited behind the dam, which could quickly reduce the amount of water the reservoir can hold.

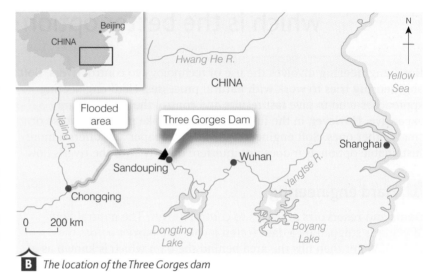

B The location of the Three Gorges dam

The water in the reservoir is becoming heavily polluted from shipping and waste. For example, Chongqing pumps in over 1 billion tonnes of untreated waste per year. Toxic substances from factories, mines and waste tips submerged by the reservoir are also being released into the reservoir.

To make way for the dam, reservoir and power station, at least 1.4 million people were forcibly moved from their homes. These people were promised compensation for their losses, plus new homes and jobs. Many have not yet received this. Newspapers in China have shown that over $30 million of the funds set aside for this has been taken by corrupt local officials.

D The Three Gorges Dam Project fact file

Dimensions	181 m high and 2.3 km wide
Area flooded	632 km²
Cost	$25.5 billion
Built	Started 1994; finished 2009
Increased depth	110 m (reduced to 80 m when flood risk downstream)

C The Three Gorges Dam

■ Soft engineering

Soft engineering tries to work with the natural processes of the river to reduce the effects of flooding. One approach is actually to do nothing at all. This can be the best option where small floods are frequent. However, there are many other approaches that can reduce the risk of flooding.

Flood warnings and preparation go together. Telling people when a flood may happen gives them time to prepare for it. The Environment Agency identifies areas at risk of flooding and gives warnings.

For example, information was given on local radio, television and the internet during the Tewkesbury flooding of 2007. A flood watch was issued on 20 July at 18.32, followed by a flood warning about 20 minutes later. This gave people time to take things upstairs, turn off gas, water and electricity and take some basic precautions against flooding. The Environment Agency's website tells people how to prepare for a flood and what to do during and afterwards.

Floodplain zoning involves creating zones of different land uses on a floodplain (diagram **E**). Notice that on diagram **E** the most expensive land uses are on higher land, away from the river.

In some river basins, flooding is encouraged on low value land, like marshes or grassland. This then prevents more valuable land downstream getting flooded.

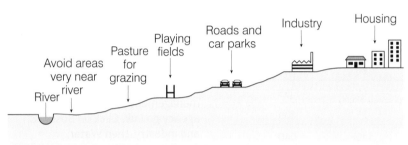

 *Floodplain zoning*

⨋links

You can find out more about the Three Gorges Dam at **www.ctgpc.com**.

The Environment Agency gives extensive advice about flooding, which you can investigate at **www.environment-agency.gov.uk**.

Key terms

Floodplain zoning: controlling what is built on the floodplain so that areas that are at risk of flooding have low-value land uses.

Economic: this relates to costs and finances at a variety of scales, from individuals up to government.

Social: this category refers to people's health, their lifestyle, community, etc.

Environmental: this is the impact on our surroundings, including the land, water and air as well as features of the built-up areas.

Activities

1   Study map **B**, photo **C** and table **D**.

a   Produce a fact file giving six key items of background information on the Three Gorges Dam. Include such things as its location, when it was completed, etc.

b   Now consider the benefits (advantages) and costs (disadvantages) of the scheme. Present this information in the form of a table as part of your factfile.

	Benefits	Costs
ECONOMIC (relates to money)		
SOCIAL (relates to people)		
ENVIRONMENTAL (relates to the environment)		

2   Study diagram **E**.

a   Make a large copy of the diagram.

b   Use the internet to find photos to illustrate each of the land uses, and stick them on your diagram.

c   Draw a single large arrow across your diagram to show how land value increases away from the river.

3   Access the Environment Agency website from the link above. Working in pairs, produce a leaflet or poster on 'What to do in the event of a flood'.

Include information on:

■   warnings available

■   how people can get the information they need

■   what people should do before, during and after a flood in their home.

Make your leaflet or poster clear, eye-catching, informative and colourful.

5.7 How are rivers in the UK managed to provide our water supply?

People in the UK use an average of 151 litres per person per day. Look at table **A** to see how water is used in a typical house. The maps in **B** show how the demand for water is expected to increase in the future. The amount of rainfall over England and Wales varies, as does **water stress** (map **C**). Areas with high water stress can be seen as **areas of water deficit** while those with low stress are often **areas of water surplus**

A *Water use for a selection of activities*

Activity	Average weekly use	Litres used per activity	Total number of litres
Bath	2	80	160
Flushing the toilet	35	8	280
Power shower	7	80	560
Washing machine	3	65	195
Dishwasher	4	25	100
Watering the garden	1	540	540
Washing car with bucket	1	32	32
Washing car with hose pipe	1	450	450

In this section you will learn

why there is an increasing demand for water in the UK

how there are areas of deficit and areas of surplus and that transfer occurs between them

the economic, social and environmental issues resulting from this transfer.

∞ links

You can find out more about water management at **www.environment-agency.gov.uk**. Click on Business and industry, then Water.

a Actual household use, 2005–06

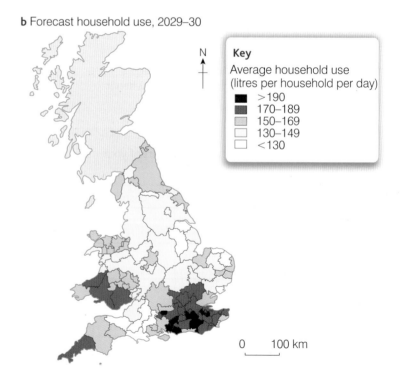

b Forecast household use, 2029–30

N

Key
Average household use
(litres per household per day)
- >190
- 170–189
- 150–169
- 130–149
- <130

0   100 km

B *Household water use in England and Wales*

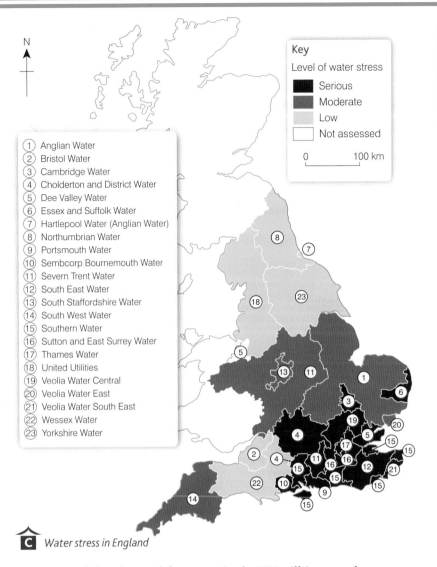

Key terms

Water stress: this happens when there is not enough water available. This may be because of an inadequate supply at a particular time or it may relate to water quality.

Areas of water deficit: areas where the rain that falls does not provide enough water and there may be shortages.

Areas of water surplus: areas that have more water than is needed. Often these are areas that get a lot of rain and don't have a lot of people living there.

Sustainable: making sure there is enough water in the long term without harming the environment.

C Water stress in England

It is expected that demand for water in the UK will increase because:

- the population is increasing
- modern lifestyles need more water as people use more time-saving devices
- people want food out of season which also increases water use (through irrigation).

There is a need to make sure that demand can be met in a **sustainable** way. There are several ways that this can be done.

- Houses are being designed with better water efficiency.
- Devices are fitted to toilets to reduce water use.
- Rainwater can be collected and used to water the garden and wash the car.
- Bath water can be recycled to flush toilets.
- People can take showers rather than baths.

Some water is also lost in leaking pipes so repairing these is also important.

Case study

Water transfer

One way of solving water shortages has been to transfer water from areas where there is a surplus to areas that do not have enough. In the late 1800s the River Vyrnwy in Powys was dammed to supply Liverpool with Welsh water (photo **D** and map **E**). Building began in 1881 and was finished in 1888. In all, 2 chapels, 3 inns, 10 farmhouses and 37 houses were to be lost under the reservoir. A new village, which retained the name Llanwddyn, was built 3 km from its original site.

D The dam at Vyrnwy

Since the dam was built, new transfer schemes have been proposed. In 1973 three new reservoirs were built (Brenig in Wales, Kielder in Northumberland and Carsington in Derbyshire), but other plans have not happened.

In 1994 there was a plan to transfer water from the River Severn to the Thames and the Trent. However, costs were high and in 2004 it was decided that local schemes, including small reservoirs, could meet the demand for water in areas such as the south-east. If, in the future, this is not possible, transfers may become a possibility.

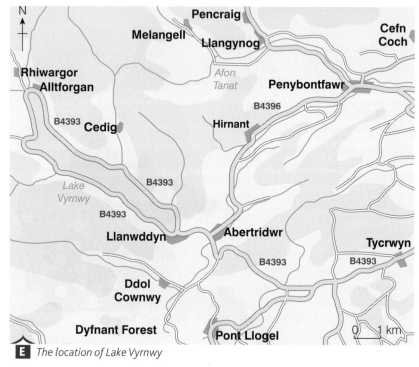

E The location of Lake Vyrnwy

Activities

1 Study table **A**, which shows how much water gets used for a range of different activities.

a List the number of times you have used water for the activities in the table during the last 24 hours.

b Multiply the number of times by the litres shown.

c Add this up to give the total number of litres.

2 a What activity in table **A** uses the most water each time this activity is carried out?

b Suggest ways of reducing the amount of water used for this activity.

3 Study map **C**.

a What is meant by 'water stress'?

b Which parts of England face 'serious' stress in the future?

c Describe how water transfers and water conservation can address this problem

d Which option in c) do you favour and why?

6 Ice on the land

6.1 How has climate change affected the global distribution of ice?

Temperature fluctuations

Today many people are worried about global warming. However, concern about climate change is nothing new. In the 1970s, some scientists thought that the climate was cooling and there would be another ice age.

Climate change in the past has been entirely natural. Scientists think that natural climate change happens:

- when there are small changes in the earth's orbit or its tilt towards the sun
- when there are changes in the pattern of ocean currents around the world.

Today, slight changes in the ocean currents near South America result in the **El Niño effect**. This has an impact on patterns of rainfall and on the development of tropical storms in some parts of the world.

Climate change during the Pleistocene period

Geological time is divided into periods. The most recent (apart from the present warm Holocene period) is called the Pleistocene period. This is known as the Ice Age. It happened over 2 million years ago and global temperatures changed a lot during this period (graph **A**).

> **In this section you will learn**
>
> the fluctuations of temperature in the recent geological past
>
> changes in the extent and distribution of ice in the world resulting from changes in global temperature.

> **Key term**
>
> **El Niño effect**: a periodic 'blip' in the usual global climate caused by a short-term warming of the cold ocean off the west coast of South America. This results in unusual patterns of temperature and rainfall and can lead to droughts and floods in certain parts of the world.

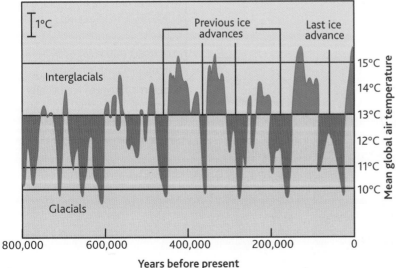

A *Fluctuating temperatures during the Pleistocene period*

Glacials

Scientists think there may have been as many as 20 cold periods during the Pleistocene period. During these **glacial periods** ice moved south to cover large parts of Europe and North America. Just 18,000 years ago ice reached its maximum extent (map **B**). Map **C** shows how ice covered almost all of the British Isles at this time. Even southern England would have been completely frozen, rather like parts of northern Canada today.

Interglacials

Between the glacial periods were warmer **interglacials**, which were at least as warm as today's climate if not warmer. There is evidence, for example, that hippopotamuses lived as far north as Leeds.

These big changes in temperature had nothing to do with human activities – there were no power stations or cars. These changes happened over thousands of years.

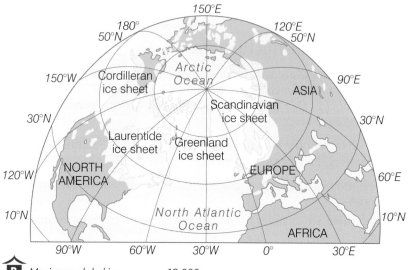

B Maximum global ice coverage 18,000 years ago

Key
→ Ice movement
▨ Tundra

Scandinavian ice

Limit of ice 18,000 years ago

Maximum limit of ice sheet during the Pleistocene period

Britain still joined to Europe

0   200 km

C Ice coverage over the British Isles 18,000 years ago

Key terms

Glacial period: a period when ice advances due to to falling temperatures.

Interglacial: a period when ice retreats due to rising temperatures.

Ice sheet: a large body of ice over 50,000 km² in extent.

Ice cap: a smaller body of ice (less than 50,000 km²) usually found in mountainous regions.

Glacier: a finger of ice usually extending downhill from an ice cap and occupying a valley.

Present-day global ice coverage

Today there are two large areas of ice in the world called **ice sheets** (map **D**).

- Antarctica is the largest ice sheet. It covers an area of 14 million km² and holds 90 per cent of all fresh water on the earth's surface. In places it is several kilometres thick.

- The Greenland ice sheet covers an area of 1.7 million km² (over 80 per cent of Greenland). At the moment it is showing signs that it is melting due to global warming.

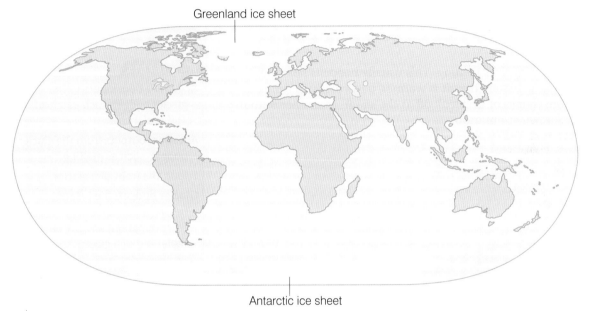

Greenland ice sheet

Antarctic ice sheet

D *Present-day distribution of ice sheets and ice caps*

Smaller bodies of ice covering an area of less than 50,000 km² are called **ice caps** or ice fields. They are usually found in cold, mountainous areas, such as in Iceland and the European Alps. Spreading out from ice caps are **glaciers**. Glaciers are like rivers except they are made of ice!

⭕⭕ links

You can find out more about ice sheets, ice caps and glaciers on the Wikipedia website at **http://en.wikipedia.org/wiki/Ice_sheet**.

Activities

1 Study map **B**. This shows how ice covered the land 18,000 years ago.

a How many ice sheets existed in the northern hemisphere 18,000 years ago?

b What were the names of the ice sheets in North America?

c Using an atlas, estimate which countries and present-day major cities would have been covered by ice 18,000 years ago.

2 Study map **C**, which shows how ice covered what is now the British Isles 18,000 years ago.

a On a blank outline map, make a copy of the maximum extent of ice covering the British Isles. Include the arrows to show the direction of ice flow.

b Using an atlas, label the four upland areas in the British Isles from where ice spread onto lower ground.

c Why do you think these areas were source areas for ice during this glacial period?

d Locate your nearest town or city on your map.

6.2   What causes glaciers to move?

◼ Glaciers

Inputs

The main input to glaciers is snow. When snow falls it becomes compacted as more snow settles on top. In the same way that fluffy snow is squeezed into a hard snowball, the ice becomes denser and eventually turns into clear glacier ice. Avalanches of snow and ice (see page 141) also provide inputs into the system. Inputs are known as **accumulation**.

Outputs

An output mostly involves melting. This usually happens near the **snout** of the glacier where the air is warmer, particularly in summer. Calving, where chunks of ice break off at the snout, is another output. Outputs are known as **ablation**.

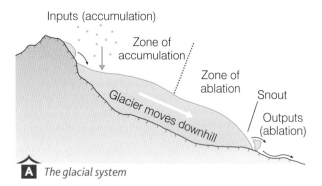

A *The glacial system*

◼ The glacier budget

The **glacier budget** is the balance between the inputs and the outputs. If there are more inputs than outputs, the glacier will get bigger (advance). If there are more outputs than inputs over several years, the glacier will get smaller (retreat).

The glacier budget varies between the seasons (graph **B**). In the winter there will be a lot of input. In the summer, when it is warmer, there will be more output.

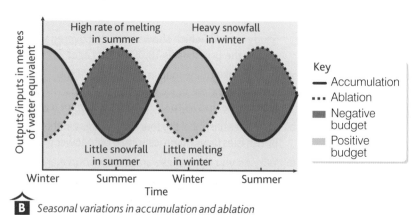

B *Seasonal variations in accumulation and ablation*

In this section you will learn

the components of the glacier budget

how the glacier budget affects glacier movement

how some glaciers have been retreating in recent decades.

Key terms

Accumulation: inputs to the glacier budget, such as snowfall and avalanches.

Ablation: outputs from the glacier budget, such as melting.

Snout: the front of a glacier.

Glacier budget: the balance between the inputs (accumulation) and the outputs (ablation) of a glacier.

Study tip

Make sure you learn glacier terms and understand how a glacier changes both seasonally and yearly.

Activity

1. Study diagram **A**. This shows the glacial system.

   a. Make a copy of the diagram.

   Add the following labels to your diagram:
   - ◼ snowfall
   - ◼ avalanches
   - ◼ melting
   - ◼ calving.

   b. Why is there mostly accumulation in the upper part of the glacial system?

   c. Why is ablation at its greatest near to the snout?

The retreat of South Cascade Glacier, USA

The South Cascade Glacier in Washington State, USA has been monitored by the United States Geological Survey (USGS) for over 40 years. Data have been collected on stream run-off, air temperature and glacier budget.

Look at the photos in **C**. They show how the South Cascade Glacier changed between 1900 and 2008. Table **D** shows the changes that have taken place in the glacier budget since 1985. Like other glaciers in the world, the South Cascade Glacier has shown a marked retreat. Many people believe this is caused by global warming.

1928

2006

C   *Changes in the South Cascade Glacier*

D   *Glacier budget data for South Cascade Glacier, 1985–2005*

Year	Winter (metres of water equivalent)	Summer (metres of water equivalent)	Net glacier budget (metres of water equivalent)	Year	Winter (metres of water equivalent)	Summer (metres of water equivalent)	Net glacier budget (metres of water equivalent)
1985	2.18	−3.38	−1.20	1996	2.94	−2.84	
1986	2.45	−3.06	−0.61	1997	3.71	−3.08	
1987	2.04	−4.10		1998	2.76	−4.62	
1988	2.44	−3.78		1999	3.59	−2.57	
1989	2.43	−3.34		2000	3.32	−2.94	
1990	2.60	−2.71		2001	1.90	−3.47	
1991	3.54	−3.47		2002	4.02	−3.47	
1992	1.91	−3.92		2003	2.66	−4.76	
1993	1.98	−3.21		2004	2.08	−3.73	
1994	2.39	−3.99		2005	1.97	−4.42	
1995	2.86	−3.55					

Activities

2 Study the photos in **C**. They show changes to the South Cascade Glacier between 1928 and 2006.

a Describe the changes between the two photos.

b Why do you think the lower part of the glacier has melted between 1928 and 2006?

3 Study table **D**. This gives the glacier budget data for the South Cascade Glacier from 1985 to 2005.

a Copy and complete the table by calculating the figures for the net glacier budget column. The first two have been calculated for you. Calculate the figures by taking the summer figure away from the winter figure for each year.

b Describe the pattern of the net glacier budget.

c Does the pattern support the evidence of glacier retreat shown by the photos in **C**?

6.3 Which processes operate in glacial environments?

Freeze–thaw weathering

If you visit a glacial area you will see huge piles of jagged rocks on the sides of the valleys (photo **A**). These are piles of scree and they happen because of freeze–thaw weathering (page 38).

Glacial erosion

Although glaciers move slowly – usually by only a few centimetres a year – they carry out a huge amount of erosion. There are two main types of glacial erosion:

- **Abrasion** – this is where the rocks trapped underneath the ice (diagram **B**) work like sandpaper smoothing the valley floor and sides. Scratches caused by large rocks beneath the ice are called striations.
- **Plucking** – the bottom of the glacier may be frozen to the rocks underneath. As the glacier moves, any loose rocks are plucked away. This leaves behind a jagged rocky surface not like the smooth surface resulting from abrasion.

In this section you will learn

the process of freeze–thaw weathering in a glacial environment

the mechanisms of glacier movement

the processes of glacial erosion, transportation and deposition.

Key terms

Abrasion: in glacial environments, a process of erosion involving the wearing away of the valley floor and sides by a glacier.

Plucking: a process of glacial erosion where individual rocks are plucked from the valley floor or sides as water freezes them to the glacier.

Rotational slip in hollow on mountainside

Scree slope

Mer de Glace moves by basal slip and internal deformation

A *Glacier movement in the French Alps and its valley*

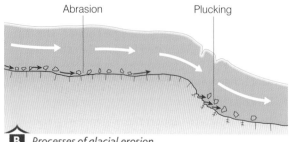

Abrasion

Plucking

B *Processes of glacial erosion*

Glacial movement

All the time glacial ice is moving very slowly downhill. This is because of the weight of the ice and the influence of gravity.

In summer, melting ice produces a lot of meltwater which helps the glacier to slide downhill. This type of movement is called basal slip and it can sometimes cause sudden movements of a glacier. In hollows high up on the valley sides, this may be more curved, in which case it is called **rotational slip** (photo **A**).

Glacial transportation

Bits of rock from freeze–thaw weathering and those that have been eroded by the ice are transported (moved) by the glacier. They can be transported on the ice, in the ice (having been buried by snowfall) and below the ice.

Deposition

Most deposition happens when the ice melts. As most melting occurs at the snout of a glacier, this is where most of the material carried by the ice ends up. As the glacier moves downhill, it pushes this material further downhill rather like a bulldozer, which is why this process is called **bulldozing**.

As a glacier slowly retreats, it leaves behind broken rock fragments. Although some of this sediment may form **hummocks**, a lot of it is washed away by meltwater rivers.

Key terms

Rotational slip: slippage of ice along a curved surface.

Moraine: sediment carried and deposited by the ice.

Bulldozing: the pushing of deposited sediment at the snout by the glacier as it advances.

Hummock: a small area of raised ground, rather like a large molehill.

Study tip

Make sure that you learn the terms associated with the glacial processes described.

Activities

1 Study photo **A**.
   a What is the evidence that freeze-thaw weathering is active in this landscape?
   b Why does the surface of the glacier look so dirty?
   c Can you work out what 'Mer de Glace' means in English.

2 Study diagram **B** carefully. It shows the processes of glacial erosion.
   a Make a copy of the diagram.
   b Add labels and annotations to your diagram to describe how abrasion and plucking work.

3 Imagine you are in a glaciated area standing on a rocky surface that has been eroded by a glacier. You can see the following signs.
   ■ smooth surface
   ■ scratches
   What glacial erosion process was responsible: abrasion or plucking (or both)?

4 Why does most of the material eroded by a glacier end up being deposited at the snout?

6.4 What are the distinctive landforms resulting from glacial processes?

Landforms of glacial erosion

Ice is a very powerful force and it can create amazing landforms in mountainous areas (photo **A**).

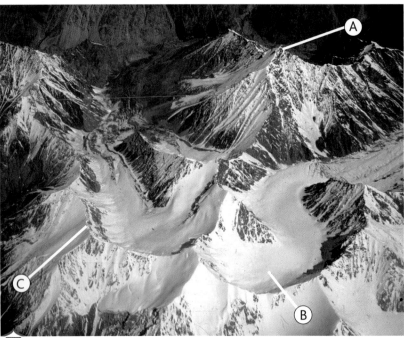

A *Glaciers with major features of erosion*

Corries

Corries, are large hollows found on the upper slopes of glaciated valleys. They are also known as cirques and cwms. They have a steep back wall and a raised lip at the front.

Diagram **B** shows how a corrie is formed. Snow builds up in a hollow. Gradually the snow turns to ice and a small corrie glacier is formed. Through rotational slip, the glacier scoops out a hollow (like an ice cream scoop, scooping ice cream). At the front of the corrie the ice is thinner so erosion is less and a raised lip is formed. Often when the ice melts, a small lake known as a tarn, forms in the hollow.

Arêtes and pyramidal peaks

An **arête** is a narrow ridge often found at the back of a corrie or between two glaciated valleys (diagram **C**).

An arête forms when erosion in two corries cause the land in between to become ever narrower. If three or more corries have formed on a mountain, erosion may lead to the formation of a single peak rather than a ridge. This is called a **pyramidal peak**.

Key terms

Corrie: a deep depression on a hillside with a steep back wall, often containing a lake.

Arête: a knife-edged ridge, often formed between two corries.

Pyramidal peak: a sharp-edged mountain peak.

Glacial trough: a wide, steep-sided valley eroded by a glacier.

Truncated spur: an interlocking spur that has been 'cut off' by ice leaving a very steep cliff.

Hanging valley: a tributary glacial trough perched up on the side of a main valley, often marked by a waterfall.

Ribbon lake: a long narrow lake in the bottom of a glacial trough.

Long profile: this shows the changes in height and shape along the length of a glacier, from its source high in the mountains to its snout.

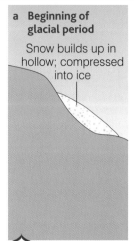
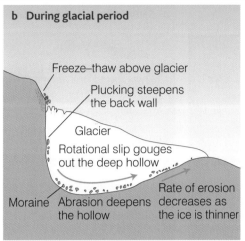
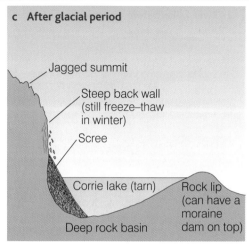

a Beginning of glacial period

Snow builds up in hollow; compressed into ice

b During glacial period

Freeze–thaw above glacier

Plucking steepens the back wall

Glacier

Rotational slip gouges out the deep hollow

Moraine   Abrasion deepens the hollow

Rate of erosion decreases as the ice is thinner

c After glacial period

Jagged summit

Steep back wall (still freeze–thaw in winter)

Scree

Corrie lake (tarn)

Rock lip (can have a moraine dam on top)

Deep rock basin

B *The formation of a corrie*

Glacial valley landforms

Glaciers usually flow along river valleys. They tend to carve quite straight courses (diagram **D**). Their power helps them to form dramatic features such as deep **glacial troughs**, **truncated spurs**, **hanging valleys** and **ribbon lakes**.

A glacial trough is a valley with steep-sides and a wide and flat bottom. It is formed mainly by the process of abrasion. Over many hundreds of years, the moving glacier grinds into the base and sides of the valley. Protruding spurs of rock are cut through to produce vertical truncated spurs (diagram **D (b)**). Smaller river valleys, carved by smaller glaciers are left perched up on the valley side as hanging valleys. These often form amazing waterfalls.

Erosion of the valley floor is usually erratic. This results in an uneven **long profile**. Some parts of the valley are eroded more, for example where the ice becomes thicker after a smaller glacier has joined. When the glacier has retreated, ribbon lakes can be formed in these linear hollows. Ribbon lakes are common in Scotland, with one of the most famous being Loch Ness.

Pyramidal peak   Third corrie behind pyramidal peak

Arête

Arête

Arête

Corrie lake (tarn)

Corrie

C *Arêtes and pyramidal peaks*

Activities

1 Study photo **A**. This shows a scene of glacier and erosional features.

Name the glacial features labelled A, B and C. Select the three right answers from the following list:

◾ truncated spur

◾ pyramidal peak

◾ corrie

◾ drumlin

◾ arête.

2 Study diagrams **B** and **C**.

a Draw some simple diagrams to show how the erosion of two corries that are back-to-back results in an arête. Add some labels to describe what is happening.

b Why are arêtes dangerous features to walk along? (Especially if it is foggy and icy!)

c How does a pyramidal peak form?

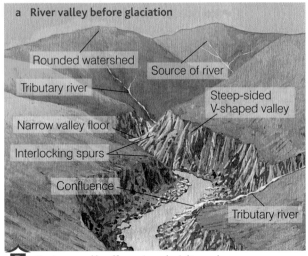

a River valley before glaciation

Rounded watershed
Source of river
Tributary river
Steep-sided V-shaped valley
Narrow valley floor
Interlocking spurs
Confluence
Tributary river

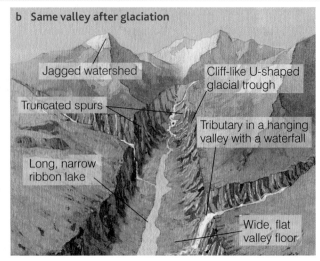

b Same valley after glaciation

Jagged watershed
Cliff-like U-shaped glacial trough
Truncated spurs
Tributary in a hanging valley with a waterfall
Long, narrow ribbon lake
Wide, flat valley floor

D *Features and landforms in a glacial trough*

Landforms of glacial transportation and deposition

Moraine

Moraine is the term given to the fragments of rock transported and then deposited by the ice. There can sometimes be so much that it forms a thick blanket of material. The deposited material is called till or boulder clay.

There are a number of types of moraine (diagram **F**):

- **Ground moraine** – material that was dragged underneath the glacier which is left behind when the ice melts. It often forms uneven hummocky ground.
- **Lateral moraine** – forms at the edges of the glacier. It is mostly scree that has fallen off the valley sides after freeze–thaw weathering. When the ice melts, it forms a slight ridge on the valley side.
- **Medial moraine** – when a smaller glacier joins the main glacier, two lateral moraines merge to produce a single line of moraine that runs down the centre of the main glacier. When it melts, the medial moraine forms a ridge down the centre of the valley.
- **Terminal moraine** – huge amounts of material pile up at the snout of a glacier to form a high ridge. This is a terminal moraine. It shows the maximum extent of glacial advance.

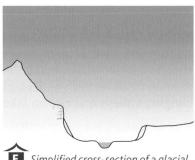

E *Simplified cross-section of a glacial trough*

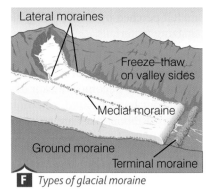

Lateral moraines
Freeze–thaw on valley sides
Medial moraine
Ground moraine
Terminal moraine

F *Types of glacial moraine*

OS map study: glacial features in the Nant Ffrancon valley, Wales

During the last ice advance, North Wales lay under a thick sheet of ice. Glaciers created spectacular landforms – like the Nant Ffrancon valley (map extract **G** and photo **H**). Take a few moments to find where the photo is located on the map. (Cwm is the Welsh term for corrie and llyn the Welsh term for a lake.)

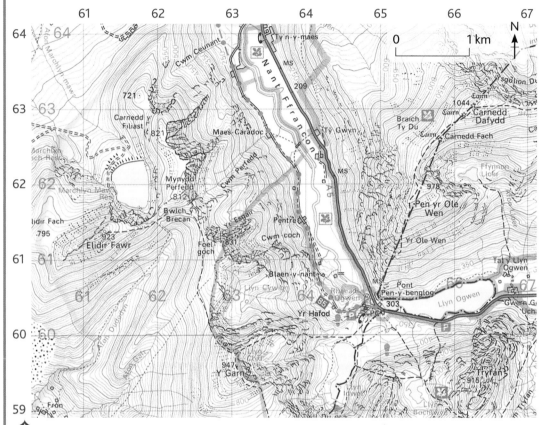

G 1:50,000 OS map extract of Nant Ffrancon valley, part of map sheet 115

H Aerial photo of Nant Ffrancon valley

Study tip

Practise drawing glacial features and adding labels to describe their features and how they were formed.

Did you know ??????

In 1967, in his boat Bluebird K7, Donald Campbell used a ribbon lake called Coniston Water in the Lake District to try to beat his existing world water speed record of 444 kph. Tragically, he was killed as Bluebird flipped and somersaulted at 515 kph.

Drumlins

Drumlins are smooth, egg-shaped hills. Most are about 10 m in height and up to a few hundred metres in length. They often occur in clusters on the floor of a glacial trough (photo **I**). They are made of moraine, but instead of simply being dumped they were moulded and shaped by the moving ice. Drumlins usually have a blunt end, which faces up-valley, and a more pointed end facing down-valley. This makes them useful as they show which way the glacier was moving.

Key term

Drumlin: an egg-shaped hill found on the floor of a glacial trough.

I *Drumlins near Alberta, Canada showing the steeper up-valley and the gentler down-valley slopes*

Activities

4   Study map extract **G** and photo **H**: a map and a photo of Nant Ffrancon valley. Use the place names on the map to answer the following questions:

a   What is the name of the river that flows along the flat valley floor at label **A**?

b   What is the name of the corrie lake (tarn) at **B**?

c   What is the name of the peak at **C** and how high is it?

d   Glaciers start in corries and flow downhill from corries along their valleys. In what direction do you think the glacier flowed along the valley? Support your answer with evidence from the map.

e   What attractions are there for tourists to the area? Include references to the map in your answer.

5   Study map extract **G**. Complete a summary table to help with your revision. For each of the following features, select an example from the map and draw a simple sketch of the contour patterns. Include scales, contour values and place names. Keep it simple but make it accurate.

▪ corrie (cwm)

▪ arête

▪ ribbon lake

▪ glacial trough

⦾ links

A useful glossary with photos can be found at **www.uwsp.edu/geo/ faculty/Lemke/alpine_glacial_ glossary/glossary.html**.

6.5 What opportunities do glacial areas offer for tourism?

Tourism in the French Alps: Chamonix

Chamonix is in the north-west of the Alps, just 15 km from the Swiss border and 15 km from Italy via the Mont Blanc tunnel (map **A**). Chamonix and its valley are dominated by Mont Blanc, Europe's highest mountain at 4,808 m (photo **B**).

Chamonix has been a centre for tourism for over 250 years. There are lots of things to do in this stunning landscape. Only 10,000 people live in Chamonix but there are up to 100,000 visitors a day in summer and about 60,000 a day in winter.

In this section you will learn

the attractions and opportunities available for tourism in the Alps

the need for responsible tourism and sustainable management.

Case study

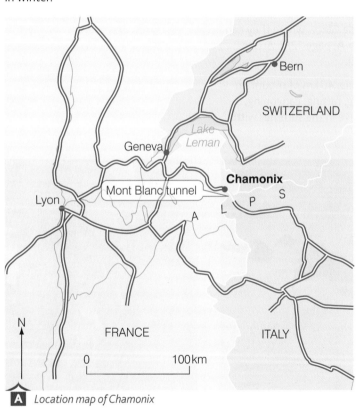

A *Location map of Chamonix*

B *Chamonix and Mont Blanc*

Winter attractions

Chamonix provides lots of options for skiers and snowboarders of all abilities (map **C** and photo **D**). Cable cars and cog railways provide easy access to the pistes. Cross-country skiing has become popular and two local courses have been built nearby. People also go ice climbing, free riding, paragliding and snowshoeing. Chamonix has hotels, restaurants, heated swimming pools and spas for the tourists. With its museums, shops and historical buildings, there is much to do away from the slopes.

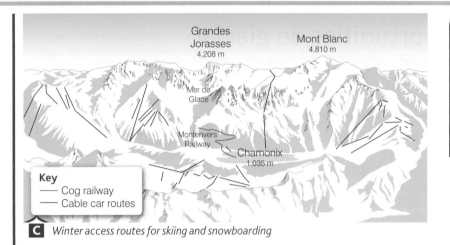

C Winter access routes for skiing and snowboarding

Summer attractions

The mountain landscapes give people a lot to do in summer as well. The famous Montenvers railway takes visitors to the Mer de Glace, where they can see the glacier and the valley that it has carved (photo **A**, page 128). An ice cave allows visitors to step inside the glacier (photo **E**).

The Chamonix area has 350 km of marked walking trails, 40 km of mountain bike tracks, rock climbing, mountaineering, paragliding, rafting, canyoning, pony trekking and summer luging. The town comes alive in the summer with live music and outdoor cafés.

D Winter sports in Chamonix

E Tourists explore the ice grotto in the Mer de Glace

Impacts of tourism in the French Alps

Tourism to Chamonix and the surrounding area brings both benefits and problems.

Benefits of tourism:

- Tourists bring huge economic benefits. They provide jobs for people in hotels and restaurants, as guides and instructors and in building and maintenance.

- The extra money supports local services such as shops. Local people benefit from improvements in public transport and health care.

- Chamonix is well looked after to keep attracting tourists. People have safe access to shops and the town is clean and well lit.

Problems of tourism:

- The town can become noisy and congested at peak times. Getting to Chamonix via motorway is good, but in Chamonix itself the roads are narrow and become jammed easily.

- Footpaths have become eroded by the number of walkers and mountain bikes.

- The shops, cafés and restaurants are for tourists and are expensive. Local people often have to pay more for everyday items. Houses are expensive and many are second homes for wealthy visitors.

- Conflicts can arise between different groups of people. Some tourists are noisy and can damage the environment which can upset other tourists doing more peaceful activities such as walking or bird watching. Local people can also be upset. Farm animals can be harmed by thoughtless actions of tourists, such as leaving gates open or dropping litter.

Managing tourism in Chamonix

- Chamonix wants to promote **responsible tourism** to try to balance the demands of tourism with the need to protect the environment.

- The Chamonix municipality (local authority) provides an environmentally friendly transport service with clean energy buses and free public transport.

- France, Italy and Switzerland are all involved in a project called Espace Mont-Blanc. This looks at issues of transport, nature conservation, forests and water resources.

- A further initiative called Tomorrow's Valley brings together people from the local community and tourist groups to plan for **sustainable management**. Current projects include:

    - burying service networks such as electricity lines underground
    - looking after historic buildings and monuments
    - preserving natural wetlands and peat bogs
    - protecting the environment from skiing by planting trees and using local building materials that blend in
    - maintaining and way-marking footpaths and cleaning rivers – this provides seasonal employment for local people
    - supporting local traditional employment sectors, particularly farming.

Key terms

Responsible tourism: the idea of encouraging a balance between the demands of tourism and the need to protect the environment.

Sustainable management: a form of management that ensures that developments are long lasting and non-harmful to the environment.

⚭ **links**

The main Chamonix tourism site, which has plenty of excellent information, is at **www.chamonix.com**.

The Espace Mont-Blanc website is at **www.espace-mont-blanc.com**.

A detailed map of Chamonix can be found at **www.skifrance.com/chamonix/resortmap.html**.

Activity

1   Study the photos, maps and text in the Chamonix case study.

a   Create a table with two columns, one column headed Winter activities and one column headed Summer activities. Complete the table for Chamonix.

b   Tourism brings money to the local economy. But tourism could bring problems for local people too: think of three types of problem that tourists bring.

c   In what ways can tourism have a negative impact on the environment? Give at least two examples.

6.6 What is the impact of climate change on Alpine communities?

Evidence for recent climate change

Many of the Alps' most popular resorts, such as Morzine and Megève, are in danger of running out of snow as the world warms up.

The UN estimates that in 30 years' time the snowline will have risen by 300 m and that up to half of all resorts in Europe will be forced to close by 2050. Hotels, restaurants and shops will be forced to close due to lack of business. Switzerland could lose up to £1 bn a year if its resorts close down.

Responses in lower-level resorts

Lower-level resorts have responded in a number of ways in order to cope with the problem:

- Tourists have been taken by bus to higher-level resorts for skiing. Artificial snow is put onto the slopes (photo **A**). In low-level parts of Austria and Italy, up to 40 per cent of resorts now have to make their own snow. This is expensive. It can also have an effect on vegetation, which may take 30 years to recover.

- Resorts have had to change what they offer. Some have started to promote themselves as centres for cross-country skiing, hiking, climbing, sledding or snowshoeing.

- There are plans to build new ski lifts to link resorts, but this could cause a lot of damage to the environment.

In this section you will learn

how climate change poses a threat to communities dependent on tourism

how Alpine environments are fragile and need careful sustainable management.

Key terms

Fragile environment: an environment that is easily unbalanced and damaged by natural or human factors.

Did you know ???????

The snow cannon was developed in 1950. It uses over 1 million litres of water to cover 0.4 ha to a depth of 30 cm.

A A snow cannon in action on the Alps

Abondance, France

Abondance is a typical Alpine ski resort in the Haute-Savoie region of France (photo **B**). It is one of many ski resorts in the area that depends on income from skiers.

In 2007, after 15 years of little snowfall, the ski lifts in Abondance closed for the last time. The local council is considering two options to try and secure its future and provide jobs for local people:

- To develop other forms of winter sports, such as ski touring, snowshoeing and snow-mobiling which do not need deep snow.
- To develop its summer programme of activities to include hiking, water sports and mountain biking. This would help the town to become an all-year round resort rather than just a winter one.

New developments

The High Alps are rich in wildlife and free from pollution. With low-level resorts in decline, there is a lot of pressure to develop these areas. However, tourism can harm **fragile environments** in a number of ways:

- The building of roads, ski lifts, houses and hotels can have a big impact on natural ecosystems and habitats.
- Trees are often cut down to make way for developments. They were binding the soil on steep slopes and breaking up avalanches.
- Overuse of slopes for skiing can strip a hillside of its natural vegetation, which can take many years to grow back. Mountain biking can lead to gullies, which scar the landscape.
- With more noise and visual pollution, the natural landscape loses some of its appeal for tourists.

B *The Abondance valley in the French Alps*

In Austria new ski lifts and cable cars are being built to open up the Gepatsch Glacier to skiers above 3,500 m. However, with almost all Alpine glaciers retreating, glacier skiing may not last for long. At Lisenser Fernerkogel new cable cars and pistes are being developed (photo **C**). In other areas there are plans to link resorts by cable car so low-level resorts can stay open even if tourists have to travel further to ski.

Should the environment be protected at all costs or should some development be allowed in order to give local people jobs and secure the region's economic future?

C *Off piste skiing in the Alps*

Activities

1 Study photo **B**. This shows the Abondance valley in the French Alps.

a Why are low-level ski resorts like Abondance suffering from a decrease in winter tourism?

b How has this affected the lives of local people living in these resorts?

c Imagine that you are the mayor of Abondance. Which of the two following options do you favour and why? Perhaps you think that both options should be adopted:

- develop support for winter activities that do not reply on deep snow
- develop a better programme of summer activites.

2 Study photo **C**. This shows an off piste group snowing in the Alps.

a What is meant by 'off piste' skiing?

b Make a list of the advantages and disadvantages of developing new areas such as photo **C** as ski resorts.

c Do you think the area in photo **C** should be developed as a ski resort? Explain your answer.

Study tip

Know the arguments for and against developments in the Alps. Be prepared to express your own opinion.

⬭ links

The BBC has information at **www.bbc.co.uk**. Type 'Alpine future' into the search box.

6.7   What is the avalanche hazard?

What are avalanches?

Avalanches are masses of snow, ice and rocks that move downhill at speeds of up to 300 kph. They happen naturally in mountain environments. They are only a hazard when they impact on people or human activity, such as roads or houses.

There are two main types of avalanche:

- **Loose snow avalanche** – this type of avalanche usually starts from a single point on the hillside and involves loose, powdery snow (photo and diagram **A**).
- **Slab avalanche** – this tends to be a more deadly type of avalanche. A large slab of ice and snow comes away from a hillside and moves quickly downhill, carrying rocks and trees (photo and diagram **B**). It has huge power and can cause a lot of damage.

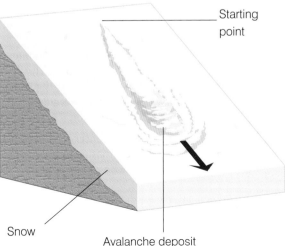

Starting point

Snow

Avalanche deposit

A *Loose snow avalanche*

In this section you will learn

the risk posed by avalanches

the factors contributing to the avalanche hazard and ways of reducing the hazard.

Key terms

Avalanche: a very fast downhill movement of a mass of snow, ice and rocks.

Loose snow avalanche: a powdery avalanche usually starting from a single point.

Slab avalanche: a large-scale avalanche formed when a slab of ice and snow breaks away from the main ice pack.

Did you know ??????

If you are buried by an avalanche, you have a 90 per cent chance of surviving if you are found in the first 15 minutes. This drops to 30 per cent after 35 minutes.

Study tip

Be aware that avalanches usually happen because of many factors, although there is usually a single trigger such as heavy snowfall or an earthquake. Use the internet to update your case studies.

B *Loose snow avalanche that may trigger the collapse of the huge slab in the top left*

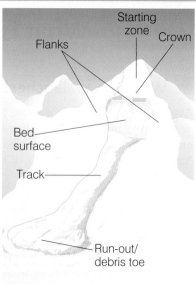

C *Slab avalanche*

Causes of avalanches

There are a number of things that add to the risk of avalanches:

- Heavy snowfall – this makes existing snow heavier and more likely to move downhill.
- Steep slopes – avalanches are more likely to occur on steep slopes of over 30°.
- Tree removal – cutting down trees can make avalanches more serious. Trees can break up an avalanche and stop it becoming too large.
- Temperature rise – sudden rises in temperatures and melting snow often lead to avalanches in the spring.
- Heavy rainfall – this can make the slope slippery and start an avalanche.
- Human factors – almost all people who die in avalanches started them. Off-piste skiing is a major cause of avalanches because it often involves skiing in areas that have not been assessed for the avalanche risk.

Avalanches as hazards

Deaths, injuries and property damage due to avalanches have increased in the last 50 years. This is mainly because of the growth of winter sports and ski resorts.

- In Switzerland an average of 40 people die each year from avalanches. Over 80 per cent were doing winter sports.
- In 2007–08, avalanches in France killed 15 people. Four were climbing and the rest were skiing or snowboarding.

⚭links

Up-to-date case studies are important, so make use of online resources and the internet. The main media sites, such as the BBC (www.bbc.co.uk) are excellent sources of information.

The Avalanche Center is an excellent source of information at **www.avalanche-center.org**.

More people are putting themselves at risk from avalanches. If there are more avalanches as the climate warms, the death toll and damage to property may well increase.

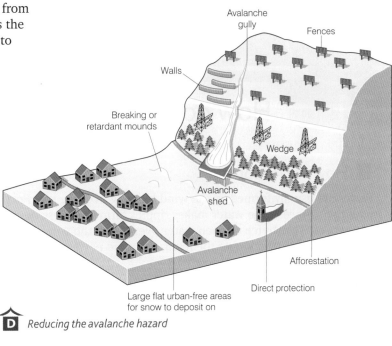

D Reducing the avalanche hazard

Recent avalanches

Europe, 2006 and 2009

The winter of 2005–06 was a record year for deaths in the French Alps, with 49 people being killed in off-piste avalanches alone. Irregular weather patterns, with changing temperatures and amounts of rain and snow, led to more avalanches than usual. The fashion for extreme sports was also thought to put more people at risk from avalanches.

In 2009 heavy snow triggered avalanches in many locations across Europe. Altogether these avalanches killed more than 20 people who had been skiing, climbing and hiking.

Salang, Afghanistan 2010

A freak snowstorm in the Hindu Kush mountains in Afghanistan led to a series of avalanches at Salang, which is north of Kabul. There were at least 36 avalanches in this series. The avalanches buried 3.5 km of road (photo **C**), killing over 170 people and trapping more than 2,000 travellers on the road. Strong winds and heavy rain contributed to the cause of the avalanches.

Case study

E Rescuers search for survivors in avalanche debris at Salang

Activities

1 Read the information about the factors that contribute to the risk of avalanches.

a Create a poster to be used in a ski resort that tells visitors what danger signs to look out for that might indicate a risk of avalanche.

b Add some illustrations to help identify the hazards.

2 Study diagram **D**. This shows ways in which the avalanche hazards can be reduced.

a Draw a simple version of the diagram.

b Add notes to describe how each measure reduces the avalanche threat.

c Which of the measures in your diagram do you think are most appropriate for poor mountainous parts of the world such as Afghanistan? Give reasons for your answer.

3 Use the internet to research recent avalanches. The Planet Ski website at **www.planetski.eu/news** is a great place to start.

7.1   How do waves shape our coastline?

How waves form

Waves are usually formed by the wind blowing over the sea. Friction with the surface of the water makes ripples form and these develop into waves. The stretch of open water over which the wind blows is called the **fetch**. The longer the fetch, the more powerful a wave can become.

Waves can also be formed when earthquakes or volcanic eruptions shake the seabed. These waves are called tsunamis. In December 2004 huge tsunami waves devastated the countries around the Indian Ocean and 240,000 people were killed (photo **A**).

Did you know ??????

When the volcano Krakatoa erupted in 1883, a tsunami said to be 35 m high killed 36,000 people on the Indonesian island of Sumatra.

A *The Indian Ocean tsunami, 2004, Sri Lanka*

When waves reach the coast

Diagram **B** shows what happens as waves approach the land. As the land rises it changes the movement of the water from circular to more egg-shaped. This causes the **crest** of the wave to rise up and then eventually to topple onto the beach. The water that rushes up the **beach** is called the **swash**. The water that flows back towards the sea is called the **backwash**.

C *Surfers on a beach in Newquay*

Top of wave moves faster

Wave begins to break

Water from previous wave returns

Water rushes up the beach

Circular orbit in open water

Friction with the seabed distorts the circular orbital motion

Increasingly elliptical orbit

Shelving seabed (beach)

B *Waves approaching the coast*

Types of wave found at the coast

There are two types of wave at the coast.

Constructive waves have a powerful swash. They carry large amounts of sediment and 'construct' the beach, making it bigger. These are the waves that surfers love (photo **C**). They are formed by storms which can be hundreds of kilometres away. There is a large space between the waves and they are powerful when they reach the coast (diagram **D**).

Destructive waves are formed by storms close to the coast. They are called destructive waves because they 'destroy' the beach. Destructive waves are close together and can get caught up with each other forming a swirling mass of water. They form high waves before crashing down onto the beach (diagram **E**). There is little forward motion (swash) when a destructive wave breaks, but a powerful backwash. This takes sediment away from the beach – destroying it.

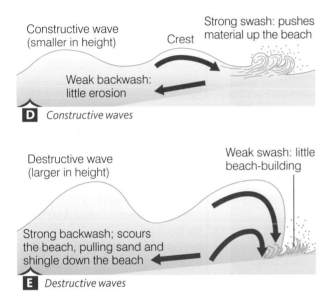

D *Constructive waves*

E *Destructive waves*

links

You can find out more about the Indian Ocean tsunami at **www.guardian.co.uk/world/tsunami2004**.

Watch the surfers by webcam at **www.fistralsurfcam.com**.

Activities

1   Look carefully at photo **A**. This shows the impact of the Indian Ocean tsunami at a coastal settlement in Sri Lanka.

 a   What sort of damage and destruction would this tsunami cause to people's houses, belongings and way of life?

 b   Many of the people who died in 2004 lived in small coastal communities around the Indian Ocean. Why do people choose to live close to the sea?

2   Study photo **C**, which shows a constructive wave. They are sometimes known as a surging waves because they 'surge' up the beach. Also study diagrams **D** and **E**, which show the differences between constructive and destructive waves.

 a   Why do surfers prefer constructive waves to destructive waves? Use the terms swash and backwash in your answer.

 b   Are constructive waves generated by storms close to the coast or a long way off?

Study tip

Practise drawing a labelled sketch of a wave type. It is a good way to learn its features.

7.2 Which land processes shape our coastline?

Weathering

Weathering affects rocks at the coast. Look at pages 37 to 39 to find out how weathering happens.

At the coast, freeze–thaw weathering is very effective if the rock is porous (contains holes) and permeable (allows water to pass through it). Look at photo **A**. The autumn of 2000 was very wet and the chalk rock became saturated with water. During late winter, long periods of frost weakened the rock, leading to several **rockfalls** along the south coast of England, including the one shown.

A *Rockfall at Beachy Head, Sussex*

Mass movement

The rockfall shown in photo **A** is one example of mass movement. Mass movement is the downhill movement of material. In 1993, 60 m of **cliff** slid onto the beach near Scarborough in North Yorkshire, taking with it part of the Holbeck Hall Hotel (photo **B**). The hotel had to be demolished. Diagram **C** describes some of the common types of mass movement found at the coast.

> **In this section you will learn**
>
> how weathering affects rocks at the coast
>
> how processes of mass movement operate at the coast.

> **Key term**
>
> **Cliff**: a steep or vertical face of rock often found at the coast.
>
> **Rockfall**: the collapse of a cliff face or the fall of individual rocks from a cliff.

> **Did you know ??????**
>
> The Belle Tout lighthouse at Beachy Head was built in 1832 and stopped operating in 1907. It was moved inland by 17 m in 1999 to prevent it falling into the sea because of coastal erosion. It is now bed and breakfast accommodation.

B *Landslip at Holbeck Hall, Scarborough*

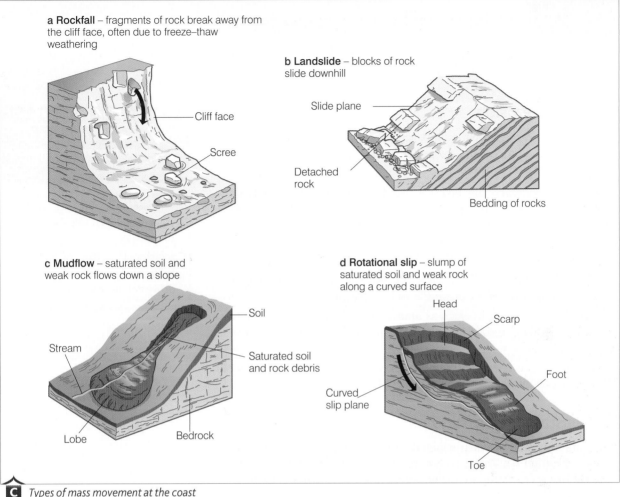

a Rockfall – fragments of rock break away from the cliff face, often due to freeze–thaw weathering

Cliff face

Scree

b Landslide – blocks of rock slide downhill

Slide plane

Detached rock

Bedding of rocks

c Mudflow – saturated soil and weak rock flows down a slope

Stream

Soil

Saturated soil and rock debris

Lobe

Bedrock

d Rotational slip – slump of saturated soil and weak rock along a curved surface

Head

Scarp

Foot

Curved slip plane

Toe

C *Types of mass movement at the coast*

Most of the material that falls from both mass movement and weathering is carried away by the waves to be deposited further along the coast.

Activities

1 Which of these statements is the best explanation of how freeze-thaw weathering occurs on a chalk cliff?

- When chalky mud dries out it cracks and pieces fall off.
- When water in cracks in the chalk freezes it expands and widens the crack, weakening the rock.
- When a chalk cliff is frozen in an ice age and then thaws it makes the cliff fall down.

2 Study photo **A**. Imagine the local council has decided to place an information board at the top of the cliff to warn people of the dangers of cliff collapse. It wants to inform people why the cliff is dangerous.

- Design an information board explaining why the cliff is vulnerable to rockfalls.
- Use diagrams to illustrate your board and do not forget to warn people to keep well away from the cliff edge!

Study tip

Weathering takes place over long periods of time. Always refer to the correct terms when writing about weathering and mass movement.

∞ links

You can find out more about a Beachy Head rockfall in 1999 at **www.bbc.co.uk**. Enter 'Beachy Head rockfall' into the search box.

There is a spectacular video of a rockfall in Cornwall at **www.guardian.co.uk**. Search for 'massive Cornwall rock fall'.

7.3 Which marine processes shape our coastline?

Coastal erosion

When a wave crashes down on a beach or smashes against a cliff, it carries out the process of erosion (photo **A**). There are several processes of coastal erosion:

- **Hydraulic power** – this involves the sheer power of the waves as they smash onto a cliff (photo **A**). Trapped air is blasted into holes and cracks in the rock, eventually causing the rock to break apart.
- **Corrasion** – this involves bits of rock being picked up by the sea and thrown at a cliff. The bits of rocks scrape and gouge the rock.
- **Abrasion** – this is the 'sandpapering' effect of pebbles grinding over a rocky platform, often causing it to become smooth.
- **Solution** – some rocks, such as limestone and chalk, are dissolved by seawater. Limestone and chalk form cliffs in many parts of the UK.
- **Attrition** – this is where fragments of rock carried by the sea knock against one another, making them smaller and more rounded.

Coastal transportation

There are four main ways in which material is transported (moved) by the sea (diagram **B**). The size and amount of rock transported by the sea depends on the strength of the waves and tidal currents. During storms, quite large pebbles can be flung up on to the land where they can damage buildings and cars.

In this section you will learn

the processes of coastal erosion, transportation and deposition.

Key terms

Hydraulic power: the sheer power of the waves.

Corrasion: the effect of rocks being flung at the cliff by powerful waves.

A *Waves crashing onto cliffs in Iceland*

Solution: dissolved chemicals often derived from limestone or chalk

Suspension: particles carried (suspended) within the water

Traction: large pebbles rolled along the seabed

Saltation: a 'hopping' or 'bouncing' motion of particles too heavy to be suspended

B *Types of coastal transportation*

The way that sediment on a beach moves depends on the direction of wave approach. Look at diagram **C**. Where the waves approach 'head on', sediment is moved up and down the beach. However, if the waves approach at an angle, sediment moves along the beach in a zig-zag pattern. This is called **longshore drift**.

Key terms

Longshore drift: the transport of sediment along a stretch of coastline caused by waves approaching the beach at an angle.

Headland: a ridge of land jutting out into the sea.

Bay: a broad coastal inlet often with a beach.

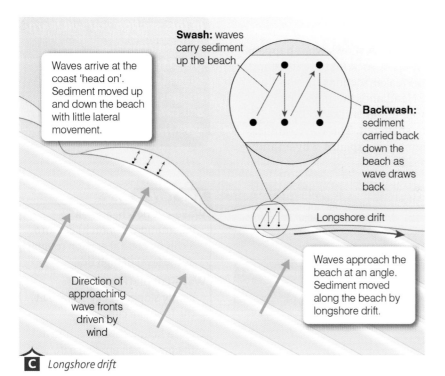

Swash: waves carry sediment up the beach

Waves arrive at the coast 'head on'. Sediment moved up and down the beach with little lateral movement.

Backwash: sediment carried back down the beach as wave draws back

Longshore drift

Direction of approaching wave fronts driven by wind

Waves approach the beach at an angle. Sediment moved along the beach by longshore drift.

C *Longshore drift*

Coastal deposition

Deposition is when the sea deposits or dumps the material it has been carrying. It happens when the flow of water slows down. Most coastal deposition is in **bays**, where the energy of the waves is reduced. This is why there are beaches in bays and no beaches at **headlands**, where wave energy is much greater.

Study tip

It is important to use the correct terms when describing coastal processes and to make sure that you can say what each one involves. Diagrams work well here.

Activities

1   Design a set of flashcards for the five processes of coastal erosion: abrasion, attrition, corrasion, solution, hydraulic power.

a   Write the term on the front of the flashcard, and a definition on the back.

b   Once you've finished, test yourself or a partner. How many can you get right?

2   Study diagram **C**. This shows how longshore drift operates.

a   Draw your own diagram to show how the process of longshore drift operates. Add labels to describe what is happening.

b   Longshore drift can end up moving all the sand off a beach. See what ideas you can come up with for ways to slow down the effect of longshore drift and keep sand on the beach.

links

A good summary of coastal processes and landforms can be found at **www.georesources.co.uk/ leld.htm**.

A fun animation using a rubber duck to show the process of longshore drift can be found at **www.geography-site.co.uk/pages/ physical/coastal/longshore.html**.

7.4 What are the distinctive landforms resulting from erosion?

Headlands and bays

Cliffs do not erode at the same pace. Diagram **A** shows what happens when rock is eroded along a coast. Sections of rock that are resistant to erosion stick out to form **headlands**. Weaker sections of coastline that are more easily eroded form **bays**. Headlands are most open to the power of the waves, so there are more features created by erosion such as cliffs. In contrast, bays are more sheltered. The waves are less powerful so there is more deposition here. This explains why a sandy beach is the most common feature found in bays.

In this section you will learn

the formation and characteristics of features of coastal erosion (headlands and bays; wave-cut platforms and caves; caves, arches and stacks).

a

Less resistant (softer) clay

Resistant (harder) sandstone

Waves

Clay

Resistant (harder) chalk or limestone

Clay

b

Less resistant rock worn away to leave a bay

Resistant (harder) rock left as a headland

Waves

Sheltered bay – sand is deposited

Headland

Bay

A *The formation of headlands and bays*

Key terms

Wave-cut notch: a small indentation (or notch) cut into a cliff by coastal erosion roughly at the level of high tide.

Wave-cut platform: a wide, gently sloping rocky surface at the foot of a cliff.

Cave: a hollowed-out feature at the base of an eroding cliff.

Arch: a headland that has been partly broken through by the sea to form a thin-roofed arch.

Stack: an isolated pinnacle of rock sticking out of the sea.

Cliffs and wave-cut platforms

- When waves break against a cliff, erosion takes a 'bite' out of the cliff to form a feature called a **wave-cut notch**.
- Over hundreds of years the notch gets deeper until the cliff above it falls.
- This happens over and over again so the cliff line gradually moves back. In its place will be a gentle slope of rock with rock pools. This is called a **wave-cut platform** (photo **B**).
- During long periods of constructive waves, the wave-cut platform may become covered by sand or shingle. Local winter storms bring destructive waves which take away the sand, so the wave-cut platform can be seen again.

B *Wave-cut platform and cliff near Beachy Head*

Caves, arches and stacks

Rocks in a headland have weak points such as joints or faults. The waves erode the rock along these lines of weakness to form a **cave** (diagram **C**). Over time, erosion may lead to two back-to-back caves breaking through a headland to form an **arch**. Gradually, the arch is made bigger by erosion at the base and sides. The roof collapses eventually to form a pillar of rock known as a **stack**.

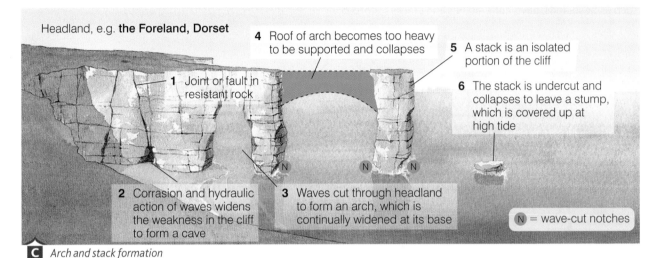

Headland, e.g. **the Foreland, Dorset**

4 Roof of arch becomes too heavy to be supported and collapses

5 A stack is an isolated portion of the cliff

1 Joint or fault in resistant rock

6 The stack is undercut and collapses to leave a stump, which is covered up at high tide

2 Corrasion and hydraulic action of waves widens the weakness in the cliff to form a cave

3 Waves cut through headland to form an arch, which is continually widened at its base

Ⓝ = wave-cut notches

C   *Arch and stack formation*

Activity

Study diagram **C**, which shows how arches and stacks are formed. Imagine you have been asked to brief an animation to explain the way arches and stacks are formed. To do this you will need to:

a   Design a storyboard to show the animator the six different stages. This storyboard should have six boxes, one below the other, which are big enough to draw clear pictures of each of the six stages. It also needs room next to each box to write notes for the animator.

b   In the first box, sketch out what the animator should show first: a joint or crack in a sea cliff face. Add notes to make sure the animator makes it clear that this cliff face is going to erode backwards (from right to left) through the animation.

c   In the second box, sketch out the stage in which corrasion and hydraulic action wide the crack into a cave. Maybe the animation should zoom in to show how these processes work?

d   Use the rest of the storyboard boxes to complete the remaining stages of the animation brief.

Compare your brief with animations of arch and stack formation on the internet. Can you find one as good as your brief out there?

Study tip

Practise drawing annotated diagrams to describe the formation of these features of erosion.

∞**links**

Good diagrams of coastal features can be found at **www.georesources. co.uk/leld.htm**.

Check out Geography at the Movies at **www.gatm.org.uk**

7.5 Coastal erosion at Swanage, Dorset

OS map study: coastal erosion at Swanage, Dorset

The coast at Swanage in Dorset is a classic stretch of coastline in the UK. There are several of the key features of erosion that you have been studying such as headlands, bays, cliffs, arches and stacks (photo **B**).

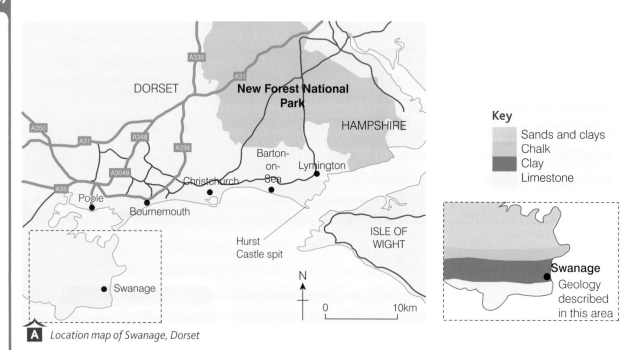

A Location map of Swanage, Dorset

Key
Sands and clays
Chalk
Clay
Limestone

Swanage
Geology described in this area

B Old Harry Stacks and the Foreland, Dorset

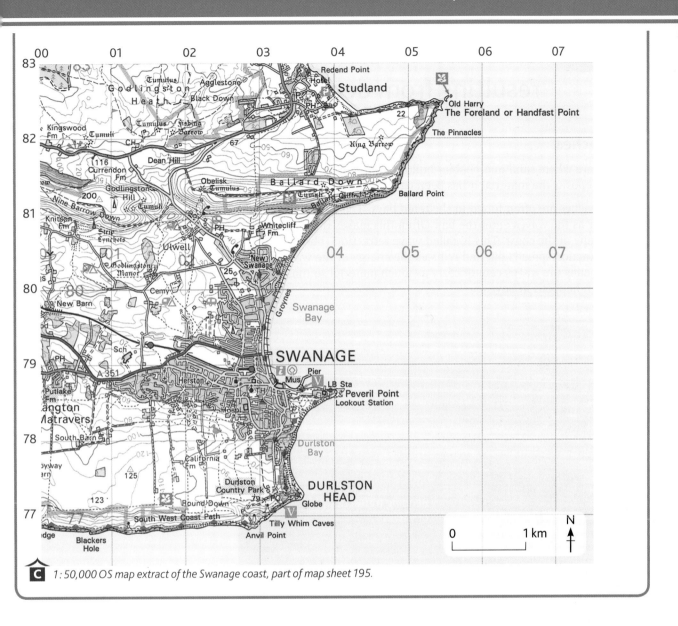

C 1 : 50,000 OS map extract of the Swanage coast, part of map sheet 195.

Activities

1 Study map extract **C**. This shows part of the Swanage coast.

a The Foreland, Peveril Point and Durlston Head are all examples of which coastal landform? Are they:

- headlands
- stacks
- wavecut platforms?

b In which grid square is the Foreland? Is it:

- 0377
- 0478
- 0582?

2 Study map **A** and map extract **C**.

a Why have headlands formed where there is chalk or limestone and bays formed where there is clay?

b Look at Swanage Bay on map extract **C**. What are the 'groynes' that are labelled on the map, and what is their purpose?

3 Study photo **B** and map extract **C**.

a What are the features labelled A, B and C on the photo?

b What processes of erosion have led to the formation of feature A?

c Use map extract **C** to give the local name of feature C.

7.6 What are the distinctive landforms resulting from deposition?

Beaches

Beaches are where sand and pebbles build up. They are found where the sea deposits the material it has been carrying.

Sandy beaches are often found in sheltered bays. The water gets shallower as the waves enter the bay. Often this makes the waves bend in the shape of the coast. This is called wave refraction (photo **A**). Wave refraction spreads out and reduces the energy of the waves. Less energy means the waves cannot carry as much material so that's why deposition happens in bays.

Key terms

Spit: a finger of new land made of sand or shingle, jutting out into the sea from the coast.

Salt marsh: low-lying coastal wetland mostly extending between high and low tide.

Bar: a spit that has grown across a bay.

Sea

Bending (refraction) of waves

Land

A *Wave refraction at the head of a bay*

Pebble beaches are often found in areas where cliffs are being eroded and where there are higher-energy waves, such as along the south coast of the UK. These stronger waves carry away the sand and leave behind the heavier pebbles.

Ridges or berms are common features of a beach (photo **B**). They are small ridges of pebbles that build up at high-tide lines. Some beaches may have several berms for different high-tide levels.

Spits

A **spit** is a long, narrow finger of sand or shingle jutting out into the sea from the land (diagram **C**). As material is moved along the coast by longshore drift, it is deposited where the coastline changes direction or where there is a river mouth. Gradually, as more and more sediment is deposited, it gets bigger and grows into the sea. The tip of the spit can become curved as it is hit by waves from different directions.

B *Berms on a beach at Deal on the Kent coast*

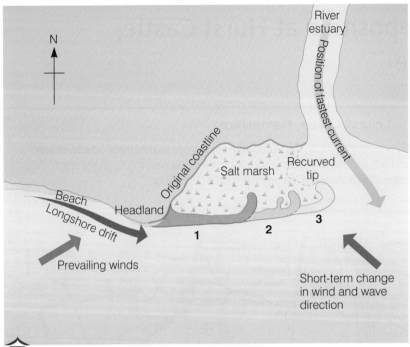

C   *The formation of a spit*

D   *Coastal bar at Slapton Ley, Devon*

Did you know ???????

At 15 km in length Orford Ness on the Suffolk coast is the longest vegetated shingle spit in Europe.

Over time, the sediment builds up until it breaks the surface of the water to form new land. This is a spit. Grass, bushes and eventually trees will grow there. On the land side of a spit where the water is calm, mudflats and **salt marshes** form. These are important habitats for plants and birds. Being close to sea level, spits may be eroded or flooded, especially during storms.

Study tip

A spit is a land feature, so it does not get covered at high tide. On a map, it will be clearly bordered by the high tide line. Be careful not to confuse it with sediment exposed only at low tide.

▉ Bars

Occasionally, a spit may grow right across a bay, trapping a lake behind it. This feature is called a **bar** (photo **D**). The lake is called lagoon.

Activity

Study diagram **C** and photo **D**. The diagram shows how a spit is formed. The photo is of a bar.

a   Draw a set of three simple diagrams to show how a spit is formed spit. Add detailed labels to describe what is happening using the text and diagram **C** to help you.

▪ In the first diagram, show material being moved along a coast and deposited on a 'corner', where the coastline changes direction suddenly. Make sure you label the direction of longshore drift.

▪ In the second diagram, show how longshore drift extends the spit out from the coast.

▪ In the third diagram, show a salt marsh forming behind the spit and show how the end of the spit gets curved over by changes in the wave direction.

b   What is the difference between a spit and a bar?

⚭ links

Information on Dungeness spit in Washington state in the USA can be found at **www.reefnews.com/reefnews/oceangeo/washngtn/dnwr.html**.

7.7 Coastal deposition at Hurst Castle, Hampshire

Skills study

OS map study: coastal deposition at Hurst Castle, Hampshire

Hurst Castle spit (map extract **A** and photo **B**) is a shingle spit on the Hampshire coast close to the city of Southampton. Longshore drift has been shaping the landform for hundreds of years. Henry VIII built a castle near the tip of the spit to help defend England. Today, English Heritage manages the castle and it is a popular tourist destination.

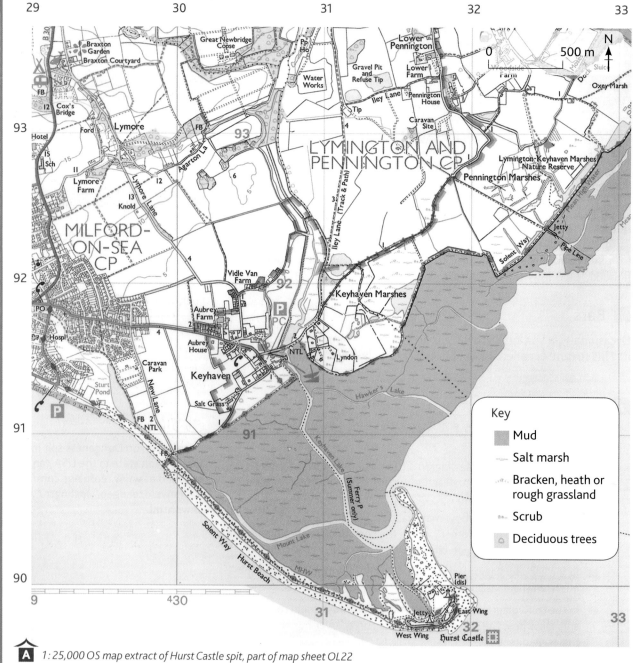

Key
- Mud
- Salt marsh
- Bracken, heath or rough grassland
- Scrub
- Deciduous trees

A *1 : 25,000 OS map extract of Hurst Castle spit, part of map sheet OL22*

B *Hurst Castle spit, Hampshire*

Activities

1 Study map extract **A** and photo **B**.

a In what direction is the photo looking?

b How long is the spit? Is it roughly 1 km, 2 km or 3 km in length?

c Use a ruler to measure the width of the spit in grid square 3090. Give your answer to the nearest 50 m. Remember that the spit is the area of land above the high-tide line, shown by the bold blue line on the map.

d Which symbol is used to indicate that the spit is made of shingle (pebbles)?

e In what direction do you think longshore drift is operating? Explain your answer.

2 Study map extract **A**.

a Draw a sketch map to show the spit and its main features. Use a pencil for the sketch and a pen for adding labels.

b Begin by drawing a grid of squares to represent the grid squares on the map. This will enable you to copy the spit accurately. Use the same scale: 4 cm = 1 km or enlarge it if you wish.

c Carefully draw the spit. Remember to follow the bold blue high-tide line. This marks the outline of the spit.

d Locate Hurst Castle on your map and label it.

e Add the following additional labels to your sketch:

■ spit

■ recurved tip

■ salt marsh

■ direction of longshore drift.

f Complete your sketch by adding a north point, scale and title.

7.8 How will rising sea levels affect the coastal zone?

The causes of rising sea levels

One of the effects of global warming is that sea-levels will rise. Over the last 15 years, sea levels have risen around the world by about 3 mm a year. By the end of the century sea levels will have risen between 28 and 43 cm.

In this section you will learn

the causes and possible consequences of rising sea levels on the coastal zone.

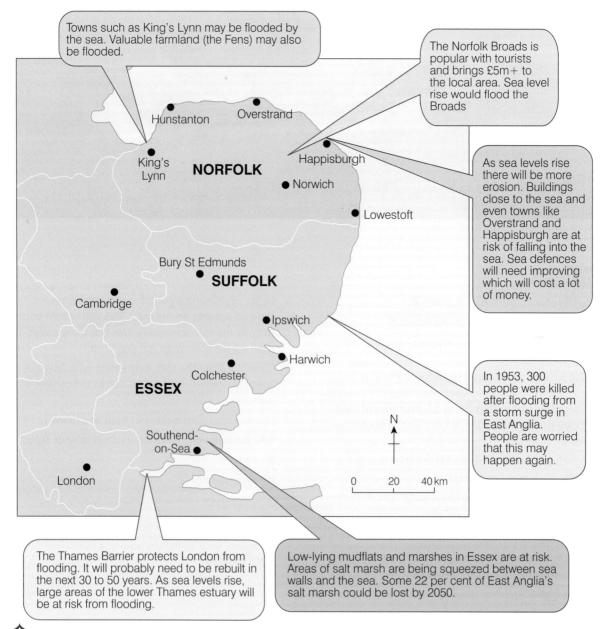

Towns such as King's Lynn may be flooded by the sea. Valuable farmland (the Fens) may also be flooded.

The Norfolk Broads is popular with tourists and brings £5m+ to the local area. Sea level rise would flood the Broads

As sea levels rise there will be more erosion. Buildings close to the sea and even towns like Overstrand and Happisburgh are at risk of falling into the sea. Sea defences will need improving which will cost a lot of money.

In 1953, 300 people were killed after flooding from a storm surge in East Anglia. People are worried that this may happen again.

The Thames Barrier protects London from flooding. It will probably need to be rebuilt in the next 30 to 50 years. As sea levels rise, large areas of the lower Thames estuary will be at risk from flooding.

Low-lying mudflats and marshes in Essex are at risk. Areas of salt marsh are being squeezed between sea walls and the sea. Some 22 per cent of East Anglia's salt marsh could be lost by 2050.

Hunstanton · Overstrand · King's Lynn · **NORFOLK** · Happisburgh · Norwich · Lowestoft · Bury St Edmunds · **SUFFOLK** · Cambridge · Ipswich · Harwich · Colchester · **ESSEX** · Southend-on-Sea · London

N

0 20 40 km

A *Possible impact of sea-level rise in East Anglia*

The main cause of sea-level rise is that seawater expands as it gets hotter. This is called thermal expansion. The melting of ice on the land, for example from glaciers on Greenland, will also increase the amount of water in the oceans. Melting sea ice, such as from the Arctic, will have no direct effect on sea levels.

The actual amount of sea-level rise will vary from place to place.

In the UK, East Anglia (diagram **A**) is likely to be hardest hit as rising sea levels threaten coastal defences and natural ecosystems. In the rest of the world, huge low-lying areas such as Bangladesh and islands such as the Maldives and Tuvalu could disappear.

Already, two Pacific islands have been submerged, and many others have been flooded. Since more than 70 per cent of the world's population live on coastal plains, the effects of rising sea levels are likely to be devastating.

Did you know ??????

If sea levels rise by 1m, several major cities of the world will be affected by flooding including London, Tokyo and New York.

Study tip

Try to understand the meaning of economic (money), social (people), environmental (natural world) and political (decision-making) when describing the possible impacts of sea-level rise.

links

http://.floodlondon.com is an excellent source of information.

www.floodlondon.com looks at what might happen if London was flooded.

B   *The islands of the Maldives are under threat from sea-level rise*

Activities

1   Study diagram **A**, which lists some possible impacts of rising sea levels for East Anglia.

Using the information in this diagram, copy out and complete the following sentences:

Sea level rises could have a major impact on people's lives in ____ Anglia because it is a ____-lying part of the UK. If the Norfolk Broads were flooded, the area would lose a lot of money from ____. Sea defences would have to be strengthened to protect buildings from ____. Valuable farmland would be flooded and salt ____ would be lost. There could be a greater risk from storm ____.

Words to use in this activity:

erosion   low   surges   tourism   marshes   East

2   This activity will involve internet research.

a   Select a coastal zone under threat from sea-level rise, such as Bangladesh, the Mississippi delta in the USA or the Maldives.

b   Conduct an internet search ('sea level rise + Maldives', for example) to find out about the problems sea-level rise would cause for your chosen coastal zone.

c   Draw a diagram like diagram **A** for your chosen coastal zone, using a photo or map of your locality in the centre.

7.9 How can cliff collapse cause problems for people at the coast?

There are many reasons why cliffs collapse.

- Freeze-thaw weathering can weaken cliffs resulting in rockfalls.
- Mass movement, such as **slumping** and **sliding**, are common at the coast.
- Waves can undercut cliffs leading to collapse.

Various parts of the UK coastline are at risk of cliff collapse, including Christchurch Bay in Hampshire, where Barton-on-Sea is sited.

> **In this section you will learn**
>
> the causes and consequences of cliff collapse for people living in the coastal zone.

Case study

Barton-on-Sea, Hampshire

Find the small settlement of Barton-on-Sea on map **B**. This stretch of coastline in Christchurch Bay has been affected by coastal erosion and cliff collapse for a long time. Over the years a number of buildings, and most recently a café, have been lost to the sea.

Many coastal defences have been built to try to stop coastal erosion. However, in 2008 there was a new **landslip** (photo **A**). This has once again raised concerns among local people about the risk of cliff collapse. An older development of houses in Barton Court is just 20 m from the cliff edge. The local authority predicts that the houses will be lost in the next 10 to 20 years.

A Cliff collapse at Barton-on-Sea, 2008

There are several reasons why the cliffs at Barton-on-Sea may collapse:

- The rocks are weak sands and clays. They are easily eroded by the sea.

- Permeable sands sit on top of impermeable clay. This means that water saturates the cliffs as it can't soak through the clay. The increase in water pressure within the cliffs (called pore water pressure) encourages collapse.

- This coastline faces the direct force of the prevailing wind. With a long fetch, the waves at Barton-on-Sea are powerful and can carry out a lot of erosion. Rates of erosion have been as much as 2 m a year in places.

- Several small streams (with the local name 'Bunny') flow towards the coast but disappear into the permeable sands before they reach the sea. This adds to the amount of water in the cliffs.

- Buildings on the cliff tops have increased the weight on the cliffs, making them more at risk of collapse. They can also interfere with drainage.

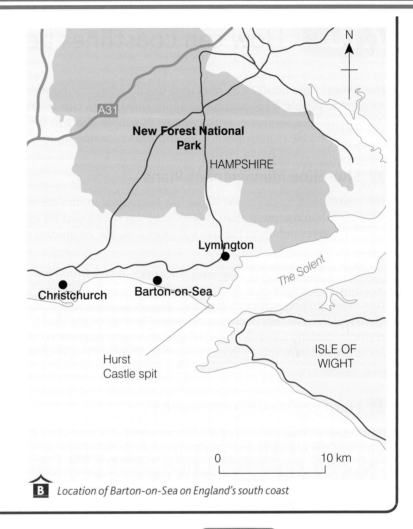

B *Location of Barton-on-Sea on England's south coast*

Activity

Study photo **A**, which shows the cliff collapse at Barton-on-Sea in 2008.

a   What evidence is there that there has been a cliff collapse?

b   Estimate the drop in the grass surface due to the collapse. The person standing next to the collapse is probably about 1.5 m tall.

c   Describe how the following factors have made the cliffs prone to collapse:

- the weakness of the cliffs (soft clay and sand)

- the permeable sand layer on top of the impermeable clay

- buildings near the cliff

- the cliffs facing towards the south west.

d   The car park in the photo is often full. Why do you think this is a popular place for visitors?

e   Why might the owner of the white house find it difficult to sell the house?

Key terms

Slumping: a type of mass movement involving material moving downhill under its own weight.

Sliding: a type of mass movement involving material moving downhill on a flat surface (a landslide).

Landslip: a type of mass movement common at the coast involving material slipping downhill usually along a curved slip surface.

⊂⊃ links

A website with fantastic photos is at www.southampton.ac.uk/~imw/barteros.htm

Study tip

Cliff collapse usually happens for many reasons. Make this clear in any explanation you need to give.

7.10 How can coastlines be managed?

The coastal zone needs to be managed to find a balance between nature and people. The coastline is under threat from cliff collapse, flooding and sea-level rise. With millions of people living in the coastal zone, sustainable management is an important consideration.

Shoreline Management Plans

The coastline of England and Wales has been divided into areas. A **Shoreline Management Plan** (SMP) has been developed for each area. This gives details of the natural processes, the environment and human uses.

Plans have been made to deal with coastlines at risk from erosion or flooding. In most cases, a decision has been made to 'hold the line'. This means taking action to keep the line of the coast as it is now. Occasionally, planners decide to 'advance the line' of the coast, for example, making a beach larger, to give the coast more protection. There are different things that can be done if authorities do decide to take action.

Hard engineering approaches

Hard engineering means building structures to try to control the actions of the sea and protect buildings from flooding and erosion. For many decades people have used hard engineering structures such as sea walls (photo **A**) and groynes (photo **B**). Table **C** gives examples of hard engineering used in coastal management.

In this section you will learn

the options of coastal management including hard and soft engineering and managed retreat.

Key terms

Shoreline Management Plan (SMP): an integrated coastal management plan for a stretch of coastline in England and Wales.

Hard engineering: building artificial structures such as sea walls aimed at controlling natural processes.

Soft engineering: a sustainable approach to managing the coast without using artificial structures.

Did you know ??????

In 1902 a sea wall was built at Galveston, USA after the devastating hurricane of 1900. The wall is 16 km long, 5.2 m high and 4.9 m thick at its base. So far, it has never been overtopped.

A The sea wall at Dawlish, Devon

B Groynes at Eastbourne

C *Hard engineering schemes*

Hard engineering	Description	Cost	Advantages	Disadvantages
Sea wall	Concrete or rock barrier built at the foot of cliffs or at the top of a beach. Has a curved face to reflect the waves back into the sea. Usually 3–5 m high.	Up to £10 million per km (south sea zones).	• Effective at stopping the sea. • Often has a walkway or promenade for people to walk along.	• Can block views and is unnatural to look at. • Very expensive to build and look after.
Groynes Beach sand	Timber or rock structures built out to sea from the coast. They trap sediment being moved by longshore drift, and broaden the beach. The wider beach acts as a buffer to the incoming waves, reducing wave attack at the coast.	Up to £5,000 per metre.	• A bigger beach can attract more tourists. • Provide useful structures for fishing. • Not too expensive.	• They stop other beaches from getting the sediment and often lead to more erosion elsewhere. The problem is not so much solved as shifted. • Groynes are unnatural and can be unattractive.
Rock armour	Piles of large boulders dumped at the foot of a cliff. The rocks force waves to break, absorbing their energy and protecting the cliffs. Barges are used to transport the boulders by sea.	Approximately £1,000 –£4,000 per metre.	• Quite cheap and easy to look after. • Can provide interest to the coast. Often used for fishing.	• Rocks come from other parts of the coastline or even from abroad. Can be expensive to transport. • They do not fit in with the local geology. • Can block views.

Hard engineering approaches are less commonly used today. They are expensive and look unnatural. They can cause problems elsewhere. For example, wave patterns can be altered which can increase rates of erosion further along the coast.

Soft engineering approaches

Soft engineering approaches (table **D**) try to fit in and work with the natural processes. They do not involve large man-made structures. They are often cheaper and better for the environment. Soft engineering approaches such as beach nourishment (photo **E**) are more sustainable. They are becoming increasingly popular options today in protecting the UK's coast from erosion and flooding.

Key terms

Sea wall: concrete or rock barrier built at the foot of cliffs or at the top of a beach.

Groyne: timber or rock structure built out to sea to trap sediment being moved by longshore drift.

Rock armour: piles of large boulders dumped at the foot of a cliff to protect it by forcing waves to break and absorbing their energy.

D *Soft engineering schemes*

Soft engineering	Description	Cost	Advantages	Disadvantages
Beach nourishment	Adding sand or shingle to a beach to make it higher or broader. The sediment is usually from local areas so that it blends in with the existing beach material.	Approximately £3,000 per metre	• Quite cheap and easy to maintain. • Blends in with existing beach. • A bigger beach can attract more tourists.	• Needs constant maintenance unless structures are built to retain the beach, such as groynes.
Dune regeneration Marram grass Fence	Sand dunes are good buffers to the sea but they are easily damaged, especially by walkers. Marram grass can be planted to stabilise the dunes and help them to develop. Areas can be fenced to keep people off newly planted dunes.	Approximately £2,000 per 100 m	• Keeps a natural coastal environment that is popular with people and wildlife. • Quite cheap.	• Takes time to plant the marram grass and fence off areas. • People do not like being stopped from accessing certain areas. • Can be damaged by storms.
Marsh creation (managed retreat) Breached sea wall Sea New salt marsh created	This involves allowing low-lying coastal areas to be flooded by the sea to become salt marshes. This is an example of managed retreat. Salt marshes are effective barriers to the sea.	Depends on the value of the land. Arable land costs somewhere in the region of £5,000 to £10,000 per hectare	• A cheap option compared with hard engineering. • Creates habitat for wildlife.	• Land will be lost as it is flooded by sea water. • Farmers or landowners will need to be paid for this lost land.

Managed retreat

Another option for coastal management is to allow the coastline to retreat (move back). This is called **managed retreat**. It is a real option if there is a high risk of flooding or cliff collapse and where the land is low value. For example, it is not worth spending lots of money protecting poor quality grazing land (see Marsh creation in table **D**). As sea levels rise, this approach is likely to become increasingly popular.

> **Key term**
>
> **Managed retreat**: allowing controlled flooding of low-lying coastal areas or cliff collapse in areas where the value of the land is low.

> **Study tip**
>
> Be clear about the differences between hard engineering and soft engineering. Appreciate that there is a great deal of debate about the option of managed retreat. Make sure that you know both sides of the argument.

E *Beach nourishment in operation at Poole in Dorset*

Activity

Use tables **C** and **D** to help you answer the following questions.

 a Why is a sea wall an example of hard engineering?

 b What are the advantages and disadvantages of a sea wall?

 d What are groynes and what are they designed to do?

 e What problems can groynes cause for other beaches?

 f Beach nourishment is a good example of soft engineering. What is soft engineering?

 g Outline some of the advantages of beach nourishment.

 h Imagine a local council wishes to defend a 1 km stretch of coastline.

  ■ Use tables **C** and **D** to calculate the costs for each of the following: a sea wall, groynes, rock armour, beach nourishment. Remember that all amounts need to relate to a 1 km length of coast.

  ■ Which solution would you recommend and why?

Coastal defences at Minehead

Case study

Minehead on the north coast of Somerset is an important tourist resort. There is a large Butlin's resort and every year it is visited by many thousands of people.

By the early 1990s it became clear that the sea defences were not going to be enough to protect the town in the future. The Environment Agency developed a plan to defend the town and improve it. Work started in 1997 and the new sea defences were opened in 2001. The total cost was £12.3 m, which was a lot less than it would have cost to repair the town after storm damage (estimated at £21m).

The main features of the scheme (diagram **F**) are:

■ A 0.6 m high sea wall with a curved front to stop waves going into the town. The top of the wall is curved so people cannot walk on it.

■ Rock armour at the base of the wall to break up some of the wave energy.

■ Beach nourishment (sand) to build up the beach by 2 m in height. This forces the waves to break further out to sea. It provides a great sandy beach for tourists.

■ Four rock groynes to help keep the beach where it is and stop longshore drift moving sand to the east.

■ A wide walkway with seating areas alongside the sea wall. This is popular with tourists and local people.

The scheme has been very successful. Not only does it protect the town from storms and high tides, but it has also made the seafront more attractive (photo **G**).

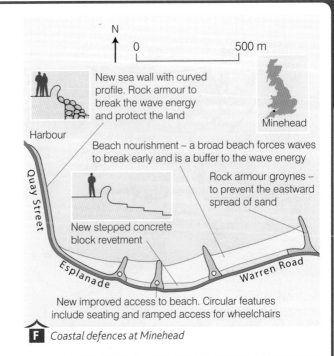

F *Coastal defences at Minehead*

G *The beach at Minehead*

Coastal defences at Wallasea Island

Wallasea Island is a low-lying coastal island formed where the River Crouch and River Roach meet in Essex (map extract **H**). Until recently it has been mostly used for growing wheat.

The government decided to allow limited flooding on the northern part of the island by breaching the old sea defences (map extract **H**). The new mudflats and salt marsh will help to protect the new sea wall and offer more protection to land and property to the south.

The £7.5 m scheme aims to replace bird habitats lost to development, improve flood defences on the island and create new leisure opportunities.

In 2006 the old sea wall was breached to allow 115 hectares of land to be flooded (photo **I**). Eventually the flooded area will contain islands and a number of salty lakes. Much of it will revert to salt marsh, providing a much-needed breeding ground for birds. The site is managed by the RSPB.

I *Managed flooding on Wallasea Island*

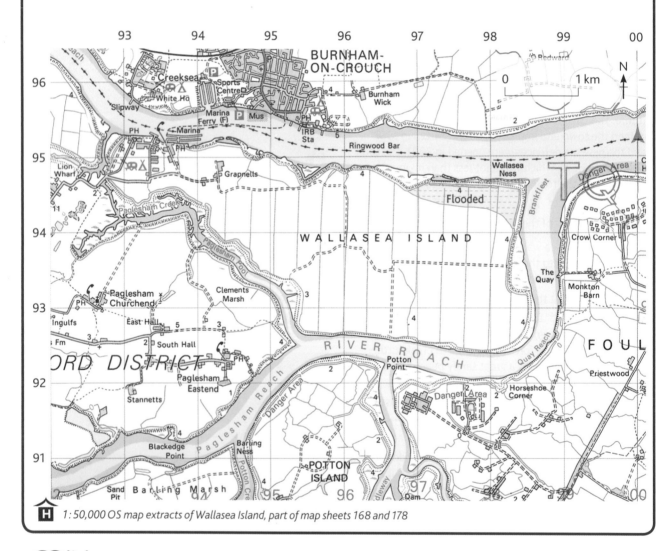

H *1 : 50,000 OS map extracts of Wallasea Island, part of map sheets 168 and 178*

∞links

The Geography Site has information at
www.geography-site.co.uk/pages/physical/coastal/defences.html.

7.11 What are salt marshes and why are they special?

Salt marshes are low-lying areas near to the coast which are sometimes flooded by the sea. They are often rich in plants, birds and animals (photo **A**).

A　*Keyhaven Marshes*

A salt marsh starts when mud and silt build up in a sheltered part of the coastline, for example in the lee of a spit or bar. As more deposition takes place, the mud appears above the sea to form mudflats. Plants such as cordgrass soon start to grow on the mudflats. These early plants are called **pioneer plants**. Cordgrass can grow in the saltwater and its long roots stop it from being swept away by the waves and the tides. Its tangle of roots also helps to trap sediment and stabilise the mud.

As the level of the mud rises, it is less frequently covered by water. Rainwater begins to wash out some of the salt and rotting plants improves the fertility of the soil. More new plants such as sea asters start grow and gradually, over hundreds of years, a succession of plants develop. This is known as a **vegetation succession** (diagram **B**).

In this section you will learn

the characteristics of a salt marsh environment

sustainable approaches to the management of salt marshes.

Key terms

Pioneer plant: the first plant species to colonise an area that are well adapted to living in a harsh environment.

Vegetation succession: a sequence of vegetation species colonising an environment.

Did you know ???????

In France, salt is produced commercially from salt marshes.

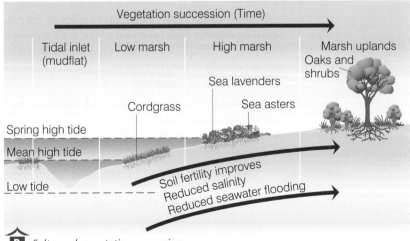

B　*Salt marsh vegetation succession*

Keyhaven Marshes, Hampshire

Keyhaven Marshes is an area of salt marsh formed in the lee of Hurst Castle spit (map **A**, page 156). It supports a range of habitats including grassland, scrub, salt marsh and reed beds. This variety of habitats means that there are lots of wildlife in the area (table **C**).

C *Common wildlife species found at Keyhaven Marshes*

Species detail	Image	Species detail	Image
Plant: cordgrass – spiky, untidy-looking grass that grows fast on mudflats		Bird: ringed plover – feeds intertidally and nests on the salt marsh	
Plant: sea lavender – attractive, colourful flowers attract wildlife		Butterfly: common blue – resident butterfly commonly found on higher marshes	
Bird: oystercatcher – feeds and nests in salt marshes		Spider: wold spider – clings for hours to submerged stems of cordgrass waiting for low tide and food	

In common with many areas of salt marsh in the UK, Keyhaven Marshes is under threat:

- The salt marsh is getting smaller by up to 6 m a year. Further sea-level rise threatens a 'squeeze' of the salt marsh as it lies between a low sea wall built in the early 1990s and the sea.

- The salt marsh has been under threat from the breaching of Hurst Castle spit during severe storms. In December 1989 storms pushed part of the ridge over the top of the salt marsh. This left a stretch of salt marsh some 50–80 m in length exposed to the sea. It disappeared in less than three months.

- More people want to visit the marshes. Careful management is needed to stop damage by trampling, parking and pollution. The area is popular with sailors who use the many creeks to moor their boats.

- In 1996 rock armour and beach nourishment were used to increase the height and width of the spit to try to stop breaching. Since the completion of the £5 m sea defences, the spit has not been breached and Keyhaven Marshes seems safe … at least for the time being.

- Keyhaven Marshes is an important site for wildfowl and wading birds. The area is officially a Site of Special Scientific Interest (SSSI) and part of the salt marsh is also a National Nature Reserve. This means that the area is carefully monitored and managed. Access is limited and development restricted.

- For the future, with sea levels expected to rise by 6 mm a year, the big issue concerns the 'squeeze' between the low sea wall and the rising sea.

D *The salt marsh at Keyhaven*

∞ **links**

An excellent case study based on Chichester harbour can be accessed at **www.conservancy.co.uk/learn/ wildlife/saltmarsh.htm**.

Activities

1 Study the photos **A** and **D** together with the other information about Keyhaven Marshes.

a Describe the landscape of the saltmarsh.

b Cordgrass is a 'pioneer species'. What does this mean?

c How is cordgrass well suited to living in a salt marsh?

d Use table **C** to describe how Keyhaven attracts a variety of wildlife.

e Use the internet to find your own photo of Keyhaven marshes. Stick it in your work and add some labels to describe its characteristics.

2 Using the information about Keyhaven Marshes from the Case Study box, answer these questions:

a How fast is the salt marsh retreating at Keyhaven Marshes (give your answer in metres per year).

b What is an SSSI and why has Keyhaven Marshes been awarded this status?

c What damage could people do to the salt marsh environment at Keyhaven Marshes?

d How did the breaching of Hurst Castle spit in 1989 damage the salt marsh environment at Keyhaven Marshes (use facts and figures in your answer)?

e What has been done to try and protect the marshes from human pressures?

f What has been done to try and protect the marshes from storm damage and coastal erosion?

■ Exponential growth

The world's population has grown exponentially (more and more quickly). The fastest period of population growth was during the late 20th and early 21st centuries. By 2000, there were 10 times as many people as there had been in 1700. Between 2008 and 2009, 220,980 people were added to world population *every day*. In 2011 the world's population reached 7 billion. Population is likely to rise to 9 billion by 2050 and finally peak a century later in 2150 at 10.8 billion. This should be followed by a more stable period of **zero growth** or even **natural decrease (ND)**.

Population growth is usually shown as a line graph. **Exponential growth** makes a line that becomes steeper over time, taking the shape of a letter J. Today, growth rates are slowing down (although the numbers being added daily are still high), so the shape of the graph is levelling off into an S curve (graph **A**).

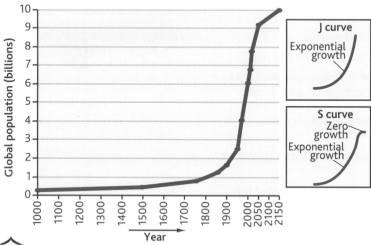

A *Global population growth*

Key terms

Zero growth: a population in balance. Birth rate is equal to death rate, so there is no growth or decrease.

Natural decrease (ND): the death rate is greater than the birth rate.

Exponential growth: a pattern where the growth rate constantly increases – often shown as a J-curve graph.

Birth rate (BR): the number of babies born per 1,000 people per year.

Death rate (DR): the number of deaths per 1,000 people per year.

Natural change: the difference between birth rate and death rate, given as a percentage.

Natural increase (NI): the birth rate is greater than the death rate.

Activities

1 Study table **B**. This table gives data on European population changes between 1800 and 2010.

a Use the data from the table to draw a line graph for Europe.

■ Plot the years along the x-axis.

■ Plot the population data along the y-axis.

b Describe the population growth pattern that you have drawn. Give details of the graph's shape and quote figures from the graph to support your answer. Use key terms such as exponential, J-shaped, S-shaped, levelling off, zero growth and population decline.

■ Birth rate and death rate

Birth rate (BR) is the number of babies born alive per 1,000 people every year. Today, birth rates for different countries varies at between 5 per 1,000 per year and 40 per 1,000 per year.

Death rate (DR) is the number of deaths per 1,000 people every year. Usually, death rates lie between 5 deaths per 1,000 people per year and 20 deaths per 1,000 people per year. Things like health epidemics, famine and war can all hugely increase the death rate. Between 1348 and 1353 the Black Death killed about a third of all the people in Europe.

Birth and death rates are given per 1,000 people so that countries of different sizes can be compared. Huge nations like China (1.3 billion people) and India (1.2 billion people) can be compared with smaller countries such as Singapore (4.7 million people) and Luxembourg (503,302 people) (2011 figures).

■ Natural change

Natural change is the difference between birth and death rates in a country. Until recently, all countries have had higher birth rates than death rates so they have had **natural increase (NI)**. Today, some countries birth rates have dropped so much that they are now experiencing **natural decrease (ND)**. This means the population is getting smaller.

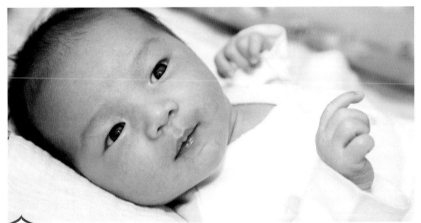

C Birth rate is the number of babies born for every 1,000 people every year

D Death rate is the number of deaths per 1,000 people every year

B *European population, 1800–2010*

Year	Population (millions)
1800	203
1900	408
1950	547
1975	676
1985	706
1995	727
2005	725
2010	830

Did you know ??????

According to United Nations estimates, the 7 billionth person was born on 31 October 2011. An organisation called Plan International, which works for more rights for children, chose a baby girl born on that day as a symbol for this 7 billionth person. They picked a baby called Nargis, born just after midnight (UK time) on 21 October, in India.

Examples

Natural change calculations

UK

BR = 10.7 per 1,000 per year

DR = 10.1 per 1,000 per year

NI = $BR - DR$

    = 10.7 – 10.1

    = 0.6

Natural change is always given as a percentage, so the answer must be divided by 10.

Therefore:

NI = 0.06% per year

Czech Republic

BR = 9.0 per 1,000 per year

DR = 10.6 per 1,000 per year

ND = $DR - BR$

    = 10.6 – 9.0

    = 1.6

ND = 0.16% per year (sometimes written as –0.16%)

Population change and development

Data on birth rates, death rates and natural increase or decrease give us information on the level of development of a country. Whatever their stage of development, all countries now have low death rates. People often think that the death rate in countries at lower stages of development must be high because people are poor and **life expectancy** may not be long, but this is not true. Two factors affect the death rate:

- health care has improved in poorer countries, lowering death rates
- having so many people under the age of 15 reduces the chance of death.

Death rates in countries at higher stages of development are often higher. This is because their populations are older, causing the death rate to rise. Birth rate is a better indicator of development. This is because, even though family size has got smaller in most countries at lower stages of development, parents in richer parts of the world still have fewer children.

E *Birth and death rates for selected countries, 2011*

Country	Continent	Birth rate (per 1,000)	Death rate (per 1,000)
Afghanistan	Asia	37.8	17.4
Brazil	South America	17.8	6.7
China	Asia	12.3	7.0
Czech Rep.	Europe	8.7	10.9
Ethiopia	Africa	43.0	11.0
France	Europe	12.3	8.8
Germany	Europe	8.3	10.9
Hong Kong	Asia	7.5	7.1
India	Asia	21.0	7.5
Ireland	Europe	16.1	6.3
Italy	Europe	9.2	9.8
Nigeria	Africa	35.5	16.1
Pakistan	Asia	24.8	6.9
Romania	Europe	9.6	11.8
South Korea	Asia	8.6	6.3
UK	Europe	12.3	9.3
USA	North America	13.8	8.4

Key term

Life expectancy: the number of years a person is expected to live, usually taken from birth.

Activities

2 Study table **E**. This shows birth rates and death rates for a range of different countries.

a Calculate the natural change for the following three countries. Set out your calculation clearly so that your teacher can follow each stage of your working.

- Afghanistan
- China
- UK

You can remind yourself how to calculate natural change on page 171.

b Death rates are now low in countries at every stage of development. Give two reasons to explain this.

c Would you expect birth rates in rich countries to be:

- higher than in poor countries because rich people can afford to have more children?
- lower than in poor countries because poor families need lots of children to help farm and look after their parents when they get old?

8.2 What is the demographic transition m...

Demography is the study of population. Transition means change. The **demographic transition model (DTM)** is a way of explaining how populations change over time. This model is shown in diagram **A**.

The model explains birth and death rate patterns across the world and through time. It includes the main period of a country's development and shows the links between demographic and economic changes.

The diagram is divided into five stages, showing change from high birth and death rates in Stage 1 to much lower ones in Stages 4 and 5.

In this section you will learn

the trends in the demographic transition model

how to interpret the demographic transition model and use it to compare the situations of different countries.

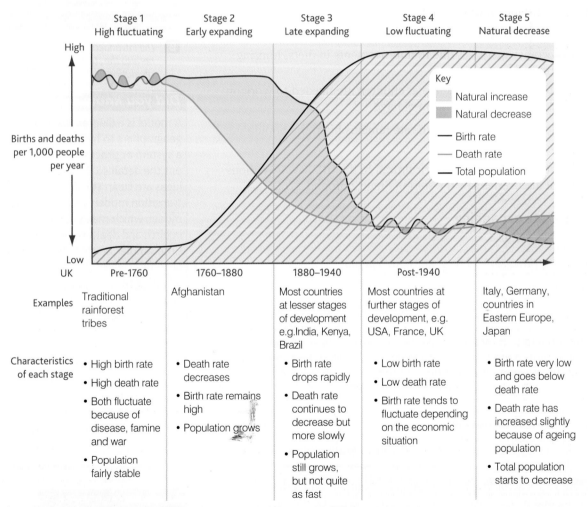

	Stage 1 High fluctuating	Stage 2 Early expanding	Stage 3 Late expanding	Stage 4 Low fluctuating	Stage 5 Natural decrease
UK	Pre-1760	1760–1880	1880–1940	Post-1940	
Examples	Traditional rainforest tribes	Afghanistan	Most countries at lesser stages of development e.g.India, Kenya, Brazil	Most countries at further stages of development, e.g. USA, France, UK	Italy, Germany, countries in Eastern Europe, Japan
Characteristics of each stage	• High birth rate • High death rate • Both fluctuate because of disease, famine and war • Population fairly stable	• Death rate decreases • Birth rate remains high • Population grows	• Birth rate drops rapidly • Death rate continues to decrease but more slowly • Population still grows, but not quite as fast	• Low birth rate • Low death rate • Birth rate tends to fluctuate depending on the economic situation	• Birth rate very low and goes below death rate • Death rate has increased slightly because of ageing population • Total population starts to decrease

Key — Births and deaths per 1,000 people per year (High / Low)

Key
Natural increase
Natural decrease
— Birth rate
— Death rate
— Total population

 A Demographic transition model

Key term

Demographic transition model: a theoretical model that shows changes in population information (birth and death rates and population growth) over a period of time.

■ Characteristics of each stage

Stage 1 – high fluctuating

This stage of high birth and death rates happens where:

- there is poor health care and medicine
- disease outbreaks and famines are common
- there is no means of birth control.

Remote rainforest areas in the Amazon and Indonesia are the only places where this stage might happen today. These are traditional societies, largely cut off from the rest of the world. The UK was at Stage 1 before around 1760.

Stage 2 – early expanding

Countries move into stage 2 when:

- the death rate gets lower because heath care improves
- life expectancy increases due to improvements in diets, housing, sanitation and health care
- birth rate stays much the same as children are needed to work on the land and support parents in old age
- as the death rate falls and birth rate remains high, the population starts to increase.

Most economies in Stage 2 are agricultural. In the UK, new inventions and medical discoveries saw the start of Stage 2 around 1760.

Stage 3 – late expanding

In stage 3:

- the death rate keeps falling, but more slowly.
- the birth rate starts to fall quickly.

There are a number of reasons why the birth rate falls quickly. Lower rates of infant mortality (child deaths) and the increasing cost of bringing up children mean that women choose to have smaller families. Children are less likely to be able to work in factories or on the land. Increasingly during Stage 3 birth control becomes more common. The UK entered Stage 3 around 1880.

Stage 4 – low fluctuating

Birth and death rates are both low. The lines on the graph are close to each other.

Birth rate varies according to the economic situation. When the economy is growing and people have jobs and earn a good living, they are more likely to afford children. In times of unemployment and low wages, people wait to have a family until times are better. In the UK in the 1960s, the economy was growing and the birth rate rose slightly, but in the 1970s, with world economic recession, the birth rate fell again. Overall, there is still population growth, but it is slow. Birth rates in the USA have been declining since a record high in 2007. It is thought that this decline could be explained by the economic recession that began in 2008.

B *The introduction of machines heralds the start of the agricultural revolution*

Did you know ??????

A model is a diagram used by geographers to help explain a system or process. It leaves out the detail so that the basic ideas are clear. The demographic transition model is a geographical model, which makes changes in birth and death rates over time simpler, so that the pattern becomes clearer and the factors affecting these changes can be explored.

Study tip

Learn the characteristics of the five stages carefully and be able to identify the differences. Know examples of countries in each stage today and know when the UK was at each of Stages 1 to 4.

Case study

Stage 5 – natural decrease

- birth rates are very low
- death rate gets higher because the population includes more old people.

Many European countries are at Stage 5, but for different reasons. In Eastern Europe an uncertain economy puts people off having babies, while Western European economies give young women so many career opportunities that they decide to be childless or to postpone motherhood.

Investigating countries

Stage 1: Traditional rainforest tribes

In parts of Indonesia, Brazil and Ecuador, small numbers of people live with little contact with the outside world (photo **B**). They have high birth and death rates.

Stage 2: Afghanistan

Afghanistan is a very poor country, where there is war and political instability. Table **E** on page 172 shows that it has one of the world's highest birth rates at 37.8 and a much lower death rate of 17.4. Natural increase is therefore 2.04 per cent every year. Most people (79 per cent) are farmers, often nomadic (photo **D**), so need children to help farm. Cities such as Kabul, the capital, have even higher rates of natural increase because easier access to medical care reduces the death rate while high numbers of young adults (who have moved to the cities) increase the birth rate.

Stage 3: Brazil

Brazil is a newly industrialising country (NIC). Although it is a country at a lesser stage of development, it is developing fast. Brazil's population will have almost doubled between 1975 and 2015, from 108 million to 210 million people. As a Roman Catholic country, it still has a high birth rate. This is getting lower though as standards of living get better and people can see the benefits from having fewer children.

Stage 4: USA

The USA is the largest and most developed economy in the world. In 2011 it had a population of 313 million. Its population growth is mostly due to immigration. Many immigrants come from Central America, where birth rates are traditionally quite high. There are also highly trained Asian people now moving to the USA who are likely to have lower birth rates.

Stage 5: Germany

Germany's economy is almost as large as the USA, but it has moved a stage further in the demographic transition model. Many German women have very good careers and choose not to have children or have them late. Plus, Germany has an ageing population. One of the first countries to enter this stage, Germany's birth rate is well below **replacement rate**. The government has to cope with the costs of a large elderly population and a workforce which is getting smaller.

C   *Rainforest tribeswoman, Ecuador*

D   *Afghan nomads*

Key term

Replacement rate: a birth rate high enough for a generation to be the same size as the one before it.

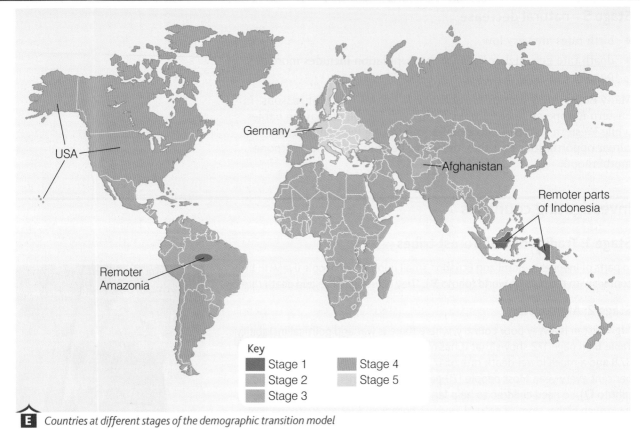

E *Countries at different stages of the demographic transition model*

Key
Stage 1
Stage 2
Stage 3
Stage 4
Stage 5

Major factors affecting population growth

Agricultural change

Changes in agriculture happen early in a country's development. Improvements in technology increases yields and mean that fewer workers are needed. In the Industrial Revolution in the UK, factories needed a large workforce, so for a while big families were a benefit. Soon, however, improvements in technology meant few people were needed for labour and smaller families were more desirable. This reduced population growth.

Urbanisation

Rural-to-urban migration is common in poorer countries as cities have greater opportunities for work, education and healthcare. There is less need for child labour in cities so, over time, families tend to become smaller than in rural areas. Highly urbanised societies tend to have lower rates of population growth.

Education

Teaching people about birth control leads to lower birth rates. Also, many parents see education as their children's best chance in life. Fewer children mean that parents have more money to spend on each child, giving them better chances. More educational opportunities tends to mean lower rates of population growth.

Key terms

Urbanisation: the growth in the proportion of people living in towns and cities

Rural-to-urban migration: moving home from a rural area to settle in a town or city.

Emancipation and status of women

The status of women changes as a country and its economy develops. This has a huge impact on the country's population.

- Better education means that women know about birth control and how to plan their families. This gives women control over the number of children they have and most choose to have fewer.

- More women now go to college or university. This means they start having children later.

- More women work and want to keep working after they have had children. Childcare is expensive so families cannot afford more than a few children.

- A better education also means more highly-skilled women who have good careers. These women may choose not to have children at all or have them much later.

All of these reasons mean that most women in developed countries choose to have fewer children. Indeed more women are choosing not to have children at all. One in five women in the UK today is childless, compared with one in ten in their mothers' generation.

F   *Women at work*

Activities

1   Study diagram **A**. This shows the demographic transition model.

a   Describe what happens in Stage 1 of the demographic transition model. Why is population low in this stage?

b   Look at Stage 2. Why does population start to grow rapidly in this stage?

c   Why does the birth rate start to drop quickly in Stage 3 of the model?

d   What happens in Stage 4 of the model. Give examples of countries at this stage.

e   Describe Stage 5. Why does population start to decrease in this stage?

2   Study map **E**. Are the following statements true or false?

a   Some remote parts of Indonesia are in Stage 1

b   Afghanistan is in Stage 4

c   African countries are in Stage 3

d   Some countries in South America are in Stage 5

e   Australia is in Stage 4

3   Why might women in Germany and other Stage 5 countries choose to have small families?

8.3 How do we use population pyramids?

Population pyramids

A population pyramid is a type of bar graph. It is used to show the **age structure** and **gender structure** of a country, city or other area.

- The horizontal axis (line along the bottom) is divided into either numbers or percentages of the population.
- The central vertical axis (line running from top to bottom) shows ages: every 10 years, every 5 years or every single year.
- The lower part of the pyramid (the base) shows the younger section of the population.
- The upper part is known as the apex and shows the elderly section of the population.

Looking at a country's population pyramid tells us a great deal about its population, such as birth rates, life expectancy and the level of economic development (or stage in the demographic transition model).

Key terms

Infant mortality: the number of babies that die under a year of age, per 1,000 live births.

Child mortality: the number of children that die under five years of age, per 1,000 live births.

In this section you will learn

how to construct a population pyramid

how to interpret population characteristics from a pyramid

how to predict likely future changes in a population.

Key terms

Age structure: the proportions of each age group in a population. This links closely to the stage a country has reached in the demographic transition model.

Gender structure: the balance between males and females in a population. Small differences can tell us a great deal about a country or city.

Population pyramids and the demographic transition model

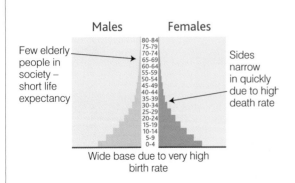

Stage 1

The Stage 1 pyramid has a very wide base due to its extremely high birth rate (up to 50 per 1,000 per year). However, **infant mortality** and **child mortality** rates are high (only half of the children born may reach their fifth birthday), so the sides of the pyramid curve in very quickly. Death rate is high in all age groups, so life expectancy is low. The result is a very narrow apex and the shortest of all the pyramids

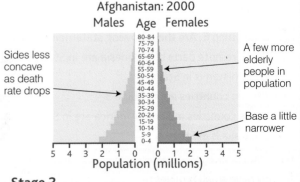

Stage 2

Stage 1 and 2 pyramids are similar in shape. Death rate begins to fall, making the sides of the Stage 2 pyramid slightly less curved. The apex shows a few more elderly people as life expectancy begins to rise.

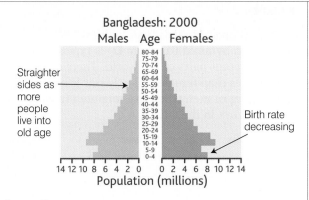

Straighter sides as more people live into old age

Birth rate decreasing

Stage 3

The narrower base shows the lower birth rate of Stage 3 countries. Birth rate is decreasing quickly. The pyramid also has straighter sides because fewer people are dying young and even more people live into old age.

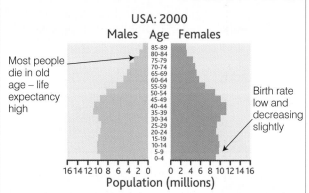

Most people die in old age – life expectancy high

Birth rate low and decreasing slightly

Stage 4

This pyramid has become straight-sided, showing a low birth rate which stays the same. High life expectancy allows most people to live into their 60s and 70s and some into their 80s.

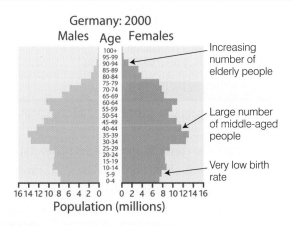

Increasing number of elderly people

Large number of middle-aged people

Very low birth rate

Stage 5

Germany has been at Stage 5 since the 1970s – one of the first countries to reduce its birth rate to this extent (photo **B**). When today's middle-aged people become elderly, there will be few adults of working age to support them. A Stage 5 population is not sustainable.

B A Stage 5 family

A Population pyramids and the demographic transition model

Future population change

Diagram **C** shows population pyramids for India in 2000, 2025 and 2050. Although India's birth rate is going to fall, its base is still wide because there are so many young adults (the group which has children). By 2025 the number of babies born each year will become stable, reducing slightly by 2050. Increasing numbers will live into old age. By 2050 most people will live into their 70s and India will have all the characteristics of a Stage 4 population.

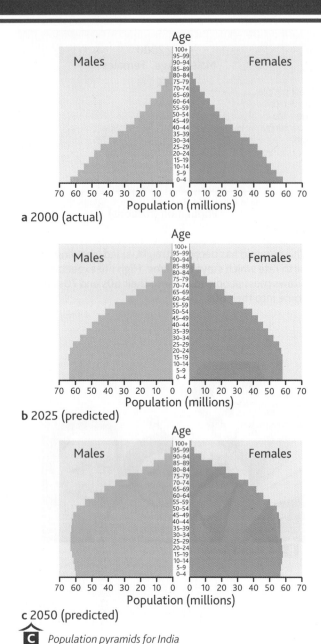

a 2000 (actual)

b 2025 (predicted)

c 2050 (predicted)

C Population pyramids for India

Kolkata

Kolkata is one of India's largest cities. The population pyramid (diagram **D**) is typical of many cities in poorer parts of the world. There are a lot more males than females. Mostly this is because of the number of men who have migrated from rural areas to work in the city.

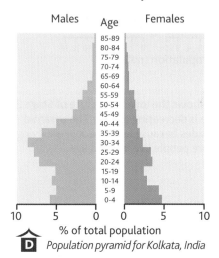

D Population pyramid for Kolkata, India

Study tip

Some tips to help you create or complete a population pyramid:

- Be careful to correctly annotate the horizontal scale.
- Mark the ends of the horizontal bars accurately.
- Use a sharp pencil and a ruler.
- If you have been asked to complete a population pyramid, make your bars as similar as possible to those that have already been drawn. .

∞ links

India's population pyramids can be used to predict future changes in the country, both demographically and economically. The same can be done for other countries. See **http://populationpyramid.net**.

Activities

1 Study diagram **C**. These are population pyramids for India.

a Which of the pyramids, **a**, **b** or **c**, shows a stage 4-type population with relatively large numbers of older people?

b Which pyramid shows a stage 3-type population, with a very youthful population?

c Would you enjoy living in a country where most of the population is under 25 years old? What would be good about it? What would not be so good (if anything)?

2 Study diagram **D**. This is a population pyramid for Kolkata, India.

a What is unusual about this pyramid, compared to others you have seen for India?

b How would you explain the distinctive shape of Kolkata's population pyramid? (Hint: what sort of people are most likely to move from the countryside into big cities?)

8.4   How can a population become sustainable?

A sustainable population is one which grows and develops slowly. This means that population growth or decline does not threaten the wellbeing of people in the future. Countries at Stage 4 of the demographic transition model, with low birth and death rates, are the most sustainable. The economy is stable or growing and the standard of living stays the same or gets better.

Stage 5 populations are not sustainable because numbers are decreasing. In Japan, they have tried to predict how long it would take the country to die out if current low birth rates continued. It is not likely to happen, but it is still a worry for the Japanese government.

In this section you will learn

the reasons for the one-child policy in China from 1979

the severity of the rules imposed

how the one-child policy has changed over recent years and the outcomes of these changes.

Will China have a sustainable population?

The early days of the one-child policy

China has the largest population of any country in the world. Between 1959 and 1961 China had a terrible famine when 35 million people died. During the 1970s the government realised that the population was growing so fast that there would soon not be enough food to feed everyone. The government stepped in to avoid another crisis.

Beginning in 1979, the one-child policy said that each couple:

- must not marry until their late 20s
- must have only one child
- must be sterilised after the first child was born or have an abortion if they became pregnant again
- would get a 5 to 10 per cent salary rise for limiting their family to one child
- would have priority housing, pension and family benefits, including free education for the single child.

Any couples disobeying the rules and having a second child were severely penalised:

- a 10 per cent salary cut was enforced (this would bankrupt many households)
- the family would have to pay for the education of both children and for health care for all the family
- second children born abroad were not penalised, but were not allowed to become Chinese citizens.

If women became pregnant for a second time, people who worked with the couple had their pay cut, so they would put pressure on the couple to have an abortion. The 'Granny Police' – older women of the community who kept everyone in line – checked up on couples of childbearing age.

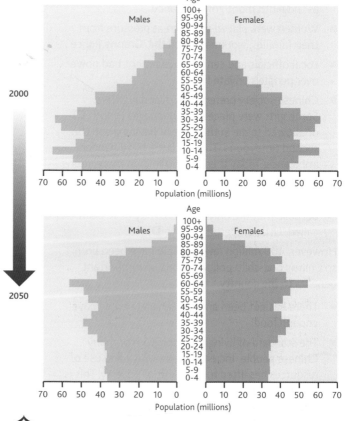

A *China's population pyramids: changes into the future?*

Case study

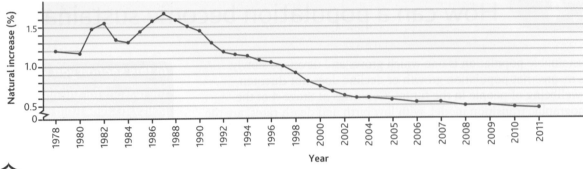

B *China's population growth through the one-child policy*

There were some exceptions to the policy. Over 80 per cent of the Chinese population is of the Han race. Minority groups could become unsustainable under the one-child policy, so these couples were allowed more than one child. In rural areas, where sons are essential to work the family land, a second pregnancy was allowed if the first child was a girl, in the hope of getting a boy next time.

The problems and benefits of the policy

Some people disagree with the policy because of some of the social effects it has:

- Some women were forced to have abortions as late as the ninth month of pregnancy.
- Women were placed under great pressure from their families, workmates and the 'Granny Police'.
- Local officials and central government had power over people's private lives.
- Chinese society prefers sons over daughters. Some girls were placed in orphanages (photo **C**) or allowed to die in the hope of having a son the second time round. This has left a huge gender imbalance. Today there are 60 million more young men than young women.
- Chinese children have a reputation for being spoilt because they are only children. They have been called 'Little Emperors' (photo **D**).

However, 400 million fewer people have been born so China's one-child policy has brought important benefits to the country.

- There has not been another famine. People have enough food.
- The standard of living has improved for many Chinese people. Increased technology and use of resources has lifted millions out of poverty. This is partly the result of the one-child policy, but new technology from other countries has helped.

Did you know ??????

There are over 15 million orphans in China, most of them girls. Missionary-run orphanages are usually very good, but in state institutions the girls are neglected and sometimes treated cruelly.

C *Children in a Chinese orphanage*

D *Only children are often spoiled*

Changes to the one-child policy in the 1990s and 2000s

- Young couples who are both only children are allowed two children, but government workers must set an example and stick to one.

- As people now have more money, more people can break the rules, pay the fine and take the other consequences of having a second child.

- Couples no longer need to obtain permission to have a first child.

- The Shanghai govenment is thinking of ways to encourage couples to have two children.

- It is now illegal to discriminate against women who give birth to baby girls and has prohibited sex-selective abortions

- The policy was relaxed in Sichuan after a devastating earthquake (2008). This was because many children died as schools collapsed in towns and cities.

Consequences of the one-child policy

- Women spend less time out of work than if they did the childcare for several children. This helps women build more successful careers in work.

- The policy won't change until 2015 at the earliest. In 2008 China still had 1 million more births than deaths every five weeks. Half of the population (600 million people) still live on less than $2 a day.

- The gender imbalance caused by boys being favoured over girls – 60 million more young men than young women in China.

> **Study tip**
>
> This topic has given you a detailed case study of China's one-child policy. Points have been made in favour of and against the policy. When you write your answer to question 3, remember to use lots of detail and make plenty of points on both sides. Clearly state your conclusion, for or against, giving your reasons or evidence.

> **Did you know** ??????
>
> Chinese couples had to get permission to try to become pregnant and take their turn. If they did not succeed in a six-month period, they had to wait for another chance.

We cannot just be content with the current success. We must make population control a permanent policy.

Adapted from the People's Daily (China's Communist Party newspaper), 2000

Beijing mother-of-one, Zhao Hui, who has a four-year-old daughter called Zhang Jin'ao, says she never wanted more than one child. 'One child is enough. I'm too busy at work to have any more,' says the 38-year-old.

Adapted from BBC News website news.bbc.co.uk, 20 September 2007

E *News items about the policy*

Activities

1 Study graph **B**. This shows Chinese population data between 1978 and 2004.

a Describe the shape of the graph.

b Do you think the one-child policy has been a success in controlling population growth? Explain your answer.

2 Produce an information poster on China's one-child policy. Complete text boxes on the following aspects:

- reasons why it was introduced
- details of the one-child policy including the rules and punishments
- benefits
- problems
- recent changes since 1990

Illustrate the text boxes with photos selected from the internet. You might be interest to watch some video clips about the one-child policy, though be prepared as some clips are upsetting.

3 Make a decision – was the Chinese government wise to introduce the one-child policy? Have the benefits outweighed the disadvantages? There is no right or wrong answer here – you simply need to justify your opinion clearly.

8.5   What are the alternatives to birth control programmes?

Transmigration in Indonesia

Indonesia is a rapidly developing country in south-east Asia (Map **A**). It comprises a group of some 17,500 islands (known as an archipelago), two of the largest being Sumatra and Java. With a population of about 240 million, it has the 4th highest population in the world. The population is growing at a rate of just over 1 per cent per year, with the birth rate at 18.1 per 1000 (2011) and the death rate at a very low 6.3 per 1000 (2011). Look back to diagram **A** (pages 178-9) to consider what stage of the demographic transition model Indonesia is in.

A   Map showing the main islands of Indonesia

What is transmigration?

In the 1950s and 1960s, Indonesia was growing rapidly and the islands of Java, Bali and Madura were in danger of becoming over-populated. This occurs when there are not enough resources (for example, food, water, jobs and housing) to adequately support the number of people.

In 1969, in an attempt to re-distribute the population, the Indonesian government embarked on an ambitious project called transmigration. This involved encouraging people to move from densely populated islands, such as Java, to the more sparsely populated outer islands, such as West Papua (Irian Jaya). Transmigration was a chance for people to escape from the poverty of overcrowded urban slums to become land owners elsewhere and earn money through farming.

Supported by the World Bank, transmigration continued into the 1980s but recent financial difficulties and changes in government have led to the policy being scaled down.

Recent developments

In 2006, an estimated 20,000 families took advantage of the transmigration programme, supported by the Department of Manpower and Transmigration. By 2010, despite there being about 250,000 families who were

In this section you will learn

how all birth control programmes in the developing world do not take the same approach.

how to compare China's one-child policy and other birth control programmes.

Key terms

Transmigration: a population policy that aims to re-distribute people from densely populated areas to sparsely populated areas and provide them with opportunities to improve the quality of their lives.

Industrialisation: a process, usually associated with the development of an economy, where an increasing proportion of people work in industry.

Study tip

To write an account contrasting two or more countries effectively, make sure you write a quick plan first, summarising the main points you are going to make. In an exam, this can be done in the spare space on the left-hand side of the lines in the answer booklet. Always support each idea with data from the diagrams given, as well as knowledge from you own notes.

keen to move, the government was only able to sponsor 10,000 families at a cost of some $US160.5 million.

Following the eruption of Mount Merapi in 2010, the government offered to re-locate tens of thousands of displaced people from Java to Kalimantan. By 2011, some 2,000 families have taken up the offer encouraged by free transportation and the promise of two hectares of land and living costs for six months.

What have been the effects of transmigration?

Whilst transmigration has probably eased overcrowding in some towns and cities, the policy has led to a number of problems.

Economic

- Rather than reducing poverty, critics suggest that transmigration has simply re-distributed poverty.
- Many new migrants lacked the necessary farming skills to make productive use of their new land. Some abandoned their new homes to become refugees.
- Settlements were often poorly planned, with few shops, roads and services such as water, sanitation and electricity.
- Re-settlement was extremely expensive, costing $US7,000 per family in the 1980s.

Environmental

- Transmigration has been blamed for accelerating the rate of deforestation in previously sparsely populated regions
- Poor land use practises, such as over-cultivation, have led to issues of soil erosion

Social

- Culture clashes have occurred between migrants and local people, particularly in more remote islands. For example, in 2001 the local Dayaks and the transmigrants from Madura clashed resulting in hundreds of deaths.
- Traditional land rights were often ignored as land ownership was granted to the new settlers.
- There have also been religious clashes between the Islamist migrants and the largely Christian local people

Political

- Some critics have suggested that transmigration was encouraged by the government primarily to increase national security and control indigenous people in the outer islands.

Despite the problems, the transmigration policy has resulted in the re-settlement of an estimated 20 million people, mostly to Sumatra and Kalimantan. Whilst the population pressures have continued to increase in cities such as Jakarta, the situation would probably have been much worse if transmigration had not occurred.

Industrialisation: another way to deal with population growth

For the future the transmigration programme will probably continue to be scaled-down. In its place, as Indonesia expands its programmes of resource exploitation (e.g. minerals, timber, oil palm and shrimp farming) and industrialisation, more people will migrate to the remoter islands looking for work. Since the 1990's the government has encouraged **industrialisation** in the remoter islands through its 'Eastward Development Policy'. This can be considered another approach to coping with a rapidly growing population.

B   *Transmigration settlement near Geumpang, Aceh in Indonesia*

Activities

1 Study this case study and answer the following questions.

a What is transmigration?

b How does transmigration address the issue of rapid population growth?

c What are the advantages of the transmigration programme to the migrants?

d How have local indigenous people been affected by the influx of new migrants?

e Do you think transmigration has been a success? Explain your answer.

2 Use the information in this case study together with your own internet research to find out more about the environmental impacts of the transmigration programme. You might choose to focus on the Mega Rice Project in Kalimantan (see Did you know?). Use maps and photos to support your study. Assess the success of the transmigration programme – did the economic benefits outweigh the environmental damage?

Did you know ??????

In 1996 the Indonesian government launched the Mega Rice Project. The aim of the project was to convert 1 million hectares of natural peat swamp forest in central Kalimantan into productive farming for growing rice. Roads were constructed, trees were cut down and the peat swamp was drained using thousands of kilometres of artificial ditches. However, the land became far too dry for paddy rice farming, wildfires broke out and the land was eventually abandoned. It was an environmental disaster!

8.6 What are the issues and opportunities for an ageing population?

Populations in richer countries are ageing because:

- low birth rates and small families mean fewer children and young people.
- better health care and medicines allow people to live longer.

These two things increase the amount of elderly people.

Today's older people in rich countries are often wealthy, fit and have a wide range of interests, with the spare time to enjoy these. But this is the age group with the most expensive needs, especially in terms of health care. The 85+ age group – the very elderly – is growing fastest, increasing stress on health and social welfare systems (photo **A**).

■ The issues

The government has to find more money to support older people. As there are more elderly people and the proportion of working people is decreasing, so the taxes must increase to pay for support in the following areas.

Health care

Older people need more health care because more illness happens in old age. The elderly visit their GP (doctor) more often. They have more hospital visits and spend more time in hospital than younger or middle-aged people.

Social services

Elderly people need other services such as nursing homes, day-care centres and people to help them to care for themselves at home.

The pensions crisis

Life expectancy is higher in developed countries than in developing countries. In rich countries, people expect to be able to retire from work and have a pension (an income) for the rest of their lives.

The state pension began in 1908 when life expectancy for men was 67 and retirement age was 65. This means the average person would get their pension for only two years.

Today, it's very different. Life expectancy is now nearly 80. This means the retirement age will have to go up. Unless people retire later, there won't be enough money to pay pensions.

A *The 85+ age group is growing fast. This couple is living in a care home*

Key term

European Union (EU): a group of countries across Europe that work towards a single market, i.e. they trade as if they were one country, without any trade barriers.

The opportunities

More and more younger retired people (those in their later 60s and early 70s) are quite wealthy and have lots of leisure time. They spend money on travel and recreation, providing jobs in the service sector (photo **B**). Many do voluntary work. Some still do paid work and therefore pay taxes.

B   *Younger retired people contribute a lot to the UK's economy*

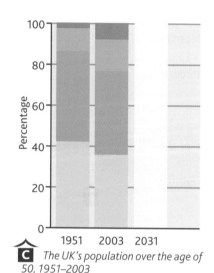

C   *The UK's population over the age of 50, 1951–2003*

Key
- ■ 85 and over
- ■ 75 – 84
- ■ 60 – 74
- ▢ 50 – 59

D   *UK population aged over 50, 2031*

Age group	%
50–59	28
60–74	44
75–84	20
85 and over	8

Ageing in the EU

Table **E** shows **European Union** (EU) birth rates are very low – in fact, they have never been so low and they may get even lower. Having few children later in life could soon mean that populations in some countries get a lot smaller. In each generation there are fewer parents, so fewer children are born. In 2003, 1.5 babies were born in the EU for every woman, but 2.1 are needed for a population to be sustainable.

E   *Selected EU birth rates (2011)*

Country	Birth rate (per 1,000)
Ireland (W)	16.1
France (W)	12.3
UK (W)	12.3
Netherlands (W)	10.2
Poland (E)	10.0
Bulgaria (E)	9.3
Latvia (E)	10.0
Germany (W)	8.3

The average global birth rate was 19.95 per 1,000 in 2009.

Note: (W) Western European country
        (E) Eastern European country

Activities

1   Study graph **C**. This shows the percentage of UK's population over the age of 50, 1951–2003

a   Make a copy of the graph and add in space for a new bar on the right.

b   Complete the graph, adding a similar bar for 2031 by using the data in table **D**.

c   Describe the changes shown by the bars between 1951 and 2031.

d   Explain why these changes are happening.

2   Work in pairs for this Activity.

a   In what ways can a country like the UK benefit from having an ageing population?

b   What are some of the problems facing a country with an ageing population?

France's solution

France is trying to solve the problems of an ageing population by encouraging people to have children and more of them. The idea is that this improves the **dependency ratio**, so in the future there will be more workers to help pay for older people.

Couples are given a range of reasons to have children:

- three years of paid parental leave, which can be used by mothers or fathers
- full-time schooling starts at the age of three. It is fully paid for by the government
- day care for children younger than three is subsidised by the government
- the more children a woman has, the earlier she will be allowed to retire on a full pension.

This has had some effect, but has not been entirely successful as graph **F** shows.

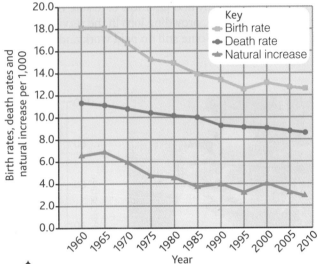

F *French birth and death rates, 1960–2007*

How does it work?

Nicole Falcou is 53. She lives in Muret, close to Toulouse in south-west France. She is married with three daughters aged between 14 and 22. She works locally with disabled children. She has three children of her own, so she can get extra benefits from the government, including retiring in her early 50s on a full state pension if she chooses. Although a pension is always less than a salary, as her children grow up and become less financially dependent this is a tempting offer.

Activity

3 Study graph **F**. This shows French birth and death rates, 1960–2007

a Describe the pattern of the birth rate line.

b Is there any indication that the policy of increasing births is working?

c Try to suggest some other government incentives that might increase the birth rate.

d Why are countries with low birth rates like France keen to increase the number of births?

8.7 What are the impacts of international migration?

In this section you will learn

the concept of migration and people's reasons for moving home (push–pull factors)

the positive and negative impacts of international migration

who moves within the EU and why

who comes to the EU and their reasons for wanting to live here

the differences between voluntary economic migrants and refugees

the benefits and difficulties of international migration for EU countries.

Push–pull factors

People move home for many reasons. Each person decides to move because of **push–pull factors**.

- Push factors are things that a person doesn't like about their home. These make them want to leave. For example, not being able to find a job.
- Pull factors are attractions of somewhere else which make the person want to move there. For example, available jobs which you would like to do.

A *Push–pull factors for a family in West Africa*

Family member	Situation
Father	Subsistence farmer – crops unpredictable due to climate. Part-time fisherman – catches are reducing because of overfishing.
Mother	Housewife with limited primary education.
Adult son	Secondary education completed. Would like the chance to go to university or obtain an interesting job.
Daughters	Part-way through school. Want to get as well qualified as possible. School resources are sometimes in short supply.

Key term

Push–pull factors: push factors are the negative aspects of a place that encourage people to move away. Pull factors are the attractions and opportunities of a place that encourage people to move there.

Activities

1 Sort the factors listed below into two groups of push and pull factors:

well paid job   natural disasters

low income   housing shortages

good health care   no shops or leisure opportunities

high standard of living   high unemployment

good shops and leisure opportunties

attractive environments   high wages

improved housing   political or social unrest

good schools   hostile climate

2 Study table **A**, which shows the factors affecting a family in West Africa who are considering moving to the EU. The family has two parents, an adult son and two younger daughters who are still at school.

a The father wants to move. Which of the factors you've just sorted out might be pushing him to move, and which factors might be pulling him to the EU?

b Why do you think the mother is less keen to move?

c If the family moves to the EU, how might the individual members benefit?

d Suggest any possible problems or issues that the family might face if they move to the EU.

Impacts of international migration

The impacts of **migration** on both the **country of origin** and the **host country** can be positive or negative.

Economic

Migration brings workers with skills and the economies of the UK and the EU have benefited from this. However, some people argue that **immigrants** take jobs which UK citizens could do. As migrants will sometimes agree to work for lower wages than UK citizens, some people argue this reduces wages for everyone.

Migrant workers often send money back to their country of origin to help their families. This is a disadvantage to the host country but brings huge benefits to the country of origin.

Housing

High levels of migration into the UK in recent years has added to housing demands. Property prices rose quickly in the early 2000s so many young people from the UK and overseas could not afford their own home. Finding somewhere to live can be hard for migrants. Some have been helped by social services and this causes resentment from some UK citizens.

Exploitation

Exploitation does happen and not everyone earns as much as they had expected. Tragedies have occurred when gang masters, who often control large numbers of workers in agriculture and shellfish harvesting, have been negligent. The deaths of 23 Chinese cockle-pickers in Morecambe Bay in February 2004 was perhaps the worst example in recent years.

Social

Too many migrants can be a burden on services like schools and doctors. Schools taking many immigrant children may be under pressure. British parents sometimes feel their own children do not get the help they need because teachers are too busy with pupils whose first language is not English. On the other hand, many people think immigration brings new cultures and ideas which benefit everyone.

Migration within the EU

There are two types of migrants within the EU:

- those moving between EU countries
- and those coming in from outside the EU.

Migrants usually go from poorer to richer countries searching for work and a better lifestyle. Poland and other Eastern European countries joined the EU in 2004. Since that date, many people have moved to the UK and other Western EU countries for work.

Key terms

Migration: the movement of people from one permanent home to another, with the intention of staying at least a year.

Host country: the country where a migrant settles.

Country of origin: the country from which a migration starts.

Immigrant: someone entering a new country with the intention of living there.

Polish workers migrating to UK

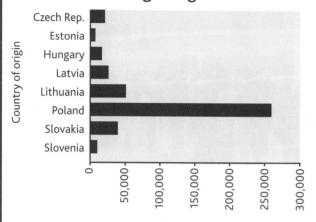

B　*Eastern European migration to the UK, 2007*

C　*Occupations of Polish workers in the UK, 2008*

Occupation	Total
Administration, business, management	33%
Hospitality and catering	22%
Agriculture	10%
Manufacturing	8%
Health service	6%
Food processing	5%
Retail	5%
Construction	5%
Others	6%

- Since 2004, 1.5 million Eastern Europeans have entered the UK. Two-thirds of these people are from Poland.

- Most have found jobs with much better pay than they would receive at home. Polish workers in the UK earn on average five times as much as they would at home, while the UK cost of living is only twice that in Poland.

- Most migrants pay tax, which helps the UK's economy. However, some work in the informal economy – working for cash and not paying tax.

- Migrants also use UK health and education services, which add to the government's costs.

Overall, the UK economy has gained from the Polish migrants. There are now more Poles in the UK than any other foreign national.

A Slovak girl working in Sussex

Jana Susinkova came to the UK in 2002 with her Czech boyfriend. She was only 18 and he a little older. She worked as a cleaner in people's homes, charging less than local cleaners charged by at least £1 per hour. She had enough work to keep busy six days a week. Her boyfriend was a mechanic and odd-job man, and his job provided a house for them.

Late in 2007 Jana returned home to Slovakia. Her boyfriend had already left to find a job in the Czech Republic, where the growing economy offered jobs for skilled people. While in the UK they had saved enough money to buy the materials and labour to build a four-bedroom house in the Czech Republic. This gave them an excellent start to their married life. Jana's English had become good, so she quickly found a well-paid job where she uses it every day.

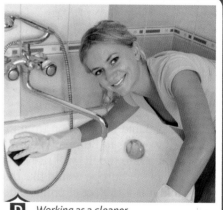

D　*Working as a cleaner*

Activities

3　Study graph **B**. This shows data on Eastern European migrants to the UK.

a　From which country were the majority of applicants from? State the number of applicants for this country.

b　How many applicants were there from Lithuania?

c　Why have a large number of Polish workers migrated to the UK?

4　Study table **C**. Represent the occupations of Polish workers as a pie chart. Remember that to convert percentages to degrees you need to multiply each value by 3.6. Clearly label each sector of your pie chart.

5　Suggest the benefits and difficulties of migration within the EU. Who benefits and who does not?

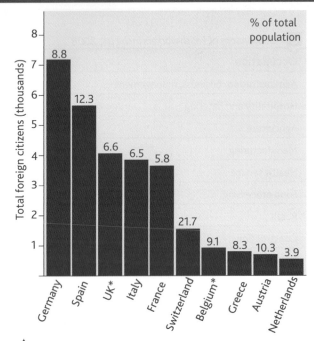

Total foreign citizens (thousands)

8.8 12.3 6.6 6.5 5.8 21.7 9.1 8.3 10.3 3.9

Germany Spain UK* Italy France Switzerland Belgium* Greece Austria Netherlands

E 'Top ten' EU countries with the highest total of foreign citizens (2009)
(* UK and Belgium 2008)

F Passport control at Heathrow Airport – a popular point of entry for economic migrants

Migration from outside the EU

Every year over 2 million immigrants arrive in Europe. This is more than any other world region. The population of Europe is being changed more by immigration than by changes in birth and death rates.

About 8.6 per cent of the EU's people are born outside the EU. This is compared with 10.3 per cent in the USA and almost 25 per cent in Australia. Most of these immigrants come from Africa and Asia.

Labour migration

Cheap travel and information from the internet attract skilled and unskilled workers to Europe. The United Nations predicts that immigration into the EU will rise by 40 per cent over the next 40 years. Many people in Europe would like the number of immigrants to be lower and it is a subject of political debate in all EU countries. Spain's immigrant population grew by 400 per cent in the first 10 years of the 21st century. Italy expects 100,000 Romanians in the years following Romania's joining of the EU. Although Italy needs workers, not everyone is happy with such a large number of new people.

Europe needs immigrants because birth rates have fallen and countries need workers. Highly skilled workers often come to the EU to fill shortages in areas such as teaching, nursing and high-tech computer jobs. About 20 per cent are graduates. Nevertheless, many people see immigrants as a problem rather than as an opportunity.

Study tip

Proportional symbols, such as circles or cubes, are used to show information drawn to scale. Proportional circles can be drawn where the radius of the circle is proportional to the value

Activities

6 Study graph **E**.

a On a sheet of plain paper, draw proportional circles to scale to show the total foreign citizens as a percentage of total population. Use the per cent figures to give the radius of each circle. Cut them out carefully.

b On a blank outline map of Europe, stick each circle on or beside the country it represents.

c Give your map a title and explain the scale of your circles in a key.

d Describe the pattern shown in your completed map.

Case study

International labour migration to the EU: Senegal to Italy

Children in Senegal love football. Many support Lazio, AS Parma and other Italian teams as well as teams in Senegal. Why is this? It is because many of these children's fathers and brothers already work in Italy.

G   *Many Senegalese fishing villages have been abandoned*

Opportunities are limited in Senegal. Many people there are subsistence farmers. There is a lot of unemployment in the cities and towns. This means that many young men want to go to the EU to find work. Senegalese workers in the EU often send money home to their families. This money helps children in Senegal get educated. It also helps improve living conditions too and economic development. For example, in the village of Beud Forage money has been used to set up water and electricity supplies.

Refugee movements to the EU

Refugees are people who have been forced to leave their homes. People can become refugees for many reasons but the most common ones are war, persecution, famine or other natural disasters. Persecution is when people are treated badly because of their race, religion, gender, political beliefs or sexual preference. Two-thirds of the world's refugees live in camps in developing countries but some manage to travel to more developed countries in the hope of a better life.

One-third of EU immigrants claim to be refugees. When they arrive they become **asylum seekers**. This means they have to wait for the authorities of the country they arrive in to decide if they are genuine refugees. If it is decided they are refugees, then they are granted 'asylum' and allowed to stay in that country. If it is decided they are not, then they are sent back to their own country. Some **economic migrants** have claimed to be refugees, believing this would give them a better chance of being allowed to stay in the EU. Unfortunately, this has sometimes caused strong feelings against all asylum seekers.

Today, the wars in Iraq and Afghanistan – in which EU forces are involved – provide most asylum claims. Two million Iraqis have already left the country, some for neighbouring countries and some to the EU. Another 1.8 million refugees live away from their homes in Iraq and many feel sufficiently threatened to want to leave. Christians are particularly persecuted.

Sweden is particularly generous to asylum seekers (table **H**). By 2007, 70,000 Iraqis already lived there – half of those coming to the EU. The Netherlands, Germany, Greece, Belgium and the UK have given homes to most of the rest. With the Iraq war coming to an end, asylum requests to EU countries from Iraqis decreased to 19,176 in 2010 from a peak of 38,286 in 2007. Afghans are now the largest group seeking refuge in the EU with 22,939 asylum requests in 2010

⊂⊃ links

To investigate further why Eastern European migrants are returning to the UK, visit **www.migrationwatchuk.com**.

Key terms

Asylum seekers: people who believe that their lives are at risk if they remain in their home country and who seek to settle in another (safe) country.

Economic migrant: someone trying to improve their standard of living, who moves voluntarily.

H   *Annual asylum applications (2010)*

EU country	Number of applications
Sweden	31,820
Netherlands	13,330
Belgium	9,940
Germany	41,330
Denmark	4,970
Ireland	1,940
UK	22,090
Spain	2,740

Activities

7 a Who are 'asylum seekers' and how do they differ from economic migrants?.

  b Why do wars often produce large numbers of asylum seekers?

  c Represent the data in table **H** in the form of bars on an outline map of Europe.

  d Why do you think the countries in table **H** are popular destinations for asylum seekers?

  e Use the internet to make your own study into asylum seekers associated with a recent world conflict, such as civil war in Libya (2011).

9.1 What are the characteristics and causes of urbanisation?

In 2008, for the first time ever, more than half the people in the world lived in towns and cities. **Urbanisation** is the increase in the proportion of people living in towns and cities. The rate of urbanisation varies around the world, (graph **A**) as does the percentage of people living in towns and cities (map **B**).

> **In this section you will learn**
>
> the process of urbanisation and how it varies throughout the world and over time
>
> the causes of urbanisation.

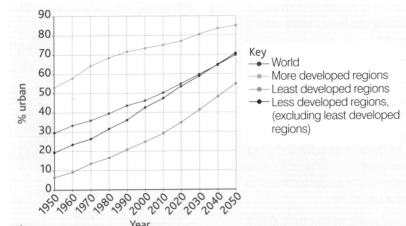

Key
- World
- More developed regions
- Least developed regions
- Less developed regions, (excluding least developed regions)

 A *Urban population, 1950–2050*

> **Key terms**
>
> **Urbanisation:** a process where an increasing proportion of the population lives in towns and cities resulting in their growth.
>
> **Rural-to-urban migration:** moving home from a rural area to settle in a town or city.

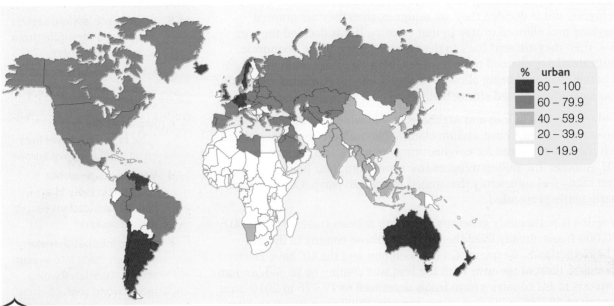

% urban
- 80 – 100
- 60 – 79.9
- 40 – 59.9
- 20 – 39.9
- 0 – 19.9

B *Global urban population, 2000*

■ Causes of urbanisation

There are two causes of urbanisation: **rural–urban migration** and natural increase.

- Rural-urban migration is the result of push–pull factors, as shown by the photos in **C**. People move from the countryside to the towns to find work and to improve the quality of their lives.

- Rates of natural increase may be high, particularly if the migrants are young people about to start families. Improved health care in the towns means more babies survive.

66 Recent droughts have meant my crops haven't grown, so I've struggled to find enough food for my family to eat. I have only a small amount of land and can't afford to buy any fertilisers. 99

66 I came here because I thought we would be better off. I believed we would have a better house and I would have a good job and some money. My children would be able to go to school and we would get better medical help if we become sick. 99

C   *Reasons why people leave the Ethiopian countryside*

Activities

1
a   What is meant by the term urbanisation?

b   What are the two causes of urbanisation?

c   Describe two problems that might be caused by lots of young people moving to a city.

d   Describe two problems that might be caused by lots of young people leaving a village.

2   Study graph **A**. This shows changes in urban populations between 1950 and 2050. Which three of these five statements are correct interpretations of the graph?

- Some of the data in the graph are predictions because it goes up to 2050.

- The less developed countries have the highest percentage of people living in cities.

- The least developed countries have the slowest growth in urbanisation.

- The most developed countries have the highest percentage of people living in cities.

- The least developed countries have the fastest growth in urbanisation.

3   Study the photos in **C**. Imagine you live in the rural area shown in the photo. Relatives have come back to your village and described the city shown in the second photo. Explain why you really want to move there.

Study tip

Make sure that you can give examples of push and pull factors to explain the process of rural–urban migration.

⚭links

You can find out more about urbanisation at
http://esa.un.org/unup.

9.2 How does land use vary in an urban area?

In all towns and cities the **land use** varies. In some areas, there may be lots of shops but in other parts there may be lots of houses. Some areas have mixed land use where the **function** varies.

In most UK cities, there are distinct areas with particular land uses. For example, the central area tends to be the shopping area or **central business district** (CBD). The area around this is likely to be the oldest part. This is called the **inner city**. Newer areas are found on the edge of the city. These are known as the **outer city or suburbs**. The photos in **A** show the key areas and their features.

In this section you will learn

how urban areas have a variety of functions

the characteristics and locations of some urban areas.

a CBD

b Redevelopment

c Suburbs

d Inner city

A *Characteristics of different parts of Sheffield*

∞links

Visit **http://www.bing.com/maps** to see a complete range of maps at different scales. You can overlay them with satellite images to see how land use varies in Sheffield or a city near to where you live.

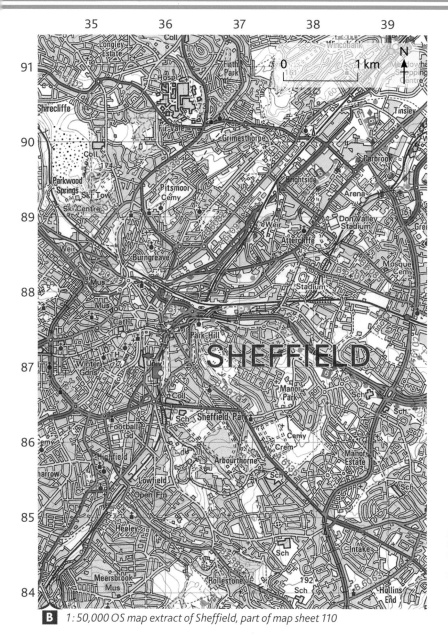

B 1 : 50,000 OS map extract of Sheffield, part of map sheet 110

Study tip

Practise drawing a simple sketch map showing typical land uses in a British city. Think about why each land use is found where it is.

Did you know

The Burj Dubai is the world's tallest building, with 141 storeys and 828 m in height. The Freedom Tower at the World Trade Center will be 110 storeys and, including the spire, 541 m high when it is completed in 2013.

Activity

1 Study the four photos of Sheffield's CBD, redevelopment area, suburbs and inner city.

a What evidence can you see in photo **a** that this is in the main shopping and service area of Sheffield?

b Using the photo of the inner city **d**, draw a labelled sketch to show the characteristics of the houses and the environment. Think about:

- the density of the housing (how close or far apart the houses are)

- the age of the houses (do they look modern or old-fashioned?)

- the facilities you can see (for example, do the houses have garages, places to leave rubbish for collection, areas for children to play, etc).

c Looking at map **B**, showing central Sheffield, do you think the CBD is located in:

- 3885 (Manor Estate)

- 3587 (where the cathedral is located)

- 3888 (near the Don Valley Stadium)?

Give reasons for your choice.

9.3 What are the issues for people living in urban areas in richer parts of the world?

There are many issues in towns and cities such as lack of housing or too much traffic. The photos in **A** highlight some of the issues.

 Issues in urban areas in the UK

In this section you will learn

the range and nature of issues that face people living in urban areas related to housing

inner city, traffic, CBD and multicultural societies

the success of strategies introduced to ease the problems.

Activity

Study the photos in **A**. These show a crowded city market and urban traffic congestion. Work in pairs.

a   Write three questions to identify key features shown in one of the two photos. Your partner should do the same for the other photo. Think about:

- What are these urban environments designed to do – what needs are they meeting?

- How easy is it for people to get what they need in this environment?

- Is this a pleasant, friendly environment to be in, or an unpleasant, unfriendly one?

- Does the environment feel too crowded or does everyone have enough space to feel comfortable?

■ Are there more efficient ways for these urban environments to do their jobs?

b   Swap questions. Answer the questions your partner has written for their photo. You should give full and detailed answers to the questions.

c   Swap your answers and read and discuss them. Do you agree with the answers given? How good were the questions asked? How could they be improved?

d   Together, summarise the issues you think are shown.

Issue 1: housing

Population in the UK has grown by 10.5 per cent since 1971. It is still growing and by 2025 there are predicted to be 65 million people in the UK. The number of **households** has risen by 30 per cent since 1971. Most of this increase is because more people live alone. This is due to people leaving home to rent or buy younger than in the past, marrying later, getting divorced and living longer.

The government wants to build 240,000 new houses every year by 2016. Many of these new homes will be built in existing towns and cities. They want 60 per cent to be built on **brownfield sites**. These are areas that have been built on in the past, usually in the inner city. However, some housing will have to be built on **greenfield sites**. These

Did you know ???????

Three blocks of high-rise flats in Everton, Liverpool were nicknamed 'The Piggeries' because of the living conditions there.

have not been built on in the past and are usually on the edge of the city. Table **B** gives points in favour of each of these two alternatives. The photos in **C** show the different types of housing being built in different parts of the city.

B   *Advantages of building on brownfield and greenfield sites*

Advantages of building on brownfield sites	Advantages of building on greenfield sites
Easier to get planning permission as councils want to see brownfield sites used	New sites do not need clearing so can be cheaper to prepare
Sites in cities are not left derelict and/ or empty	No restrictions of existing road network
Utilities such as water and electricity are already provided	Pleasant countryside may appeal to people who want to buy houses
Roads already exist	Some shops and business parks on outskirts provide local facilities
Near to facilities in town centres, e.g. shops, entertainment and places of work	Land is cheaper on outskirts so houses can be larger
People are close to where they work	More space for gardens

a Riverside apartments, Bridgewater Place, Leeds

b Gentrified housing, Cambridge

c Retirement bungalows, Scartho, Grimsby

d Family homes, Scartho Top, Grimsby

C   *Types of housing*

Activities

2 Study table **B** on page 199. This lists the advantages of building on brownfield and greenfield sites

a Draw up a table of your own with two columns. In the first column copy out the advantages of building on brownfield sites.

b In the second column, work out some disadvantages of building on brownfield sites. (The advantages of greenfield sites will give you some useful clues.)

3 Study the photos in **C** on page 199. These show four different types of housing.

a In groups, take on the following roles:

- professional accountant working in a city-centre office, aged 26 and single
- a 68-year-old pensioner, widowed and living alone
- a couple seeking an old, modernised house as a first home together
- a family with two children aged 10 and 12.

b For each role, identify which of the four houses shown in **C** would be most suitable and explain the advantages of living there.

Issue 2: the inner city

Many governments have tried to improve living conditions in inner cities. In the 1960s and 1970s they built cheap, high-rise blocks of flats as a 'quick fix'. But these were not popular. Many have been demolished now. Since the 1980s there have been three main strategies for inner city living.

Strategy 1: UDCs

Urban Development Corporations (UDCs) were a major strategy introduced in the 1980s. The London Docklands Development Corporation (LDDC) and Merseyside Development Corporation (MDC) were set up in 1981. Eleven more UDCs followed. These were large-scale projects paid for by government and by private businesses.

> **Key term**
>
> **Urban Development Corporations (UDCs):** set up in the 1980s and 1990s using public funding to buy land and improve inner areas of cities, partly by attracting private investment.

UDC example: The London Docklands Development Corporation

The LDDC was at work for 17 years. In its final report in 1998 it summed up its success as:

- £1.86 billion in government investment
- £7.7 billion in private business investment
- 431 hectares of land sold for development
- 144 km of new and improved roads
- the construction of the Docklands Light Railway
- 2.3 km² of commercial/industrial floorspace built
- 762 hectares of derelict land reclaimed
- 24,046 new homes built
- 2,700 businesses trading
- contributions to 5 new health centres and the redevelopment of 6 more
- funding towards 11 new primary schools, 2 secondary schools, 3 post-16 colleges and 9 vocational training centres

- 94 awards for architecture, conservation and landscaping
- 85,000 people now at work in London Docklands.

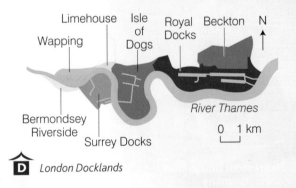

D London Docklands

Strategy 2: City Challenge

City Challenge was the name of a plan for **regenerating** areas in the 1990s. Local authorities, private companies and the local community worked together to put together a plan. The Hulme (Manchester) City Challenge Partnership tried to improve the housing built in the 1960s. Part of this involved trying to improve the environment, community facilities and shops (photo **E**).

City Challenge example: Hulme, Manchester

- Crescents were built in the 1960s and pulled down in the 1990s.
- Through City Challenge, Hulme received £37.5 million.
- Some old buildings were kept.
- Homes were designed to save water and energy and be nice to live in.
- There was a return to a traditional layout – Stretford Road (at the end of which is Hulme Arch) was rebuilt.
- Local schools and a new park were built.
- The views of local people were taken into account.

E   *Hulme, Manchester*

Strategy 3: Sustainable communities

Sustainable communities began in 2003. The idea is to plan an area with good houses and access to jobs, education and health care. This will help people to have a reasonable **quality of life**. One area affected is in east Manchester. It used to be called Cardroom but has been renamed New Islington Millennium Village. As diagram **F** shows, it seeks to provide for a good quality of life in inner-city Manchester in the 21st century.

Sustainable communities example: What's coming to New Islington?

New homes
- 66 houses
- 1,300 apartments.

Waterways
- 3,000 metres of canalside
- 50 moorings for narrow boats.

Urban amenities
- 10 new shops, new offices
- 2 pubs, 2 restaurants, cafés and bars
- Metrolink stop in 10 minutes' walking distance
- New bus lines and bus stops
- 1,400 car-parking spaces.

Parks and gardens
- 300 new trees, 2 garden islands, an orchard, a beach
- play areas and climbing rocks
- secured courtyard gardens.

Community facilities
- a primary school, a crèche and play areas
- a health centre with 8 GPs
- 2 workshops and a village hall
- a football pitch.

Sustainability
- boreholes will provide up to 25 litres per second of water
- central heat and power to generate 600 kW electrical energy and 1,000 kW thermal energy
- recycling collection points.

 Living in New Islington, Manchester

Activity

4 Study diagram **D** and photo **E**. You could work in groups of three for this task, with each member of the group doing one of the strategies.

a For each of the three strategies (UDCs, City Challenge and sustainable communities), complete a fact file including the following information:
- location
- dates
- what was done
- who was involved
- where funding came from
- what has been done to improve housing, the environment and the community.

b Create a table to show the advantages and the disadvantages of each of the three strategies.

c Which of the three strategies do you think is best? Give full justification for your answer. You should stress its advantages and the disadvantages of the other two.

- Air pollution from vehicles
- Noise from heavy vehicles
- Buildings discoloured
- Impact on health – respiratory conditions, asthma
- Unsightly.

G *Environmental problems resulting from traffic congestion*

Issue 3: traffic

As the number of cars has increased so has the problem of traffic congestion. Photo **G** shows some of the problems caused by traffic and congestion. Diagram **H** shows some ways that have been used to reduce the use of cars including **park-and-ride schemes** and congestion charging.

Key term

Park-and-ride scheme: a bus service run to key places from car parks on the edges of busy areas in order to reduce traffic flows and congestion. Costs are low to encourage people to use the scheme – they are generally cheaper than fuel and car parking charges in the centre.

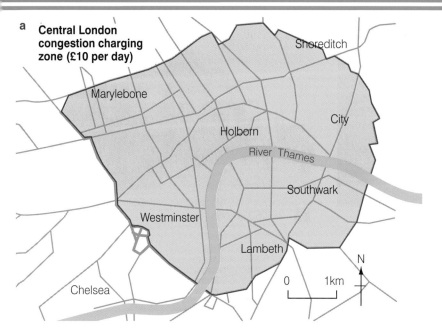

a Central London congestion charging zone (£10 per day)

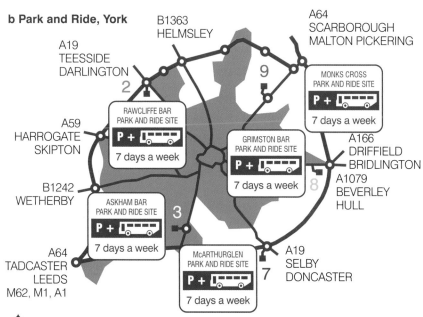

b Park and Ride, York

H Attempts to solve the problem in London (top) and York (below)

Issue 4: the central business district (CBD)

During the 1960s to the early 1980s, the CBD struggled to attract businesses. Out-of-town shopping areas and regional shopping centres became popular with lots of shops and free parking. In contrast, city centres were seen as busy and crowded with poor air quality.

However, there have been many changes in CBDs and their image is now, once more, a positive one. Some have become vibrant and pleasant places as a result of a number of initiatives (photos in **I** and **J** on page 204). Walkways have been created alongside the waterways, trees have been planted and a variety of building materials have been used to smarten up the image of Leeds CBD.

Activities

5 Study diagram **H**. This shows how traffic congestion has been tackled in two cities.

a How does the congestion charge aim to reduce the amount of traffic in central London?

b Why is there a free through-route? What sort of drivers is this designed for?

c Why do you think some London residents get a discount on the congestion charge? (Hint: think about the local trips people make: would you be happy if you had to pay a fee every time you were driven from home to school?)

d How do park and ride schemes work and why has York got so many of them – why can't everyone just drive to one big park and ride site?

I Revitalising the image of Leeds CBD

J The CBD in Leeds

Issue 5: multicultural mix

Many cities have a problem with **segregation**. There are many reasons why people choose to live with people from similar countries and cultures:

- Support from others
  People feel safe and secure when they are with other people from the same background. There is a sense of belonging and protection from racial abuse.
- A familiar culture
  There is comfort from being with people who have similar ideas and beliefs and speak the same language.
- Specialist facilities
  People from the same countries and cultures need facilities which may not be available in some areas. Examples are places of worship like gurdwaras or mosques or shops selling food from a particular country.
- Safety in numbers
  People have a stronger voice if they are heard as a group, rather than individually.
- Employment factors
  Immigrant groups often have low-paid jobs or can't find work. They have little money and so can only afford cheaper housing in certain parts of the city.

In Leeds, they are trying to reduce segregation by:

- improving education, including trying to improve English where it is a second language
- improving basic skills and access to information and training for adults so they have a chance of getting better jobs
- increasing community involvement by making sure that the needs of all groups are understood and met
- providing places and encouraging meetings of all people in a community rather than separate ethnic groups.

Key term

Segregation: occurs where people of a particular ethnic group choose to live with others from the same ethnic group, separate from other groups.

⚭ links

Find out more about Leeds CBD and its plans for the city and Chapeltown at **www.leeds.gov.uk**.

9.4 What are the issues for people living in squatter settlements in poorer parts of the world?

Rural–urban migration is happening very fast in many poorer countries. There is no time to build proper houses and for the economy to grow to provide jobs for people moving to the cities. People find empty areas of land and begin to build their own makeshift homes. These are known as **squatter settlements.** As there are few official jobs available an **informal sector** of the economy grows. This means that people create their own work, for example, making and repairing items, selling in shops or market stalls or acting as cleaners or gardeners.

In this section you will learn

why squatter settlements have developed, their characteristics and effects on people's lives

different strategies to try to improve squatter settlements and evaluate them

how to apply general concepts relating to squatter settlements to a case study.

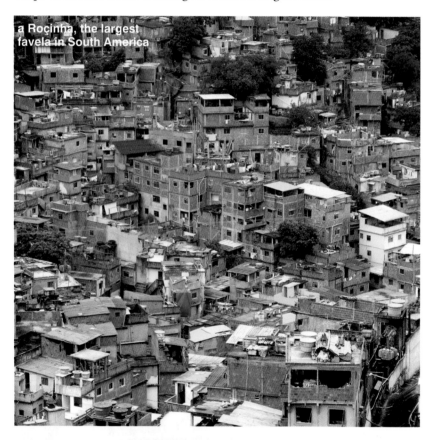

a Roçinha, the largest favela in South America

Key terms

Squatter settlements: areas of cities (usually on the outskirts) that are built by people from any materials they can find on land that does not belong to them. They have different names in different parts of the world (e.g. favela in Brazil) and are often known as shanty towns.

Informal sector: that part of the economy where jobs are created by people to try to get an income (e.g. taking in washing, mending bicycles) and which are not recognised in official figures.

b Close-up of Roçinha

c Mumbai

A *Typical shanty towns*

■ Living in squatter settlements

The photos in **A** (page 205) include views of Roçinha, a favela in Rio de Janeiro, Brazil, where 100,000 people live. Close-up views give a clearer impression of what life is like in the favela.

■ Most houses have no basic infrastructure such as sanitation, water, electricity or roads/access.

■ Shelters are made from any materials people can find – bits of iron, wood, pieces of board, etc.

■ Large families live in a small shack often with just two rooms – a living and a sleeping area.

■ There are no toilets. Water must be collected and carried back.

■ Rubbish is not collected and the area quickly becomes a place of filth and disease.

■ People have little money. They create their own low-paid jobs or work in low-paid jobs in the formal sector.

■ Children often do not go to school.

■ Crime is a problem.

Quality of life is poor and people do not have the money to improve their lives. The focus is on trying to survive from one day to the next.

■ Strategies to improve living conditions

People try to improve their living conditions by 'doing up' their homes (photo **B**). This means replacing flimsy materials with bricks and concrete, catching rainwater in a tank on the roof and getting electricity (often illegally, by tapping into a nearby source). However, this can take time and not all the problems of poor living conditions can be solved.

Self-help is where local authorities help the people living in the squatter settlements to improve their homes. This involves the improvements above, but it is better organised.

■ People work together to remove rubbish.

■ The local authority offers grants, cheap loans and sometimes materials to help people improve their homes.

■ Standpipes are often given to help get water to people's homes.

■ The residents, with help from the local authority, may begin to build health centres and schools.

■ Sometimes people become the legal owners of the land their homes are built on. This encourages them to improve the quality of their homes.

B DIY improvements in Roçinha

> ### Key terms
>
> **Self-help**: sometimes known as assisted self-help (ASH), this is where local authorities help the squatter settlement residents to improve their homes by offering finance in the form of loans or grants and often installing water, sanitation, etc.
>
> **Site and service**: occur where land is divided into individual plots and water, sanitation, electricity and basic track layout are supplied before any building by residents begins.

Site and service schemes are a more formal way of helping people in squatter settlements. Land is found for the scheme. Water, sanitation and electricity are properly supplied to individually marked plots before building starts. People then build their homes using whatever materials they can afford at the time. They can add to and improve the structure if they have more money later.

Local authority schemes can take a number of different forms. There may be large-scale improvements made to some squatter settlements or new towns may be built. In Cairo, new settlements such as 10th of Ramadan City were built to reduce pressure on the city (photo **C**). High-rise blocks of flats were built, together with shops, a primary school and a mosque. Industries were also planned to provide jobs for people.

C   *10th of Ramadan City, Cairo*

Activities

1   Study the photos in **A** and **B**. These show shanty housing in Roçinha and Mumbai.

Imagine you are a 14-year-old resident of a squatter settlement such as Roçinha. Your name is Eduardo Camila. You were born in Roçinha and have lived there all your life. You are being interviewed by a well-known journalist from a national paper. The reporter wants to know all about your house, your surroundings, your life, what you think the future holds for you and what you think are the good and bad points about living in Roçinha. Write down what you say. Include a labelled photo of a shanty town.

2   Use the internet to find a photo that shows life in Roçinha. Stick it into your book and add detailed labels to describe the main features shown in your photo.

3   a   What is the difference between 'self-help' schemes and 'site and service' schemes?

   b   Many local people prefer self-help. Can you suggest why?

Kibera, a squatter settlement in Nairobi, Kenya

Map **D** shows the location of Kibera in the capital city of Nairobi in Kenya. Some 60 per cent of people in Nairobi live in slums, over half of them in Kibera.

Specific facts about Kibera are uncertain.

- It is believed that between 800,000 and 1 million people live in the shanty town.
- Kibera covers an area of 255 ha so it is extremely crowded. People only have 1 m² of floor space each.
- Over 100,000 children are believed to be orphans as a result of HIV/Aids.

Photos **E** and **F** show the squatter settlement.

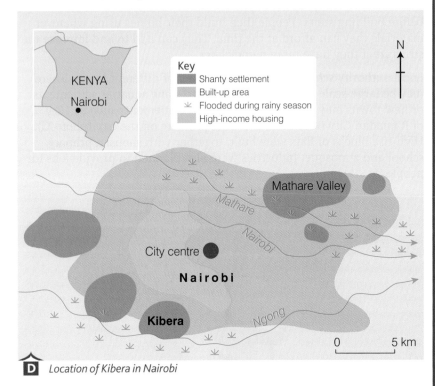

Key
- Shanty settlement
- Built-up area
- Flooded during rainy season
- High-income housing

KENYA
Nairobi

Mathare Valley

Mathare

Nairobi

City centre

N a i r o b i

Kibera

Ngong

0   5 km

D *Location of Kibera in Nairobi*

The area smells of human waste and of the charcoal used for fuel.

Homes are made of mud, plastered-over boards, wood or corrugated iron sheeting.

The paths between the houses are narrow and often have a ditch running down the middle that has sewage in it.

There is a good community spirit, homes are kept clean and visitors are welcomed.

There is a lot of crime. Gangs protect people but it costs a lot of money. Police won't go there.

A standpipe may supply water for up to 40 families.

Rubbish is not collected.

E *General view of Kibera*

Finding solutions

There are signs that things are getting better.

- Practical Action, a British charity, has helped develop roofing tiles. Made from sand, clay, lime and natural fibre, they are cheap and easy to produce.
- The United Nation's Human Settlement Programme (UN-Habitat) has provided affordable electricity to some parts at 300 Kenyon shillings (about £2.25) per shack.
- There are two mains water pipes – one provided by the council and the other by the World Bank – at a cost of 3 Kenyon shillings (about 2¼p) for 20 litres.
- Improving sanitation is more difficult and progress is slow.
- Medical facilities are provided by charities.

There are bigger schemes. In a 15-year project that began in 2003, there are plans to re-house thousands of residents of Kibera. This is a joint venture between the Kenyan government and UN-Habitat. In its first year, 770 families were rehoused in new blocks of flats with running water, toilets, showers and electricity. Residents have been involved in plans and funding of 650 million Kenyan shillings (£4.9 million) had been set aside for the first year. It is hoped funding will be provided by charities and by setting up private loans.

F   *Close-up view of Kibera*

Activities

4   Look carefully at photos **E** and **F**. Describe the living conditions in Kibera by answering the following questions.

a   How is sewage disposed of?

b   Is electricity available?

c   How is water stored?

d   What materials are used to build the houses?

e   What is it like when it rains?

f   What services exist in the settlement?

5   Make a list of the ways people have tried to improve living conditions in Kibera.

∞links

Investigate Kibera at www.bbc.co.uk and www.mojamoja.org.

9.5 What are the problems of rapid urbanisation in poorer parts of the world?

◼ Examples of problems

Environmental problems: Bhopal disaster, India (1984)

On 3 December 1984, the world's worst industrial accident happened in the Indian city of Bhopal. Poisonous gas escaped from a chemical plant and killed thousands of people (photo **A**). Unofficial estimates put the number of dead between 8,000 and 10,000. Around 50,000 people suffered permanent disabilities and more died later. This is one example of how rapid urbanisation and **industrialisation** can lead to environmental problems in poorer parts of the world. As cities get bigger very quickly there are problems like air and water pollution and **disposal of waste**, including toxic waste from plants like the one at Bhopal.

Electronic waste in India

Electronic waste (or e-waste) is parts of computers which people no longer need. It is another major problem in a rapidly industrialising country like India. The country imports more than 4.5 million new computers a year, plus many second-hand ones. In the cities, poor people scrape a living by breaking down PCs and monitors (photo **B**). They boil, crush or burn parts in order to get valuable materials like gold or platinum. But what they do not realise is that the toxic chemicals inside, like cadmium and lead, can cause serious health problems. India's hospitals are starting to see patients with ten times the expected level of lead in their blood. E-waste is literally leading to a brain drain.

Waste and pollution: urbanisation in Shanghai, China

- The building boom in Shanghai creates 30,000 tonnes of waste a day.
- Shanghai's industry is responsible for 70 per cent of China's carbon dioxide emissions.
- In Shanghai, 400,000 deaths a year are linked to these environmental problems.

A *Deaths caused by the industrial accident in Bhopal*

B   *Breaking down PCs and monitors in India*

Did you know ? ? ? ? ? ?

People who live in Dhaka in Bangladesh create 3,000 tonnes of solid waste each day. Only 42 per cent of this is collected. In Mexico City, each person creates 248 kg of waste each year.

■ Reducing the problems

Waste disposal

Different solutions are used to the problem of waste: here are some examples:

- In São Paulo, Brazil, 7,500 tonnes of waste is burnt every day. This is not good for the environment and is a waste of useful resources. It does mean the streets are cleaner, though, which helps to prevent disease.
- In Shanghai, China, a waste disposal unit has been installed in most houses and the waste is used as a fertiliser in surrounding rural areas.
- After the Bhopal accident in 1984, the site was polluted by toxic waste. This could not be disposed of safely in India. The waste was packed up and sent to the USA where it was safely destroyed.
- In Bangalore, there are many call centres and therefore a lot of electronic waste. Companies are supposed to get rid of electronic waste safely. But there are not enough people employed to make sure this law is obeyed.

Greenpeace believes that the high-tech companies that make the electronic products should take responsibility for the waste created. This would involve getting rid of the dangerous chemicals from the equipment at the end of its life.

Recycling plants are more common in cities around the world (photo **C**). Recycling waste means less rubbish goes into landfill.

Waste can also be a good thing. It can provide a resource and a means of making a living for many people who live in shanty towns. Children and adults search **landfill** sites for things they can reuse or sell. For example, car tyres may be made into sandals and food waste is fed to animals or used as a fertiliser on vegetable plots.

Key terms

Landfill: a means of disposing of waste by digging a large hole in the ground and lining it before filling it with rubbish.

Recycling: collection and subsequent reprocessing of products such as paper, aluminium cans, plastic containers and mobile phones, instead of throwing them away.

C   *A recycling centre in Beijing, China*

Air pollution

Air pollution is a real issue. Most industrial production is in the biggest cities. The use of new technologies that can cut emissions of greenhouse gases is an option. However, coal is a lot cheaper and there is lots of it! In China, for example 80 per cent of electricity comes from coal. To make companies change from coal to cleaner fuels, governments may need to bring in a carbon tax. This would make coal more expensive and encourage them to find other, cleaner fuels. In Shanghai, China, industries use low sulphur coal to try to reduce pollution.

There needs to be greater safety checks if disasters such as Bhopal are to be avoided. Limits need to be set on emissions, and companies, including **transnational corporations** (TNCs), must be checked to make sure that emissions of greenhouse gases are reduced.

Transport is another area to look at. Reducing the number of cars through congestion charging and public transport are examples which could be used. In Mexico City odd-numbered cars are allowed on one day and even-numbered cars on another to cut the amount of traffic.

Water pollution

If water quality is to be improved in rapidly industrialising countries then governments need to set limits and guidelines. In 1986, the Ganga Action Plan brought water treatment works to the River Ganges in India. This cleaned up the water for a while but the growing number of people in the city was not taken into account. Water quality has got worse again (photo **D**). Such attempts have been tried in other countries. In Shanghai, the Huangpu and Suzhou rivers have been the target for improving water quality. A World Bank loan of $200 million was granted for this cause in 2002.

D *The River Ganges, India*

Activities

1. Study photo **B**.
   a. What is the man in the photo doing?
   b. What are the dangers of his work?
   c. Do you think high-tech companies should be responsible for disposing of e-waste? Why?

2. Study photo **D**.
   a. How is the R. Ganges being polluted?
   b. Why do you think it is proving so difficult to clean up the R. Ganges?

3. How has the Chinese city of Shanghai tried to tackle pollution?

9.6   How can urban living be sustainable?

A **sustainable city** has a plan for a long-term future. They are the cities of the future! In a sustainable city:

■ The environment is not damaged and there are low levels of pollution.

■ There is a good economic base with secure jobs.

■ There is a strong sense of community, with local people involved in decisions made.

■ Sustainable cities have lots of public transport rather than everyone using their own cars.

■ Waste is managed very efficiently.

■ There are lots of green spaces and gardens.

Photos **A** and **B** show two contrasting urban scenes in Los Angeles and Belfast.

In this section you will learn

attempts made to ensure that city life is environmentally and socially sustainable

the characteristics of a sustainable city.

A   *Los Angeles: non-sustainable urban living?*

B   *Belfast: sustainable urban living?*

Activity

1   Study photo **A** which shows Los Angeles in USA.

a   Some people say that Los Angeles was designed for the car. Do you agree?

b   Why do you think so many people rely on their cars in Los Angeles?

c   What other characterstics of a 'non-sustainable' city can you see in photo **A**?

2   Study photo **B**. Do you think Belfast shows sustainable urban living? Explain your answer.

Key term

Sustainable city: an urban area where residents have a way of life that will last a long time. The environment is not damaged and the economic and social fabric are able to stand the test of time.

Seeking environmental sustainability

Conserving the historic environment: Liverpool, UK

The Liverpool Maritime Mercantile City is an example of how a historic environment can be conserved (looked after). Many of the buildings look the same as when they were built in the 18th and 19th centuries (photos in **C**), even though they are now used for very different purposes. The Liverpool waterfront was made a World Heritage Site in 2004. The award shows how important this area and its buildings were in the past. It should mean that these places continue to be well looked after.

a Liver Building

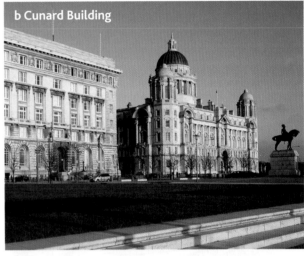
b Cunard Building

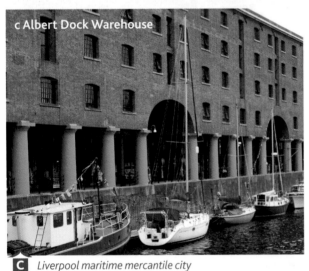
c Albert Dock Warehouse

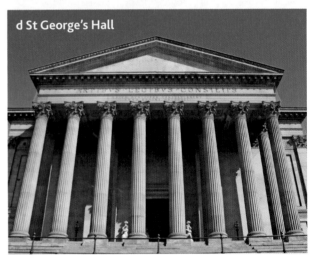
d St George's Hall

C *Liverpool maritime mercantile city*

Activity

3 Study the photos in **C**. Produce a leaflet for Liverpool City Council in the form of an illustrated report to show how the city has used and conserved its industrial heritage in a sustainable way. Use the Internet to help you with your research.

Key term

Sustainability: development that looks after future resources and considers the needs of future generations.

Conserving the natural environment

The natural environment (or countryside) can be conserved by controlling the amount of building on the edge of the existing built-up area. **Green belts** have been created around many towns in England (map **D**). These were set up to stop **urban sprawl** and to make sure that countryside on the edge of towns is protected. This provides open space for people from the town to enjoy.

Stopping building on the edge of the city means that other places for development must be found if growth is to continue. This means that building on brownfield sites is encouraged (photo **E**).

> **Key terms**
>
> **Green belt:** land on the edge of the built-up area, where restrictions are placed on building to prevent the expansion of towns and cities and to protect the natural environment.
>
> **Urban sprawl:** the spreading of urban areas into the surrounding rural/rural-urban fringe areas.

D   *Green belts in England*

- Provides an economic use of derelict land
- Provides jobs
- Foundations often in place for new construction
- Improves environment
- No need to develop greenfield sites
- Prevents urban sprawl

E   *Advantages of building on a brownfield site*

Reducing and safely disposing of waste

By 2008, the UK was producing 400 million tonnes of waste each year. That's enough rubbish to fill the Royal Albert Hall in London every hour! Much of this was mining and quarrying waste, but 30 million tonnes was from households. In 2011, around 40 per cent of household waste was recycled in the UK. That is a big improvement from 2001, when only 11 per cent was recycled. But there is much more that could be done.

> **Did you know** ??????
>
> In the UK we produce 517 kg of waste per person every year.

One way of reducing waste is to reduce the amount of packaging on goods and items sold in shops. Recently, people have been encouraged to use re-usable bags rather than plastic bags. A huge range of waste items are now collected from households to be recycled.

However, some waste will always need to be got rid of. There are two main options: incineration (burning) and landfill (photos **F** and **G**). Only 9 per cent of household waste in the UK is incinerated. People don't like to have incinerators near where they live because of pollution and all the traffic bringing in the waste to be burnt. A problem with landfill is that we are running out of space. By 2015 we will run out of landfill sites.

F *Incineration: Sheffield energy recovery facility*

G *A landfill site in Liverpool*

Activities

4 Study map **D** and photo **E**.

a Which major cities have green belts around them?

b What is the purpose of a green belt?

c What is the evidence that the land in photo **E** is a brownfield site?

d What are the advantages of building on a brownfield site?

5 Study photos **F** and **G**. Summarise the advantages and disadvantages of the following as a means of waste disposal.

■ landfill

■ incineration

6 a What materials are collected by the council from your home?

b What other items do you recycle at home?

c How do you reuse items at home?

d Describe how you try to reduce waste at home.

e What efforts are made at school to reduce, reuse and recycle?

f How effective do you think efforts are at home and at school? How could they be improved?

Providing adequate open spaces

It is not just in the countryside that building is controlled. Many areas in cities have areas of open space in the form of parks, playing fields and individual gardens. There are restrictions which mean these areas cannot be built on. Map **H** shows the open space in Greater London and some of the types of open space available.

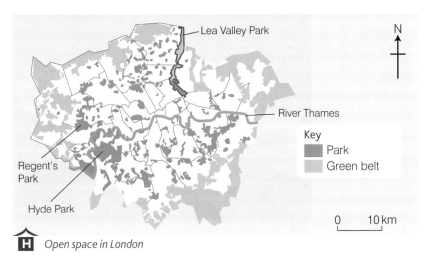

Key
■ Park
■ Green belt

H Open space in London

I Hyde Park, London

Involving local people

If people have their ideas heard and feel involved they are much more likely to care for the building and environment in which they live. Talking and listening to people when building is planned is important. This is happening more and more. People often join together and form associations to give them a stronger voice.

Providing an efficient public transport system

The number of cars is a barrier to a city being sustainable. London has tried to cut the number of cars by using congestion charging. However, there needs to be an alternative to cars. This means a public transport system that is efficient, reliable and comfortable. The mayor of London is keen to make a public transport system which the capital can be proud of and one that is sustainable. This means a focus on the Underground and improvements in buses and train links.

J Residents' meeting

London 2012: the sustainable Olympics?

The London Olympics 2012 has been designed to have a lasting positive impact on the local area.

During the Olympics

- The huge Olympic Park has been built in a derelict and run-down area in Stratford, East London. The physical environment has been hugely improved with the creation of parks and landscapes areas.

- Most of the events will take place in the Olympic Park and most of the athletes and coaches will stay in the Olympic Village so they won't need transport to and from the Games. This will reduce traffic congestion and pollution.

- No car parking will be provided, so people coming to watch the events will have to use public transport which has been massively improved

- 97% of materials from demolished buildings have been re-used in the construction of the Olympic Park. Timber has been sourced from sustainable forests.

K *The 2012 Olympic site*

- Several buildings, such as the Velodrome, have been designed to use as little energy as possible by making use of natural light and ventilation.

- Rainwater will be collected and used to flush toilets and water the gardens and lawns

- Rubbish has been cleared and green spaces have been created with footpaths and tracks created for cyclists. Some 4,000 new trees have been planted and bird and bat boxes have been installed.

After the Olympics

- The Olympic Park Legacy Committee intends the sports stadiums to be used in the future. The Olympic Stadium itself will be used again by hosting the 2017 World Athletics Championships. The Aquatic Centre is to be used by local people.

- The high-tech International Broadcast Centre may be used in the future by media and IT companies and could create up to 3,000 jobs.

- Some of the housing used by athletes in the Olympic Village will become cheaper housing for local people.

- Developments such as the massive Westfield Shopping Centre will be a permanent legacy of the Olympics, providing local jobs and shopping opportunities.

Only the future will tell quite how sustainable the London Olympics 2012 will turn out to be. You will have to judge for yourself!

⚭ **links**

For more information about the 2012 Olympics visit **www.london2012.com**

Activity

8 Use the internet to find out more about sustainability at the London Olympics 2012. Produce a Powerpoint presentation or a poster showing how the people running the Olympics are trying to make it sustainable both during and after the Olympics. To what extent do you think the Olympics will leave a sustainable legacy?

Sustainable urban living in Curitiba

Curitiba is the capital city of the Brazilian state of Parana. It is the seventh largest city in Brazil with a population of 1.8 million. The city is seen as a role model for planning and sustainability in cities worldwide. In 1968 the Curitiba Master Plan began. It tried to control urban sprawl, reduce traffic in the city centre, develop public transport and preserve the historic sector. The emphasis has been on ensuring a good and sustainable quality of life for the people of Curitiba. There is now a network of 28 riverside parks creating almost 100 miles of city trails. Lakes have been created within these parks that fill and flood the surrounding parkland in periods of heavy rain reducing the risk of flooding in the city itself.

The 'green exchange' programme means that families in shanty towns can exchange rubbish for bus tickets and food. 70 per cent of the city's rubbish is recycled by its residents.

The Bus Rapid Transport (BRT) System

Curitiba was the first Brazilian city to have bus lanes. The BRT system has four elements:

- direct line buses, which operate from key pick-up points
- speedy buses, which run on the five main routes into the city and have linked stops
- inter-district buses, which join up districts without crossing the city centre
- feeder mini-buses which pick people up from residential areas.

Housing in Curitiba

In Curitiba, COHAB, the city's public housing programme, believes that residents should have 'homes – not just shelters'. They have introduced a housing policy that will provide 50,000 homes for the urban poor.

L *The innovative bus system in Curitiba*

Activities

9 Study the information in this case study about Curitiba.

a How have the city authorities tried to improve housing for poor people in the city?

b Why do you think the Curitiba Bus Rapid Transport System is an example of sustainable urban living? Is it:

- because people are too poor to afford cars?

- because it allows people to travel around the city really easily and quickly by public transport?

- because the buses go really fast and have few stops – perfect for commuters?

c Use the internet to put together your own illustrated project on Curitiba as a sustainable city?

10 Changing rural environments

10.1 What pressures are being placed on the rural–urban fringe?

The **rural–urban fringe**, is a transitional zone (area of change) between countryside and city. It is the area where urban land use is gradually replaced by rural land use. Cities rarely have clear edges but usually merge into the countryside.

As town and cities grow outwards (known as urban sprawl) the rural–urban fringe is under more and more pressure. The land is wanted for shops, leisure (golf courses, horse-riding, etc.), houses (growth of villages) and transport (ring roads, airports, etc.).

Retail outlets

The areas of land on the outskirts of cities are prime land for building out-of-town **retail parks**. A retail park is a huge area of shops and leisure facilities such as cinemas and restaurants. The shops are often under cover and next to large car parks.

Bluewater Park, Kent

Bluewater Park is in Kent (map **C**). It is a large **regional shopping centre**. It is a **high-access location** within London's rural–urban fringe. Some 12 million people live within two hours' drive of Bluewater. It may also attract customers from France as it is 4 km from the Ebbsfleet station on the Channel Tunnel rail link.

A *Bluewater Park regional shopping centre*

In this section you will learn

what is meant by the rural–urban fringe and know why people are attracted to live there

the impacts of out-of-town retail outlets and leisure provision

how transport networks have expanded in the rural–urban fringe

what is meant by commuting and its impacts on landscape and settlement

the characteristics of a suburbanised village, how they grow, their characteristics and the type of people who live there.

Key terms

Rural–urban fringe: an area around a town or city where there is a mix of urban and rural land uses.

Retail parks: large warehouse-style shops often grouped together on the edge of a town or city, aiming to serve as many people as possible.

Regional shopping centre: a major indoor shopping centre with a large car parking area. Usually located close to a large urban area at a high access point, such as a motorway junction.

High-access location: an area with excellent transport links, making it easy to reach for people and goods.

Bluewater was built in a disused chalk quarry. Some people think the shopping centre is better than what was there before. The buildings themselves and the communication links (roads, etc.) put a lot of pressure on the rural–urban fringe. This part of Kent is much more urbanised and congested than it used to be. Massive engineering works took place in 2008 to improve the link from the M25 to Bluewater.

Bluewater Park opened in 1999. Since then, three other 'regional' centres have been built: the Trafford Centre in Manchester, Braehead in Glasgow and the Westfield Centre in west London. However, these are within the existing urban area. It is unlikely that any more developments like Bluewater will be built in the rural–urban fringe.

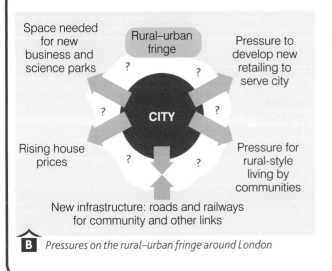

B   *Pressures on the rural–urban fringe around London*

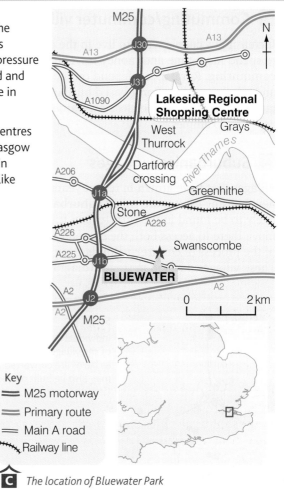

C   *The location of Bluewater Park*

Leisure

People from towns and cities use the rural–urban fringe as a leisure area. Fields and woodlands close to towns and cities are ideal places for people to enjoy walking, riding horses, cycling or fishing. Can you think of leisure opportunities in the rural–urban fringe near where you live?

> **Study tip**
>
> Be clear about the pressure put on the rural–urban fringe. Make sure that you can explain some of the conflicts that arise as a result of these pressures.

Activities

1   Look at the case study on Bluewater Park in Kent.
a   Describe the location of Bluewater Park. Is it:
- a long way away from where lots of people live
- close to major communication routes (motorway, A roads, rail)
- difficult to reach by car (with nowhere to park when you get there)?

b   Why do you think the owners of Bluewater Park located it where they did? Use the term 'high-access location' in your answer.

Commuting/commuter villages

Increasingly, people want to live in the countryside and they are willing to spend more time and money travelling to work. This is known as **commuting**. Rural areas depend on the urban zone for jobs, services and administration. Rural-based businesses do well because of the larger number of people close by. Garden centres and market gardens are good examples.

Suburbanised villages

Villages that have grown in recent years with new people moving in to new housing estates are called **suburbanised** villages. They are most likely to be found in the rural–urban fringe. This is because people move there to access both the city and the countryside. They are part of the process of **counter-urbanisation**, i.e. moving out of the city. These villages develop in stages (diagram **D**):

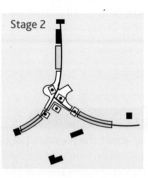

Stage 1:

Individual new houses are built on the edge of the village. Non-residential buildings such as barns are converted into homes. Houses may also be built on vacant land in the village. Growth is minimal at this stage.

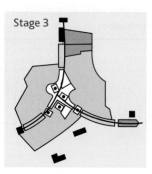

Stage 2:

Linear development (ribbon development) takes place along the main roads. Stages 1 and 2 are common in villages all over the country.

Stage 3:

Housing estates are built on land between roads entering the village. These modern estates can change a village's character. Many of these newer homes are bought by people from nearby towns and cities. They hope to find a balance between urban and rural lifestyles. As they work outside the village and do not shop there, they may add little to village life. Sometimes there is conflict between long-term and newer village residents.

Key

✿ Original village core

◄ Isolated houses

◈ Infill and conversions

⬗ Early ribbon development

▢ New housing estate development

▨ Most recent additions to the village

— Roads

D *Stages in the development of a suburbanised village*

Chalgrove, Oxfordshire

Chalgrove is on the edge of the rural–urban fringe between Oxford and London (map **E**). People who live there can commute to work in either city. Although some villages in Oxfordshire are growing, others are getting smaller. Location and planning regulations are key factors. Reasons for the growth of Chalgrove include the following (map **E**):

- The village is close to the M40 motorway, which goes to London.
- It has A-road access to Oxford (for much of the route).
- It is close to railway stations in nearby Thame and Wallingford.
- These towns provide a range of local services, including health and education.
- New job opportunities are growing in the Didcot–Thame development axis.
- Chalgrove is outside both the green belt and the Area of Outstanding Natural Beauty, so is not limited by their planning restrictions.
- Since 1993 the South Oxfordshire Development Plan has encouraged the development of larger villages like Chalgrove.

Chalgrove's typical 'suburban' residents:

- are highly mobile (90 per cent of households have cars)
- work in the professions or in management (40 per cent)
- have lived in the village for less than 10 years.

Did you know ??????

The rural–urban fringe should serve the needs of both city and countryside. It should include parks and green spaces. Public transport should allow access and daily travel. The rural–urban fringe should serve the city for recreation and sustainable waste management. More woodland could be planted.

∞ links

Find out more about Chalgrove at **www.chalgrove-parish.org.uk**.

Average house prices in Chalgrove

Beds	2008	2011	
All	£415,000	£404,540	−2.5% ⬇
2	£259,000	£234,700	−9.4% ⬇
3	£348,000	£294,400	−15.4% ⬇
4	£575,000	£449,000	−21.9% ⬇

Key

- ═══ M40 motorway
- ═══ Main roads
- ▬▬ Didcot–Thame development axis
-    Green belt
-    Chilterns, Area of Outstanding Natural Beauty (AONB)
- ▮ City
- ■ Small to medium-sized towns
- • Village

E *Factors affecting the development of Chalgrove*

F *Chalgrove*

Transport developments

G Parts of the M25 were built on green belt land

Transport is quite good in the rural–urban fringe because of road and rail networks. However, as more people move into the rural–urban fringe, the road and rail networks have to get bigger to serve their needs. It is said, however, that more roads encourages more cars which makes the problem worse.

Did you know ??????

Car pooling is when people share lifts with others. This cuts costs, is sociable and environmentally friendly. Councils and companies are increasingly running sharing schemes.

Activities

2 Study diagram **D** on page 222. This shows the three stages of how a village turns into a suburbanised village. Read these three statements and decide which one is describing stage 1, which is for stage 2 and which is for stage 3.

Farmer John: '*Well, a couple moved out here from the city and I agreed that they could buy my old cow barn. They turned it into a five bedroom house. Very nice it is, but it's still the old cow barn to me though.*'

Pensioner Pete: '*I can't say I recognise the place anymore – there's been that much new building. New estates here and there, all of them with cars so you can't properly get in nor out of the place these days.*'

Vicar Angela: '*It is a little more difficult for people to park near the church now that there are houses out along the London Road: we always used to park there when it was just hedges. But it is good to see the village growing.*'

3 Look at photo **G**. It shows the M25 that forms a ring road around London.

a Why do you think it was built in the rural-urban fringe?

b Can you suggest some disadvantages of using the rural-urban fringe for building motorways?

10.2 What social and economic changes have happened in remote rural areas?

Locations of remote rural areas in the UK

There is a close link between uplands, hill sheep farming and remote rural areas (map **A**). Snowdonia is an example of a remote rural area. The climate is harsh, with low temperatures, lots of rain and heavy snowfall. The landscape is challenging, with steep slopes, bare rock outcrops and thin soils. This is **marginal land**. The landscape is dramatic and beautiful, but these remote areas can make people's lives very difficult.

Remote farming areas, usually used for hill farming

North-west Highlands
Grampian Mountains
Southern Uplands
Lake District
Pennines
SNOWDONIA
Cambrian Mountains
Brecon Beacons
Exmoor
Dartmoor

N

0   200km

A *Remote rural farming areas in the UK*

Rural depopulation in Snowdonia

Rural depopulation is the net emigration of people from a rural area. In other words, more people move out than move in. The 2001 Census showed there were 3 per cent less people living in Snowdonia than in 1991. During the 1980s there had been a 6.2 per cent growth, but there was no growth in the 1990s.

As one of the highest and steepest regions in the UK, there has never been a lot of people living in Snowdonia. Now, more people are leaving every year. Those leaving are local people whose families have lived there for a very long time.

People have left Snowdonia for different reasons:

1. Decline in hill farming

All over the UK the number of hill sheep farmers is getting smaller. This is mostly because of economic reasons.

In the 1990s it cost a lot more to raise a lamb than farmers could get from selling them. At the same time, fuel and other costs were rising. Farm vehicles need diesel and in such remote rural areas people often have no choice but to travel by car. Making a living became impossible. Average farm income dropped as low as £8,000 a year. Many farmers were simply driven out of business.

In this section you will learn

the reasons for rural depopulation and the impacts it brings

how village characteristics change during decline

the growth of second homes and the impact this has on village decline.

Key terms

Marginal land: land that is only just good enough to be worth farming. It may be dry, wet, cold, stony or steep.

Rural depopulation: people leaving a rural area to live elsewhere, usually in a town or city.

Did you know ??????

The 1990s saw the worst agricultural recession for almost 100 years in the UK. The average family farm suffered a 90 per cent drop in income over five years.

B *Snowdonia: a remote rural area with limited economic opportunities*

2. Competition from abroad

Competition from abroad was also a problem. For example, New Zealand can produce cheaper lamb and ship it around the world to British supermarkets. To increase income, hill farmers have tried **diversification** by working in other rural industries such as tourism and forestry. Some farms run B&B businesses, but this is not a secure income.

3. Job losses

Farming is not the only industry which is struggling in Snowdonia.

- Quarrying has reduced its labour force.
- The Trawsfynydd Nuclear Power Station closed in 1993 with 500 job losses.

People who had lost their jobs were forced to move to the towns to look for work.

4. Better job opportunities elsewhere

Many young people leave Snowdonia to go to college or university. But then there aren't many chances of getting a graduate-level job in Snowdonia. So most graduates have to go to towns or cities to find suitable careers.

5. Housing shortage

To protect the landscape the Snowdonia National Park Authority does not allow planning permission for building new homes. There aren't enough houses for all the people that want to buy them. That means sellers can charge more for houses, especially when rich people from big cities are looking to buy a country cottage as a holiday home. Local people are priced out of the market and are forced to rent or move out of the area.

> ### Key terms
>
> **Diversification**: moving into new activities to try to make a better living, e.g. a farmer offering tourist accommodation.
>
> **Second home**: a home bought to stay in only at weekends or for holidays.

6. Loss of services

As people leave rural areas, services like village shops, post offices, banks, primary schools and doctors' surgeries close. This can make even more people move away. Unless new jobs and sources of income can be put in place, as well as new housing being built, many villages have little chance of surviving.

7. Growth in ownership of second homes

A **second home** is bought by someone whose main home is outside the region. They are used for holidays and weekends and the owners often do not use local services, bringing all they need with them. This means that the owners of second homes are rarely part of the community, so they are not well accepted. Across Wales, 1.2 per cent of houses are second homes. In the Snowdonia National Park it is a huge 13.7 per cent.

Rhyd, Snowdonia

Rhyd is a small village in Snowdonia. It is linked to other settlements by a minor road. Local jobs used to be in farming, lead mining and clay works, but all have been in decline. In 2003 there were 15 homes and 37 residents in the village. Five of the houses were holiday homes. In the past Rhyd had a primary school, chapel, post office and shop. There are no services and no jobs in the village today. The only service now is two buses passing daily.

D   *Distances to essential services for Rhyd's population*

Service	Distance (km)
Primary school	3
Pub	3
Doctor's surgery/pharmacy	7
General store	11
Clothes shop	11
Bank	11

Case study

C   *The village of Rhyd*

Activities

1   Construct an information poster to describe the causes of rural depopulation in Snowdonia. Use the internet to find a photo of Snowdonia to go in the centre of your poster, ideally showing signs of depopulation. Add text boxes, with illustrations from the internet, around your central photo to describe the various reasons for depopulation. Don't forget to add a title to your poster!

2   a   Study the information about Rhyd above. Write a paragraph to describe the difficulties faced by the population of Rhyd in Snowdonia.

   b   Living in Rhyd has its advantages too. Consider whether you would like to live there or not. Explain the reasons for your answer.

Study tip

Think of the social and economic changes that have taken place in remote rural areas.

10.3 How can rural living be made sustainable?

Conserving resources and protecting the environment

To live sustainably means looking after resources for us and for our children. If we waste what we have, and do not protect our environment, not only will our economy and standard of living suffer, but so will the generations that follow us.

There are several government schemes that try to look after the rural environment.

1 Environmental Stewardship Scheme

This scheme is open to all farmers to improve their sustainability. Run by the Department for Environment, Food and Rural Affairs (Defra), it aims to:

- conserve wildlife
- increase biodiversity (photo **A**)
- improve landscape quality
- provide flood management
- promote public access to the countryside.

Annual payments from UK government to farmers vary from around £30 to £60 per hectare or more, depending on the level of involvement of the farmer.

2 Rural Development Programmes

The new Rural Development Programme for England (RDPE) began in 2007 and will run until 2013. It will give £3.9 billion to make rural life more sustainable. Most funding (£3.3 billion) will help farmers to manage their land more sustainably, and encourage biodiversity and good water quality.

In this section you will learn

how rural environments can be protected and conserved

ways in which the needs of the rural population can be supported

government initiatives aimed at supporting the rural economy and environment.

A *Meadow land developed under the Environmental Stewardship Scheme*

The remaining £600 million will make agriculture and forestry more competitive and sustainable. This will also provide rural job opportunities. Three types of project grants exist:

- the Forestry Commission can support sustainable woodland schemes
- Natural England runs the Energy Crops Scheme
- the Regional Development Agencies give new economic and social funding in rural areas.

Supporting the needs of the rural population

People need to get to work and access services as easily as possible. Some schemes have been put in place to help improve the quality of rural life.

1 Rural Transport Partnership

Rural transport is a difficult issue. There are fewer customers and longer distances than in towns and cities. Making public transport networks pay can be almost impossible. Many parts of the country have schemes to try and tackle these issues.

- From 1999, the Devon Rural Transport Partnership was started. It gives financial grants and advice on setting up services.

- In rural east Surrey students aged over 16 who need to travel to college courses can get discounts on bus, coach and train fares. The moped loan scheme allows them to travel where public transport does not go. Safety helmets and clothing are provided.

- Buses4U is a minibus scheme open to everyone in east Surrey. Journeys need to be booked at least an hour in advance and the minibus routes are then planned (photo **B**).

B   *The Buses4U scheme*

2 Village Shop Development Scheme

This scheme aims to help village and farm shops and other local services to provide for their communities. The idea is to stop people from getting in their cars and driving to the nearest town. This is important because:

- people save time and energy and carbon emissions are lowered
- people who do not have cars can still access services
- local shops, post offices and pubs provide jobs for people in the village
- more money is spent within the community rather than going outside
- a sense of community is improved.

Shops use the money to widen the range of goods and services they offer. For example, by offering banking which is usually only found in towns.

Some village businesses are run by community groups and may even use church and village halls for premises. For example, the village of Redmire in Wensleydale, North Yorkshire, lost both its shop and post office. Now, both have re-opened, based in a garage and run by community volunteers.

Case study

Harting village store, West Sussex

In this village shop, the owners wanted to retire but could not find a buyer. The villagers of Harting set up an action committee. They formed a Village Shop Association. This gave them access to government funding and they raised £60,000. A new owner was then able to pay the rest of the value of the shop. Harting kept its shop and social lifeline (photo **C**). The store is being used by people from the surrounding area more and more. Environmentally it is also a success as people drive less often to towns, saving 'shopping miles'.

C *Harting village store*

Activities

3 If you live in a rural area, this question applies directly to you. If you are an urban person, put yourself in the position of someone living in the countryside.

a What are the most difficult things about living in a rural area?

Think about things like: shopping, getting to school or college, transport in general and finding a job.

b Choose three of these problems. How might the projects discussed on pages 229–31 help with each of these three difficulties?

c Are there any ways in which you would improve the existing schemes?

4 Work in pairs for this Activity. Imagine you were taking over the running of a declining village shop. What actions would you take to try to turn it into a thriving business? Consider opening times, the stock you would sell and the services you would offer.

Supporting the rural economy

There are two important programmes aimed at supporting the local economy in rural areas.

1 Rural Challenge

Rural Challenge involved 11 rural regeneration schemes in the 1990s to generate jobs, improve **living standards** and tackle social disadvantage. £75 million created 3,000 jobs and 18,000 weeks of training for young people. Around 200 new community facilities were set up. One example is in Bishop's Castle, Shropshire, which has 37 small business units with an IT resource centre and childcare facilities. Grants for arts, tourism, transport and social projects are available.

Key term

Living standards: people's quality of life, mostly measured economically but also socially, culturally and environmentally.

Latest initiatives by the government to support the economy of rural areas include:

- £100m of funding from the Rural Development Programme for England aimed at rural businesses
- £530m spent on superfast broadband
- £25m used to promote tourism in rural areas
- £15m to help communities tap into the renewable energy potential of rural areas.

2 Objective 1

Objective 1 regions are the poorest parts of the EU. Money comes from four funds:

- the European Regional Development Fund
- the European Social Fund
- the Agricultural Guidance and Guarantee Fund
- the Financial Instrument for Fisheries Guidance.

Any money from the EU has to be matched by money from the country being helped, too. The aim is to help failing industries and tackle economic and social problems.

Study tip

Be able to summarise the government initiatives aimed at supporting the rural economy and environment.

South Yorkshire (2000–2008)

In 2000, South Yorkshire was one of the most deprived regions in Europe. Then over a period of 8 years, £2.4 billion was invested in the region. This boosted the economy and created new jobs. Funding went to both urban and rural areas. 250 organisations and 650 projects received money to help them grow. Here are some examples:

- training so people could learn rural crafts, like building dry stone walls
- money to help farmers start new businesses, like changing a barn into a childcare centre
- money for local tourist attractions, like the 'Maize Maze' at a farm in Cawthorne (near Barnsley), with its 'Maizie Moo' ice cream
- planting trees for forestry projects. For example, South Yorkshire Forest Partnership received £2 million to plant 1 million trees. This helps to support 50 businesses that use timber products.

D *Maize maze in Cawthorne*

Case study

10.4 How does commercial farming operate in the UK?

Factors affecting farming

Farming is affected by both physical and human factors (figure **A**). Farmers decide what to do with their land based on:

- the quality of land
- the climate
- supermarket pressure to produce certain crops
- and what people want to buy.

Farming is a system. A system is when **inputs** are processed to produce **outputs**.

- Inputs into the **farm system** are things like climate, land, seeds, labour, livestock.
- The farmer **processes** the inputs by doing things like ploughing the land, harvesting the crops, milking the cows.
- Farm outputs are processed things like milk, crops, eggs – plus waste products. Profit from the farm is another output. This can be put back into the system, for example to buy new machinery to improve processing.

Key terms

Commercial farming: a type of farming where crops and/or livestock are sold to make a profit.

Inputs: anything entering the farm system, e.g. climate, soil, seed, labour.

Outputs: products leaving the farm system, usually for sale.

Farm system: the operation of a farm, where inputs are processed to produce outputs.

Processes: jobs done on the farm to produce outputs.

Livestock farming: rearing animals.

Intensive farming: high inputs of capital and/or labour to achieve maximum productivity.

Mixed farming: farming both crops and animals.

Arable farming: growing crops.

Study tip

Give better answers to a question by using facts and figures to support what you say. Using numbers like this gives a much clearer picture and allows you to compare more accurately.

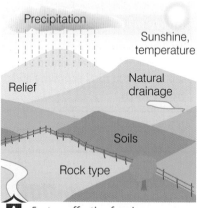
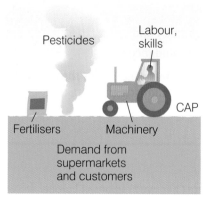

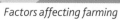
A Factors affecting farming

Activities

1. For each of the following, either draw a simple picture to illustrate this type of farming or find a photo to illustrate it
   a intensive farming   b livestock farming
   c mixed farming   d arable farming.

2. Read the Case Study on the next page and put together a factfile about commercial farming in East Anglia. Make sure you include the following:

- How much of the region is used for farming.
- What types of crops are grown and what livestock are reared (include facts and figures).
- The physical factors that make East Anglia suitable for commercial farming.
- The things that make this farming intensive and commercial: size and scale of farms, machinery, etc.

Commercial farming in East Anglia

East Anglia covers Norfolk, Suffolk, Essex and Cambridgeshire (map **B**). It is one of the most productive agricultural landscapes in the world. Three-quarters of East Anglia is used for farming.

Crops

The region is well known for its cereal crops.

- More than a quarter of England's wheat and barley is grown in East Anglia.
- Well over half the UK's sugar beet crop and a third of all potatoes come from Norfolk, Suffolk and Cambridgeshire.
- Market gardening and horticulture are also important: peas, beans, salad crops, strawberries and other fruits, as well as flowers, are grown there.

Livestock

East Anglia is the centre of the UK's pig and poultry industry. Most **livestock** farms are **intensive**. Every week 2.2 million eggs and 25 per cent of chickens eaten in the UK come from the region. More than 1 million pigs live on 1,900 farms. Beef and dairy cattle herds and sheep flocks are small compared with other regions, such as the south-west. Raising crops, feed and livestock is known as **mixed farming**.

Physical factors

East Anglia's climate is ideal for intensive **arable** production.

- Low rainfall (around 650 mm per year) comes mainly in spring and summer when it helps crops grow.
- Warm summers (July = 18 °C), with plenty of sunshine hours, make sure crops ripen.
- Cold, frosty winders help to break up the soil and kill pests and diseases.

Human factors

Most farms in East Anglia are hundreds of hectares in size – some of the largest in Europe. Large farm machinery is essential to production on this scale. Farms often share the most expensive equipment such as combine harvesters. During harvest time in August, farmers work all day and at night using floodlights.

Many farms are owned by large companies that employ a manager to run one or more farms. Financial inputs are high. Much is spent on chemical fertilisers, pesticides and weed killers.

B The location of East Anglia

C Sugar beet factory in East Anglia

∞links

Research in your school library and on the internet into different types of farming areas in the UK. Try the NFU's FACE website at **www.face-online.org.uk**. Look particularly at Lynford House Farm, Cambridgeshire.

10.5 What are agribusinesses in the UK?

Agribusiness is large-scale farming of crops or livestock. The aim is to produce as much as possible, usually for major supermarkets. Farms are highly mechanised and **capital intensive**. Few workers are needed. Farms may be owned by companies and one company often runs many farms.

Impacts of agribusiness

Agribusiness is sometimes criticised for the following reasons.

1 Use of chemicals

Agribusiness farms use a lot of chemicals to maximise profits.

- Pesticides are used to control pests, diseases and weeds. Without them, yields would be 45 per cent lower. However, chemicals don't just kill 'pests' they also kill important wildlife such as bees.
- Artificial fertilisers put more nutrients into the soil. This makes the soil more fertile so it produces bigger crops. Fertilisers are very expensive. They can also leach into the water table and run into rivers, leading to **eutrophication**.
- Phosphates from animal manure pollute water supplies.

2 Damage to ecosystems

Farming on such a huge scale has caused the loss of important wildlife **habitats**.

Wetlands, such as marshes and peat bogs act as sponges. They soak up rainwater and stop flooding. They also support lots of animals and birds. In some areas, wetlands have been drained to make high-quality farmland. This increases flooding as well as destroying wildlife habitats.

Hedgerows (photo **A**) are an important wildlife habitat. They also act as windbreaks and their roots bind soil together. This reduces soil erosion. Between 1945 and 1990, over 25 per cent of UK hedges were removed. In some arable areas like East Anglia, the figure was over 60 per cent. Hedgerows take up valuable cropland. Getting rid of them also makes large machinery more efficient. However, attitudes have now changed and hedges are being replaced, even on very large farms.

In this section you will learn

what is meant by the term 'agribusiness' and what its impacts are

the demands of the supermarket chains and food processing firms on farmers.

Key terms

Agribusiness: running an agricultural operation like an industry. Inputs and outputs are both high.

Capital intensive: farming to achieve maximum production through buying fuel, fertilisers and buildings that will allow maximum output.

Eutrophication: pollution of fresh water from agricultural waste or excess fertiliser run-off.

Habitat: the home to a community of plants and animals.

Genetically modified (GM) crops: involves putting genes from other species into a crop to give it certain characteristics that increase yield.

A *A hedgerow in winter*

3 Use of genetically modified (GM) crops

Agribusiness farms are more likely to use **genetically modified (GM) crops**. These aim to prevent food shortages and cut prices for the customer. However, environmental groups are very against the use of GM crops. If the added genes get into the natural environment, ecosystems could be changed forever.

Study tip

Labelling a field sketch is similar to labelling a photo. Labels should be placed around the sketch rather than on it. Link the label to the relevant part of the sketch with a clear, ruler-drawn arrow. Make labels detailed.

Grain storage: environmentally controlled, temperature and humidity
Indoor intensive livestock production: food supply controlled by computer, as well as temperature and humidity
Removing hedges: can lead to soil erosion. Large open fields help big machinery be efficient
Combine harvester: efficient at harvest time, but its weight compacts the soil, making it drain poorly
Crops have been treated with:
• chemical fertilisers
• pesticides
which have an impact on wildlife

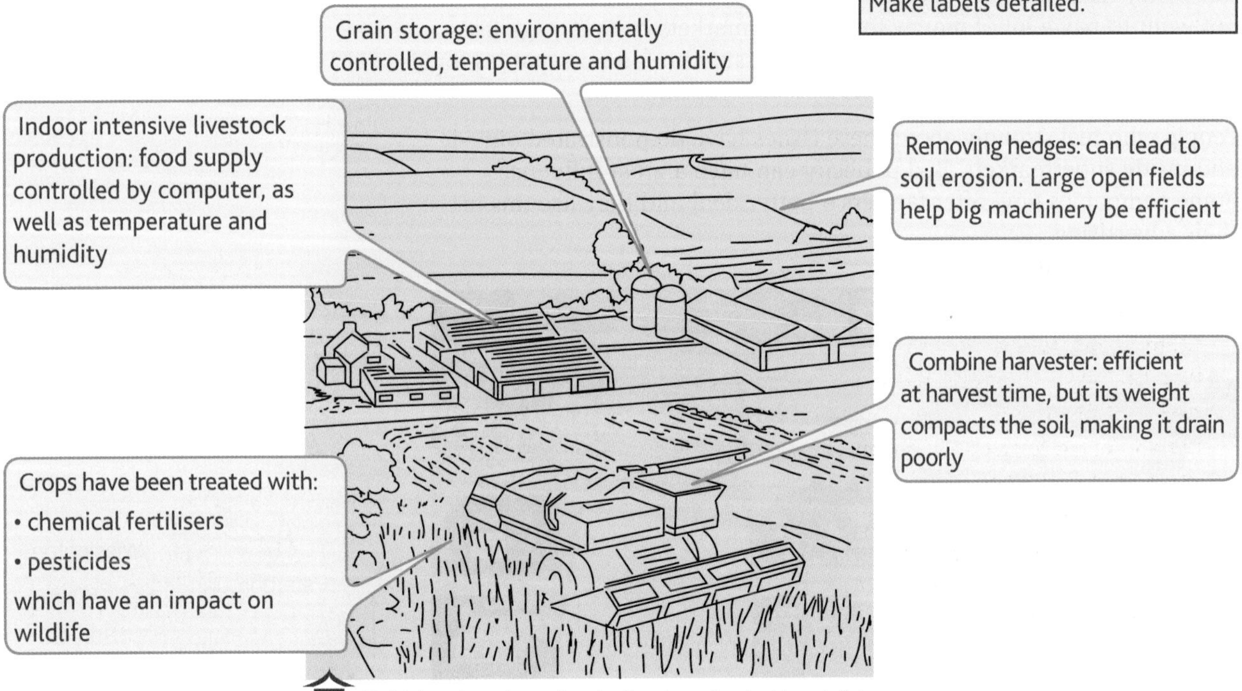

B *Field sketch to show chemical and mechanical inputs into agriculture today*

Activities

1 Draw a concept map (spider diagram) to show the main features of agribusiness.

a Write 'agribusiness' in the centre of your page and define it. Use a photo from the internet too if you can.

b Around the edges, add information to describe the main features and impacts of agribusiness.

2 Copy and complete the table below to describe the advantages and disadvantages of agribusiness practices:

	Advantages for agribusinesses	Disadvantages to the environment
Use of chemicals		
Drainage of wetlands		
Removal of hedges		
Use of GM crops		

The influence of supermarkets on UK farming

The major supermarkets have a lot of power and control over the whole food supply system. Almost all food is bought in supermarkets. If farmers want to sell their produce, they often have to take what the supermarkets offer them.

UK dairy farmers receive the lowest price for their milk in the EU. In 2010 they received 25p per litre. Milk is a daily basic food so people do not want to pay a lot of money for it. Supermarkets compete against each other to keep prices low. They put pressure on food companies for lower prices, so they in turn pay farmers less for milk too.

People who feel strongly about these issues have demonstrated outside and inside supermarkets. Bad publicity can have a great influence. Some companies now offer farmers a better deal and they use this in their advertising.

C What can the customer do?

D British Sugar factory locations

The influence of food processing firms

Food processing turns raw foods from farms into packaged, often ready-cooked food for people and livestock. The food processing industry in East Anglia alone is worth £3 billion. Factories are usually located close to their raw materials or their market. British Sugar processes all sugar beet grown in the UK. Its five factories are all within the growing region for sugar beet (map **D**). Warburton's makes 750,000 loaves of bread in Oldham. All of this is sold within 48 km of the factory.

Food processing companies are put under pressure by supermarkets to produce food at low prices. To make money the companies try to buy their raw materials as cheaply as possible from farmers. Farmers have to accept low prices rather than not sell their produce at all.

10.6   How can we reduce the environmental effects of high impact farming?

The importance of organic farming

Organic farming does not use chemical fertilisers, pesticides or livestock feed additives. Instead, it relies on **crop rotation**, manure, compost and biological pest control. Since 1990 the market for organic produce has been growing by 20 to 25 per cent each year. In 2010 organic produce was worth £36 billion in the UK. The amount of organic land is also growing: 0.9 per cent globally and 4.3 per cent in the UK (2009).

Advantages of organic farming

- It is considered to be more sustainable because it looks after the soil and natural habitats.
- It produces healthier food for people.

Beneficial organisms are introduced, such as ladybirds to eat aphids. Bees and other insects thrive without the chemicals that kill them, in turn improving pollination.

Weeds are controlled mechanically, which is more time-consuming, and by mulching (adding a layer of organic material on top of the soil to prevent weed germination).

Disadvantages

- Organic food is expensive. This is because it requires more labour and yields tend to be lower.
- Organic pesticides can be toxic. This may be worse for the environment than some modern, biodegradable pesticides.
- Dairy production is a major source of greenhouse gas emissions, mainly methane, which is more than 20 times as powerful as carbon dioxide. Organically reared cattle produce twice the amount of methane of other cattle because of their diet.
- Organic crops produce less per hectare but cost the same amount of energy to harvest.
- The Department for Environment, Food and Rural Affairs (Defra) estimates that organic tomato production in the UK takes 25 per cent more water than non-organic production. On the other hand, organic wheat uses less water and less energy per kilogram harvested than non-organic wheat.

> **In this section you will learn**
>
> government policies to reduce environmental effects of high impact farming
>
> how to compare and contrast intensive and organic farming systems

> **Key terms**
>
> **Organic farm**: a farm that does not use chemicals in the production of crops or livestock.
>
> **Crop rotation**: changing the use of a field regularly to help maintain soil fertility.

A *Organic produce in a supermarket*

How do government policies affect farming today?

Governments want to support farmers to make sure that enough food is produced and the countryside is protected.

Farmers are the main people working to conserve the countryside. The Environmental Stewardship Scheme gives farmers money to look after their land and maintain and restore wildlife habitats by:

- replacing hedgerows and keeping them well trimmed
- leaving a strip of land along both sides of a hedge to increase wildlife habitats
- planting trees and managing woodland
- looking after ditches and ponds (photo **B**)
- maintaining hay meadows and grassland.

The National Farmers' Union (NFU) has calculated that farmers carry out £400 million of unpaid work in maintaining the British landscape.

The European Union gives money to support farmers in the Single Farm Payment system. To receive this money, the farmer has to keep livestock and land in good condition. The amount of money given, depends on the size of the farmland. This means that larger farms benefit the most.

> **Did you know** ???????
>
> British farmers are now growing biofuels such as oilseed rape. This helps to lower carbon dioxide emissions, as well as creating new jobs.

B *Ponds are an essential wildlife habitat on farmland*

Activities

1. Study photo **A** on page 237. This shows organic produce in a supermarket.
   a. Can you identify some of the organic produce being sold?
   b. What is meant by 'organic farming'?
   c. How do organic farmers cope with pests?
   d. Why is organic food often more expensive than intensively grown food?
   e. Would you buy organic food? Explain your answer.

2. The Environmental Stewardship Scheme helps farms to restore wildlife habitats.

   Suggest three reasons why wildlife habitats should be preserved.

3. Look back at the factfile you created on East Anglia's commercial farming. What objections might the agribusinesses of East Anglia have if they were told to all use organic farming methods?

10.7 How do countries change from subsistence to cash crop production?

Having borrowed money to support economic development many poor countries are in debt. One solution is to turn land currently used for subsistence crops into cash crop production. Subsistence means that the crops grown are eaten by the farmer and their family. This is how they survive. Cash crops are crops which can be sold to make money for the farmer. Governments encourage cash crop production as it makes money for the country.

> **In this section you will learn**
>
> how cash crop cultivation impacts on subsistence food production.

Cash crop production in Kenya: flowers

Poorer countries like Kenya are using more land for cash crop production (map **A**). The land was previously used for growing subsistence crops for local people or belonged to small-scale producers of tea and coffee.

Kenya's flower industry is the oldest and largest in Africa. Kenya's main flower crops are roses and carnations. No other country exports as many roses as Kenya. Just look in your local supermarket – it will almost certainly have Kenyan roses (photo **B**).

◻ Main flower-producing area
⊗ Nairobi – main airport for exports

A *Major flower-producing area in Kenya*

B *Kenyan roses on sale in a UK supermarket*

Today, Kenya's flower exports earn the country $250 million a year, and this business is growing by 20 per cent a year. One fifth of the year's business takes place in February and this is when workers put in maximum hours. This is because of Valentine's Day in Europe. Millions of roses are flown from Nairobi to Europe every year. The USA is also an expanding market.

Case study

C   *Worker in Kenya's flower cash crop industry*

Kenya has some of the largest flower farms in the world. Even though Kenya has a good climate for flower growing, most roses are grown in greenhouses to protect them from rain, which rots them, and wind and hail, which can damage them. Flowers are grown close to the Rift Valley lakes because they provide a reliable source of water.

The flower business employs tens of thousands of workers (photo **C**). Two-thirds of them are casual labourers with no job security or benefits. Pregnancy usually means you lose your job. Wages of £1 per day – Kenya's minimum wage – are just above the globally accepted poverty level of $1 per day.

∞ links

See p.293 for more on flower production in Kenya. This will help inform your activity answers.

See p.293 for more on flower production in Kenya.

Study tip

There are always at least two points of view to any issue. First, you need to write about all sides of the situation. In your conclusion, give your own opinion but it must be backed up with reasons.

Activity

Think about what you have read about Kenya's flower industry.

a   Describe the location of Kenya's flower-producing area.

b   Why is Kenya well suited to growing flowers for the European market?

c   Why are flowers grown in greenhouses?

d   How much does Kenya earn from flower exports each year?

e   How much do Kenyan workers earn a day on the flower farms?

f   Why do countries like Kenya want to use land for cash crops rather than for food crops for Kenyan people?

10.8 How do forestry and mining impact on the traditional farming economy?

Traditional farming in the Amazon Basin

Shifting cultivation (also called 'slash and burn' agriculture) is the traditional form of rainforest subsistence farming. Native tribes have used the system for thousands of years. Most nutrients are stored in rainforest plants. Soils are poor quality and it takes at least 20 years for the soil to recover after being used for only 2 or 3 years. Usually, a family has three or four plots under cultivation each year and ten times as many **fallow** ones.

Rainforest destruction

When rainforest plants are taken away (deforestation), the soil quickly breaks down. Heavy rain then washes it away. Once clearance has happened, traditional farming cannot restart because the soil is ruined. Tribal people often have no legal right to the land they farm. This means that governments can use the land however they want or sell it to transnational corporations (TNCs).

There are four main reasons why the rainforest is being destroyed.

1 The impact of cash crops and ranching

To get money, governments of poorer countries use rainforest land to grow cash crops. In the Amazon, huge areas of rainforest have been cleared for soya production. This is mainly used to feed beef cattle in the USA or Brazil itself to produce beef for export. In Indonesia, cassava – another fodder crop – is grown for export to the EU. Large areas of forest have been cleared for cattle ranching, especially in the Amazon Basin. On average one animal requires two hectares of land.

> ### In this section you will learn
>
> the scale of deforestation for forestry and mining in the Amazon Basin
>
> the impacts of this on traditional farmers
>
> whether some forms of large-scale exploitation are more acceptable than others.

> ### Key term
>
> **Fallow:** land that has been left unseeded to recover its fertility.

A   *A farmer burns the rainforest*

B   *Deforestation*

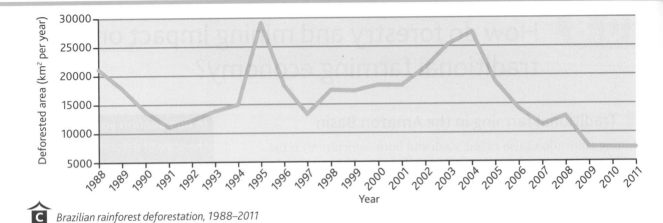

C *Brazilian rainforest deforestation, 1988–2011*

2 The impact of forestry

Governments also use the trees themselves to make money. Wood from the rainforest can be used for building or for making expensive furniture. This has many impacts.

- Deforestation destroys the land.
- Rivers dry up with silt from soil erosion.
- Water and soil are polluted by the machines which cut down and move the logs.
- Logging has devastated tribes such as the Moi people in Indonesia. Their way of life threatened, they tried to stand up to the Intimpura Timber Company. The government sent in the army to support the company over its own people.

3 The impact of mining

The mining industry in the Amazon is worth billions of pounds. Carajas Iron Ore Mine in Brazil, for example, is one of the largest working mines in the world. Most companies are foreign-owned, although Brazilian investment is increasing.

Mining has many impacts on the rural environment:

- Rainforest has to be cleared on a huge scale so rocks and minerals can be dug out of the ground (photo **D**).
- Pollution is high for both water and land.
- The landscape has been complete changed and ecosystems destroyed.

4 The impact of growing infrastructure

Road construction in the Amazon has led to great losses too. Roads provide access to logging and mining sites, as well as allowing farmers to get deeper into the forest. The Trans-Amazonian Highway, for example, was a huge project. It involved constructing a 3,200 km long highway through the rainforest region.

D *Large-scale mining in the Amazon Basin*

Case study

Rainforest clearance in Indonesia, 1997–1998

From September 1997 to June 1998, much of South-east Asia suffered major air pollution caused by thousands of rainforest fires. Some fires were started by new farmers clearing land and they were largely blamed. However, 80 per cent were due to large forestry companies clearing land for large-scale mining and agriculture projects.

Indonesia has lost 20,000 plant species and 17 per cent of the world's birds. Thousands more species face extinction due to deforestation. From 1997 to 1998, rainforest fires polluted the whole region.

E *Advantages and disadvantages of large-scale rainforest exploitation*

Advantages	Disadvantages
Wood and minerals make a lot of money for the country which can be spent on development projects to help local people.	Local people lose their homes and way of life.
TNCs help local people learn new skills.	Businesses are often owned by TNCs who get all the profits.
Jobs are provided for local people.	Local people usually only get the low paid jobs – senior jobs are given to people from overseas.
Infrastructure (roads and services) can be used by local people.	Land can be destroyed forever – once the logging and mining has stopped, there are no jobs and no way of farming the land again.

Activities

1 a   Use the data below to draw a pie chart to show the causes of deforestation in the Amazon Basin. The diameter of your pie chart should be at least 6 cm for clarity.

Causes of deforestation in the Amazon Basin by land area (2000–2005)	
Cattle ranching	60%
Small-scale subsistence agriculture	30%
Fires, mining, urbanisation, road construction and dams	4%
Logging, legal and illegal practices	4%
Large-scale commercial arable agriculture	2%

b   Why do you think cattle ranching is by far the main cause of deforestation?

2   Study photo **A**.

a   Why is the farmer burning the rainforest?

b   Suggest some environmental effects of what he is doing.

3   Study photo **D**.

a   What is happening in the photo?

b   What might be the environmental effects of this mining operation?

Did you know ??????

Between 1970 and 2006, over 600,000 km² of Amazon rainforest were destroyed, mostly by logging and some by mining concerns.

∞ **links**

Research deforestation in the Amazon Basin at **www.mongabay.com/brazil.html**.

10.9 What are soil erosion issues?

What is soil erosion?

Soil erosion occurs when the soil is either blown away by wind or washed away by rain (photo **A**). It is common in areas with steep slopes. Deforestation destroys the tree roots that bind the soil together and the shelter that limits the impact of the wind. Poor farming techniques make the problems worse because they weaken soil structure and make it more likely to be eroded. Population increase puts pressure on farmers to grow more with the chance that the soil will be over-cultivated.

> **In this section you will learn**
>
> why soil erosion happens
>
> methods for solving soil erosion problems.

A Severe soil erosion in East Africa

> **Key term**
>
> **Salinisation**: the deposition of solid salts on the ground surface following the evaporation of water. Also, an increase in the concentration of salts in the soil, reducing fertility.

What are the impacts of soil erosion?

As soil erodes it can support fewer plants. The more erosion happens the less can grow. In the world as a whole, an area 10 times the size of the UK has become so severely degraded that it can no longer produce food. This is a serious problem as world population keeps growing.

Where does soil erosion occur?

Today Iraq has the worst soil problems in the world: erosion, **salinisation** and deforestation. The USA, Australia and China also have serious soil erosion problems. In Madagascar, the best farmland is used to grow coffee for export. Local people have had to clear more and more forest to grow subsistence crops. Half the island's forest vanished between 1950 and 1985. Losses of topsoil are huge. Air and satellite photos show red staining in the Indian Ocean due to topsoil being washed out to sea (photo **B**).

In Democratic Republic of Congo and Nigeria, increasing demands for food meant shifting cultivators could not leave soil plots long enough to grow again between crops. They cleared too many areas too close together, which allowed heavy rain to wash the soil away. This whole farming system has broken down as a result.

B Satellite photo showing eroded soil washed into the Indian Ocean

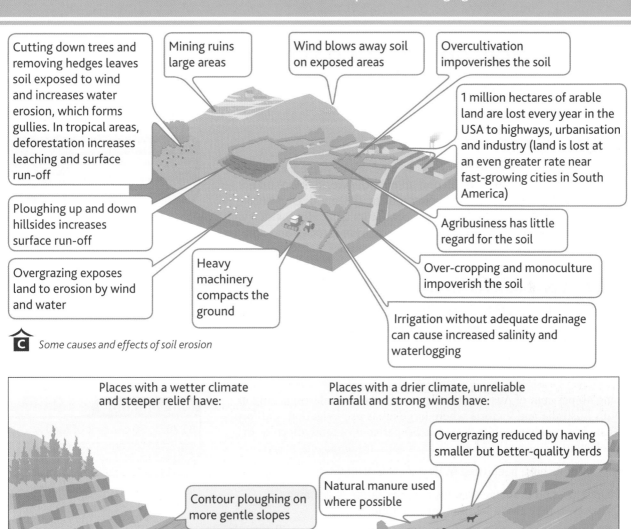

Cutting down trees and removing hedges leaves soil exposed to wind and increases water erosion, which forms gullies. In tropical areas, deforestation increases leaching and surface run-off

Mining ruins large areas

Wind blows away soil on exposed areas

Overcultivation impoverishes the soil

1 million hectares of arable land are lost every year in the USA to highways, urbanisation and industry (land is lost at an even greater rate near fast-growing cities in South America)

Ploughing up and down hillsides increases surface run-off

Overgrazing exposes land to erosion by wind and water

Heavy machinery compacts the ground

Agribusiness has little regard for the soil

Over-cropping and monoculture impoverish the soil

Irrigation without adequate drainage can cause increased salinity and waterlogging

C *Some causes and effects of soil erosion*

Places with a wetter climate and steeper relief have:

Places with a drier climate, unreliable rainfall and strong winds have:

Overgrazing reduced by having smaller but better-quality herds

Natural manure used where possible

Contour ploughing on more gentle slopes

Strip cultivation with alternate crops in same area

Crops alternated with grass to prevent overcultivation and soil exhaustion

Gullies filled in with soil and replanted

D *Some attempts to reduce and prevent soil erosion*

Activities

1   Study photo **A** and diagram **C**.

  a   What is the evidence that the land in the photo is suffering from soil erosion?

  b   Use diagram **C** to suggest some possible causes of the soil erosion in photo **A**. Think carefully as some of the causes are more likely than others!

2   Draw your own version of diagram **D**. Locate and add the following labels to your diagram:

  ■   terracing on steep slopes

  ■   hedgerows replanted to hold the soil together and act as windbreaks.

  ■   planting trees (afforestation) on the steepest slopes to bind the soil together and protect it from heavy rain.

10.10 How do irrigation schemes increase food production?

What is irrigation?

Irrigation is the artificial watering of the land. It has played a huge role in increasing farming production all over the world. More than half of rice and wheat are already grown using irrigation. One-third of the world's food is grown on 17 per cent of its land, all of which is irrigated. This shows just how important irrigation is today and will continue to be in the future as the population grows.

What problems does irrigation bring?

California and Australia have used irrigation schemes on a huge scale. Yields were dramatically increased, but after several years problems emerged. Up to half the irrigated land in these countries now suffers from salinisation – where salt damages the land. This puts the land out of production until the problem can be solved – an expensive process.

Some 40 per cent of Australian soils are affected by salt, especially in South Australia and Victoria where large areas use irrigation. California has similar problems while Syria has 50 per cent of land affected. In Uzbekistan, a staggering 80 per cent of soils are damaged by salt.

Two solutions have been tried in Egypt's Nile Valley:

- Underground drainage systems take the saline water away. However, they cost a lot of money to build.
- Changing land use is a cheaper alternative. Some grass will grow in salt. So turning arable land to pasture keeps it productive while the salt washes away slowly with the rain.

Irrigation in sub-Saharan Africa

Sub-Saharan Africa includes many of the world's poorest countries. It suffers from unreliable rainfall. At the moment, only 3.5 per cent of land is irrigated (photo **A**).

Africa lags behind Asia and the rest of the world in all aspects of irrigation. In West Africa, 1 in 20 of Senegal's farmers has irrigation and this is one of the better-served countries. In Asia, one in three farmers has irrigation. This means that opportunities for growing more food and improving lives are being lost.

Due to lack of technology, most African irrigation systems use the water only once. It is not recycled within the system. Most technology improvements are funded by aid.

> ### In this section you will learn
> how irrigation schemes can change agriculture.

> ### Did you know ??????
> By 2025, 80 per cent of food is expected to come from irrigated land.

A An irrigation scheme in sub-Saharan Africa

Types of irrigation

- **Drip irrigation** – pipes are laid across fields. Water flows through slowly and drips out through holes in the pipe. It soaks into the soil and quickly reaches the roots over a long period of time (diagram **B**).

- **Sprinkler irrigation** – water is piped to one or more central spots in the field. Pressure sprinklers then spray water to the crops (photo **C**). More developed countries, including the UK, use this method. However, it is expensive to set up and run.

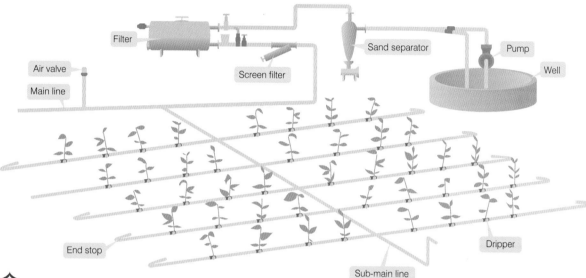

B   *A drip irrigation scheme*

C   *Sprinkler irrigation*

D   *Advantages and disadvantages of drip and sprinkler irrigation*

	Drip	Sprinkler
Advantages	• Uses a small amount of water • Little chance for water to evaporate • Can be laid in the ground, so even less water is wasted • Plants have regular supply of water • Easy to control • Inexpensive to set up • Can use recycled water • Farmer can control soil moisture • Minimises soil erosion • Leaves stay dry; no rot	• Flexible – can be fed by hose from water source • Can be moved easily around a field • Can use recycled water
Disadvantages	• Only works with crops grown in rows • Needs gently sloping land to work efficiently • Pipes and holes can become clogged with silt • Needs a pump to flow well on flat land	• Expensive to start up • May need a pump to run • Leaves get wet and might rot • Uses more water • Higher rate of evaporation

Water use in Jordan

Jordan is a particularly dry country in the Middle East. Only 6 per cent of the country is farmed. Irrigation is essential and 70 per cent of all water is already used for food production (photo **E**). Treated waste water is now used for extra irrigation water. Sixteen treatment plants put 60 million m³ of clean water into irrigation schemes or into the River Jordan where it can be used downstream. The World Bank financially supports the companies involved. Other countries might be able to learn from Jordan's experience.

E *Intensive production of tomatoes using pumped water in the Badia desert, Jordan*

Appropriate technology

Sometimes, aid projects have introduced technology at too high a level to work. It should be appropriate to the needs and technology of the people who are to make use of it. It should be:

- Affordable to buy.
- Cheap to run (fuel is expensive).
- Easy to use (so training isn't needed).
- Easy to repair with simple tools.

For example, small, handheld ploughs may be more appropriate in a remote part of Africa than tractors. In the same way, simple irrigation systems, like the drip method, may turn out to be more effective than others.

Activities

1. a Write a short definition of 'irrigation'.

    b Explain why irrigation is important in world farming today. Use facts and figures in your answer.

    c If many Sub-Saharan African countries suffer from drought and many Sub-Saharan Africans do not have enough to eat, why do you think these countries do not make more use of irrigation? Think about the following factors when writing your answer:

    - cost of introducing irrigation
    - whether irrigation means a big change in traditional farming techniques
    - whether the crops that work best with irrigation are expensive to buy (as seeds)
    - how technical knowledge is needed to introduce and maintain an irrigation system.

2. a Explain what is meant by the term 'salinisation'.

    b What percentage of Uzbekistan's soil is affected by salinisation?

    c How can the problem be solved or reduced?

3. Imagine you are a consultant on a new irrigation scheme in a less well-off country. What advice would you give on the following points?

    - the best type of scheme to be used
    - the construction of the scheme
    - avoiding future problems of salinisation.

    Present your advice in the form of a short report using photos and diagrams.

10.11 How does rural-to-urban migration affect rural areas?

■ Reasons for rural-to-urban migration

Rural-to-urban migration is caused both by rural push factors and by urban pull factors.

Rural push factors

- Poor rural standards of living make people want to do better for themselves and their children.
- Subsistence farms may not be able to support large families.
- Often there are not many jobs or educational opportunities in the country.
- Droughts, natural disasters and war force people to leave.

Urban pull factors

As a country develops, more opportunities become available, but most of these are in the cities. The city is seen as the place where more and better paid jobs can be found and where there are better schools and healthcare facilities.

■ Impacts of rural–urban migration on the rural area

Benefits

Migrants send money home to those in the villages. This can be used to improve farming – increasing livestock, buying new tools or better seed – or to help the family by paying school fees.

Problems

- Sometimes whole families move, but often it is the main breadwinner – the husband and father. Wives, children and the elderly are less able to carry out the hard physical labour involved in farming. Crop yields may be reduced and rural development may become limited.
- Children are brought up with less influence from their fathers. They may have to help more on the farm, which can affect their education.
- Although the money sent home helps, the family and farming system are put under pressure.

In this section you will learn

- the reasons for rural-to-urban migration
- the impact rural-to-urban migration may have in the rural areas from which people move
- why some agricultural systems are failing.

A *Poor quality land in Lesotho, Africa acts as a 'push' factor encouraging rural–urban migration*

Case study

Crisis in Lesotho

Farming employs 57 per cent of Lesotho's labour force, mostly on small subsistence farms. This is low compared with other poor countries. The reasons vary:

- Lesotho has lots of mountains. This limits the amount of agricultural land available. Much of the land suffers from serious soil erosion, partly because of drought.

- Some 35 per cent of men leave home to work in the cities and mines of South Africa (map **B**). If they were all at home on the land, farm labour would be a much higher 86 per cent of the national workforce.

- It is difficult to manage farming in such circumstances. Also, since the area of productive land has got smaller, 40 per cent of families are landless.

B The location of Lesotho in southern Africa

Table **C** shows the main crops produced in Lesotho. Maize is the main crop. Along with other crops its production has dropped since 2000/01. Crop production in Lesotho is high risk and yields are low because of poor soil quality and the harsh, unpredictable climate (photo **A**). About 10 per cent of the country is arable land, but only 1 per cent is high quality. Lesotho has to import a lot of grain as well as some other food. Livestock production is important to rural income because animals cope better with poor land than crops, although drought in the 1980s and 1990s limited the amount of pasture.

With so many men and older boys leaving to find paid work elsewhere, much of the farm labour is left to women, children and the elderly.

On a more positive note, Lesotho has one of the most advanced soil conservation programmes in Africa. It is beginning to solve some of the problems by terracing the land and introducing irrigation systems.

C Agricultural production, 2000–2008 (thousands of tonnes)

Crop	2000/01	2001/02	2002/03	2003/04	2004/05	2005/06	2006/07	2007/08
Maize	158.2	111.2	82.1	81.0	75.0	76.9	60.3	59.6
Sorghum	45.4	11.9	12.0	10.3	10.3	12.1	7.8	10.1
Wheat	37.3	19.0	13.1	11.7	11.1	2.9	1.2	3.7
Beans	7.9	4.4	3.7	4.8	5.2	5.3	5.3	3.1
Peas	3.7	3.0	3.0	1.5	1.4	0.7	0.7	1.0

Activity

a Explain why rural–urban migration is causing this decline in the amount of land being farmed in Lesotho.

b How has the climate affected agricultural production in Lesotho?

c Suggest ways that the men may be encouraged to remain as farmers in rural areas?

11 The development gap

11.1 What are the traditional ways of dividing up the world?

■ What is meant by 'development'?

The word 'development' means change. It usually means change for the better. In geography, development is a word used to describe how rich or how poor a country is. Generally, a highly developed country has more wealth than a less developed country. However, it is not just about money. It is about improving people's lives. Today, there are lots of different ways that development is measured (see section 11.2 pages 254–256).

All countries are different from each other but countries are often grouped together by how developed they are. This section will look at the different ways in which the world has been divided up.

■ North/South

In 1971 the Brandt Report came up with a simple way of dividing the world. It used GNP (Gross National Product) which is how much money a country earns. It split the world into two:

- Rich countries with lots of different types of industry.
- Poor countries with few industries (mostly agriculture).

A line called the North-South divide was drawn on a world map to make this difference clear (map **A**). This system is not used any more because it is just too simple.

> **In this section you will learn**
>
> the traditional ways of dividing up the world in terms of development
>
> a modern division based on wealth.

> **Did you know** ??????
>
> Gross Domestic Product (GDP) is an indication of the value of goods produced within a country's borders. Gross National Product (GNP) relates to the value of goods produced by citizens of the country.

> **Did you know** ??????
>
> Map **A** shows Gross Domestic Product (GDP) per capita (per person) across the world. The type of map used to show this is called a choropleth map. It is a shaded map where the depth of colour increases as the value gets higher. The darker colours show higher values and paler ones show lower values. The map helps us to understand it easily and quickly.

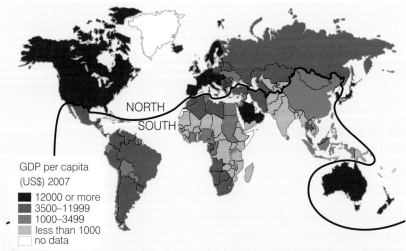

GDP per capita (US$) 2007

- ■ 12000 or more
- ■ 3500–11999
- ■ 1000–3499
- ■ less than 1000
- □ no data

NORTH
SOUTH

Source: International Monetary Fund 2008

A Choropleth map showing GDP per capita, 2007

LEDCs and MEDCs

The North-South divide was seen as too simple because it only looked at how much money a country had. It was not fair to suggest that culture, for example, was at a low level just because the country was economically poor. This led to new terms which made it clear that money was the only factor being looked at – 'less economically developed country' (LEDC) and 'more economically developed country' (MEDC).

However, these terms were also seen as too simple because there were sometimes huge differences between countries classed as LEDCs. Although they are still used today, the LEDC/MEDC division is becoming much less useful.

The five-fold division based on wealth

This puts countries into five groups. The groups are also based on financial wealth (map **B**). The problem is that not all countries fit into one group only.

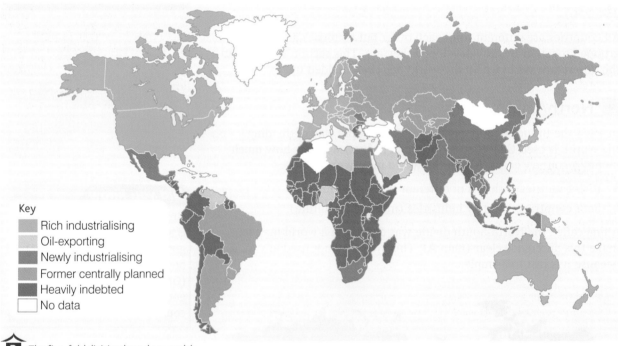

Key
- Rich industrialising
- Oil-exporting
- Newly industrialising
- Former centrally planned
- Heavily indebted
- No data

B *The five-fold division based on wealth*

1 Rich industrialising countries

These are the richest countries in the world which have lots of different types of industry. The UK would be classed as a rich industrialising country. We are still wealthy, but our manufacturing industry has declined recently.

2 Oil-exporting countries

Huge amounts of money are made from countries which sell oil. However, the oil companies are owned by only a few people in those countries and sometimes they keep the money for themselves. Most people remain poor in oil-exporting countries. Some profit is used for development projects to help the poor people, so this may change. Some UK football clubs have been bought by billionaires from oil-exporting countries (photo **C**).

3 Newly industrialising countries

These are countries which are still very poor but where more trade and industry is happening. Some are growing faster than most developed countries. China's economy is growing extremely quickly – its speed of industrialisation has been amazing.

4 Formerly centrally planned economies

These are countries where most things used to be owned and run by the government. This is no longer the case but their development is still affected by their past. There is a lot of overlap between this category and category 3. For example, Russia is *both* a newly industrialising country and *also* a formally centrally planned economy.

5 Heavily indebted poor countries

These are countries where development has never really got going. This is often because of debt. Many poor countries were loaned large sums of money by other countries and by the World Bank back in the 20th century. Most of what they earn now goes on paying for their debt and not enough is left to develop the economy.

C *Manchester City football club was bought by a Middle Eastern company*

Activities

1   Study map **A** (page 251). This shows GDP per capita in different countries around the world. GDP is a measure of a country's wealth. It is expressed 'per capita', which means 'per person'.

a   Use an atlas to help you name two countries with less than $1000 per capita per year and two with $12,000 or more.

b   Describe the pattern of GDP per capita across the world in 2007.

■   Where are most of the richest countries located?

■   Where are most of the poorest countries located?

2   Now compare map **A** with map **B**, which shows five different categories of countries. Which of these statements would you agree with?

■   There is a close match between the poorest countries (GDP per capita) and 'heavily indebted' countries.

■   The oil exporting countries are the richest countries in terms of GDP per capita.

■   There is a concentration of newly industrialising countries in Asia.

■   Some of the newly industrialising countries have very low GDP per capita.

11.2 How can we measure development?

Correlating different measures of development

Things that tell us a great deal about a country and allow us to compare countries are called indicators. Any **development measure** that tells us about wealth, poverty or economic development should link up (correlate) with other indicators. For example, a country with low **GNP** per capita (money earned per person) is likely to have low levels of education and health care. There isn't much money to pay for education and health, so living standards for most people are low.

Birth rate is closely linked to levels of development. The more developed a country, the lower its birth rate. The demographic transition model shows that birth rate gets lower as countries become more developed (map **A**).

Key term

Development measures: statistics used to show the level of development, which allows countries to be compared.

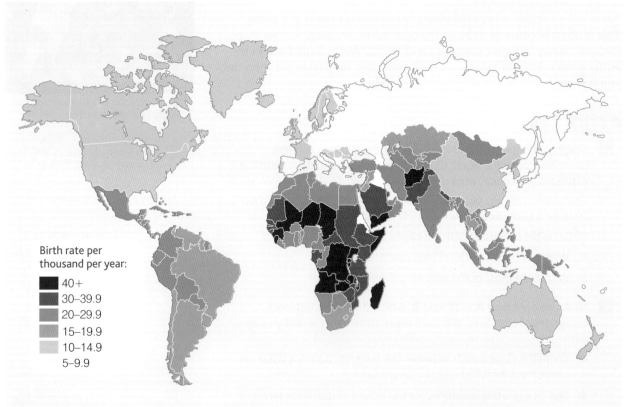

Birth rate per thousand per year:
- 40+
- 30–39.9
- 20–29.9
- 15–19.9
- 10–14.9
- 5–9.9

A Birth rate as a development indicator

A country at a further stage of development is likely to have:

- a high **human development index (HDI)**
- a low **infant mortality** rate
- widespread access to clean water
- many doctors for the number of people
- high **literacy rates**.

Key terms

Infant mortality: the number of babies that die under a year of age, per 1000 live births.

Literacy rate: the percentage of adults in a country who can read and write sufficiently to function fully in work and society.

Poorer governments do not have enough funds to provide high-level services. Often even the basics like clean water and a living wage are not possible (table **B**).

B *A range of development indicators for selected countries*

Country	GNI per capita (US $) (2010)	HDI (2010)	Birth rate per 1,000 per year	Death rate per 1,000 per year	Infant mortality per 1,000 live births per year	Number of doctors per 1,000 people	Literacy rate (%)	Percentage of population with access to clean water
USA	47,020	0.902	13.8	8.4	6.1	2.3	99.0	99
Japan	34,790	0.884	7.3	10.1	2.8	2.0	99.0	100
UK	36,580	0.849	12.3	9.3	4.6	2.2	99.0	100
Turkey	14,580	0.679	17.9	6.1	23.9	1.3	88.7	99
Romania	14,050	0.767	9.6	11.8	11.0	1.9	97.6	61
Brazil	10,920	0.699	17.8	6.4	21.2	2.1	90.0	97
China	7,570	0.663	12.3	7.0	16.1	1.5	95.9	89
Ivory Coast	1,650	0.397	31.0	10.2	64.8	0.1	48.7	80
Bangladesh	1,620	0.469	23.0	5.8	50.7	0.3	53.5	80
Zimbabwe	460	0.140	30.0	15.0	56.0	0.6	90.7	82

Activities

1 Study table **B**. This gives a range of development indicators for some different countries.

a Which country has the highest GNI per capita?

b Which country has the lowest GNI per capita?

c Now look at the other indicators for the country with the lowest GNI per capita. Do they also suggest that this is a poor country? Remember that:

- poorer countries tend to have high birth rates because families rely on children for work and care of the elderly

- poorer countries may have quite low death rates because most of the population is young

- infant mortality (death rate for babies) is a good measure of development – wealthier countries can afford the healthcare that saves more infant lives

- number of doctors per 1,000 people: the richer the country, the more doctors it can afford

- literacy rate: the richer the country, the better the education system it can afford

- access to clean water: you'd except 100% in a wealthy country so anything much less than this suggests lower development.

Key terms

GNI: Gross National Income – the total value of goods and services produced within a country including income received from and payments made to other countries.

GNP: Gross National Product – the total value of all goods and services produced by a nation in a particular year.

Human development index (HDI): an index based on three variables: life expectancy at birth; level of education, including both literacy rate and years spent in school; income adjusted for purchasing power (how much it will buy). Maximum HDI = 1. Wealthy countries like Japan have an HDI of over 0.9, whereas poor countries are around half that figure or less.

Graph **C** shows a clear correlation between two development indicators, although there are a few anomalies. An anomaly is a figure that does not fit in with the pattern. For example, Romania has a lower birth rate than expected, given its low GNI.

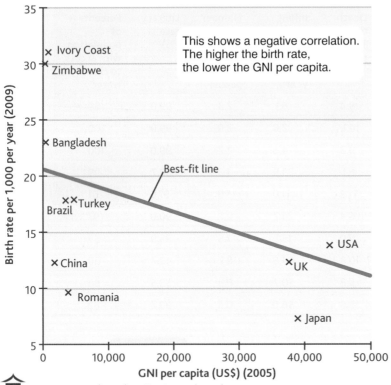

This shows a negative correlation. The higher the birth rate, the lower the GNI per capita.

C *GNI per capita (2005) and birth rate (2009)*

Limitations of using a single development measure

Some measures of development can give a narrow or confusing picture if just used by themselves.

- Birth rate is an excellent measure of development. In highly developed countries, more women have high levels of education and career prospects so have fewer children.
- Death rate is a bad indicator of development because almost all countries have low death rates today. It doesn't show at what age people are dying or what they are dying from.
- GNP or GNI per capita are only economic measures so they do not give a clear indication of what people's lives are like. For example, people can be quite poor but still be educated, live to a good age and have healthy children.

Multi-variable indicators

Combining several indicators together can give a better idea of what life is actually like for people:

- **Physical quality of life index (PQLI)** combines literacy rate, life expectancy and infant mortality to measure quality of life.
- **Human Development Index (HDI)** uses life expectancy, literacy rates and measures of how much people earn to give an indicator for overall development. It is the most commonly used indicator of development.

11.3 What factors make global development inequalities worse?

Physical factors

The physical geography of some countries does not help development. For example, high mountains and hot deserts can make farming, building, trade and transport difficult and slow down the processes of development.

Natural hazards are also more common in some parts of the world. For example:

- Drought regularly strikes some parts of Africa.
- The location and height of the land means some countries such as Bangladesh are often flooded.
- Hurricanes often hit the Caribbean and central America.

These limit future development and destroy what may already have been achieved.

In this section you will learn

different factors that contribute to development inequalities

the impacts of a natural hazard on development (a physical factor)

the effects of social, economic and political factors on development.

Hurricane Ivan (2004)

Hurricane Ivan was one of the Caribbean's most powerful hurricanes. It hit several Caribbean countries as well as the USA. Ivan struck the island of Grenada on 7 September 2004 (map **A**). Winds of 200 km per hour caused major damage.

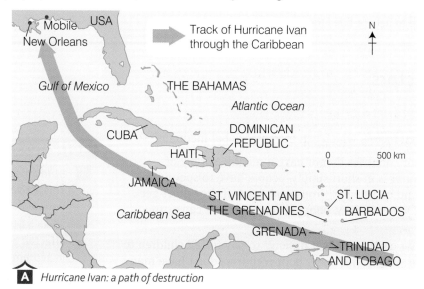

A *Hurricane Ivan: a path of destruction*

Effects of the hurricane

The southern part of Grenada was the worst affected. Services and buildings were destroyed (photo **B**). Roads were blocked by fallen trees. Coastal defences did well against the storm surge and stopped many parts from being flooded. Thirty-seven people died in Grenada. Around 90 per cent of houses were damaged or destroyed.

Most people were affected in some way, half being made homeless. Almost all schools were damaged. Water, power and telecommunications systems were also disrupted. Water supply was seen as the most important problem and was fixed within three weeks of the storm.

Case study

B *Hurricane Ivan's damaged landscape*

Impact on development

In terms of development, long-term damage is often more of a problem than short-term damage. In Grenada, agriculture, tourism and the country's infrastructure were badly affected. This slowed down the pace of development and has been costly to put right. Many of the people affected were poor and did not have insurance to help re-build their lives.

■ Human factors

Social

There are many social factors which can increase global inequalities:

- **Water:** Many poor countries do not have a reliable supply of clean water. If water is in short supply, people have to spend time searching for it and carrying it. Crops can't grow if they don't get enough water. If water is dirty, people become ill and can't support their families.

- **Education:** A poor country finds it difficult to pay for all children to go to school. This means that many poor countries don't have many well-educated people to work and help their country develop.

- **Health:** Many poor countries have serious health problems. Tropical Africa, South America and Asia suffer from more climate-related diseases, such as malaria than cooler parts of the world. Sub-Saharan Africa has suffered particularly badly from HIV/Aids. Poor countries cannot afford a good healthcare system to stop illness and help people once they get ill. Sick people can't work and many children are orphaned which affects the economy of that country.

Activities

1   Study map **A** on page 257. This shows Hurricane Ivan's path of destruction.

a   Make a list of the countries affected by Hurricane Ivan in September 2004.

b   Describe the short-term impacts of Hurricane Ivan on Grenada.

c   How has the impact of Hurricane Ivan affected Grenada's long-term development?

Economic

A country's income is mainly measured by its gross domestic product (GDP) per capita. The welfare of its people is measured by the human development index (HDI). In general, when the income is low, so is the level of welfare (table **B**). In other words, the more money a country makes, the more is spent on improving people's lives. A major part of how countries make money is through trade – when countries buy and sell from each other. We'll look at trade in the next section.

Political

- Corrupt politicians become rich at the expense of their country's development. When this happens, money is not available for education, health services, roads and clean water.

- Corrupt governments put people off investing or giving aid to that country because they do not know what that money will be used for. Foreign investors and aid providers are discouraged from putting funds into such a country because they cannot rely on the money reaching the target. Economies that are already weak cannot afford to miss out on this income.

- War seriously affects the development of a country. A civil war is a war between two or more different groups in one country. Many of the world's poorest countries have been affected by civil wars. Examples include the Democratic Republic of the Congo, Somalia and Sierra Leone.

C *GDP per capita and HDI compared, 2010*

Continent/ country	GDP per capita ($) (2010)	HDI (out of 1) (2010)
Africa:		
Chad	1,600	0.36
Comoros	1,000	0.43
DR of Congo	300	0.31
Ethiopia	1,000	0.41
Ghana	2,500	0.49
Somalia	600	0.28 (2001)
Sudan	2,300	0.48
Zimbabwe	500	0.18
Asia:		
India	3,500	0.59
Indonesia	4,200	0.69
Iran	10,600	0.74
Malaysia	14,700	0.77
Pakistan	2,500	0.53
Philippines	3,500	0.68
Latin America:		
Mexico	13,900	0.79
Peru	9,200	0.76

Activities

2 Study table **C**.

a Draw a scattergraph to show HDI and GDP per capita for the countries shown in the table **C**. Put GDP ono the horizontal (*x*) axis and HDI on the vertical (*y*) axis.

b Draw a best fit line and describe the relationship.

c Which continent has the poorest and least developed countries according to the scattergraph?

3 a Why does a lack of clean water slow down the rate of development?

b Name two diseases that affect people in Africa.

c Some countries have decided to invest in education to encourage development. Do you think this is a good idea? Why?

Study tip

Be clear as to the differences between 'physical', 'economic', 'social' and 'political' factors in relation to global inequalities and be able to give at least one example of each.

links

Find out more about the importance of clean water at www.wateraid.org.uk

11.4 How does trade increase global inequalities?

The trade imbalance

No country has everything that it needs or wants. They have to buy and sell from other countries. This is known as trade. The money that a country makes from trade can then be spent on improving the lives of people, for example by building hospitals and paying for people to go to school. To do this though, the country has to make more money from trade than it spends.

The problem is that poor countries sell mostly primary goods (such as rice, bananas, metal ores). Rich countries sell mostly secondary products (such as computers and cars). Primary goods are cheaper than secondary products so the rich countries make more money than they spend and poor countries spend more money than they make.

A *Trade between rich and poor countries*

Other problems with trade

- Sometimes **tariffs** are placed on goods by the country buying them. This means that the country selling the goods does not get as much for the goods as they are worth.
- Often poorer countries rely on just one or two products for trade. If the price for these products falls or a natural disaster strikes this can have a huge impact on that country's income.
- Most trade happens between rich countries and between countries that are geographically close to each other. The existence of trading groups, such as the EU, can prevent free trade across the world and can disadvantage poorer countries.

In this section you will learn

how the trade balance imbalance means poor countries stay poor

other problems with trade which means that poor countries do not benefit as much as rich countries do.

Did you know ??????

As a rule, Africa exports raw materials (mainly minerals and petroleum) and imports manufactured goods. The production of export goods employs around 2 million people over the whole continent, a fraction of the total population of over 934 million. Companies involved are transnational corporations (TNCs), so profits go to their bases abroad. African governments have sometimes squandered their profits, so trade has been of little help towards true development.

Key term

Tariffs: government taxes on imported or exported goods.

Activity

1 Study diagram **A**.
a What is trade?
b What are the main differences between the products sold by poorer countries and those that are bought?
c How can trade lead to development in poorer countries?

11.5   How can international efforts reduce global inequalities?

■ Loans

Loans are sums of money that have to be paid back with interest at some time in the future. A country in need of money for development projects can borrow from other countries, world financial organisations (e.g. IMF, World Bank) or international banks. If the project is a success, the money is repaid. However, often things do not go according to plan and the debt (money owed) has to be paid back over a longer period. This means that the interest on the loan gets bigger and bigger so more and more money is owed. This is what is meant by the 'debt crisis'.

Debt relief and abolition

Poorer countries can be helped by debt relief, which means reducing the interest rate or the amount of the loan. Sometimes debts are abolished or written off so the loan does not have to be repaid. Debtor nations (those who have borrowed) benefit hugely as they can begin to spend money on improving people's lives. Today many people in rich countries think that all the debts of the poorest countries should be written off. But many rich countries and international banks now have money problems themselves, so this would be more difficult to achieve.

> **In this section you will learn**
>
> how debt results from loans and how individuals and countries are affected
>
> the concept of fair trade, and its advantages and disadvantages for producers and consumers
>
> the advantages and disadvantages of different types of aid for both recipient and donor countries.

> **Did you know** ??????
>
> Loans from governments, world organisations and banks from countries at lesser stages of development total $1.2 trillion.

Making handkerchiefs in Peru

Loans on a small scale may be the way forward. Non-profit groups in the USA have been lending money to people in poor countries. Sara Garcia in Lima, Peru borrowed $1,845 in 1984. She invested in equipment to make handkerchiefs. She hired extra workers and family members to help. This meant that she could make 500 in one day, instead of 20. So she had more to sell and met her repayments on time. The technology used allowed the business to become sustainable and successful.

This is typical of what can be done on a small scale. Today, this system has expanded greatly. Small businesses are the basis of any economy. They employ a surprising number of people and support their families.

Case study

> **Did you know** ??????
>
> Each year Africa gives more money to Western bankers in interest on its debts than it gets in foreign aid from these countries.

■ Conservation swaps

As poorer countries try to develop, they want to use every natural resource available to them. For example, they might want to cut down an area of rainforest to build a factory. This is not good for the environment but many people think it's unfair that the poor country loses out. 'Conservation swaps' try to solve this problem.

> **Key terms**
>
> **Debt repayment:** paying back money borrowed to support development to banks or governments.
>
> **Conservation swaps:** agreements made between countries where some debts are written off in exchange for conservation projects being done.

In a swap, a rich country agrees to write off some of the poor country's debt. In return, the poor country agrees to a conservation project. Usually, areas of valuable land are protected, especially tropical rainforest. The first swap took place in Bolivia, South America. A North American conservation group took over $650,000 of Bolivia's national debt in return for the Bolivian government setting aside a large area of rainforest as a nature reserve. Other countries that have taken part in conservation swaps include Guatemala, Peru, Ecuador, Costa Rica and Poland.

A Bolivian rain forest

Did you know ??????

The US government gave the Guatemalan government $15 million towards the cancellation of its debt. Conservation groups added more. The total contributed from all sources was $24 million. Threatened forests, including high-altitude 'cloud forests', were protected in this trade. Hundreds of rare and endangered species were assisted.

⃝⃝ links

More on Guatemala's debt for nature swap can be found at www.wildlifeextra.com/go/news/guatemala-debt.html.

Fairtrade

Fairtrade is an international movement that aims to make sure people in poor countries get a fair deal for products they sell. They receive a minimum price and long-term contracts for their crop. This means they have more money to live on and develop their businesses.

Table **B** shows the fast growth in Fairtrade goods bought in the UK between 1999 and 2009. Around 7 million farmers, farm workers and their families in 58 poorer countries benefit from the improved trading conditions brought about by Fairtrade.

B Fairtrade goods consumed in the UK, 1998–2008/9 (£ millions)

Product	Year						
	1999	2001	2003	2005	2007	2008	2009
Coffee	15.0	18.6	34.3	65.8	117.0	137.3	157.0
Tea	4.5	5.9	9.5	16.6	30.0	64.8	68.1
Cocoa/chocolate	2.3	6.0	10.9	21.9	25.5	26.8	44.2
Honey	–	3.2	6.1	3.5	2.7	5.2	4.6
Bananas	–	14.6	24.3	47.7	150.0	184.6	209.2
Flowers	–	–	–	5.7	24.0	33.4	30.0
Wine	–	–	–	3.3	8.2	10.0	16.4
Cotton	–	–	–	0.2	34.8	77.9	50.1
Other	–	2.2	7.2	30.3	100.8	172.6	219.4
Total	21.8	50.5	92.3	195.0	493.0	712.6	799.0

Aid

Aid is gifts of money, goods, food, machinery, technology and trained workers. The aim is to make people's lives better. True aid does not need to be paid back. However, in the real world some 'aid' really is a loan because some form of payback is required.

Did you know ??????

The Kuapa Kokoo cooperative in the Ashanti region at the heart of Ghana's cocoa belt is working with fairtrade organisations. It is helping 35,000 members to get their fair share of the profits generated by cocoa.

⃝⃝ links

You can find out more about Kuapa Kokoo by entering the name of the organisation into the search box on www.fairtrade.org.uk.

C   *Short-term aid being distributed in Haganoy, the Philippines*

Different types of aid

- **Short-term aid** can help to save lives by providing things like food, water and clothing for people in a disaster.

- **Long-term aid** can build schools and hospitals, and invest in industry and agriculture.

- **Bilateral aid** is given by one government to another government.

- Governments also give money to international organisations which run projects in developing countries. This is called **multilateral aid**.

- Charities are not run by governments (Non-Governmental Organisations, or NGOs). People donate money and resources to charities like Oxfam or ActionAid which run their own development projects.

There are many advantages and disadvantages of aid (table **D**, page 264). Some aid is lost to corrupt governments and people. The lack of infrastructure can prevent development happening as planned, for example schools and hospitals cannot work without roads and power. Trained staff may not be available. Too much aid has been tied. This means that the **donor country** has given money but, for example, the **recipient country** has to buy products from the donor country or can only spend the money on certain things.

Possible effects of the recent global recession

The recent global economic recession has affected most countries in the world, though at differing rates. The problems of the wealthier countries will spread to all those with whom they trade or exchange loans or debts. Countries that normally donate aid will have less to give away in aid or to lend. As world prices decrease, poorer countries will receive less for their exports. These countries will no longer be able to repay the interest on their debts to richer countries and to global financial institutions. They may therefore go even further into debt.

Study tip

Know the different types of aid given to countries and be able to give advantages and disadvantages of each.

D *Advantages and disadvantages of aid for donor and recipient countries*

Type of aid	Donor countries		Recipient countries	
	Advantages	Disadvantages	Advantages	Disadvantages
Short-term aid	People want to help in a disaster – 'feel-good' factor	None	Saves lives! Flow of aid may continue after the 'disaster' is over	Sometimes the aid is not exactly what is needed
Long-term aid	Projects in developing countries give companies and individuals work Trade between donor and recipient may continue even after project has ended	None	New industries improve skills and provide work Agriculture improves Schools and hospitals are built which help local people in the future Trade between donor and recipient may continue even after the project has ended	Tied aid – recipient country relies on donor country Local people may not have the skills and training for all the jobs Agricultural changes might not last Lack of money to keep things running Local people may lose land to projects
Top-down aid (government)	Feel in control as give money to government or international organisations	May feel that money is wasted or too much is given as projects are very expensive	Aims to improve country as a whole Large projects improve infrastructure	Most ordinary people do not benefit directly
Bottom up aid (individuals and communities)	'Feel-good' factor for people giving to charities Feel that there is a direct link between the donor and recipient – e.g. sponsorship schemes like ActionAid	None	NGOs work with recipient community Money not lost to corruption Appropriate technology used, so projects are sustainable	Donors might give less in a recession

Activities

1
a What is the difference between loans and aid?

b What is the difference between short-term aid and long-term aid?

c Explain why interest payments on international debt can stop countries being able to develop themselves effectively.

2 Study table **D**. This shows some of the advantages and disadvantages of aid for donor countries (those giving the aid) and recipient countries (those receiving the aid).

a In groups, act out dialogues between donor countries and recipient countries that explain how each feels about different types of aid.

■ For example, donors of short term aid could say how good giving short term aid makes them feel. Recipients could explain that they are grateful for the help, but they need the aid to be specific to their needs: for example, it costs a lot to ship heavy donated clothing to recipient countries and the clothes might not be that appropriate anyway.

b Each group could take a different type of aid and each group could then act out their dialogues in front of the whole class in turn.

c Remember to capture both donor and recipient in your dialogues. Consider the advantages and disadvantages.

11.6 How successful are development projects?

A large-scale aid project
The Cahora Bassa dam, Mozambique – an example of bilateral aid

The Cahora Bassa dam was started by the Portuguese government of Mozambique in the 1960s. Civil war (1977–1992) damaged the dam and stopped people working. Work did not begin again in 1995 and it was finished in 1997.

It is the largest hydro electric power scheme in southern Africa, with five huge turbines and a large lake. Three other major dams have also been constructed in the River Zambezi Basin but the Cahora Bassa dam is the most recent and potentially the most important (fact file **A**).

Has it been a success?

- Only 1 per cent of Mozambique's rural homes have a direct electricity supply. This level has hardly changed during the life of the dam.

- Most of the power is sold to South Africa, which makes money for the Mozambican economy but does little for its people.

- The Cahora Bassa dam has much greater potential than it produces today. It could provide the whole of Mozambique with all the power it needs as long as some natural gas, solar and wind projects are also developed to serve the most rural areas.

- The River Zambezi often flooded and destroyed people's crops and homes. It was hoped that the Cahora Bassa dam would stop this. Whilst it has reduced the flooding, with more careful control, much more could be achieved.

- Having three dams in one basin has caused environmental damage. River flow is low because so much water is held in reservoirs. The shrimp fishing industry in the lower valley has been almost destroyed. A new dam, has been planned downstream from Cahora Bassa. The environmental consequences of this are uncertain, but risky.

In this section you will learn

detailed case studies of aid at different scales and from different donors.

Case study

Fact file

- Catchment area: 56,927 km²
- Length of lake: 292 km
- Maximum width of lake: 38 km
- Surface area of lake: 2,739 m
- Average depth of lake: 20.9 m
- Maximum depth of lake: 157 m

 Cahora Bassa dam fact file

B *The Cahora Bassa dam*

A medium-scale aid project
ActionAid, Kolkata, India

ActionAid is a UK charity working in local communities in poorer countries of the world to try and improve people's lives. Its six target areas of relief are:

- HIV/Aids
- hunger and food
- women's rights
- the right to education for all
- the right to security
- the right to good government.

ActionAid works in the poorest districts of Kolkata such as Dharavi, known as the world's worst slum. This area has a large number of people in a small area and few services.

Some of ActionAid's work is done through sponsorship schemes. Donors give monthly to general projects or to sponsor a child and his or her family or community. This is a successful approach. Donors like the idea of improving the life chances of an individual, especially that of a child.

ActionAid's donors feel they are doing something worthwhile for real people. Low technology is used. Local people benefit, both individuals and communities, and costs remain low. Environmental quality is improved as sustainability is an important aspect of ActionAid's work.

A small-scale aid project
Community Youth Empowerment Programme, Uganda

Restless Development (formerly Student Partnership Worldwide) is based in the UK. It places gap-year students in development projects in countries like Uganda. They work with school pupils and farmers. Volunteer UK and Ugandan students work together to:

- raise awareness of HIV/Aids risk to try and stop people getting infected. They use things like role-play and drama in schools to educate young people
- improve knowledge of environmental health concerns such as healthy eating, hygiene and waste management
- teach energy conservation methods such as how to make a fuel-efficient stove or how to start a tree nursery to provide wood for fuel
- promote sustainable farming ideas.

Projects have included the following examples:

- **1** In Kebager village, the three natural springs were polluted. Restless Development students built a

C *Restless Development works with school pupils in countries like Uganda*

covered water tank to keep pollution out. People took their supplies from this by tap, so water never lay open to risk. Appropriate technology has improved living standards as well as the environment.

- **2** In Bwanyanga village, schools received Restless Development students as volunteer teachers, who gave lessons and workshops on sexual health awareness and improving life skills. These projects were well received but due to issues with school fees some pupils could not attend.

Activities

1 Study the case study on the Cahora Bassa dam.

a Who are the winners and who are the losers in this project? Make two lists to show who has benefited and who has suffered.

b Decide whether the dam should have been built, giving reasons for your answer.

2 Study the case study on the Community Youth Empowerment Programme in Uganda.

a 'Small-scale aid projects don't help as many people as large-scale projects. So all aid projects should be large-scale ones.' Do you agree with this statement? Give a reason for your answer.

b If you had money to either fund SPW in Uganda in cleaning up a village water supply or teaching all teenagers in a village about sexual health and how to avoid Aids, which would you choose?

- Explain what short-term benefits influenced your choice.
- Explain what long-term benefits influenced your choice.

11.7   How do levels of development vary within the EU?

What is the EU?

The European Union (EU) is a group of countries in Europe which do not have any trade barriers between them. Today, 27 countries are members of the EU (map **A**).

A   *The 27 EU member countries*

The EU is one of the richest areas of the world. However, there is still a development gap between EU countries. Table **B** (page 268) shows three measures of development for all EU countries. They have been selected to show you that there are many similarities and some differences.

- HDI is high for every member country. All are in the top 60 in the world.
- Life expectancy is always over 70 years, but some are over 80, which shows a very high standard of living.
- GDP per capita is the indicator that really shows up the clearest differences. Luxembourg's GDP per capita is almost seven times higher than that of Bulgaria. The older members have higher GDP per capita than the newer ones.

B *EU comparative development indicators (2012/2011)*

Country	HDI rank in the world	Human Development Index (HDI) (2010)	Life expectancy at birth (years) (2011 est.)	GDP per capita ($) (2010)
Ireland	5	0.90	80.2	37,300
Sweden	9	0.89	81.1	39,100
Netherlands	7	0.89	79.7	40,300
France	14	0.87	81.2	33,100
Finland	16	0.87	79.3	35,400
Spain	20	0.86	81.2	29,400
Denmark	19	0.87	78.6	36,600
Austria	25	0.85	79.8	40,400
UK	26	0.85	80.1	34,800
Belgium	18	0.87	79.5	37,800
Luxembourg	24	0.85	79.6	82,600
Italy	23	0.85	82.0	30,500
Germany	10	0.89	80.1	35,700
Greece	22	0.86	79.9	29,600
Slovenia	29	0.83	77.3	28,200
Cyprus	35	0.81	77.8	21,000
Portugal	40	0.80	78.5	23,000
Czech Rep	28	0.84	77.2	25,600
Malta	33	0.82	79.7	25,600
Hungary	36	0.81	74.8	18,800
Poland	41	0.80	76.1	18,800
Slovakia	31	0.82	75.8	22,000
Lithuania	44	0.78	75.3	16,000
Estonia	34	0.81	73.3	19,100
Latvia	48	0.77	72.7	14,700
Bulgaria	58	0.74	73.6	13,500
Romania	50	0.77	74.0	11,600

Contrasting two EU countries: Bulgaria and Ireland

Bulgaria

Bulgaria's population in 2011 of 7,364,570 was lower by almost one million than in 1998. People are leaving to find jobs in the rest of the EU, which Bulgaria joined in 2007. Today it is a democracy, but previously it was dominated by the USSR and was a Communist country. With the break-up of the Communist bloc in the 1990s, its standard of living fell by 40 per cent. Although Bulgaria is the second poorest country in the EU and is in its **economic periphery**, new funding and projects are improving people's quality of life.

Ireland

Ireland's population of 4,581,269 (2011) is growing slowly because of natural increase and migrant labour. Until it joined the EU in 1973, it was a poor country within Europe. Membership has helped Ireland. It's changed its focus from agriculture to a high-tech service economy. Every year between 1995 and 2000 Ireland's economy grew by 10% earning it the title 'Celtic tiger' and brought it from being on the economic periphery to be very much part of the **economic core**.

EU policies to reduce inequalities

The Common Agricultural Policy (CAP)

The CAP includes a system of subsidies (money) paid to EU farmers. Its main aims are to:

- set minimum levels of production so that there is enough food for Europe's people
- make sure farmers have a fair standard of living
- make sure prices for customers are fair.

Many people agree with the CAP but some people are against it.

Supporters of the CAP say:

- farmers and rural communities wouldn't be able to survive without it
- more than half of people in the EU live in the countryside and so benefit from it
- some of the money is spent on helping the environment and making sure that animals are treated well.

Critics of the CAP say:

- only 5 per cent of people in the EU work in agriculture so it doesn't help many people
- agriculture generates only 1.6 per cent of GDP but over half the EU budget is spent on the CAP
- it stops developing countries being able to get a fair price for their products in the EU.

C *Good and bad points about the CAP*

Did you know ???????

CAP costs about £34 billion (€43 billion in 2008) a year, just over half the total EU budget of £60 billion. Most of this goes straight to farmers. Another £5 billion (€7.7 billion) is spent on rural development. This adds £9 to a family of four's weekly food bill.

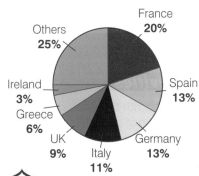

D *CAP – who gets the money?*

European Investment Bank (EIB)

Money from the European Investment Bank is invested in regional development. Some regions of the EU have problems because local industry is not doing well or farmers are not earning enough to live on. This money helps set up new businesses and trains people with new skills.

Urban II fund

Most Europeans live in urban areas (towns or cities). That's where most jobs are and where there are lots of things to do. However, all cities have areas with social, environmental and economic problems. The Urban II fund money is for **sustainable development** in troubled parts of European cities. It aims to improve the lives of people who live in these areas.

This includes:

- improving living conditions (e.g. renovating older buildings)
- creating new jobs in services that benefit the whole population
- improving education and training to help people get good jobs
- developing environmentally friendly transport systems
- making greater use of renewable energy.

Urban II has 70 different programmes that affect 2.2 million people. Money is given according to need, which is measured by population numbers and unemployment rates (see table **E**).

E *Urban II fund across Europe, 2000–06*

Country	Urban II fund (Euros)
Austria	8,400,000
Belgium	21,200,000
Denmark	5,300,000
Finland	5,300,000
France	102,000,000
Germany	148,700,000
Greece	25,500,000
Ireland	5,300,000
Italy	114,800,000
Netherlands	29,800,000
Portugal	19,200,000
Spain	112,600,000
Sweden	5,300,000
UK	124,300,000

Case study

Teruel, Spain

The town of Teruel in northern Spain has a new ring road, paid for by Urban II funds. It reduces traffic flows through the town by at least 20 per cent. This cuts congestion, improves air quality and makes travel times shorter. The new road also links previously isolated neighbourhoods. There are paths for cyclists and joggers. The project cost a total of €16.6 million.

Structural funds

Structural funds are used to support poorer parts of Europe. The money is used particularly to support transport development.

These funds go to regions where GDP per capita is less than 75 per cent of the EU average. The aim is to help these places develop so they catch up with other parts of Europe. The budget for 2007–13 is €347.41 billion.

Activities

3 Describe the effects of the Urban II fund on the town of Teruel. Try to find some information and photographs from the internet to support your study.

4 The EU's structural funds focus on improving transport in the EU's poorest countries.

a What sort of developments do you think this will involve?

b Do you agree that improvements in transport will lead to economic improvement? Why?

12   Globalisation

12.1   What is globalisation?

Have you heard the saying 'the world is shrinking'? It is used to describe the way people can now travel and send and receive information and goods from all over the world. This is **globalisation**. Today everyone uses good and services from all over the world. Our **independence** on each other has increased.

This has happened because:

- laws were changed to allow foreign investment in countries. This encouraged the rise of transnational corporations, or TNCs

- transport has improved and become cheaper

- the use of telephone, e-mail and internet communications (like Skype) means that people do not have to be in the same country to communicate with each other.

Nike is a TNC that manufactures footwear and clothing. It has 124 plants in China, 73 in Thailand, 35 in South Korea, 34 in Vietnam and others elsewhere in Asia. It also has factories in South America, Australia, Canada, Italy, Turkey and the USA. Africa is the only populated continent where Nike does not have any factories.

In this section you will learn

what is meant by the term 'globalisation'

the increased interdependence and interrelationships that result from greater connectivity between the different countries.

Key terms

Globalisation: the increasing links between different countries throughout the world and the greater interdependence that results from this.

Interdependence: the relationship between two or more countries, usually in terms of trade.

A   *Nike shoes on sale in China*

Study tip

Ensure that you explain the meanings of the terms 'globalisation', 'interdependence' and 'transnational corporation' (defined on page 276).

The production of a Wimbledon tennis ball

Dunlop Slazenger makes the 48,000 balls that are used at the Wimbledon tennis championships. From the 1940s to 2002, the tennis balls were made in Barnsley, south Yorkshire. However, to try and increase profits by cutting labour costs, from 2002 the balls have been made in Bataan in the Philippines.

Table **B** shows where the components for making the tennis balls come from. All the components are sent to Bataan where they are made into tennis balls. The final product is then sent to London.

B *The manufacture of a Wimbledon tennis ball*

Ingredient	Origin	Destination
Wool	New Zealand	UK
Cloth (made from wool)	UK	Philippines
Dyes	UK	Philippines
Silica	Greece	Philippines
Zinc oxide	Thailand	Philippines
Rubber	Malaysia	Philippines
Tins	Indonesia	Philippines
Clay	USA	Philippines
Magnesium carbonate	Japan	Philippines
Sulphur	South Korea	Philippines
Tennis balls (product)	Philippines	UK

C *Tennis at Wimbledon*

Did you know ??????

300 million tennis balls are made each year, 90 per cent of them in South-east Asia. Wimbledon tennis balls are recycled to provide homes for the harvest mouse, which is a threatened species.

∞ **links**

Find out more about globalisation by typing the word into the search box at **www.bbc.co.uk**.

Activities

1 a   Write down a definition of 'globalisation' and give one example to illustrate it.

   b   Compare your answer with a partner's and agree on a definition.

   c   Now work together to make a list of international companies that have shops or businesses in your local town or city centre.

2   Study table **B**.

   a   On a world political map outline, draw flow lines to show the movement of materials from the different countries to the Philippines and then the completed tennis balls to the UK.

   b   Describe how your map illustrates the concept of 'globalisation'.

   c   Why are the tennis balls now made in the Philippines rather than the UK?

12.2 How has globalisation changed manufacturing and services worldwide?

▇ The influence of developments in ICT

Advances in transport and communication are the main reasons for the increase in globalisation. Graph **A** shows the rapid decline in the costs of transport and communications.

Many of the advances made in communication are because of satellites. A satellite is an object that revolves around the earth. It is usually built for a specific purpose, for example, to study the weather. Can you think how satellites are used in TV and other forms of communication?

Also, cables have been laid under the sea across the world. These allow people all over the world to send information to others very quickly.

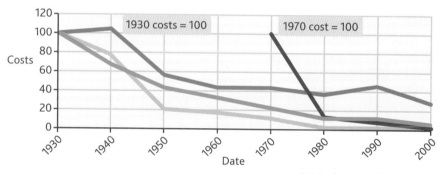

Original source: HM Treasury

[1] Cost of three-minute telephone call from New York to London
[2] Average ocean freight and port charges per short ton of import and export cargo
[3] Average air transport revenue per passenger mile

A *Falling transport and communication costs*

Activities

1. Study graph **A** (transport and communication costs). Notice that the costs all relate to a starting index value of 100. So, for example, the cost of a transatlantic phone call was just 20 in 1950, a fifth of the cost (100) in 1930.

    a. Describe the changes in costs of sea freight between 1930 and 2000.

    b. Describe the changes in satellite charges between 1970 and 2000.

    c. Why do you think satellite charges fell so dramatically between 1970 and 1980?

    d. Predict the relative cost of sea freight in 2010.

    e. How do cheaper transport and communication costs increase globalisation?

Did you know ??????

Submarine cables can be accidentally damaged. On 26 December 2006, an earthquake damaged SEA-ME-WE3 cables off Taiwan and, on 30 January 2008, a ship's anchor damaged the SEA-ME-WE4 off Egypt.

Small industrial region with global connections

Developments in ICT have allowed very fast access to people all over the world. They have also led to clusters of similar businesses developing in the same area because they can benefit from being close together. In the UK, between Northampton and Oxford there is a cluster of companies associated with motor racing (map **B**). This area is known as Motorsport Valley®.

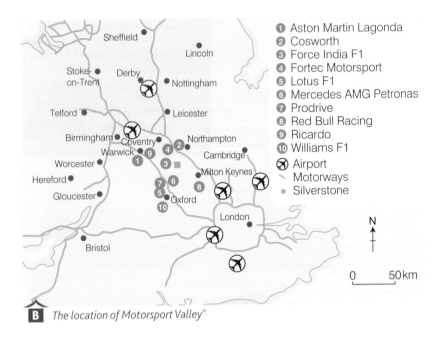

❶ Aston Martin Lagonda
❷ Cosworth
❸ Force India F1
❹ Fortec Motorsport
❺ Lotus F1
❻ Mercedes AMG Petronas
❼ Prodrive
❽ Red Bull Racing
❾ Ricardo
❿ Williams F1
✈ Airport
＼ Motorways
■ Silverstone

B *The location of Motorsport Valley®*

Motorsport Valley® fact file

• Almost 40,000 people are employed, including over 25,000 world-class engineers.

• 2,200 businesses relating to design, research and development, and event organisation.

• Over 80 per cent of the world market in high-performance engineering.

• Sales of around £6 billion, of which 60 per cent are exports.

• About a third of the total profits are reinvested into research and development.

C *Sebastian Vettel, Red Bull Racing*

Did you know ???????

Several F1 teams are based in Motorsport Valley® including the 2010 and 2011 Constructor's Champions, Red Bull Racing. Silverstone is the home of the British Grand Prix and attracts many racing based industry including the Force India F1 team. Rockingham Motor Speedway near Corby, Mallory Park near Leicester and Donington Park near Derby also host major race meetings.

■ The development of call centres abroad

Banks and other finance companies such as insurance were the first to develop **call centres** in the UK. These were set up so that people could answer customer's questions. Today, many companies have call centres. A total of 400,000 people work in UK call centres, often in small towns such as Harrogate, Carlisle, Gateshead and Warrington.

More and more companies now use call centres overseas. Companies such as ASDA, Tesco, BA, BT, Barclays, Lloyds TSB, HSBC and Virgin Media have all set up call centres in India. The location of the major call centres and reasons why companies choose India are shown in Map **C**. Other important places for call centres abroad are South Africa and the Philippines.

** Key term **

Call centres: offices where groups of people answer telephone queries from customers. Employees use a computer to give them information that helps them answer questions.

About 10 per cent of the population (some 100 million people) speak good English

About 80 per cent of Indian people who live in towns can read. 18 per cent are graduates.

It costs between 10 and 60 per cent less to run a call centre in India than in the UK.

The average salary in India is about £1,200 a year, compared to £12,000 a year in the UK.

Development of ICT allows fast and clear communication.

Staff are less likely to leave than in Britain and will work nine-hour shifts at all hours of the day and night.

 Telephone call centres in India

2 Study map **D**, which shows telephone call centres in India. Work in pairs for this activity.

Imagine you are director of customer relations for a call centre in India. You are being interviewed for national television news about the reasons your company chose to locate the call centre in India.

- One of you should be the interviewer and come up with three interview questions to ask (such as: How do your call centre staff deal with calls in English?)

- One of you should be the customer relations director and should reply to these questions using the information around map **D**.

⊙⊙ links

You can find out more about submarine cables at **www.telegeography.com**.

More information on Motorsport Valley® can be found at **www.thebritishmidlands.com**.

Visit **www.call-centres.com** for more on call centres.

12.3 What are the advantages and disadvantages of TNCs?

Transnational corporations (TNCs) are large international companies that have their headquarters in one country, but often have many other branches spread across the world.

Most TNCs have their headquarters in richer areas of the world, especially the USA, UK, France, Germany and Japan. Research and development is usually centred here. Products are often made in poorer countries where labour costs are lower. Many TNCs are hugely wealthy. Table **A** shows the world's biggest TNCs according to their value.

In this section you will learn

what advantages and disadvantages result from the presence of TNCs in countries

the characteristics of Toyota as a case study of a TNC.

A *The top ten non-financial TNCs, 2008*

Rank	TNC	Headquarters	Product
1	General Electric	USA	Electrical/electronic equipment
2	British Petroleum	UK	Petroleum
3	Toyota	Japan	Motor vehicles
4	Royal Dutch/Shell	UK/Netherlands	Petroleum
5	ExxonMobil	USA	Petroleum
6	Ford	USA	Motor vehicles
7	Vodafone	UK	Telecommunications
8	Total	France	Petroleum
9	Electricité de France	France	Electricity/gas/water
10	Wal-Mart	USA	Retail

Key terms

Transnational corporation (TNC): a corporation or enterprise that operates in more than one country.

Multiplier effect: where initial investment and jobs lead to a knock-on effect, creating more jobs and providing money to generate services.

Leakage: where profits made by the company are taken out of the country to the country of origin and so do not benefit the host country.

Advantages of TNCs

- They provide jobs making and selling their products. The income that people have from working for TNCs helps local businesses, creating a **multiplier effect**.
- The TNCs bring new technology as well as money.
- People get more training and skills paid for by the TNC.
- Often, the infrastructure and communications are improved which helps local people.

Did you know ??????

The income of Ford and General Motors added together is greater than the GDP of all of sub-Saharan Africa.

Disadvantages of TNCs

- Most profits go to the country of origin and not poorer countries where factories are often based. This is known as **leakage**. In some places wages are very low and local people do not get the best jobs.
- If there are problems economically, the branch plants in poorer countries are more likely to close than those in richer countries.
- TNCs make their own decisions. If they decide to close a factory in a country, there's nothing the government of that country can do to stop them.

- In some areas, working conditions are bad and people are expected to work long hours, with little time for breaks. Safety can be an issue and workers' health can be put at risk.
- Higher levels of air and water pollution may be allowed in poorer countries where factories are based.

Activities

1 Study table **A** on page 276. Work with a partner.

a Find out the identity of a further 10 large TNCs.

b Produce a collage to display the name, logo and line of business in which they are involved. Try to do this in a limited amount of time – say, 20 minutes – to see how you can work under pressure.

2 On a large copy of the table below, summarise the economic, social and environmental advantages and disadvantages of TNCs. One category has been partly done for you to illustrate the types of answers you could include.

Category	Advantages	Disadvantages
Economic		
Social	People may feel more secure with a job and regular income.	Working conditions are poor. Workers have to suffer crowded, hot conditions and work for many hours at a stretch.
Environmental		

Toyota

Toyota began in Toyota, Aichi, Japan in 1937. Seventy years later, it was the biggest producer of cars in the world, with profits of $11 billion in 2006. Map **B** shows (in red) the countries where Toyota plants are present and table **C** shows production in different regions in 1996 and 2009.

B *The global location of Toyota*

Toyota production by region, 1996 and 2009 (1 = 1,000 vehicles) **C**

Region	1996	2009
North America	782.9	1,189.1
Latin America	3.2	181.5
Europe	150.3	507.3
Africa	85.0	102.8
Asia	257.0	1,501.4
Oceania	67.6	96.8
Overseas total	1,346.0	3,579.0
Japan	3,410.1	2,792.2
Worldwide total	4,756.1	6,371.3

Case study

Toyota began to develop outside Japan in the late 1950s. Today, its headquarters in Tokyo manages 250,000 workers in 26 countries. The company decided to start making cars in the UK in the early 1990s. The reasons for this are outlined on p.278 . Toyota's first factory in Britain was built near Burnaston (map extract **D** and photo **E**).

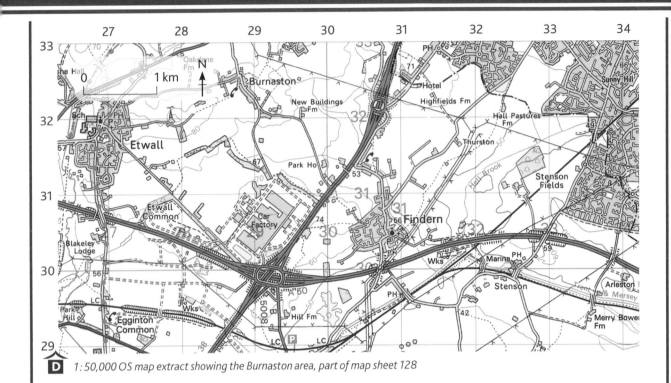

D 1 : 50,000 OS map extract showing the Burnaston area, part of map sheet 128

E The Toyota plant at Burnaston

Reasons why Toyota started making cars in the UK.

- Large UK market to buy the cars
- Good transport links to component factories and markets
- English is the second language in Japan
- Supportive British government
- Britain has a strong tradition of making cars

∞ links

You can find out more about Toyota at **www.toyotauk.com**.

Activities

3 Study map **B** and table **C** on page 277.

a With the help of an atlas, on an outline world map shade and label 10 countries where Toyota is present.

b For each of the seven regions (including Japan), work out their percentage of production (divide the region's 2009 figure by the worldwide total for the same year, and multiply by 100).

c Write the percentages for each region onto your map.

d Describe the pattern shown by your map.

e Where and why do you think Toyota should locate future new factories?

4 Study map extract **D** and photo **E** above.

a Draw and label a sketch map to describe and explain why the location at Burnaston is a good one.

b Why do you think Toyota decided to locate a new factory in the UK?

c Suggest some advantages of encouraging major companies such as Toyota to locate factories in the UK.

12.4 How and why is manufacturing in different countries changing?

▇ Changes in relative importance of world regions

In some parts of the world the manufacturing industry (making things) has got smaller, while in other places it has grown. The changes in high-tech manufacturing are shown in graph **A**. In many of the richest areas of the world, manufacturing has declined. For example, in Britain the number of people employed in manufacturing fell from just over 6 million in 1981 to 2.49 million in 2010. This is because of de-industrialisation and the growth of the financial and service sectors.

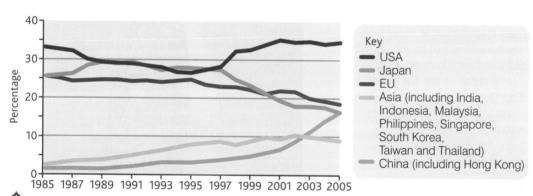

A *World share of high-tech manufacturing, 1985–2005*

▇ Reasons for changes

There are many reasons why manufacturing has grown in some places and declined in others.

1 Government legislation

The laws set by the government of a country can affect the manufacturing industry. For example:

- setting the amount of money that people can be paid. Some countries have a minimum wage. In the UK, this is currently £6.19 per hour for those aged 21 years and older. In Sri Lanka, some workers are paid a fraction of a much lower minimum wage. This means that labour costs in some countries are much lower than others.

- limiting the number of hours people can work. People in some EU countries can work a maximum of 48 hours a week. The average South Korean works 2,390 hours a year in contrast to 1,652 in the UK. This means that workers in some countries can produce more than others.

- setting up areas (**assisted areas/enterprise zones**) which help new industry.

- providing **advanced factories** of various sizes.

Key terms

De-industrialisation: a process of decline in some types of industry over a long period of time. It results in fewer people being employed in this sector and falling production.

Assisted areas/enterprise zones: areas that qualify for government help. Enterprise zones are on a smaller scale than assisted areas.

Advanced factories: where buildings for production are built in the hope they will encourage businesses to buy or rent them.

2 Health and safety regulations

Working conditions vary in different countries. In the UK, workers have the right to:

- know how to do their job safely and to be trained to do so
- know how to get first aid
- know what to do in an emergency
- be given protective clothing.

Other countries do not have these regulations or if they do, they are not enforced. To comply with health and safety laws costs money. Therefore, companies can cut costs by setting up in countries which do not have them or where they are not as strict.

3 Prohibition of strikes

In the 1970s, there were many **strikes** in the UK. This led to companies losing a lot of money and choosing to place their factories in countries where there weren't so many strikes. Companies such as Nissan and Toyota only came to the UK in the 1980s on the understanding that strike action would not be allowed. Many newly industrialising countries (NICs) don't allow strikes.

4 Tax incentives and tax-free zones

Tax incentives take many forms, but all try to reduce the costs a company has to pay. For example, One NorthEast (the development agency that was responsible for the north-east of England) offered job-creation grants, business rate or rent-free periods and helped in preparing a business plan while the government gave a grant towards the cost. Regional Development Agencies were abolished in March 2012.

Tax-free zones are free from the paying of tax and include zones such as areas of Dubai (photo **B**) and Zambia.

■ China: the new industrial giant

Most of the things we use every day are made in China (photo **C**). For example, China makes 60 per cent of the world's bicycles (photo **D**) and 72 per cent of the world's shoes. Between 2000 and 2006, cloth manufacture more than doubled (photo **E**) and car production increased by more than six times. The National Bureau of Statistics of China is predicting economic growth of at least 7 per cent to 2018.

> **Key term**
>
> **Strikes**: periods of time when large numbers of employees refuse to work due to disagreements over pay or other grievances.

B Burj Al Arab Hotel, Dubai

C In 2010 China became the world's largest exporter

D *60 per cent of the world's bicycles are made in China*

E *Chinese knitwear factory, part of a rapidly growing textile sector*

Study tip

Look for links between ideas when writing an answer. For example, in explaining why China has become one of the world's most powerful economies in such a short time, you might say, 'Labour costs are low in China and so it can make products more cheaply than richer countries, which means it is able to gain easy access to world markets.'

■ Reasons for China's rapid growth

There are many reasons why China is the new economic giant.

1 Government legislation

China became Communist in 1949. This meant that the government planned and ran all economic activity and China was closed off to the rest of the world.

In 1977, Deng Xiaoping, the leader of China, changed this. The government still had overall control over the economy but foreign investment and trade was encouraged. Special economic zones (SEZs) were set up between 1980 and 1994 (map **F**). Here, there were tax incentives to attract interest from outside China.

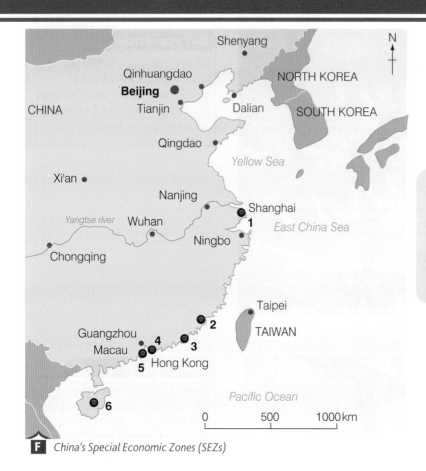

F *China's Special Economic Zones (SEZs)*

Special Economic Zones (SEZ)
1 Pudong District, Shanghai Muncipality
2 Xiamen, Fujian Province
3 Shantou, Guangdong Province
4 Shenzhen, Guangdong Province
5 Zhuhai, Guangdong Province
6 Hainan Province

2 The home market

China has the largest population of any country in the world. 500 million people live in China's towns and cities. As people have become wealthier, they have more money to spend on products.

3 The Olympics factor

The 2008 Olympics were held in Beijing (photo **G**). The eyes of the world were on China! The opening ceremony, based on the theme 'One World, One Dream', helped to show China as a modern, open and friendly country.

4 Energy

Industrial development on a large scale needs large resources of energy. Although China is a vast country, it doesn't have much coal, oil or gas. At the moment, two-thirds of China's electricity comes from coal-fired power stations, which need a lot of imported coal and cause serious air pollution.

Hydroelectric power (HEP) accounted for 14 per cent of electricity in 2010. China produces more HEP than any other country in the world and is keen to develop new sources of energy such as the Three Gorges Project (photo **H**).

G *The Olympics in Beijing*

The Three Gorges Dam, part of the Three Gorges Project which produces HEP and reduces flooding on the Yangtse River.

5 Labour

Cheap labour is a key reason why foreign companies are attracted to China. Wages are 95 per cent lower than in the USA. This means that products can be made cheaply.

Activities

1   Study graph **A** on page 279. It shows the world shares of hi-tech manufacturing between 1985 and 2005.

  a   What percentage of high-tech manufacturing was produced in the EU in 1985 and in 2005?

  b   What percentage of high-tech manufacturing was produced in China in 1985 and in 2005?

  c   Why do you think high-tech manufacturing has declined in Japan and the EU but increased in China?

2   Study map **F** (China's Special Economic Zones) and the text on pages 282 and 283.

  Produce an information poster (preferably A3 size) identifying the main factors responsible for China's recent economic growth.

  ■   Use the internet to find maps and photos to support text boxes.

  ■   Choose a striking image for the centrepiece of your poster.

links

There are many statistics relating to China that can be found in the National Bureau of Statistics of China at **www.stats.gov.cn/english**.

Research information about China and economic policy, including SEZs, at **www.china.org.cn**.

You can find out more about the Three Gorges Dam at **www. timesonline.co.uk**.

12.5 What are the causes and effects of increasing global demand for energy?

■ Why are we using more energy?

1 World population growth

The number of people in the world is growing fast! Table **A** and graph **B** show the overall increase in population and the relative importance of different regions.

Notice how global population has rocketed since the 1950s? This growth has meant a surge in demand for energy. Population growth is the main reason for the increased use in energy around the world.

A *Overall global increase in population, 1750–2050*

Year	1750	1800	1850	1900	1950	1999	2050
World population (billions)	0.79	0.98	1.26	1.65	2.52	5.98	8.91

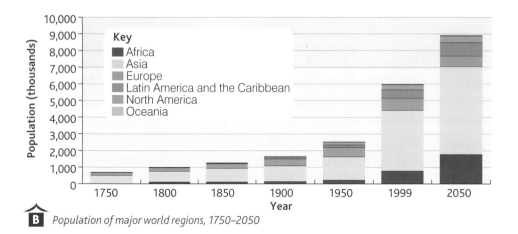

B *Population of major world regions, 1750–2050*

2 Increased wealth

Think about the things your family might have: a fridge, washing machine, tumble drier, dishwasher, microwave, television, computer, car. These all use a lot of energy. The chances are that you will have many, if not all, of these items. This was not always the case. As people have earned more money, they have spent it on things to make their lives easier and better. Making these goods uses lots of energy too.

Think about the impact on energy use of the following:

- The average wage in China is four times higher than in 1995.
- In 1997, there were hardly any private cars in China. In 2009 there were 26 million!
- In the UK, more and more families own cars. In 2009, there were more households that owned two cars than there were households with no car at all.

1 Study table **A** on page 284. This shows the overall increase in population from 1750 to what is predicted for 2050.

a Draw a line graph to show the total world population figures from 1750 to 2050.

b Where would you say global population numbers really 'took off'?

2 Study graph **B** on page 284. This shows population growth by global regions.

a Which region has seen the biggest increase in population?

b Why do bigger populations usually mean a higher demand for energy?

3 Technological advances

Technological advances have given us more energy and more and more products that we can buy.

- Technological advances have enabled new sources of energy to be developed, such as solar, wave and tidal power. Oil and gas can be extracted from deep underground in hostile environments.

- New products get developed as technology improves and these often use more energy to make and to use. This textbook doesn't need a battery to use, but what if you were reading it on an iPad or a Kindle?

■ Social and economic impacts

The social effects of increased energy use include the impacts on people's health. Using coal for energy causes air pollution and smog (see photo **C**). Poor air quality leads to asthma and other diseases.

The economic effects of increasing energy use are very important all around the world. As energy sources get used up, energy gets much more expensive. New sources of energy have to be found.

3 a List the products you and your family own that use energy.

b Ask your parents to highlight the items they would not have owned 10 and 20 years ago.

c How will the amount of energy used by you and your family have changed in the next 10 years?

4 If economic problems mean families have less money to spend, will their energy use reduce?

- Think of some examples where people would be able to cut down on energy use quite easily.

- Think of some examples where cutting down on energy use would be more difficult.

C *Smog in Beijing, home of the 2008 Olympics, before the games*

Environmental impacts

Most energy is made by burning fossil fuels (oil, natural gas and coal). This has a huge impact on the environment:

- on land, where heaps of waste rock has built up next to coal mines.
- on water, where oil has polluted the water when it is being transported.
- on air, which is polluted when energy is burnt.

Most scientists believe that burning fossil fuels is causing climate change or global warming. The possible impact of this is shown in diagram **D**.

∞links

The Environment Agency gives extensive advice at **www. environment-agency.gov.uk**.

You can investigate air quality at **www.airquality.co.uk** and global warming at **www. worldviewofglobalwarming.org**.

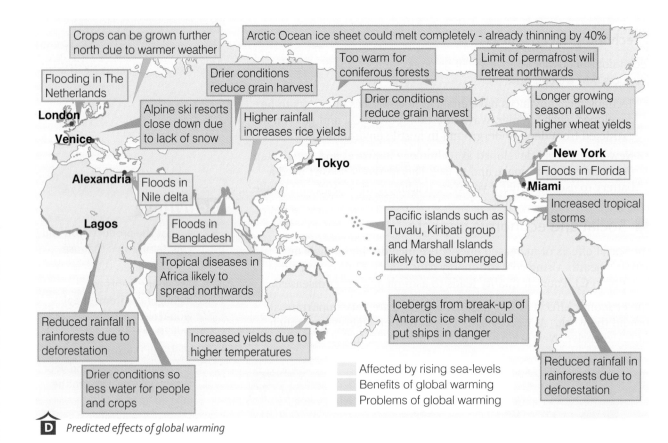

D *Predicted effects of global warming*

Activities

5 Study photo **C** and diagram **D**. Work in pairs.

Produce a research project that summarises the social, economic and environmental impacts of increased energy use. You should include at least one map, one photo and evidence of further research. There should be reference to at least two effects in each category. Try to include facts, figures and information as evidence wherever possible.

12.6 How can energy use be sustainable?

■ The use of renewable energy

Supplies of coal, oil and natural gas are limited. In other words, at some point they will run out or become too expensive to extract. Renewable energy means getting our energy from sources that will not run out. Hydroelectric power (HEP), solar, tidal and wind power are sustainable options (Fact file A). These alternatives have been used for some time but only on a small scale. They have advantages over the use of fossil fuels, but not everyone agrees with them. The recent surge in the use of **biofuels** for example, has critics as well as supporters.

> **In this section you will learn**
>
> how the use of renewable energy is sustainable
>
> why some locations are more suited to the development of renewable energy than others and the debate over locations and costs
>
> the importance of international directives and local initiatives in the drive to ensure sustainability.

> **Key term**
>
> **Biofuels:** the use of organic matter such as maize to make ethanol (an alcohol-based fuel) or biogas from animal waste. It is the use of crops that has become especially important.

> **Did you know** ??????
>
> Biofuels are sometimes known as 'deforestation diesel'. The grain needed to fill the tank of a large Range Rover is enough to feed one person for a year. The EU has a target of 5.75 per cent biofuels for transport by 2010.

 A *Wind power in the UK*

Fact file

- **Aims**: to generate 10 per cent of power by renewable energy sources.
- **Role**: to generate one-third of electricity.
- **Number of wind farms and turbines operational in 2011**: 306.
- **Location**: mostly on land.
- **The future**: offshore wind farms to become more important, with 8 GW to be generated by 2016.
- **Size of a modern wind turbine**: 100 to 120 m, including the blades. Offshore wind turbines tend to be bigger. For comparison, the London Eye is 135 m high.
- **Offshore operations**: these are usually within 4 to 6 km off the coast, but in the future some may be over 18 km away from the coast.
- **Location requirements**: the shallow waters off the coast of the UK are an advantage. Wind farms need to be able to get as much wind as possible. Small differences in distance can mean a real difference in the potential of the site, e.g. a site that is 10 per cent less windy means 20 per cent less energy is generated.

- **Reasons for**:

  Wind is free and can now be captured efficiently.

  The energy it produces does not cause greenhouse gases or other pollutants.

  Wind turbines only take up a small plot of land (a small footprint). This means that the land below can still be used, for example for agriculture.

  At sea the turbines can attract fish and have no long term affects on sea life.

  Some people find wind farms an interesting feature of the landscape.

  Turbines can be used to produce electricity in areas that are not connected to the National Grid.

- **Reasons against**:

  They are noisy and some people do not like the way they look in the countryside.

  House prices nearby may fall.

  They may affect birds and wildlife.

  Producing electricity using wind turbines is expensive.

  The strength of the wind changes so there will be times when they produce no energy at all.

  Some pollution is produced when they are being made.

  Large wind farms are needed to provide entire communities with enough electricity.

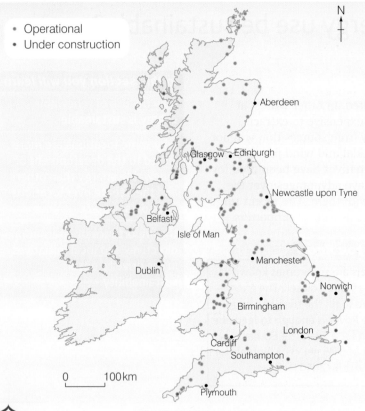

- Operational
- Under construction

N

Aberdeen

Glasgow • Edinburgh

Newcastle upon Tyne

Belfast

Isle of Man

Manchester

Dublin

Norwich

Birmingham

London

Cardiff

Southampton

0   100km

Plymouth

B *The location of wind farms in the UK*

C *The number of wind farms in the UK is increasing*

International responses to climate change

Climate change is a problem for every country in the world. To find solutions, countries need to work together.

- The Earth Summit in Rio de Janeiro in 1992 was the first real international attempt to try to cut down on greenhouse gas emissions. Richer countries agreed not to increase emissions.

- The **Kyoto Protocol** in 1997 went further. Industrialised countries agreed to reduce greenhouse gas emissions to 5 per cent below 1990 levels between 2008 and 2012. The treaty became legally binding in 2005, when enough countries responsible for 55 per cent of the total emissions had signed. 191 countries have now signed up to the agreement, although the USA has not signed up. The poorer nations, including those with many industries, do not have to reduce their emissions. Countries can trade in their carbon credits – the amount of greenhouse gases they are allowed to emit. Countries putting more pollution into the atmosphere than they should can buy carbon credits from a country below its agreed level.

- The Bali Conference in December 2007 tried, but failed, to set new targets to replace those agreed at Kyoto. However, the USA agreed to support the Bali 'roadmap', designed to lead the way into the future.

- The Durban Conference in December 2011 agreed to a legally binding deal comprising all countries, including USA, China and India, which will be preprared by 2015, and take effect in 2020

> **Key term**
>
> **Kyoto Protocol**: an international agreement to cut CO_2 emissions to help reduce global warming.

Local initiatives

The phrase 'think globally, act locally' means that we can only fix global problems if we all make the changes ourselves, in our own lives.

- Conservation can involve simple things like turning off lights and appliances when they are not being used, filling a kettle with only the water that is needed and reusing carrier bags.

- Local authorities collect paper, cans, glass, plastic, cardboard and garden waste for recycling. This reduces the amount that is put into landfill. Figures from the Department for Environment, Food and Rural Affairs (Defra) show that in 2009–10, 40 per cent of household waste was recycled. By 2015, the government wants only 35 per cent of waste going into landfill.

D   *A local authority recycling facility*

Activity

Different people have contrasting views on the development of wind farms such as Burbo Bank wind farm in Liverpool bay and onshore wind farms.

  a Choose one of the following who you think would support wind farms and one who you think would oppose them.

    i someone who lives right next to where the wind farm is going to be constructed, but who supports renewable energy

    ii a supporter of nuclear energy

    iii an electricity-generating company director

    iv a member of the Royal Society for the Protection of Birds (RSPB)

    v a member of Greenpeace for Action against Climate Change

    vi a resident who wants cheap electricity.

  b From the point of view of each person you have chosen, give your views explaining fully why you are for or against the development of wind farms.

links

You can investigate biofuels by searching **www.bbc.co.uk**. This website is also useful for information on offshore wind farms.

The British Wind and Energy Association website at **www.bwea.com** gives lots of information on wind farms in the UK.

Local authority websites provide information on recycling and waste disposal.

12.7 What are the effects of increasing global food production?

The amount of food produced throughout the world has grown in the last 50 years (graph **B**). This has had important environmental, political, social and economic impacts.

Environmental impacts

Today, people in the UK want to eat strawberries in the winter and apples in the spring. One half of vegetables and 95 per cent of fruit eaten in the UK is not grown here. Transporting food longer distances – the idea of **food miles** – increases our **carbon footprint**. The more we rely on imported food, the more we add to climate change and air pollution. Food imported by plane is of most concern. We import 1 per cent of food by air, but 11 per cent of UK carbon emissions comes from transportation of food by plane.

The Kenyan green bean debate

But the situation isn't black and white, as the example of Kenyan green beans will show (photo **A**).

- Beans in Kenya are produced in a very environmentally friendly way and the low-tech farming methods employ a lot of people.
- British beans are grown in fields where oil-based fertilisers have been sprayed and which are ploughed by tractors that burn diesel.
- So it is possible that flying Kenyan beans to the UK actually produces lower carbon emissions than producing British beans.

Apples: to store or not to store?

Apples are another interesting example. In the UK, apples are harvested in September and October. Some are sold fresh while the rest are chill stored. For most of the following year, they still represent good value (in terms of carbon emissions) for British shoppers.

However, by August those apples will have been in store for 10 months. The amount of energy used to keep them fresh for that length of time will then be higher than the carbon cost of shipping fresh apples from New Zealand.

It is therefore better for the environment if UK shoppers buy apples from New Zealand in July and August rather than British apples!

A *Kenyan beans*

Activity

1 Read the text about Kenyan green beans and New Zealand apples.

a Explain why the food miles argument says that UK customers should buy local bean and apples.

b Now explain why buying Kenyan green beans might actually mean lower carbon emissions overall than buying UK beans.

c Explain why buying New Zealand apples in July and August could mean lower carbon emissions overall than buying UK apples that have been stored since the previous autumn.

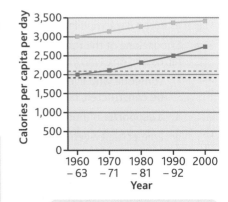

- — Developing countries
- — Developed countries
- -- Developing country requirements
- -- Developed country requirements

B *Global food production*

Farming on marginal land

As populations increase in some countries, there is pressure to grow more food. This may involve farming on marginal land – land that is not really suitable for farming.

Photo **C** shows the difficult conditions in which people try to grow food in order to survive. Here, the already poor-quality land is likely to become even poorer. As the small amount of crops are harvested, no goodness is returned to the soil. The lack of vegetation cover makes the area prone to soil erosion, where it is easily washed or blown away (photo **D**). This is known as environmental degradation.

> **Key term**
>
> **Environmental degradation:** undesirable changes to the natural environment through the removal of natural resources and disruption to natural ecosystems. Human activity is a major cause.

C *Marginal land in Darfur*

D *The effects of growing crops on marginal land*

■ Political impacts

Water is essential for farming and growing food. In areas where water is limited irrigation is essential.

The River Indus flows through northern India and Pakistan. The flow of the Indus is seasonal. A huge amount of water means flooding in summer, whereas flows are much less in winter due to less rainfall. The Indus supplies the fertile Punjab, which crosses the India–Pakistan border.

After the Independence Act of 1947, it took 13 years of talking before the Indus Waters Treaty was signed by the two countries (map **F** on page 292). The disputed region of Kashmir lies here. There had been concerns that during times of conflict India could build dams and cut off water to Pakistan, perhaps even diverting rivers. The signing of the treaty in 1960 meant that Pakistan had the westward-flowing rivers and India had the eastward-flowing rivers. The building of two dams on the Jhelum and Indus Rivers gave Pakistan water which India could not control.

> **Key terms**
>
> **Food miles:** the distance that food items travel from where they are grown to where they are eaten.
>
> **Carbon footprint:** the amount of carbon generated by things people do, including creating a demand for out-of-season food.

E The Indus River

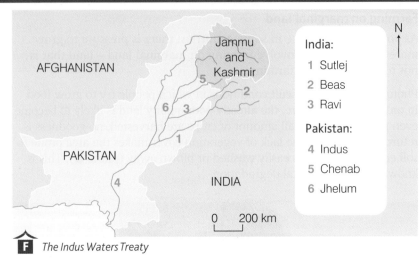

F The Indus Waters Treaty

India:

1 Sutlej
2 Beas
3 Ravi

Pakistan:

4 Indus
5 Chenab
6 Jhelum

0   200 km

Activity

2 Study map **D** (and photo **E**) on page 292.

a Draw a sketch map to show the Indus and its five tributaries, international boundaries, main regions and places.

b Label the map to show the cause of conflict linked to water.

c Draw a timeline to show the sequence of events described that contributed to the conflict.

Did you know ? ? ? ? ? ?

The River Indus is 3,200 m in length, making it the 24th longest river in the world.

Social impacts

Social issues include health, safety and quality of life. Growing cash crops for a source of income can offer economic benefits. However, socially there are potentially more problems. The areas around Lake Naivasha in Kenya and north of Mount Kenya are home to the flower industry (diagram **G**). Notice that growing flowers brings social and environmental problems.

Did you know ? ? ? ? ? ?

A quarter of Europe's cut flowers are supplied by Kenya in an industry that was worth £77 million in 2003 and 10 per cent of Kenya's export earnings.

Activity

3 Study diagram **G**, which describes some of the social problems of the Kenyan flower industry.

a List the problems that involve chemical pollution.

b List the problems that involve water shortage and conflicts over water use.

c List any remaining problems: what category would you put those into?

d What benefits do you think the flower industry has brought to Kenya?

⚭ **links**

The case study on 'Flower growing in Kenya' on **www.learningafrica. org.uk** is particularly useful, as is **www.farmersmarkets.net**.

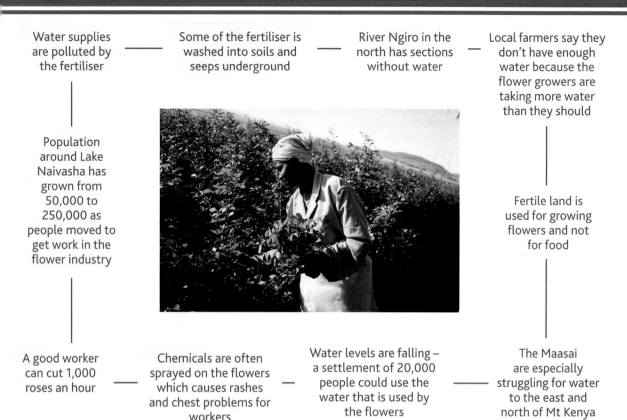

Water supplies are polluted by the fertiliser —— Some of the fertiliser is washed into soils and seeps underground —— River Ngiro in the north has sections without water — Local farmers say they don't have enough water because the flower growers are taking more water than they should

Population around Lake Naivasha has grown from 50,000 to 250,000 as people moved to get work in the flower industry

Fertile land is used for growing flowers and not for food

A good worker can cut 1,000 roses an hour —— Chemicals are often sprayed on the flowers which causes rashes and chest problems for workers — Water levels are falling – a settlement of 20,000 people could use the water that is used by the flowers —— The Maasai are especially struggling for water to the east and north of Mt Kenya

G *Growing flowers in Kenya*

Economic impacts

Growing cash crops as well as food for themselves is often the way forward for many small-scale farmers. This means that money can be spent improving the farm. However, there are problems. There is often a need to step-up production, which means increasing the use of fertilisers and pesticides. These cost money which farmers do not have so they borrow it. This can create a vicious circle (diagram **H**).

∞**links**

See spread 10.7 on p. 240 for more on flower production in Kenya.

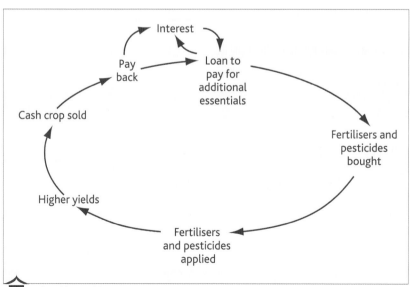

Interest

Pay back — Loan to pay for additional essentials

Cash crop sold

Fertilisers and pesticides bought

Higher yields

Fertilisers and pesticides applied

H *The effects of borrowing money*

Buying locally produced food

In the UK, farmers benefit local people buying food that they have produced. Buying from local, regional or national sources should help farms in the UK. It may also help the environment. Others might take a different view. What would the effect on Kenya be if the UK stopped importing strawberries, for example?

In the UK, we can ensure that we support local produce by:

- looking at labels in supermarkets, which often say where the food comes from
- visiting specialist local shops
- buying online from 'local' producers
- supporting local farmers' markets (photo I)
- going to regional agricultural shows, which celebrate and sell local produce

In May 2008 the 'celebrity' chef Gordon Ramsey said 'There should be stringent licensing laws to make sure produce is only used in season. I don't want to see strawberries from Kenya in the middle of March. When we haven't got it, we take it off the menu.' Do you think he's right?

I *Fresh local produce from a farmers' market*

13 Tourism

13.1 Why has global tourism grown?

Growth in tourism

Tourism is the world's largest industry. There were 940 million tourist travellers in 2009 and this is set to rise to a massive 1.6 billion by 2020. In most countries, domestic tourism (people going on holiday in their own country) is between four and five times greater than international tourism.

A *International tourist arrivals*

Region	2006	2010	Percentage change 2006–10	Percentage of world tourism (2010)
Africa	50 million	49 million	-2%	5%
Americas	136 million	151 million	+11%	16%
Asia and Pacific	168 million	204 million	+21%	22%
Europe	461 million	471 million	+2%	51%
Middle East	41 million	60 million	+46%	6%
World	856 million	935 million	+9%	100%

The tourism industry is very important for many different countries. Some parts of the world depend on tourism for money. For 83 per cent of countries, tourism is one of the top five sources of foreign exchange. Caribbean countries get half their GDP from tourism.

The top six tourist destination countries are France, Spain, the USA, China, Italy and the UK. Germans spend more on holiday per person than any other nation, followed by Americans, British, French and Japanese.

Activity

1 Look carefully at table **A**. It shows how many tourists visited different global regions.

a Which continent had the highest number of tourists in 2010?

b Why do you think this continent has such a large tourist industry?

c Which continent had the lowest number of tourists in 2010?

d Why do you think this continent has not yet developed its tourism as much as other regions?

e Which continent's tourism grew by the largest percentage between 2006 and 2010?

f Can you suggest why it grew so rapidly?

In this section you will learn

the many types of landscapes and holidays that attract people and why.

Study tip

You should be able to interpret tables of statistics. Usually, we look for patterns or trends and drawing a graph can be the easiest way to spot these. Sometimes there are few differences in the data. Nevertheless, tiny differences can still be important and may show a trend, and this is what you need to pick out.

B *Tourism in the Caribbean*

Factors affecting the growth of tourism

Growth in tourism is explained by three sets of factors.

1 Social and economic factors

- Since the 1950s many people have become richer as jobs are now better paid. Most families have two working parents whereas in the past it was usually one.

- People have more spare time. Holiday time for working people has increased from two weeks per year in the 1950s to between four and six weeks today. Most people now enjoy paid holiday.

- Life expectancy has risen (more people are living longer) so more people are retired. Many have good pensions and can afford several trips a year. They also have more time to travel.

2 Improvements in technology

- Travel today is quick and easy because of improvements in transport. Flying has become cheaper and booking online is quick and easy.

3 More holiday choice

- During the 1950s and 1960s coastal resorts were popular and in the UK the National Parks were opening and offering new opportunities. The 1970s saw a decline in seaside holidays due to competition from cheap package holidays to mainland Europe, especially Spain. Packages are now available to destinations all over the world that offer a huge variety of sights and activities. **Ecotourism** and unusual destinations such as Alaska are expanding rapidly too.

C Budget airlines have made international travel quicker and cheaper

■ Tourist attractions

Many people choose to visit cities to enjoy the museums, art galleries, shops and restaurants. Cities such as London, Rome and Paris have a huge amount to offer tourists of every age. The natural landscape is also a major 'pull' for tourists, particularly mountains such as the Alps in Europe or the beautiful stretches of coastline found in the Mediterranean or the Caribbean.

> **Key term**
>
> **Ecotourism:** tourism that focuses on protecting the environment and the local way of life. Also known as green tourism.

> **Activity**
>
> 2 Study photo **D** opposite. This shows the Italian Alps: a popular tourist destination.
>
> a Draw a field sketch of this photo. Add labels to identify the attractions of the area for tourists.
>
> b What types of tourists are most likely to be attracted to this area in the winter?
>
> c What types of tourists are most likely to be attracted in the summer?
>
> d Look at all three of these photos, **D**, **E** and **F**. Out of your family and friends, who would be most attracted to each of these three Italian holiday destinations? Why?

Italy

Italy is a country with a great variety of landscapes. Photos **D**, **E** and **F** show the three main types: mountains, cities and coastline. All the places shown have a busy tourist business, making an important contribution to the national economy.

Venice is well known for its canals and Renaissance buildings; Florence for its art galleries. Skiing in the Alps and sunbathing on the coast are popular with both Italians and visitors from other countries.

D   *Mountains: The Italian Alps*

E   *Cities: Venice is a popular tourist destination*

The example of Italy illustrates point 3 opposite – more holiday choice. People want to visit a greater variety of places and the tourist industry grows and adapts to supply what people want.

Study tip

Photos can be labelled directly with arrows to point out the features. There needs to be space around each photo because the labels need to be detailed. Keep what you write clear, straightforward and to the point.

F   *Coastline: Coastal tourism in Vernazza*

13.2 How important is tourism in different countries?

Tourism is an important part of the economies of many richer countries. For many developing countries, it is one of the best ways to earn foreign income, provide jobs and improve standards of living. Countries want to take advantage of the growing numbers of tourists and the money they have to spend.

The economic importance of tourism

Tables **A** and **B** show the top 10 countries for tourist receipts (money earned from tourism) and most tourist arrivals (number of tourists every year).

- France has had more tourists than any other country for many years. French tourism includes every type of holiday such as city breaks, holiday cottages, camping and skiing.
- The USA earns more than any other country from tourism even though it doesn't have the largest number of visitors. This is because Europeans consider a trip to the USA as more special than staying in Europe, so they are likely to stay longer and spend more money.
- China is high in both tables **A** and **B**. For many people, distance makes it too expensive to visit, but its variety of unusual landscapes and unique culture attracts increasing numbers of people. This trend is likely to continue.
- In the Caribbean almost 50 per cent of visitors come from the nearby USA, with France, Canada and the UK also important sources of business. The amount of money spent by tourists ranges between $324 per holiday in Belize to $2,117 in the Virgin Islands, which attract the wealthiest celebrity visitors.

> **In this section you will learn**
>
> the economic importance of tourism to countries in contrasting parts of the world
>
> how to compare and contrast tourist regions.

A *Countries with the largest tourist receipts, 2009*

Country	Annual tourist income ($ billions)
USA	110.1
Spain	61.6
France	55.6
Italy	45.7
China	40.8
Germany	40.0
UK	36.0
Australia	24.7
Turkey	22.0
Austria	21.8

B *Countries with the most tourist arrivals, 2009*

Country	Number of tourists (millions)
France	78.5
USA	57.9
Spain	57.3
China	53.1
Italy	42.7
UK	30.1
Ukraine	25.5
Turkey	25.0
Germany	24.9
Russia	23.7

Activity

1 Study tables **A** and **B** on page 298. .

a What do you notice about the top three countries in the two tables?

b Why does the USA have the largest income from tourism?

c Suggest reasons why France is the world's most popular tourist destination.

d Why do you think poorer countries of the world don't appear in the tables?

Jobs from tourism are created in all countries. However, rich countries have a broadly balanced economy, of which tourism is one part. On the other hand, in less well-off countries tourism can be essential. In the Caribbean, for example, several small island countries rely heavily on tourism to provide national income and employment. Around 80 per cent of Barbados's national income comes from tourism.

Benefits of tourism in poorer countries

- Many people are employed to serve tourists such as waiters (photo **C**), souvenir shop assistants and tour guides. In Antigua and Barbuda 30 per cent of the population work in these jobs, but in Jamaica only 8 per cent.

- Tourists spend their holiday money in pounds sterling, US dollars or euros. This foreign exchange is essential to poorer countries. It can be used to buy goods and services from abroad.

- Many governments tax visitors to help pay for the extra services they use such as water supply, drainage, electricity and roads.

- Extra jobs are created indirectly. Hotels buy some produce from local suppliers to feed the visitors.

- Many small businesses have been started up to serve the tourists themselves and supply the services they demand. These include taxis, bars and restaurants, builders and maintenance workers.

C *Working as a waiter*

Dubai

Dubai is located on the Arabian Gulf coast neighbouring Saudi Arabia (map **D**). Tourism in Dubai is growing quickly because it is easily accessible from Europe, Asia and Africa (120 airlines fly there). Around 2.8 million people visited Dubai in 2000, 4.9 million in 2003 and 5.4 million in 2004. These numbers are predicted to grow further to 15 million by 2015, which would make Dubai one of the world's top tourist destinations.

E   *Dubai waterfront*

D   *Location of Dubai*

The state is famous for its duty-free shopping malls, its markets and its impressive waterfront developments (photo **E**). Prices are reasonable and there is huge variety.

Sightseeing is popular – the markets, the zoo, the dhow-building yards (traditional boats). Watersports, and especially diving, are growing in popularity. Excursions out from the city allow the visitor to see the desert and its wildlife (photo **F**). Bird-watching trips take visitors to the wetland mudflat areas, where there are 400 species.

F   *Desert trekking in Dubai*

∞ links

Find out more about Dubai's ambitions at **www.nakheel.com**.

Activities

2   Study photos **E** and **F**. These show some of the tourist attractions of Dubai.

a   What are the attractions that Dubai has to offer to tourists?

b   Which groups of people do you think benefit the most from the growth of tourism in Dubai?

- ■ People who get jobs as waiters, taxi drivers or hotel cleaners?
- ■ People with regular non-tourist jobs, like factory workers, teachers, shop workers, office workers?
- ■ Rich people, for example hotel owners and restaurant owners?
- ■ The government of Dubai (they collect taxes from tourism)?

There isn't a single right answer to this question, but it's a good one for discussion.

c   Would you like to go to Dubai? Why/Why not?

Study tip

Use case studies for longer, higher-mark questions. In a short answer you do not have space to do a case study justice, so naming examples is more appropriate. Be careful to mention only the aspects of your material that are relevant to the question – do not be tempted to write everything learned from your notes.

13.3 How do we manage tourism in the UK?

Tourism in the UK – changes

In the past, almost all British people went on holiday in the UK. Only rich people were able to go abroad. Tourism in Britain grew quickly in the 1950s and 1960s as the growing economy gave people higher pay and more time off work. Having a holiday every year became common. UK seaside holidays peaked in the early to mid-1970s, with 40 million visitors every year (graph **A**).

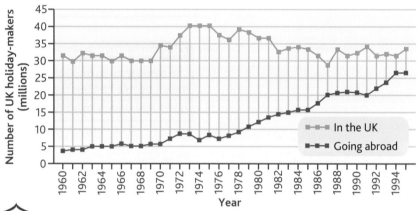

A Numbers of UK residents holidaying in the UK and abroad, 1960–95

After that, Britain's seaside resorts declined as cheap package holidays abroad with hot weather attracted people of all incomes. It was often cheaper to go to a Spanish resort like Benidorm than to go on holiday in the UK. British weather was seen as too unreliable.

B British seaside resorts were popular in the 1960s

Activities

1. Study graph **A**. This shows the numbers of UK residents taking holidays in the UK and abroad between 1960 and 1995.

   a In 1960 how many people holidayed within the UK and how many went abroad?

   b Which of these three years had the largest gap between the numbers of holidays in the UK and holidays abroad? Was it:

   ■ 1966

   ■ 1974

   ■ 1978

   c Describe the trend of the line showing people going abroad.

   d Suggest reasons for the trend described in c above.

   e What do you think the pattern of the two lines would be like today? Give reasons for your answer.

The Butler tourist resort life-cycle model

This model says that any tourist resort starts on a small scale, develops into something bigger, then either goes into decline or makes changes to maintain its attractions (graph **C**). There are six stages.

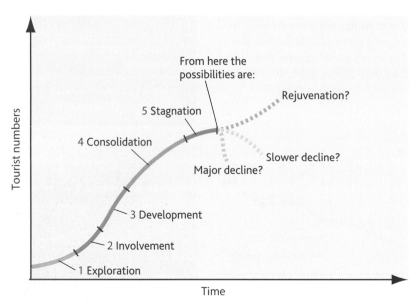

 The Butler model

1 Exploration

Small numbers of visitors are attracted by something specific, for example, good beaches, attractive landscape, historical or cultural features. Local people have not yet developed many tourist services.

2 Involvement

The local population sees the opportunities for tourism and starts to provide places to stay, food, transport, guides and other services for the visitors. At this stage most buildings are temporary and simple.

3 Development

Large companies build hotels and leisure complexes and advertise package holidays. Numbers of tourists rise dramatically. Job opportunities for local people grow rapidly bringing both advantages and disadvantages. Whilst they provide employment, they are often seasonal and poorly paid.

4 Consolidation

Tourism is now a major part of the local economy, but perhaps at the expense of other types of development. Employment is secure as the numbers of visitors are steady. However, some hotels and other facilities are becoming older and unattractive, so the type of customers attracted goes downmarket. Rowdiness becomes a problem and the environment can become damaged or polluted.

5 Stagnation

The resort becomes unfashionable and fewer people visit. Businesses change hands and often fail. Some buildings may be abandoned and fall into disrepair.

6 Decline or rejuvenation

Decline: visitors prefer other resorts. Day trippers and weekenders become the main source of income.

Rejuvenation: attempts are made to modernise the resort and attract different people to enjoy new activities, for example, shopping or conferences.

Blackpool is a good example of a resort reinventing itself.

Blackpool, a UK coastal tourist resort

Blackpool's growth and stagnation

Located on the Lancashire coast in the north-west of England, Blackpool became a major tourist centre during the 19th century. Factory workers from northern industrial towns could increasingly afford a holiday, travelling by train to the nearby coast. Blackpool boomed between 1900 and 1950.

D   *Factory workers on holiday, 1951*

However, since the 1960s people increasingly chose to travel abroad to enjoy cheap package holidays. This led to a decline of tourism in Blackpool. In an attempt to regenerate Blackpool's tourism, money from private companies and local authority grants was used to:

- upgrade hotels
- convert small hotels into self-catering holiday flats
- turn outdoor pools into indoor leisure centres
- increase car-parking provision.

Decline continued, but more slowly. Blackpool's attractions still made it a little different to other resorts.

- The famous Blackpool Tower, gives fantastic views. The complex there includes the Tower Ballroom, famous for national ballroom dancing competitions, and the Tower Circus.

- The town upgraded its zoo and a Sealife Centre was built.
- The Blackpool Illuminations – a light show stretching along the Golden Mile (the central section of the sea front) – began in 1879 and has been upgraded several times with advancing technology.

Blackpool should have been quicker to fight the competition from package holidays. Eventually it lost much of its family holiday business and came to rely on day trippers and stag and hen party business – not popular with residents and not great for the town's image.

E   *Blackpool Tower and the Illuminations*

The supercasino

Blackpool applied to the government to be the home of the UK's first supercasino, a huge leisure and entertainment complex based on those in Las Vegas and Atlantic City in the USA. The proposed sea-front site included a wide variety of entertainments. Lots of jobs and investment would have been generated but Blackpool lost the supercasino development to Manchester, coming only third in the vote. The town council was shocked.

Blackpool today

Despite the supercasino setback, Blackpool is aiming for regeneration. The Blackpool Masterplan spent millions improving the town for the casino bid, so the town now looks less run-down. A new department store (Debenhams) opened in 2008 and the council bought the famous Winter Gardens in 2010 with the aim of making them a big tourist attraction.

2 Study the information about Blackpool on p.303 together with the Butler Model (graph **C**, p.302)

a Make a large copy of the Butler Model line graph in the centre of a blank sheet of paper.

b Carefully work your way through the Blackpool case study selecting information to write in the correct stages alongside your graph. You will probably need to do this in rough first.

c Select some photos from the internet to illustrate your work.

d Do you think Blackpool is currently declining or being rejuvenated? Explain your answer.

Did you know ?????

In 2009, 30.1 million visitors to the UK spent over £15 billion in this country.

The contribution of tourism to the UK economy

Every year the UK earns over £114 billion (2008) from tourism and leisure. This amount usually grows slightly every year. Restaurants and hotels make up a large amount of these earnings. More than 100 new hotels opened in the UK between September 2004 and December 2005, creating more jobs and income.

External factors affecting UK tourism in the early 21st century

Two key issues have produced tourism difficulties in the early 21st century.

Terrorism

The destruction of the World Trade Center in New York on 11 September 2001 had a huge impact on travel. So did the London Underground bombings of 7 July 2005. After such events, people were worried about it happening again and visitor numbers fell. Security has increased around the world to try and stop terrorism. This means that it can take longer to get to places. At airports, for example check-in times have increased. This can also put people off travelling.

Exchange rates and the banking crisis

Currency exchange rates control value for money for tourists on holiday. In 2011 the euro was high against the pound, valued at around 87p (compared with 68p previously), so holidaying in Europe became more expensive. At the same time, £1 was worth $1.60, making the USA a much more attractive holiday destination.

From 2008, the whole world suffered huge economic problems. In the UK, many people lost jobs or had pay freezes when prices for food and fuel went up. These problems caused a reduction in tourism.

F *Around 1.1 million tourists travelled to London for the royal wedding in 2011.*

∞links

Find out more about Blackpool tourism at **www.visitblackpool.com**.

13.4 What is the importance of National Parks for UK tourism?

National Parks are large areas of mainly rural landscape. They have been created by Parliament to protect natural and cultural landscapes while allowing visitors to enjoy them. The first Scottish National Park was created in 2002. In England the most recent National Parks are the New Forest (2004) and the South Downs (2011).

Many National Parks are uplands such as Snowdonia (photo **B**) and the Lake District. A few are lowlands (The Broads) and others include stretches of coast (for example, Pembrokeshire Coast). Most of the land is privately owned by farmers but the Forestry Commission, the National Trust, the Ministry of Defence and the water authorities also own some areas.

In this section you will learn

the contribution of tourism to the UK economy

the importance of National Parks for UK tourism

the conflicts caused by tourism in the Lake District

how to devise management strategies for tourism in the Lake District.

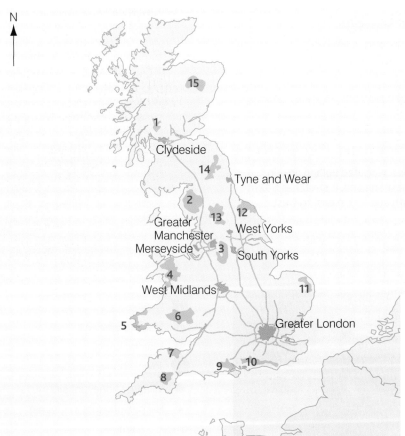

1 Loch Lomond and the Trossachs
2 Lake District
3 Peak District
4 Snowdonia
5 Pembrokeshire Coast
6 Brecon Beacons
7 Exmoor
8 Dartmoor
9 New Forest
10 South Downs
11 The Broads
12 North York Moors
13 Yorkshire Dales
14 Northumberland
15 Cairngorms

National Park
Motorway
Major urban areas

0   100 km

A *The location of National Parks in Britain*

Key term

National Park: an area where development is limited and planning controlled. The landscape is regarded as unusual and valuable and therefore worth looking after.

B *Snowdonia National Park*

Activities

1 Study map **A**.

a Out of the 15 National Parks, how many are in Scotland?

b Some National Parks are close to large urban areas. Which one is close to Greater Manchester?

c If you lived in London, where is your nearest National Park?

d What do Pembrokshire Coast, Exmoor and the North York Moors have in common?

e You are taking a family holiday in SW England. Which two National Parks could you choose to visit?

2 Study photo **B**, a scene from Snowdonia National Park. What types of activities would tourists come here to do?

3 Divide up the 15 National Parks between members of your class. Conduct internet research to discover what makes your chosen National Park special. Present your research to the rest of the class as a PowerPoint presentation using a maximum of six slides only.

The Lake District

Attractions and opportunities for tourism

The Lake District became a National Park in 1951. Famous for its stunning scenery, abundant wildlife and cultural heritage, it is considered to be England's finest landscape. What makes it so special for tourists? Landscape, culture and outdoor activities all play a major role.

The Lake District is a glaciated upland area in Cumbria, north-west England. It stretches 64 km from north to south and 53 km east to west.

Key

- ♜ Castle
- ✳ Notable gardens
- ⌂ Historic house
- ● Town – honeypot site
- ● Village – honeypot site
- ▲ Hill peak (height in metres)

0   5 km

D *Lake District attractions*

C *Hill Top, Beatrix Potter's house – a honeypot site in the summer*

Many 19th-century writers and artists, such as John Ruskin, loved the area. Beatrix Potter's family, residents of London, had a summer home there, which is why she settled there later at Hill Top beside Lake Windermere.

Walking is one of the most popular reasons why people visit the Lake District, whether for a day or an extended visit. Routes vary from short and relatively flat to extremely long and tough. Known as the 'birthplace of mountaineering', even the most experienced climbers find plenty of challenges in scaling back walls of corries and sides of U-shaped valleys (photo **E**). Public access to the fells (open uplands) is unrestricted.

E *Red Tarn and Striding Edge, Helvellyn*

The ribbon lakes and tarns are part of a unique and hugely varied landscape, as well as being a major watersports resource. On some lakes, areas are set aside for windsailing and power-boating. Small boats are allowed on many lakes and quiet areas are left for people seeking peace and quiet. Fishing from the shore or boating are increasing in popularity.

Map labels:

Keswick A66 M6
A5091
Pooley Bridge Askham
Catbells 451
Glenridding Ullswater
Derwent Water A591
Place Fell 857
Helvellyn 950
Thirlmere
Fairfield 873
A592
Harrison Stickle 736 Grasmere Dove Cottage Rydal Mount Yoke 706 Haweswater
Rosset Crag 651
Elterwater Ambleside Townend Holehird Gardens
A593
Hawkshead Windermere & Bowness A6
Coniston A591
Coniston Old Man 803 Brantwood Hill Top Kendal
Coniston Water A5074
Broughton in Furness Windermere Sizergh
A5084 A592

F *Windermere town centre*

Lake Windermere specialises in ferry cruises. Most people sail between the main centres of Windermere town (photo **F**) and Ambleside.

Historical and cultural sites attract tourists. The Lake District has been occupied since the end of the ice age 10,000 years ago and evidence of early settlement remains in the landscape.

Impacts of tourism

There are many more visitors to the Lake District National Park than people who live there. About 12 million tourists visit the Lake District each year, compared with a resident population of just 42,239. This huge popularity has led to a number of issues.

1 Traffic problems

Over 89 per cent of visitors come by car, often just for the day. Many roads are narrow and winding. Buses and large delivery vehicles have to use these for both locals and tourists. Queues are a common problem, especially towards the end of the day when people are heading home. Towns were not built for the huge volumes of traffic that arrive in the summer, especially at weekends. Congestion and parking are serious problems. In the countryside people park on grass verges, causing serious damage.

2 Honeypot sites

The Lake District has both physical and cultural **honeypot** sites. Beauty spots, small shopping centres and historic houses all attract hundreds of visitors daily. Honeypot sites need to provide access and facilities while remaining as unspoilt as possible. Across the Lake District, 4 million people walk at least 6 km every year. Catbells is quite an easy climb, so many people walk up this smaller mountain. It therefore suffers from serious footpath erosion (photo **G**). Several areas have scarred landscapes. Bowness is an extremely busy shopping and recreation centre in summer and it frequently becomes crowded.

3 Pressure on property

Almost 20 per cent of property in the Lake District National Park is either second homes or holiday let accommodation (15 per cent of all housing in 2007). Some local people make a good income from owning and letting such property. However:

- Holiday cottages and flats are not occupied all year.
- Holidaymakers do not always support local businesses, often doing a supermarket shop at home before their trip.
- Demand for property from outsiders increases property prices in the Lake District. Local people are forced to find affordable homes on the edge of the region in Kendal or Penrith. This is the most serious tourist problem affecting local communities.

4 Environmental issues

Water sports are not allowed on some of the lakes, but Windermere, the largest lake, has ferries and allows power-boating, windsurfing and other faster and more damaging activities (photo **H**). The main issue is the wash from faster vehicles eroding the shore. Fuel spills are not uncommon, causing pollution.

G Footpath erosion in the Lake District

H Boat trips, a popular tourist attraction on Lake Windermere

Activities

1. Study photo **G**. What is the evidence that this footpath is being eroded?

2. Study photo **H**.
    a. What evidence is there that taking a boat trip is a popular activity?
    b. What environmental problems have been caused by boats on Lake Windermere?

links

Find out more about the Lake District at **www.lake-district.gov.uk**.

Tourism management strategies

In 2007 the Lake District National Park launched its plan for sustainable growth of the National Park, 'Visions for the National Park in 2030'. In 2008 the Cumbria Tourist Board produced a management tourist plan 'Making the Dream a Reality 2008–2018'.

1 Traffic solutions

- Roads, often dual carriageways, have been built on the edges of the Lake District to help move traffic in and out as easily as possible.
- Distributor roads link the small towns and key tourist villages such as Ambleside.
- Traffic on smaller roads can be slowed down by traffic-calming measures, cattle grids and an overall maximum speed limit.
- Low-carbon vehicle use, such as buses, has been encouraged.
- A park-and-ride scheme called the 'Honister Rambler' runs from Keswick. This takes walkers to popular sites, such as Catbells, so that fewer cars are on the roads and also fewer car parking spaces are needed.
- Make it easier to change between parking, buses, boats, cycling and walking.

2 Honeypot management

Footpaths:

- The 'Upland Path Landscape Restoration Project (2002-2011)' meant that 145 paths were repaired by creating steps, surfacing with local stone and re-planting native plants.
- A badly eroded path at Whiteless Pike, Buttermere has been repaired using a technique called 'stone pitching'. This is where large stones are dug into the path to create solid, hard-wearing footpaths.

Parking:

- Fenced roadsides so cars cannot damage verges.
- Develop several new small car parks and hide them by landscaping using tree planting.
- Car-park surfaces have been reinforced to prevent damage.

Litter:

- Bins are provided at popular sites and emptied often.
- Signs encourage people to not leave litter.

3 Property prices

This is the most difficult issue as house prices can't be controlled. Local authorities could build more homes for rent and low-cost homes for sale. Little has yet been achieved.

4 Environmental issues

Speed limits for boats can limit the amount of wash caused. However, to prevent erosion, speeds would have to be very low, which clashes with the main pleasure of the sport – going fast! Limiting the noisiest and most damaging sports to certain parts of the lake can restrict the amount of conflict between different users.

Tourism conflicts and opportunities

1 Farming

Tourism and farming are often thought to be in conflict, which can be true. Visitors can trample crops and disturb animals, but signs and education have limited these problems. Tourists have offered farmers new ways of making money in difficult economic times. Income can be made from B&B accommodation, holiday cottages converted from farm buildings, camping and caravan sites. Activities such as pony trekking and paintballing can be offered.

2 Employment

The impact of tourism on employment is positive as so many jobs are created. Many businesses thrive and make a profit. However, these jobs are often low paid and there's less work in winter.

1 *Elterwater village*

13.5 Why do so many countries want mass tourism?

Advantages and disadvantages of mass tourism

Mass tourism involves large numbers of tourists coming to one place (photos **A** and **B**). There is usually a particular purpose and a particular type of location, such as skiing in a mountain resort or sunbathing on a beach. Many countries and regions want to develop mass tourism because they believe it will bring many advantages (table **C**).

A Mass tourism in Barcelona, Spain

B The Parthenon in Athens, Greece, is the most visited ancient monument in Europe

Key term

Mass tourism: tourism on a large scale to one country or region. This is linked to the Development and Consolidation phases of the Butler tourist life cycle model.

Did you know ??????

In the USA the first mass tourist resorts were Atlantic City in New Jersey and Long Island in New York State.

Study tip

Ensure that you can describe and explain some of the advantages and disadvantages of mass tourism to the economy and environment of a location.

C *Advantages and disadvantages of mass tourism*

Advantages	Disadvantages
• Local business such as hotel, restaurants and shops make money. Taxes make money for the governmnent.	• The activity may be seasonal – skiing only happens in winter. Local people may find themselves out of work for the rest of the year.
• These businesses provide jobs for local people, who gain regular work with a more reliable wage.	• Few local employees are well paid. The higher level jobs are often taken by people from the companies involved in developing the resort, who are not locals.
• Increased money for local people means that they will spend money as well as tourists which will help the economy grow.	• Lower- and middle-income customers are the target market for mass tourism – this type of tourism does not appeal to rich people who have more money to spend.
• Local people learn new skills which can be used in other businesses as well.	• Companies who run big resorts are usually based overseas. Profits therefore go outside the tourist country – they do not benefit the host country.
• New infrastructure must be put in place for tourists – airports, hotels, power supplies, roads and telecommunications. These can also be used by the local population.	• New construction can damage the environment, destroy habitats and cause pollution.
• Jobs building the new hotels and other facilities often go to local people, but they are temporary.	• New building developments need land. This reduces the land available for local people's homes and for farmers to grow food. Less local food is available.
• New leisure facilities may be open to local people.	• Tourists can be narrow-minded and often prefer familiar food, rather than experimenting with local dishes.
	• Culture clashes can occur. Tourism can lead to problems with drugs and alcohol. Sex tourism is a problem in some areas.

Tourism in Jamaica

Case study

Jamaica is one of the Caribbean's main tourist destinations. Tourism is the country's second biggest earner and other local businesses also depend on tourism, such as food production for visitors and other hotel suppliers. Jamaica has much to offer the tourist (map **D** and fact file **E**) including watersports, for which it is famous, wildlife sanctuaries and, increasingly, golf.

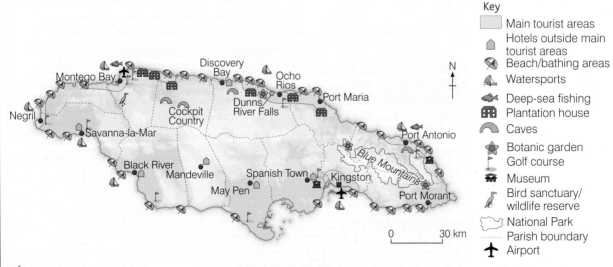

D *Jamaican tourist attractions*

Community tourism

A recent trend has been the growth in community tourism. This involves local people directly because visitors become a part of their home and village during their stay. Families provide bed and breakfast accommodation. Other local businesses, such as restaurants and bars, supply their other needs. This style of holiday provides greater interaction between tourists and local people, gives the visitors a clearer idea of local life, supports local businesses and uses fewer resources. Money goes directly to the people rather than to large international businesses.

Ecotourism

Jamaica needs to maintain its tourist resources into the future and some companies offer ecotourism. This uses areas of the island, such as the Blue Mountains as well as parts of the coast, spreading tourists further around the island. Nature reserves are increasing and eco-lodges are being built. The number of tourists are kept low in these areas, which reduces pressure on the environment.

∞ links

Find out more about Jamaican tourism at www.visitjamaica.com.

E *Jamaican tourism fact file, 2010*

Jamaican tourism facts and figures	
Total number of tourist arrivals	1.9 million
Population employed in tourism	22.6%
Contribution to GDP	24%
Passengers arriving by cruise ships	910,000
Rooms available to tourists	31,000
Visitors from USA and UK (% of total)	70% and 10%

F *Ocho Rios, Jamaica*

Activities

1 Study map **D**, fact file **E** and photo **F**. The map shows Jamaican tourist attractions and the fact file lists some key tourism information.

a Name two important tourist areas in Jamaica.

b Which tourist activities are found in these areas? Name as many as you can.

c Make two separate lists of the advantages and disadvantages to Jamaica of the holiday industry.

2 This is a group exercise. Each group should have at least three members.

■ Imagine a new tourist enterprise is being set up in Jamaica. The plan is to make this new enterprise really eco-friendly and sustainable. (You can find more information on sustainable tourism on pages 316 and 317 of this book.)

■ Your job is to present information on your proposal to a panel made up of government officials and representatives of environmental groups.

■ The government would like to see as many tourists coming in as possible and also create many more jobs for local people.

■ The environmental groups want the beautiful Jamaican environment to be conserved and respected.

a Where on Jamaica will your new development be located? What activities are going to be provided? Remember to make this sound exciting for your audience.

b What sort of accommodation will you provide? Will you use sustainable materials? Is this a massive development or a small-scale one?

c Will local people be employed as waiters, cleaners, receptionists etc, or will you recruit tourism professionals who can provide the very best service for guests?

d What are the advantages of your proposal and what difficulties will you need to overcome?

e Compare your plans with other groups' plans.

13.6 What attracts people to extreme environments?

Extreme environments and activities

Extreme environments are spread across the globe and cover a wide variety of locations including mountains, deserts, rainforests, caves and ice-covered landscapes (photos **A** to **D**). They are often dangerous landscapes which have a difficult climate and have few, if any, people living in them. Increasing numbers of tourists are attracted to extreme environments.

Extreme activities include rock climbing, paragliding and white-water rafting. Some of these activities need to be done in extreme environments. Ice-walking is one example, because you need an ice cap or glacier to walk across. But many extreme activities can be done in a variety of places, for example paragliding and microlighting are done on the South Downs in Sussex.

Adventure tourism is one of the fastest-growing types of tourism in the world. It involves an element of risk and people often choose such a trip for the adrenaline rush they get from the dangerous activities and sports involved. Examples include ice-diving in the White Sea, north Russia, with almost freezing temperatures, and travelling across the Chernobyl Zone of Alienation in Ukraine – the area devastated by nuclear contamination in 1986. In Jamaica such activities include climbing waterfalls and cliff-diving.

In this section you will learn

what we mean by 'extreme' tourism

which environments are classified as extreme

what is happening in Antarctica in tourism development and the likely consequences of this

how to assess whether particular remote landscapes should be developed for tourism on any scale.

Key term

Extreme environments: places with particularly difficult environments, such as being very hot or cold. Tourism to these places has only recently occurred due to people wanting to visit somewhere with different physical challenges.

A Exploring the icy landscape in Greenland

B Setting up camp under the stars in the desert

C Paddling in a dug-out canoe in the Amazon

D Hiking in the foothills of the Himalayas

The target market

Adventure tourists look for physical challenge and are prepared to take risks. They are often fit and well-educated professionals who can afford these expensive adventures. In recent years, there has been considerable growth in this sector as people seek to take on a challenge during their holiday rather than simply lying on a beach.

Setting up this kind of tourism is quite cheap as expensive things like building hotels and roads are irrelevant. Part of the experience is to sleep 'rough' and travel over untouched landscapes. This tourism sector is growing rapidly in Peru, Chile, Argentina, Azerbaijan and Pakistan. Northern Pakistan is one of the most mountainous and difficult landscapes in the world.

Case study

Antarctica

Small-scale tourism began in Antarctica in the 1950s when commercial shipping began to take a few passengers. The first specially designed cruise ship made its first voyage in 1969. Some 9,000 tourists in 1992–93 has now grown to nearly 34,000 in 2010–11 (table **E**).

Tourists usually fly to New Zealand or Argentina, taking a cruise ship onwards for one to two weeks. Smaller boats take them ashore at key locations for short visits, mainly to the peninsula or nearby islands (map **F**).

E *Antarctic tourist numbers, 2010–11*

Country of origin	Numbers	Percentage of total
USA	12,629	37.4
Australia	3,220	9.5
UK	2,763	8.1
Canada	2,531	7.5
Germany	2,378	7.0
Japan	936	2.8
Netherlands	889	2.6
Others	8,478	25.1
Total	33,824	100.0

There aren't many landing sites in Antarctica so they quickly become honeypots. Walking, kayaking, skiing, climbing, scuba diving and helicopter/small aircraft flights are some of the activities tourists can do (chart **G** opposite).Tourism could easily cause lots of damage to the fragile environment. This means tourism activities have to be carefully managed.

Tourists only spend a short time ashore but they want to visit the most beautiful areas with the most wildlife. Animals, especially penguins and seals, are disturbed by more than a few people (photo **H**). Not used to humans, they do not like to be touched. If they leave as a result, they may abandon eggs and young.

There have been accidents when ships have struck uncharted rocks or ice floes.

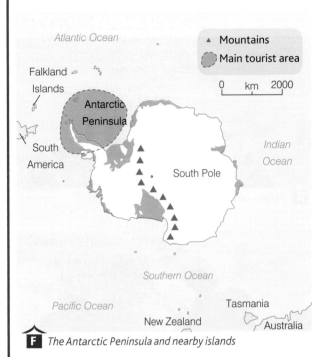

F *The Antarctic Peninsula and nearby islands*

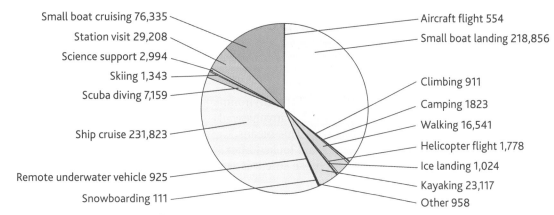

Small boat cruising 76,335
Station visit 29,208
Science support 2,994
Skiing 1,343
Scuba diving 7,159
Ship cruise 231,823
Remote underwater vehicle 925
Snowboarding 111

Aircraft flight 554
Small boat landing 218,856
Climbing 911
Camping 1823
Walking 16,541
Helicopter flight 1,778
Ice landing 1,024
Kayaking 23,117
Other 958

G *Tourist numbers in Antarctica, 2007–08*

The great majority of shipping in Antarctic waters is tourist-based. Oil spills are becoming an increasing hazard for wildlife. Tourist ships must discharge all waste materials well away from the shore of Antarctica.

Coping with tourism in Antarctica

Although tourist numbers have increased rapidly in Antarctica, protection remains a high priority.

- All tour operators are members of IAATO, which directs tourism to be safe and environmentally friendly.
- Visitors are not allowed to visit Sites of Special Scientific Interest (SSSIs) in order to conserve precious wildlife and landscapes. Bird Island on South Georgia is one example.
- A permit must be obtained for any activities on the continent.
- No ship carrying over 500 passengers can land in Antarctica.

Nevertheless, there is concern that larger ships will eventually be allowed to land and that the volume of tourists will be beyond sustainable limits.

Did you know ??????

The ice in an Antarctic iceberg is around 100,000 years old. The continent is actually a desert, with only 254 mm of precipitation each year.

Activity

Use the information about Antarctica to help you make a study of tourism in this extreme environment. Use the internet to help you investigate the following themes:

a What are the attractions to tourists?

b Where do tourists come from? (Here you could use table **E** opposite to make a flow map.)

c What are the issues associated with tourism? (Hint: impact on environment, safety issues.)

d How should tourism be controlled in the future?

∞ links

Find out more about tourism in Antarctica at **www.coolantarctic.com**.

H *The impact of tourists can be great*

13.7 How can tourism become more sustainable?

Stewardship and conservation

The term **stewardship** means careful management of the environment on a large scale, for example, in a country. Stewardship involves managing the earth's resources in a sustainable way. This means that the environment and resources are protected and looked after. We should all be stewards of our environment to make sure it is sustainable.

Conservation is stewardship on a smaller scale. People feel much more involved at this level. An individual building can be conserved and protected because of its historical importance. Habitats and landscapes in rural areas can be protected. Careful use of non-renewable resources is also a form of conservation. Planned use allows them to last as long as possible. Conservation can involve improving energy efficiency and recycling waste.

The aims of ecotourism

Ecotourism is environmentally friendly tourism that promotes sustainable development. It caters for a small but growing number of environmentally aware tourists and is the fastest expanding tourism sector.

Ecotourists want to experience the natural environment directly and do activities such as trekking and bird-watching. They want their holiday to have as little impact on the environment as possible. Ecotourists prefer accommodation in lodges that may not even have electricity, rather than in large hotels. They like to eat local food. Local people are their guides as their knowledge and experience is seen to be more valuable. The impact on the environment is low but, because ecotourism is small in scale, the price paid by each tourist is high.

In this section you will learn

the concept of sustainable tourism

different types of sustainable tourism and be able to compare them.

Key terms

Stewardship: the personal responsibility of us all for looking after things, in this case the environment.

Conservation: the thoughtful use of resources; managing the landscape in order to protect ecosystems and cultural features.

Study tip

Make sure you can use an example to explain how ecotourism can help sustainable development.

A *Ecotourism in a Costa Rican rainforest*

The Galapagos Islands

The Galapagos Islands lie 1,000 km off the west coast of South America in the Pacific Ocean. They belong to Ecuador. Around 90 per cent of these islands are National Parks or marine reserves. The islands are among the most fragile and precious ecosystems in the world, becoming the first Unesco World Heritage Site in 1979.

Today, tourists visit under strict rules. They arrive mainly by small ships that tour the islands and allow people onshore only at specific locations in limited numbers. The tour boats are owned by locals and take 10 to 16 tourists each. Many go with professional guides who give information and stop people from causing damage.

The benefits of ecotourism in the Galapagos Islands include the following:

- Environmental benefits – carefully planned ecotourism gives local people the chance to make money while keeping environmental damage low.

- Economic benefits to the local economy – local businesses have been started to provide the needs of tourists. Tourists usually stay in small guest houses, often run as family businesses. Local companies provide boat trips around islands and between the islands.

- Economic benefits to the lives of individuals – people are employed in guest houses, on boats and as guides. The income is enough to make a difference to a household. Many visitors give tips, which go directly to local people.

In supporting local communities and preventing damage to the environment, management of the Galapagos Islands is an excellent example of sustainable development. It allows development to take place but is long-lasting and protects the environment.

B   Ecotourism on the Galapagos Islands

Activities

1 **a** What sort of damage can tourism do to the environment? Consider the issues at three different scales.

- local scale – just to the environment surrounding a tourist location

- national scale – the damage tourism can cause, particularly if a country is dependent on it (e.g. development of roads and airports)

- global scale – the damage global travel can cause the environment.

b How does ecotourism aim to be more environmentally friendly than 'standard' tourism?

c If ecotourism is small scale, with basic facilities and uses local food and employs local people, why do tourists pay more for it than 'standard' tourism? (Hint: think about the sort of people attracted to ecotourism and how many people there are like this.)

2 Choose one of this chapter's case studies – Jamaica or the Galapagos Islands. Write an extract from a travel company brochure to sell this holiday to potential customers. Think of your target market and make sure you use language that would appeal to them. For your chosen tourist destination, find one or more photos from the internet to illustrate the holiday you are advertising.

3 The Geography and Biology departments at your school want to run a trip to the Galapagos Islands. Your class has been asked to help promote the trip by producing posters and PowerPoint presentations. The trip is to be as environmentally sensitive as possible so you need to stress the principles of ecotourism. Work in pairs or small groups and use the internet to help you.

Levels of response marking

Levels of response marking is normally used for answers with a mark allocation of four and above. Parts of questions with fewer marks are point marked. With point marked questions there is a mark allocated for each point made. It is possible to allocate a mark to a particular point in the answer where the candidate has made a correct and relevant response. For this reason it is possible to position ticks within the body of the answer. The question will be worded so that it is clear that a certain number of points have to be made. For example, give one advantage and one disadvantage of .... would be worth two marks. In levels marking, the mark allocated is for the overall quality of the answer as a whole and not for specific points within it.

On a Foundation Tier paper, level two is the maximum achievable. In the vast majority of cases this will mean that the total mark would be four, which gives both levels a range of two marks i.e. level one with 1–2 marks and level two worth 3–4 marks. If six marks are allocated to a question on a Foundation Tier paper then the split is likely to 1–4 and 5–6 marks.

There are descriptions for each level as follows.

■ Level 1: Basic

- Knowledge of basic information
- Simple understanding
- Little organisation with few links, little or no detail, uses a limited range of specialist terms
- Reasonable accuracy in spelling, punctuation and grammar
- Text is legible

■ Level 2: Clear

- Knowledge of accurate information
- Clear understanding
- Organised answers with some links, occasional detail/exemplar, uses a good range of specialist terms where appropriate
- Considerable accuracy in spelling punctuation and grammar
- Text is legible

In a physical geography question testing candidates' knowledge and understanding of the geomorphological formation of a landform, such as a corrie or a wave cut platform, marking would work as follows. A level one answer would consist of simple statements with either an incomplete or inaccurate sequence in the land formation and with no reference to any processes. Alternatively, there may be some explanation of processes but limited or no reference to sequence. At level two, examiners would expect a complete sequence and at least the names of the erosion or depositional processes involved and an explanation of the processes involved. You can also gain further marks if the spelling, punctuation and grammar is accurate. Well annotated diagrams can also enhance the quality of the answer although they should not simply repeat information given in the written answer.

Do not work through the levels. Write at the highest level possible at the beginning of your answer. Always try to write linked statements, because this triggers access to level two. No matter how many simple unlinked statements you write, your answer will remain in level 1. Linking two or more of these statements, by means of a conjunction or another 'joining' word, means that there has been some development or elaboration of a simple or basic fact or idea. This will get you to level two

If, after reading a point, the reader wants to say 'so what?' the answer has not been developed and so remains in level one. Consider the answer to a question such as – 'What is the advantage of a conservation swap to a country in the Poor World?' If your answer consists merely of 'It brings money into the country' the reader wants to know more. On the other hand if your answer reads 'It brings money into the country in return for agreeing not to cut down any more rainforest', there is some clarity to the answer, as a result of developing the simple idea of financial gain for the poor country. No marks to be deducted for any incorrect or irrelevant information

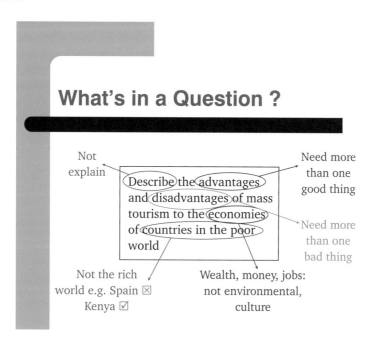

You must answer all parts of the question. For this reason it is important that you get into the habit of breaking down a question. Highlight or underline on the examination paper all the command words and any plurals etc. so you answer all parts of the question.

Consider the following questions and the examples of possible candidates' answers.

■ WATER ON THE LAND

Explain the formation of an Oxbow lake. (4 marks)

Level 1 (Basic) 1–2 marks

The answer will be made up of simple points and will jump about, with the sequence of events either incomplete or not in the correct order.

The river will cut through a meander making it straighter and leaving an ox-bow lake behind. There will be erosion and deposition so that the land across the meander gets narrower and the river cuts through.

There is much confusion here. There no clear description of where the river erodes across the neck of the meander. The answer starts off with the end of the sequence rather than taking it from the start. There is no reference to the process and therefore no explanation of the areas of erosion and deposition that lead to the cutting off of the meander to leave an ox-bow lake. This answer would have gained one out of the two marks that are available at level one.

Level 2 (Clear) 3–4 marks

The answer will have complete linked statements with a full and complete sequence. There will be reference to processes but these need not be described in detail as this question does not have the opportunity to go to level three.

On a meander the river flows fastest on the outside of the bend, which is where erosion is taking place. Deposition takes place on the inside of the bend where the river is flowing more slowly. The

erosion causes the bends on the outside of the meanders to get closer together. Eventually the river will cut through the short distance between the two bends and form a new, straighter channel. The rest of the meander is left as a curved ox-bow lake.

There is reference to the process of erosion taking place on the outside of the bend which means that the distance across the neck of the meander get smaller. It would have been useful if comment had been made to the fact that the cut off across the neck was likely to have occurred after a period of heavy rain when the river was in flood. The importance of deposition taking place on the inner bend could have been developed by showing that the build up of material here helps separate the remains of the meander from the new straighter river channel. This is not a perfect answer and would have benefitted from some simple diagrams but there is enough clarity here for the answer to get the full four marks available at the top of level two.

■ Tourism

Describe how an ecotourism development can benefit future generations.   (4 marks)

Level 1 (Basic) 1–2 marks

Simple statements and little reference to how it can benefit future generations

The resort in Brazil is a long way from anywhere. People have to walk there because there are no other forms of transport. They live in huts made of wood and eat local food. Local people are employed as waiters and cleaners. The people eat local food and are not allowed to leave rubbish anywhere. The electricity for heating the water is made by the sun. People go on nature trails to look at animals and birds.

This is largely a description of ecotourism and is an example of a 'so what' type of answer. The answer refers to the materials used for building the accommodation, the use of local food and the use of renewable energy, but fails to develop these points to show why these features are sustainable. There is a basic understanding of ecotourism and this would allow the answer to be awarded two out of the possible four marks.

Level 2 (Clear) 3–4 marks

The answer will have linked statements with some attempt to explain how future generations can benefit.

The Kapari Lodge in the Amazon near the border with Ecuador and Peru is sustainable in many ways. The water for the showers in the lodges is heated by solar panels which convert the solar energy into electricity and create four gallons of heated water a day per person. The rubbish is dealt with in three ways – all metal and plastic is flown to the city; all paper is burned and all biodegradable waste buried under the forest where it decomposes to be used as materials for the plants. Also carbon dioxide emissions are reduced as it is a ten day walk to the nearest village so there are no cars to pollute the atmosphere.

The use of a named example is always useful even if one is not specifically asked for in the question. This allows there to be more detail in the answer. However, while this answer gives details about the Kapari Lodge, it is not always linked closely enough to the needs of the question. It is only the final sentence about the atmospheric pollution which gives some idea on the effect on future generations and, even here, it could have been made more explicit. There was potential to develop the ideas of the disposal of the rubbish and the use of renewable energy on future generations. The benefits could have been to the environment, the local economy or the lives of the people. Despite this, the answer contains enough specific details to gain all four marks.

Practice questions

1 The restless earth

a)
   i)   Use Figure C on Page 9 to state why the boundary between the Nazca plate and the South American plate can be described as constructive. *(1 mark)*

   ii) Use Figure D on page 10 to explain why volcanoes form along the plate margin between the Nazca Plate and the South American Plate. *(4 marks)*

   iii) Give **one** reason why an oceanic plate can move under a continental plate. *(1 mark)*

b) With reference to a *named* volcanic eruption explain how the effects can be both positive and negative. *(6 marks)*

c) Look at Figure A on page 12. Circle **True** or **False** against *each* of the following statements: *(4 marks)*

There are ocean trenches in the Atlantic Ocean.	**True** / **False**
There is one area of young fold mountains in Africa.	**True** / **False**
Young fold mountains run along the eastern coasts of North and South America.	**True** / **False**
The longest ocean trench is in the Pacific Ocean.	**True** / **False**

d)
   i)   Study pages 29–30. Give **two** *effects* of the Haiti earthquake. *(2 marks)*

   ii) Look at page 28 and give **two** *responses* to the Kobe earthquake. *(2 marks)*

e)
   i)   State whether a tsunami is a primary or a secondary effect of an earthquake. *(1 mark)*

   ii) Explain the methods used to reduce the destructive impacts of tsunamis. *(4 marks)*

2 Rocks, resources and scenery

a) Use Figure A on page 34 to explain the difference between an era and a period. *(2 marks)*

b) Complete the following table by writing *biological, chemical or mechanical* to show the type of weathering. One has been done for you. *(4 marks)*

	Type of weathering
Freeze-thaw	Mechanical
Tree roots	
Carbonation	
Exfoliation	
Solution	

c) With the help of Figure B on page 43 explain the formation of an escarpment or cuesta. *(6 marks)*

d)
   i)   Which one of the following is **not** found in a carboniferous limestone landscape? Circle the correct answer.

          Clint   Tor   Dry valley   Stalagmite   Gryke   Swallow hole *(1 mark)*

   ii) Explain why carboniferous limestone can be described as a permeable rock. *(2 marks)*

e)
   i)   Describe an aquifer including the type of rock in which it is likely to be found. *(2 marks)*

   ii) Explain why London is able to get water from underground sources. *(4 marks)*

f) Describe how a quarry can be managed after extraction has finished. *(4 marks)*

3 **Challenge of weather and climate**

a)   What is the difference between climate and weather? *(2 marks)*

b)   i)   Study Figures Ca and Cb on page 55. Outline how the pattern of temperatures over the UK varies between January and July. *(2 marks)*

        ii)   Explain why it is wetter in the west than in the east of the UK as shown on Figure Cc on page 55. *(2 marks)*

c)   i)   Draw a line between the weather conditions described and the correct part of the depression as it passes over the UK: *(3 marks)*

Short, sharp period of heavy rain often with thunder and lightning	Warm sector
Warmer temperatures with high cumulus cloud	Cold sector
Gradually thickening cloud with prolonged period of rain	Cold front
Clearer visibility and lower temperatures	Warm front

        ii)   What name is given to a high pressure weather system over the UK? *(1 mark)*

d)   Describe the weather conditions in different parts of the UK on 4th January 2008 as shown in Figure D on page 58. *(4 marks)*

e)   i)   Give **two** advantages of global warming for the UK. *(2 marks)*

        ii)   Give **two** disadvantages of global warming for the UK. *(2 marks)*

        iii)   Give **one** way that human activity has contributed to global warming. *(1 mark)*

        iv)   Describe global and national responses to the threat of global warming. *(6 marks)*

4 **Living world**

a)   i)   Draw a labelled diagram of a *named* small scale ecosystem. *(4 marks)*

        ii)   Underline **one** producer named on your ecosystem diagram. *(1 mark)*

        iii)   Outline how a change in one part of the ecosystem can affect the others. *(2 marks)*

b)   i)   Describe the distribution of the hot deserts shown on diagram A on page 81. *(4 marks)*

        ii)   Draw a labelled diagram to show the main features of vegetation found in the hot deserts. *(4 marks)*

c)   Study the climate figures in the following table:

	Jan	Feb	Mar	Apr	May	Jun	Jul	Aug	Sept	Oct	Nov	Dec
Temp(°C)	6	8	9	12	16	19	22	21	18	15	10	7
Rainfall(mm)	80	75	50	50	55	48	75	80	72	85	101	86

        i)   What was the temperature of the warmest month? *(1 mark)*

        ii)   Which of the following is nearest to the total rainfall for the year? Circle the correct answer.

               250 mm   500 mm   800 mm   1200 mm *(1 mark)*

d)   Which of the following vegetation types will be found in a location with climate figures similar to those shown in the table? Circle the correct answer.

          Tropical rain forests   Hot desert   Temperate deciduous woodland *(1 mark)*

e)   i)   What is deforestation? *(1 mark)*

        ii)   Use a case study to show how forests can be managed sustainably. *(6 marks)*

5 Water on the land

a) i) Give **two** pieces of evidence that Figure C on page 101 was taken near the source *(2 marks)*

ii) Draw **two or more** annotated diagrams to show how a waterfall changes over time. *(4 marks)*

b) i) Using the list of forms of transportation below, write the correct letter (**A, B, C, D**) next to each definition.

      A Traction   **B** Solution   **C** Suspension   **D** Saltation

Medium sized material is bounced along the river bed

The finest material is carried along near the surface of the river

The heaviest material is rolled along the bed of the river

Some material is carried along dissolved in the water *(3 marks)*

ii) Give **two** reasons why the river will eventually start to deposit the material it is carrying. *(2 marks)*

c) i) Describe the features of the River Tees shown on map D on page 105. *(4 marks)*

ii) Name **two** uses of the floodplain of the River Tees shown in Figure I on page 107. *(2 marks)*

iii) Why are there very few buildings in the area close to the river in Figure I on page 107? *(1 mark)*

d) i) Name **one** form of soft engineering used in the management of rivers. *(1 mark)*

ii) Explain why soft engineering is a sustainable form of river management. *(6 marks)*

6 Ice on the land

a) Look at Figure C on page 124. Describe the sources and extent of the ice cover 18,000 years ago. *(4 marks)*

b) What is meant by ablation? *(1 mark)*

c) i) Draw a labelled diagram to show the formation of **one** of the following:

      Glacial trough   Hanging Valley   Terminal moraine *(4 marks)*

ii) Explain the formation of a corrie. *(4 marks)*

d) i) Use map G on page 133 to explain why many tourists visit this area. *(6 marks)*

ii) Give **two** pieces of evidence that global warming is affecting Alpine tourist communities. *(2 marks)*

iii) Give **two** reasons why this is important for these communities. *(2 marks)*

iv) Explain how Alpine tourist communities can react to the threat of global warming. *(2 marks)*

7 The coastal zone

a) i) What is the swash of a wave? *(1 mark)*

ii) Tick the **three** features of a destructive wave which are correct in the following list:

      Strong swash   Strong backwash   Material pushed up the beach

      Material removed from the beach   High Crest   Long wave length *(3 marks)*

iii) Outline **one** process of coastal erosion. *(2 marks)*

b) i) Study Figure A on page 152. Why is the south coast straighter than the east coast? *(1 mark)*

ii) Draw two or more labelled diagrams to show the formation of a wave cut platform. *(4 marks)*

c) i) Use Figure A on page 158 to support the view that the coastline of East Anglia will be very different from its present form in the future. *(6 marks)*

ii) Outline why a management strategy in one part of the coast may have a negative effect further along the coast. *(2 marks)*

d) i) Name **one** pioneer species commonly found in a named coastal habitat. *(1 mark)*

ii) State **one** change in vegetation over time as plant succession takes place. *(1 mark)*

iii) Choose a coastal habitat and explain why it is important that it is conserved. *(4 marks)*

8 Population change

a)   i)   What is the meaning of the term 'natural increase'?   *(1 mark)*

     ii)   Complete the figures for natural increase in the following table: *(2 marks)*

Country	Birth Rate/1000 people	Death rate/1000 people	Natural increase
Uganda	44	14	30
Bolivia	26	7	
UK	12	10	
Japan	9	9	0

     iii)   Suggest why there is such a large natural increase in the poor country of Uganda.   *(6 marks)*

b)   i)   Since the 1990's China's One Child Policy has been relaxed for the following groups in some areas:

         Ethnic minorities   People living in rural areas.   Parents with no brothers or sisters.

         For **two** of the above, suggest why these groups are now allowed to have more than one child.   *(4 marks)*

     ii)   Describe some problems associated with China's One Child Policy.   *(4 marks)*

c)   Sketch an outline of a population pyramid for a country in Stage 5 of the Demographic Transition Model.   *(2 marks)*

d)   i)   Explain the difference between a refugee and an economic migrant.   *(2 marks)*

     ii)   Using the case study on pages 184–5, give **two** reasons why transmigration policy in Indonesia is unpopular with some people.   *(4 marks)*

9 Changing urban environments

a)   Explain the difference between urbanisation and urban growth.   *(2 marks)*

b)   i)   There is a need for more housing in a city. Write the letter of the part of the city next to the best solution of how more housing can be provided. The first has been done for you.

         A City centre   **B** Outer suburbs   **C** Inner city   **D** Inner suburbs

         Subdivide large Victorian houses into modern flats **D**

         Modern terraced housing

         Provide flats over shops

         Build new estates   *(2 marks)*

     ii)   Describe **two** different approaches to urban regeneration used in inner cities in a country in the rich world.   *(4 marks)*

c)   i)   Name **two** problems associated with the increasing amount of traffic in cities.   *(2 marks)*

     ii)   Describe **one** solution to the problem of traffic in cities.   *(4 marks)*

d)   The following strategies have been used to manage the issues that arise as UK cities have become more multi-cultural:

- providing English classes
- developing multi-cultural areas as tourist centres
- improving employment opportunities
- discourage ethnic segregation.

     Choose **two** of the above and suggest how they help to manage the issues that arise in multi-cultural cities in the UK   *(4 marks)*

e)   i)   What is a squatter settlement?   *(1 mark)*

     ii)   Explain how people living in squatter settlements can be involved in redevelopment of their areas.   *(6 marks)*

10 Changing rural environments

a)

i) Tick the **three** correct statements about an expanding village: *(3 marks)*

There is a large proportion of elderly people living in the village.

There are many young families with children in the village.

Many people live in the village and commute to work elsewhere.

The people do most of their shopping in the village shop.

The village is served with good transport connections.

The village is in a remote rural area.

ii) Explain why there may be conflict between different groups of people in an expanding village. *(4 marks)*

iii) What is meant by commuting?   *(1 mark)*

b) Choose **two** of the strategies aimed at sustaining rural living detailed on pages 228–231.
For *each* suggest how effective it will be in achieving sustainable rural living.   *(4 marks)*

c) Suggest why the development of organic farming has slowed down in recent years.   *(2 marks)*

d) Study the pie graph showing the loss of land caused by deforestation in the Amazon Basin
by land area between 2000 and 2005.

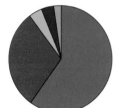

■ cattle ranching
■ subsistence agriculture
□ fires, mining, urbanisation, roads and dams
■ logging
▨ commercial agriculture

i) Approximately what percentage was lost due to cattle ranching? Circle the correct answer:
   20   40   60   80 per cent   *(1 mark)*

ii) Outline **one** difference between subsistence and commercial agriculture.   *(2 marks)*

e)

i) Give **two** reasons why there is rapid rural-urban migration in many areas of the Poor World.   *(2 marks)*

ii) Describe the effects of rural-urban migration on the rural areas of the Poor World.   *(6 marks)*

11 The development gap

a)

i) Study table B on page 255. Draw a scatter graph to show the relationship between
GNI per capita and the infant mortality rate per thousand per year.   *(2 marks)*

ii) Describe the link between these two development indicators.   *(1 mark)*

iii) Give **one** reason for this link between GNI per capita and infant mortality rate.   *(1 mark)*

b)

i) Define *each* of the following terms:
   HDI   Adult literacy rate   GNI per capita   *(3 marks)*

ii) Why is a single indicator not an accurate measure of a country's development.   *(2 marks)*

c) Tick **four** of the following statements that are correct: *(4 marks)*

Countries can only trade with other members of their trading group.

Fair trade cuts out the middleman.

Poor countries largely export primary products.

Tied aid means that a poor country can only trade with the country that has given them money.

Conservation swap means debts are written off in return for not cutting down some tropical rain forests.

Small-scale irrigation using simple technology is a good example of sustainable development.

d) i) Using evidence from Ireland and Bulgaria on pages 268–9, explain how physical and human factors cause the great difference in the development of these two countries. *(6 marks)*

ii) Name **one** way the E.U. has tried to reduce inequalities within Europe. *(1 mark)*

e) i) Give **one** political factor that may cause a slow rate of development in a poor country. *(1 mark)*

ii) Describe how a poor water supply can affect peoples' standards of living. *(4 marks)*

12 Globalisation

a) i) What is the meaning of the term globalisation? *(1 mark)*

ii) Explain how ICT developments helped the globalisation of industry. *(2 marks)*

iii) Describe the impact of globalisation on older established industrial areas. *(4 marks)*

b) i) What is a TNC? *(1 mark)*

ii) Explain some advantages of a TNC locating in a poor country. *(4 marks)*

iii) Give **one** disadvantage of a TNC locating its factories in a poor country. *(1 mark)*

c) The following are reasons for the recent rapid growth of industry in China:

- TNCs are allowed to set up in Special Enterprise Zones.
- China is densely populated.
- Ports like Shanghai are now open cities.
- There are close links between industry and universities.

For **two** of the above, state why they are important for the growth of industry in China. *(4 marks)*

d) i) Describe the environmental effects of the increasing demand for energy. *(6 marks)*

ii) Explain why any attempt at pollution control has to be international if it is to be successful. *(2 marks)*

13 Tourism

a) Study Table A on page 295.

i) Which area received the greatest number of visitors in 2010? *(1 mark)*

ii) Which area has seen the greatest percentage growth in the number of visitors between 2006 and 2010? *(1 mark)*

b) i) Choose *either* a named coastal resort *or* a National Park.
For your chosen area explain why it has become an important tourist destination. *(6 marks)*

ii) Explain the features of the development phase of the Butler model. *(1 mark)*

iii) Give **one** reason why a resort may decline in popularity. *(2 marks)*

c) Explain why Jamaica's north coast (Figure D on page 311) is an example of mass tourism. *(4 marks)*

d) i) Give **one** reason why tourists go to extreme environments like Antarctica. *(1 mark)*

ii) Refer to pages 314–5 and tick the **four** statements in the following table that show how Antarctica tries to cope with the impact of an increasing number of visitors: *(4 marks)*

All tour operators are members of the International Association of Antarctic Tour Operators.
Boats must not carry more than 100 people.
Landing stages have been built so that larger ships can dock near to the wildlife.
Cafes and shops have been built on the ice to serve the visitors.
All visitors must be accompanied by qualified guides.
Visitors can only stay for short periods in any one area.
All waste to be left in litter bins on the ice cap

e) i) What is ecotourism? *(1 mark)*

ii) Explain how ecotourism can be of benefit to the local people. *(4 marks)*

Glossary

This is a glossary of key terms that appear in the GCSE Geography specification. Additional terms are defined in the text.

A

Ablation: outputs from the glacier budget, such as melting.

Abrasion: a process of erosion involving the wearing away of the valley floor and sides (glaciers) and the shoreline (coastal zones).

Abrasion *(rivers)*: happens when larger loads carried by the river hits the bed and banks, causing bits to break off.

Accumulation: inputs to the glacier budget, such as snowfall and avalanches.

Age structure: the proportions of each age group in a population. This links closely to the stage a country has reached in the demographic transition model.

Aid: money, food, training and technology given by richer countries to poorer ones, either to help with an emergency or for long-term development.

Air pollution: putting harmful substances into the atmosphere such as carbon dioxide.

Altitude: height above sea level, usually given in metres.

Anticyclone: an area of high atmospheric pressure.

Aquifer: an underground reservoir of water stored in pores and/or joints in a rock, e.g. chalk.

Arable farming: growing crops.

Arch: a headland that has been partly broken through by the sea to form a thin-roofed arch.

Areas of water deficit: areas where the rain that falls does not provide enough water and there may be shortages.

Areas of water surplus: areas that have more water than is needed – often such areas receive a high rainfall total, but have a relatively small population.

Attrition: the knocking together of stones, making them gradually smaller and smoother.

Avalanche: a very fast downhill movement of a mass of snow, ice and rocks.

B

Bar: a spit that has grown across a bay.

Bay: a broad coastal inlet often with a beach.

Beach: a deposit of sand or shingle at the coast, often found at the head of a bay.

Biofuels: the use of living things such as crops like maize to make ethanol (an alcohol-based fuel) or biogas from animal waste. It is the use of crops that has become especially important.

Biological weathering: weathering caused by living things such as tree roots or burrowing animals.

Birth rate (BR): the number of babies born per 1,000 people per year.

Bottom-up aid: aid used to provide basic health care for communities, clean drinking water and money for education.

Brownfield sites: land that has been built on before and is to be cleared and reused. These sites are often in the inner city.

Bulldozing: the pushing of deposited sediment at the snout by a glacier as it advances.

C

Call centres: offices where groups of people answer telephone queries from customers. Employees use a computer to give them information that helps them answer questions.

Carbon credits: a means of trading carbon between organisations or countries in order to meet an overall target.

Carbon footprint: the amount of carbon generated by things people do, including creating a demand for out-of-season food.

Carbonation: weathering of limestone and chalk by acidic rainwater.

Carbon emissions: release of carbon (usually in the form of carbon dioxide) often by burning fossil fuels.

Cash crops: crops grown in order to sell to make a financial profit.

Cave: a hollowed-out feature at the base of an eroding cliff.

Cavern: a large underground cave.

Cement: mortar used in building, made from crushed limestone and shale.

Central business district (CBD): the main shopping and service area in a city. The CBD is usually found in the middle of the city so that it is easily accessible.

Channel: the part of the river valley occupied by the water itself.

Chemical weathering: the process where chemical reactions change or destroy minerals when rock comes into contact with water and/or air.

Cliff: a steep or vertical face of rock often found at the coast.

Climate: the average weather conditions recorded over a period of at least 30 years.

Climate change: long-term changes in the climate, such as cooling leading to an Ice Age or the current trend of global warming.

Commercial farming: a type of farming where crops and/or livestock are sold to make a profit.

Commuter village: a village located in the rural–urban fringe, many of whose inhabitants commute to work in surrounding towns or cities.

Commuting: The daily movement of people travelling between home and work and back again.

Composite volcano: a steep-sided volcano that is made up of a variety of materials, such as lava and ash.

Congestion charging: charging vehicles to enter cities, with the aim of reducing the use of vehicles.

Conservation: the thoughtful use of resources; managing the landscape in order to protect ecosystems and cultural features.

Conservation swaps: agreements made between countries where some debts are written off in exchange for conservation projects being done.

Conservative plate margin: a plate margin where two plates are sliding alongside each other.

Constructive plate margin: a plate margin where two plates are moving apart.

Constructive wave: a powerful wave with a strong swash that surges up a beach.

Consumer: organisms that get their energy by eating other organisms.

Continental plate: a tectonic plate made of low density continental rock that will not sink under another plate.

Corrie: a deep depression on a hillside with a steep back wall, often containing a lake.

Cross profile: a line that represents what it would be like to walk from one side of a valley, across the channel and up the other side.

Crust: the outer layer of the earth.

Curtain: a broad deposit of calcite usually formed when water emerges along a crack in a cavern.

D

Dam: an artificial structure designed to hold back water to create a reservoir.

Death rate (DR): the number of deaths per 1,000 people per year.

Debt: money owed to others, to a bank or to a global organisation such as the World Bank.

Debt repayment: paying back money borrowed to support development to banks or governments. Decomposers: organisms such as bacteria that break down plant and animal material.

Deforestation: the removal of trees and undergrowth.

De-industrialisation: a process of decline in some types of industry over a long period of time. It results in fewer people being employed in this sector and falling production.

Demographic transition model: a theoretical model that shows changes in population information (birth and death rates and population growth) over a period of time.

Deposition: the dumping (deposition) of sediment that has been transported by a river.

Depression: an area of low atmospheric pressure.

Destructive plate margin: a plate margin where two plates are moving towards each other resulting in one plate sinking beneath the other.

Destructive wave: a wave formed by a local storm that crashes down onto a beach and has a powerful backwash.

Development measure: statistics used to show the level of development, which allows countries to be compared.

Discharge: the volume of water passing a given point in a river at any moment in time.

Disposal of waste: safely getting rid of unwanted items such as solid waste.

Donor country: a country giving aid to another country.

Drainage basin: area from which a river gets its water. The boundary is marked by an imaginary line of highland known as a watershed.

Drumlin: an egg-shaped hill found on the floor of a glacial trough.

Dry valley: a valley formed by a river during a wetter period in the past but now without a river.

E

Earthquake: a sudden and often violent shift in the rocks forming the earth's crust, which is felt at the surface.

Economic: this relates to costs and finances at a variety of levels, from individuals to government.

Economic core: the centre of a country or region economically, where businesses thrive, people have opportunities and are relatively wealthy. A highly developed area.

Economic periphery: the edge of a country or region in terms of economics. It may not physically be the edge, but is a more remote, difficult area where people tend to be poorer and have fewer opportunities. A less well developed area.

Ecosystem: the living and non-living parts of an environment and the interrelationships between them.

Ecotourism: tourism that focuses on protecting the environment and the local way of life. Also known as green tourism.

Emigrant: someone leaving their country of residence to move to another country.

Environmental: this is the impact on our surroundings, including the land, water and air as well as features of the built-up areas.

Environmental degradation: undesirable changes to the natural environment through the removal of natural resources and disruption to natural ecosystems. Human activity is a major cause.

Epicentre: the point at the earth's surface directly above the focus of an earthquake.

Erosion: the sculpting of a landscape, for example by rivers, involving the removal of material.

Escarpment/cuesta: an outcrop of chalk made up of a steep scarp slope and a more gentle dip slope.

European Union (EU): a group of countries across Europe that work towards a single market, i.e. they trade as if they were one country, without any trade barriers.

Exfoliation: flaking of the outer surface of rocks mainly caused by repeated cycles of hot and cold.

Exponential growth: a pattern where the growth rate constantly increases – often shown as a J-curve graph.

Extreme environments: places with particularly difficult environments, such as being very hot or cold. Tourism to these places has only recently occurred due to people wanting to visit somewhere with different physical challenges.

Extreme weather: a weather event such as a flash flood or severe snowstorm that is significantly different from the average.

F

Fair trade: a system whereby agricultural producers in countries at lesser stages of development are paid a decent price for their produce. This helps them to attain a reasonable standard of living.

Flashy: a hydrograph that responds quickly to a period of rain so that it characteristically has a high peak and a short lag time.

Flood or storm hydrograph: a line graph drawn to show the discharge in a river in the aftermath of a period of rain, which is shown as a bar graph.

Floodplain: the flat area next to the river channel, especially in the lower part of the course. This is a natural area for water to spill onto when the river reaches the top of its banks.

Floodplain zoning: controlling what is built on the floodplain so that areas that are at risk of flooding have low-value land uses.

Floods: these occur when a river carries so much water that it cannot be contained by its banks and so it overflows onto surrounding land – its floodplain.

Focus: the point in the earth's crust where an earthquake begins.

Fold mountains: large mountain ranges where rock layers have been crumpled as they have been forced together.

Food chain: a line of linkages between producers and consumers.

Food miles: the distance that food items travel from where they are grown to where they are eaten.

Food web: a diagram that shows all the linkages between producers and consumers in an ecosystem.

Fragile environment: an environment that is easily unbalanced and damaged by natural or human factors.

Freeze–thaw weathering: weathering involving repeated cycles of freezing and thawing.

Function: the purpose of a particular area, e.g. for residential use, recreation or shopping.

G

Gender structure: the balance between males and females in a population. Small differences can tell us a great deal about a country or city.

Geological timescale: the period of time since life became abundant 542 million years ago, which geologists have divided into eras and periods.

Glacial retreat: melting of the ice causes a glacier to retreat up-valley.

Glacial trough: a wide, steep-sided valley eroded by a glacier.

Glacier: a finger of ice usually extending downhill from an ice cap and occupying a valley.

Glacier budget: the balance between the inputs (accumulation) and the outputs (ablation) of a glacier.

Global warming: an increase in world temperatures as a result of the increase in greenhouse gases (carbon dioxide, methane, CFCs and nitrous oxide) in the atmosphere brought about by the burning of fossil fuels, for example.

Globalisation: the increasing links between different countries throughout the world and the greater interdependence that results from this.

GNI: Gross National Income – the total value of goods and services produced within a country including income received from and payments made to other countries.

GNP: Gross National Product – the total value of all goods and services produced by a nation in a particular year.

Gorge: a narrow steep-sided deep valley.

Greenfield sites: land that has not been built on before, usually in the countryside on the edge of the built-up area.

Gross domestic product (GDP) : the total value of goods and services produced by a country divided by its total population. Foreign income is not included.

Ground moraine: glacial material deposited on the valley floor, often forming hummocks.

Groyne: timber or rock structures built out to sea to trap sediment being moved by longshore drift

H

Habitat: the home to a community of plants and animals.

Hanging valley: a tributary glacial trough perched up on the side of a main valley, often marked by a waterfall.

Hard engineering: building artificial structures such as sea walls aimed at controlling natural processes.

Hazard: an event where people's lives and property are threatened and deaths and/or damage result.

Hazard map: A map that shows areas that are at risk from hazards such as earthquakes, volcanoes, landslides, floods and tsunamis

HDI: Human Development Index – an index based on three variables: life expectancy at birth; level of education, including both literacy rate and years spent in school; income adjusted for purchasing power (how much it will buy). Maximum HDI = 1. Wealthy countries like Japan have an HDI of over 0.9, whereas poor countries are around half that

figure or less. HDI concentrates on people's experience rather than economic measures.

Headland: a ridge of land jutting out into the sea.

Honeypot site: somewhere that attracts a large number of tourists who, due to their numbers, place pressure on the environment and people.

Hot deserts: deserts have a rainfall of less than 250 mm per year. Hot deserts are generally found between 30°N and 30°S.

Hurricane: a powerful tropical storm with sustained winds of over 120 kph (75 mph). Also known as a tropical cyclone, a cyclone or a typhoon.

Hydraulic action: the power of the volume of water moving in the river.

Hydraulic power: the sheer power of the waves.

Hydroelectric power: the use of flowing water to turn turbines to generate electricity.

I

Igneous rocks: rocks formed from the cooling of molten magma.

Immediate responses: how people react during a disaster and straight afterwards.

Impermeable: rock that does not allow water to pass through it.

Industrialisation: a process usually linked with the development of an economy, where an increasing proportion of people work in industry.

Infant mortality: the number of babies that die under a year of age, per 1,000 live births.

Informal sector: that part of the economy where jobs are created by people to try to get an income (e.g. taking in washing, mending bicycles) and which are not recognised on official figures.

Inner city: the area around the CBD – usually built before 1918 in the UK.

Insolation: heating of the earth's surface by the sun.

Interdependence: the relationship between two or more countries, usually in terms of trade.

Irrigation: artificial watering of the land.

K

Kyoto Protocol: an international agreement to try and reduce carbon emissions from industrialised countries.

L

Landslip: a type of mass movement common at the coast involving material slipping downhill usually along a curved slip surface.

Land use: the type of buildings or other features that are found in the area, e.g. terraced housing, banks, industrial estates, roads, parks.

Landfill: digging a large hole in the ground and lining it before filling it with rubbish.

Lateral erosion: sideways erosion, for example in a river channel at the outside bend of a meander.

Lateral moraine: a ridge of sediment running along the edge of a glacier where it meets the valley side.

Latitude: determines the geographic north-south position of a point on the earth. 0° is at the Equator and 90° are at the poles.

Levees: raised banks along the course of a river in its lower course. They are formed naturally but can be artificially increased in height.

Life-cycle model: a theoretical model used to describe the changes that take place as a tourist resort develops.

Life expectancy: the number of years a person is expected to live, usually taken from birth.

Limestone pavement: a bare rocky surface, with blocks (clints) and enlarged joints (grikes).

Literacy rate: the percentage of adults in a country who can read and write sufficiently to function fully in work and society.

Living standards: people's quality of life, mostly measured economically but also socially, culturally and environmentally.

Load: material of any size carried by the river.

Long profile: a line representing the course of the river from its source (relatively high up) to its mouth where it ends, usually in a lake or the sea, and the changes in height along its course.

Long profile (glacier): this shows the changes in height and shape along the length of a glacier, from its source high in the mountains to its snout.

Longshore drift: the transport of sediment along a stretch of coastline caused by waves approaching the beach at an angle.

Long-term aid: aid given over a long period, which aims to promote economic development.

Long-term responses: later reactions that happen in the weeks, months and years after an event.

M

Managed retreat: allowing controlled flooding of low-lying coastal areas or cliff collapse in areas where the value of the land is low.

Marginal land: land that is only just good enough to be worth farming. It may be dry, wet, cool, stony or steep.

Maritime influence: the influence of the sea on climate.

Mass movement: the downhill movement of material under the influence of gravity.

Mass tourism: tourism on a large scale to one country or region. This is linked to the Development and Consolidation phases of the Butler tourist resort life-cycle model.

Meander: a bend or curve in the river channel.

Mechanical weathering: a process where physical forces break down or reduce a rock into smaller fragments.

Medial moraine: a ridge of sediment running down the centre of a glacier formed when two lateral moraines merge.

Mercalli scale: a means of measuring earthquakes by describing and comparing the damage done on a scale of I to XII.

Metamorphic rocks: rocks whose chemistry and texture has changed because of heating and/or pressure.

Migration: the movement of people from one permanent home to another, with the intention of staying at least a year. This move may be within a country (national migration) or between countries (international migration).

Moraine: sediment carried and deposited by ice.

Multiplier effect: where initial investment and jobs lead to a knock-on effect, creating more jobs

and providing money to generate services.

N

National Park: an area where development is limited and planning controlled. The landscape is regarded as unusual and valuable and therefore worth looking after.

Natural change: the difference between birth rate and death rate given as a percentage.

Natural hazard: an event over which people have little control, which threatens people's lives and possessions. This is different from a natural event as volcanoes can erupt in unpopulated areas without being a hazard.

Nutrient cycling: the recycling of nutrients between living organisms and the environment.

O

Oceanic plate: a tectonic plate made of dense iron-rich rock that forms the ocean floor.

Ocean trenches: deep sections of the ocean, where an oceanic plate is sinking below a continental plate.

Organic farm: a farm that does not use chemicals in the production of crops or livestock.

Outer city or suburbs: the area on the edge of the city. Many suburbs were built after 1945 and get newer as they reach the edge of the city.

Oxbow lake: a horseshoe or semicircular area that used to be a meander. Oxbow lakes are cut off from a supply of water and so will eventually become dry.

P

Permeable rock: a rock that allows water to pass through it.

Pervious: rock that allows water to pass through it via vertical joints and horizontal bedding planes.

Physical quality of life index (PQLI): the average of three social indicators: literacy rate, life expectancy and infant mortality.

Pillar: a calcite feature stretching from floor to ceiling in a cavern.

Plate: a section of the earth's crust.

Plate margin: the boundary where two plates meet.

Pleistocene period: a geological time period lasting from about 2 million years ago until 10,000 years ago.

Sometimes this period is called the Ice Age.

Plucking: a process of glacial erosion where individual rocks are plucked from the valley floor or sides as water freezes them to the glacier.

Porous: rock that allows water to soak into it via spaces between particles.

Precipitation: the transfer of water from the atmosphere to the ground, for example rain and snow.

Prediction: attempts to forecast an event – where and when it will happen – based on current knowledge.

Preparation: organising activities and drills so that people know what to do if an earthquake happens.

Pressure (atmospheric): pressure exerted on the Earth's surface by the mass of the overlying atmosphere.

Primary effects: the immediate effects of an event, e.g. a volcanic eruption, caused directly by it.

Producers: organisms that get their energy from a primary source such as the sun.

Protection: constructing buildings so that they are safe to live in and will not collapse.

Push–pull factors: push factors are the negative aspects of a place that encourage people to move away. Pull factors are the attractions and opportunities of a place that encourage people to move there.

Pyramidal peak: a sharp-edged mountain peak.

Q

Quality of life: how good a person's life is as measured by such things as quality of housing and environment, access to education, health care, how secure people feel and how happy they are with their lifestyle.

Quarry restoration: restoring or improving the environmental quality of a quarry, either during its operation or afterwards.

R

Recipient country: a country receiving aid from another country.

Recycling: using materials, such as aluminium or glass, time and again.

Regeneration: improving an area.

Relief: the height and slope of the land.

Reservoir: commonly an artificial lake formed behind a dam and used for water supply.

Resurgence: a stream that emerges from underground.

Retail parks: large warehouse-style shops often grouped together on the edge of a town or city, aiming to serve as many people as possible.

Retirement migration: migration to an area for retirement.

Ribbon lake: a long narrow lake in the bottom of a glacial trough.

Richter scale: a scale ranging from 0 to 10 used for measuring earthquakes, based on scientific recordings of the amount of movement.

Rock armour: piles of large boulders dumped at the foot of a cliff to protect it by forcing waves to break and absorbing their energy.

Rock cycle: connections between the three rock types, shown in the form of a diagram.

Rotational slip: slippage of ice along a curved surface.

Rural debt: money borrowed and now owed by farmers to banks or other organisations.

Rural depopulation: people leaving a rural area to live elsewhere, usually in a town or city.

Rural–urban continuum: a graduation from rural to urban areas.

Rural–urban fringe: an area around a town or city where there is a mix of urban and rural land uses.

S

Saltation: the bouncing movement of small stones and grains of sand along the river or sea bed.

Second home: a home bought to stay in only at weekends or for holidays.

Secondary effects: the after-effects that occur as an indirect effect of an event, e.g. a volcanic eruption, on a longer timescale.

Sea wall: concrete or rock barrier built at the foot of cliffs or at the top of a beach.

Sediment: loose rock debris that has been weathered or eroded before being transported and then deposited.

Sedimentary rocks: most commonly, rocks formed from the building up of sediment on the sea floor.

Segregation: occurs where people of a particular ethnic group choose to live with others from the same ethnic group, separate from other groups.

Selective logging: the cutting down of selected trees, leaving most of the trees intact.

Self-help: sometimes known as assisted self-help (ASH), this is where local authorities help the squatter settlement residents to improve their homes by offering finance in the form of loans or grants and often installing water, sanitation, etc.

Shield volcano: a broad volcano that is mostly made up of lava.

Shock waves: seismic waves generated by an earthquake that pass through the earth's crust.

Shoreline Management Plan (SMP): an integrated coastal management plan for a stretch of coastline in England and Wales.

Short-term aid: aid given to help a disaster situation, e.g. people who have been made homeless and are starving after a serious flood.

Site and service: occurs where land is divided into individual plots and water, sanitation, electricity and basic track layout are supplied before any building by residents begins.

Slash and burn: a form of subsistence farming in tropical rainforests where some trees are felled and land is cleared by burning before being replanted

Sliding: a type of mass movement involving material moving downhill on a flat surface (a landslide).

Slumping: a type of mass movement involving material moving downhill under its own weight.

Social: refers to people's health, their lifestyle, community, etc.

Soft engineering: a sustainable approach to managing the coast without using artificial structures.

Soft engineering (rivers): this option tries to work with the natural river system and involves avoiding building on areas most likely to flood, warning people of a possible flood and planting trees to increase lag time.

Soil erosion: the removal of the layer of soil above the rock where plants grow.

Solution: the dissolving of rocks and minerals by rainwater. This is a means of transportation as well as an erosion process.

Solution (coastal transportation): the transport of dissolved chemicals.

Spit: a finger of new land made of sand or shingle, jutting out into the sea from the coast.

Spring: water re-emerging from the rock onto the ground surface. Springs often occur as a line of springs (spring line) at the base of a scarp slope.

Squatter settlements: areas of cities (usually on the outskirts) that are built by people from any materials they can find on land that does not belong to them. They have different names in different parts of the world (e.g. *favela* in Brazil) and are often known as shanty towns.

Stack: an isolated pinnacle of rock sticking out of the sea.

Stalactite: an icicle-like calcite feature hanging down from a cavern roof.

Stalagmite: a stumpy calcite feature formed on a cavern floor.

Stewardship: the personal responsibility for looking after things, in this case the environment. No one should damage the present or future environment.

Straightening meanders: making the river follow a more direct, rather than its natural course, so that it leaves an area more quickly.

Strikes: periods of time when large numbers of employees refuse to work due to disagreements over pay or other grievances.

Subsistence farming: farming to produce food for the farmer and his/her family only.

Suburbanised village: a village with easy access to a large urban area much in demand. Housing estates attached to the village edges aim to fulfil this demand.

Supervolcano: a mega colossal volcano that erupts at least 1,000 km³ of material.

Suspension: small material carried (suspended) within the water.

Sustainability: development that looks after future resources and considers the needs of future generations.

Sustainable: making sure there is enough water in the long term without harming the environment.

Sustainable city: an urban area where residents have a way of life that will last a long time. The environment is not damaged and the economic and social fabric are able to stand the test of time.

Sustainable community: community (offering housing, employment and recreation opportunities) that is broadly in balance with the environment and offers people a good quality of life.

Sustainable development: this allows economic growth to occur, which can continue over a long period of time and will not harm the environment. It benefits people alive today but does not compromise future generations.

Sustainable management: a form of management that makes sure that developments are long lasting and do not harm the environment.

Swallow hole: an enlarged joint into which water falls.

T

Tectonic activity: activity (such as volcanic eruptions and earthquakes) caused by the movement of tectonic plates.

Temperate deciduous forest: forests made up of broad-leaved trees such as oak that drop their leaves in the autumn.

Terminal moraine: a high ridge running across the valley representing the maximum advance of a glacier.

Top-down aid: aid used so that governments can run more efficiently or to build infrastructure such as roads and bridges.

Tor: an isolated outcrop of rock on a hilltop, usually in granite landscapes.

Track: the path or course of a hurricane.

Traction (rivers): the rolling along of the largest rocks and boulders along the sea or river bed.

Transmigration: a population policy that aims to move people from densely populated areas to sparsely populated areas and provide them with opportunities to improve the quality of their lives.

Transnational corporations (TNCs): companies that spread their operations around the world to try to reduce costs.

Transportation: the carrying of sediment downstream from the point where it has been eroded to where it is deposited.

Tropical rainforests: the natural vegetation found in the tropics, well suited to the high temperatures and heavy rainfall associated with these latitudes.

Truncated spur: where ice has 'cut off' an interlocking spur and left a very steep cliff.

Tsunami: a special type of wave created where an event, often an earthquake, moves the entire depth of the water above it.

U

Urban sprawl: the spreading of urban areas into the surrounding rural/rural-urban fringe areas.

Urbanisation: the increase in the proportion of people living in cities, resulting in their growth.

V

Vale: in the landscape, a flat plain typically formed on clay.

Vertical erosion: downwards erosion, for example when a river gouges out a deep valley.

Volcano: an opening in the earth's crust through which molten lava, ash and gases are ejected.

W

Water pollution: putting poisonous substances into water courses, such as sewage, industrial effluent and harmful chemicals.

Water stress: this happens when there is not enough water available. This may be because of an inadequate supply at a particular time or it may relate to water quality.

Waterfall: the sudden, and often vertical, drop of a river along its course.

Wave-cut platform: a wide, gently sloping rocky surface at the foot of a cliff.

Weather: the day-to-day conditions of the atmosphere involving, for example, temperature, cloud cover and wind direction.

Weathering: the breakup or decay of rocks in their original place at or close to the earth's surface.

Index

This index shows all key terms that are defined in the book in blue. See glossary for those key terms that appear in the specification.

Acknowledgements

The author and publisher would like to thank the following for permission to reproduce material:

Source texts:
P63 Quote from BBC news article 'Is extreme weather due to Climate change?' by Paul Rincon, 23 August 2005. © bbc.co.uk/news; p111 Extract from 'Cost of deluge will be millions' from the Sheffield Star Special Edition. © 2007 by Johnston Press. Reprinted with permission from The Editor of The Sheffield Star, www.thestar.co.uk; p111 Quote from BBC news article ' Why Bangladesh floods are so bad' by Tracey Logan, 27 July, 2004. © bbc.co.uk/news; p209 Extract from BBC News article 'Nairobi slum life: Into Kibera' by Andrew Harding, 4 October 2002. © bbc.co.uk/news; p293 Quote from Gordon Ramsay, taken from 'Gordon Ramsay's war on out-of-season vegetables', by Caroline Gammell, 9 May 2008. © 2008 by Telegraph Media Group Limited. Reprinted with permission.

Photographs courtesy of:
1.3B Christian Ostrosky/Alamy; 1.3A Lonely Planet Images/Woods Wheatcroft; 1.3D Frans Lanting/Corbis; 1.4C AFP/Getty Images; 1.4E KPA/Zuma/Rex Features; 1.4F Arctic-Images/Alamy; 1.4I George Steinmetz/Science Photo Library; 1.5C Fotolia; 1.7B AFP/Getty Images; 1.7C Noboru/Corbis; 1.7E Claudia Dewald/Getty; 1.7F Hector Retemal/AFP/Getty Images; 1.8B Aflo/Rex Features; 2.1B (top & middle) Tony Waltham/geophotos; 2.1B (bottom) Fotolia; 2.3A Tony Waltham/geophotos; 2.3C Simon Ross; 2.4B Simon Lewis/www.westcountryviews. co.uk; 2.5C iStockphoto; 2.6B Tony Waltham/geophotos; 2.7B iStockphoto; 2.8C David Dunford; 2.9A West Sussex County Council; 2.9B Bell Ingram Limited; 3.2B, 3.2C Satellite Receiving Station, University of Dundee; 3.2H Clifford Rhodes/Alamy; 3.2I Andrew Parker/Alamy; 3.2J, 3.2L Satellite Receiving Station, University of Dundee; 3.3A Roland Gal/Rex Features; 3.3C Apex News & Pictures; 3.3D Simon Ross; 3.4C Arctic-Images/Corbis; 3.6A Sam Toren/Alamy; 3.6B Gerard Fritz/Getty Images; 3.7C NOAA/Science Photo Library; 4.2F geogphotos film/Alamy; 4.2G (1) Tim Gartside USA America/Alamy; 4.2G (2) Photolibrary; 4.2G (3) iStockphoto; 4.2G (4) iStockphoto; 4.3A Tony T/Alamy; 4.3B Jon Sparks/Alamy; 4.4B Nigel Dickinson/Still Pictures; 4.4C Reuters/Corbis; 4.5B Rhett Butler; 4.5C Alex Hipkiss/RSPB; 4.6B imagebroker/Alamy; 4.6D Biosphoto/Eichaker Xavier/Still Pictures; 4.6F Getty Images; 5.1A, 5.1C, 5.1D Judith Canavan; 5.2B Alistair Forrester Shankie/iStockphoto; 5.2F geogphotos film/Alamy; 5.2H Sue Ogrocki/AP/Press Association Images; 5.3F Tony Waltham/geophotos; 5.3G Ed Maynard/Alamy; 5.5B Anna Gowthorpe/PA Archive/Press Association Images; 5.5C Kirsty Wiggleworth/AP/Press Association Images; 5.5E The Environment Agency; 5.5H AFP/Getty Images; 5.6C Xinhua Press/Corbis; 5.7D The Photolibrary Wales/Alamy; 6.2C U.S. Geological Survey; 6.3A Simon Ross; 6.4A Tony Waltham/geophotos; 6.4H Photolibrary; 6.4I Dr. Marli Miller/Visuals Unlimited/Corbis; 6.5B Photoshot; 6.5D Photolibrary; 6.5E Simon Ross; 6.6A Brian North/Alamy; 6.6B Laurent Cipriani/AP/Press Association Images; 6.6C Ross Woodhall/Cultura/Corbis; 6.7A John Heilprin/ AP/Press Association Images; 6.7B Fotolia; 6.7E AFP/Getty Images; 7.1A Gemunu Amarasinghe/AP/Press Association Images; 7.1C Steve Allen Travel Photography/Alamy; 7.2A Jason Hawkes; 7.2B Peter Smith Photography; 7.3A Tony Waltham/geophotos; 7.4B Simon Ross; 7.5B Photolibrary; 7.6A Tony Waltham/geophotos; 7.6B David Lyons/Alamy; 7.6D J Farmar/Skyscan; 7.7B Jason Hawkes; 7.8B iStockphoto; 7.9A Ian West Photographs; 7.10A Robert Harding Picture Library Ltd/Alamy; 7.10B Manor Photography/Alamy; 7.10E Martin Keene/PA Archive/Press Association Images; 7.10G Flight Images LLP/Getty Images; 7.10I Defra Biodiversity team; 7.11A Peter Hutchings, Hampshire & Isle of Wight Wildlife Trust; 7.11D Peter Hutchings, Hampshire & Isle of Wight Wildlife Trust; 8.1C iStockphoto; 8.1D Lisa F. Young/Fotolia; 8.2B Threshing the wheat (colour litho) by Tunnicliffe, Charles Frederick (1901-79) Private Collection/The Stapleton Collection/The Bridgeman Art Library; 8.2C iStockphoto; 8.2D AFP/Getty Images; 8.2F Gerard Fritz/Getty Images; 8.3B iStockphoto; 8.4C Nir Elias/Reuters; 8.4D Gareth Brown/ Corbis; 8.5B Mangiwau/Getty Images ; 8.6A iStockphoto; 8.6B, 8.7D iStockphoto; 8.7F David Pearson/Rex Features; 8.7G Irene Abdou/Alamy; 9.1C(left) Philippe Bourseiller/Getty Images; 9.1C(right) Fabienne Fossez/Alamy; 9.2A(a) Paul White, Leeds the modern city/Alamy; 9.2A(b) Simon Ross; 9.2A(b) Simon Ross; 9.2A(c) Simon Ross; 9.3A (left) Christopher Pillitz/Alamy; 9.3A(right) Getty Images; 9.3C(a) Judith Canavan; 9.3C(b) iStockphoto; 9.3C(c) iStockphoto; 9.3C(d) Judith Canavan; 9.3E J Jackman/Skyscan; 9.3F Urban Splash www.urbansplash.co.uk; 9.3G Photoshot; 9.3H(top) Fotolia; 9.3H(middle) 2007 Getty Images; 9.3H(bottom) Fotolia; 9.3I, 9.3J Judith Canavan; 9.4A(a) Photoshot; 9.4A(b) Jenny Matthews/Alamy; 9.4A(c) Mark Edwards/Still Pictures; 9.4B Peter Treanor/Alamy; 9.4C Art Directors & Trip/Helene Rogers; 9.4E Sean Sprague/Still Pictures; 9.4F iStockphoto; 9.5A Getty Images; 9.5B Sipa Press/Rex Features; 9.5C Getty Images; 9.5D Amit Bhargava/Corbis; 9.6A David R. Frazier Photolibrary, Inc./Alamy; 9.6B Titanic Quarter Ltd/Handout/Reuters/Corbis; 9.6C(a) iStockphoto; 9.6C(b) Paul Thompson Images/Alamy; 9.6C(c) iStockphoto; 9.6C(d) iStockphoto; 9.6E UIG via Getty Images; 9.6F Robert Brook/Alamy; 9.6G William Robinson/Alamy; 9.6I Fotolia; 9.6J Jeff Morgan 12/Alamy; 9.6K London 2012; 10.1A Bluewater; 10.1F Martin Sookias; 10.1G Mykel Nicolaou/Rex Features; 10.2C Gary Brunning/Alamy; 10.3A FLPA/Peter Wilson; 10.3B Tandridge District Council; 10.3C Peter Cragg/Harting Stores; 10.3D Alison Thompson/ Alamy; 10.4C geogphotos/Alamy; 10.5A iStockphoto; 10.5C Andrew Olney/Getty Images; 10.6A Bubbles Photolibrary/Alamy; 10.6B Fotolia; 10.7B Art Directors & Trip/Helene Rogers; 10.7C Christophe Smets/Luna/VISUM/Still Pictures; 10.8B National Geographic/Getty Images; 10.8A Mark Edwards/Still Pictures; 10.8D South American Pictures/Tony Morrison; 10.9A Mark Boulton/Alamy; 10.9B Bombetoka Bay/Corbis; 10.10A Panos/Stefan Boness; 10.10C Fotolia; 10.11A Friedrich von Hörsten/Alamy; 11.1C Getty Images/John Powell ; 11.3B Getty Images; 11.5A Fotolia; 11.5C AFP/Getty Images; 11.6B Imagestate Media Partners Limited – Impact Photos/Alamy; 11.7C iStockphoto; 12.1A Sports Illustrated/ Getty Images; 12.1C Sports Illustrated/Getty Images; 12.2C Rex Features; 12.3E David Wootton/Alamy; 12.4B Amanda Hall/Robert Harding World Imagery/Corbis; 12.4C Scott Stulberg/Getty Images; 12.4E EIGHTFISH/Getty Images; 12.4D PhotoLink/Getty Images; 12.4G AFP/ Getty Images; 12.4H Xinhua Press/Corbis; 12.5C Peer Grimm/epa/Corbis; 12.6C Rob Bouwman/Fotolia; 12.6D Getty Images; 12.7A AFP/Getty Images; 12.7C Photoshot; 12.7D iStockphoto; 12.7E Fotolia; 12.7G 2006 Per-Anders Pettersson/Getty Images; 12.7I, 13.1B, 13.1D, 13.1E, 13.1F iStockphoto; 13.2C Arthur Tilley/Getty Images; 13.2E iStockphoto; 13.2F Weixin Shen/Alamy; 13.3B Evening Standard/Getty Images; 13.3D Topham Picturepoint; 13.3E Rex Features; 13.3F Chris Ison/PA Archive/Press Association Images; 13.4B Eli Pascall-Willis/Getty Images; 13.4F Annie Griffiths Belt/Corbis; 13.4E curved-light/Alamy; 13.4C World Pictures/Alamy; 13.4G Jason Friend/Alamy; 13.4H Peter Titmuss/Alamy; 13.4I Darryl Gill/Alamy; 13.5A Lee Christensen/Getty; 13.5B, 13.5F iStockphoto; 13.6A Nordicphotos/Alamy; 13.6B Frans Lemmens/Alamy; 13.6C Bruce Farnsworth/Alamy; 13.6D iStockphoto; 13.6H Arcticphoto/Alamy; 13.7A Martin Shields/Alamy; 13.7B Craig Lovell/Eagle Visions Photography/Alamy.

Ordnance Survey maps (2.5D, 2.7E, 4.3C, 5.1F, 5.2C, 5.2D, 5.2I, 5.5F, 6.4G, 7.5C, 7.7A. 7.10H, 9.2B, 12.3D) reproduced by permission of Ordnance Survey on behalf of HMSO. © Crown copyright 2012. All rights reserved. Ordnance Survey Licence number 100017284